KEY GUIDE

Australia's
National
Parks

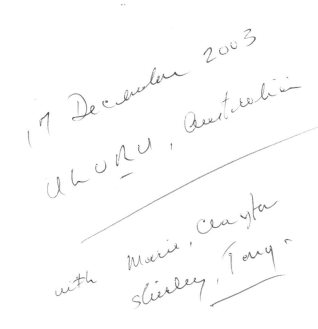

17 December 2003
ULURU, Australia

with Marie, Clayton
Shirley, Tony

KEY GUIDE

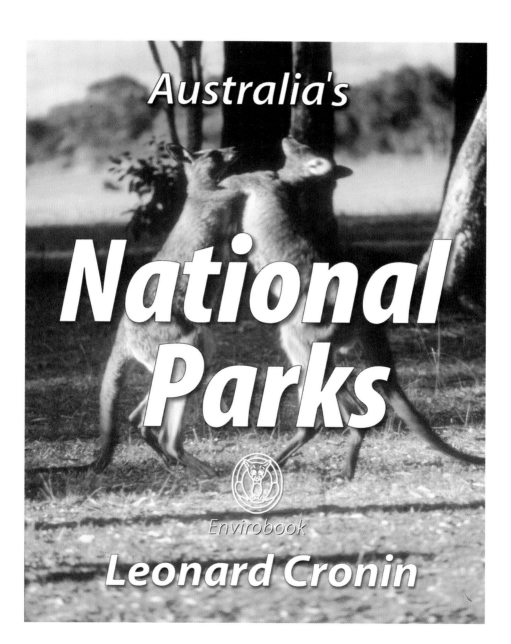

Australia's

National Parks

Envirobook

Leonard Cronin

The maps are in this book are intended as guides only, and should not be used in place of accurate topographical maps for bushwalking. Bushwalkers should select topographical maps, preferably at a scale of 1:25,000 prodcued by State mapping authorities and the Australian Surveying and Land Information Group. The maps in this book were derived from base mapping published by the Land Information Centre and Crown copyright material, used with permission of the General Manager, AUSLIG, Department of Administrative Services, Canberra, and the Land Information Centre, Panorama Ave, Bathurst.

Acknowledgement is gratefully made to the State National Parks and Wildlife Services and to individual rangers who supplied information about their respective parks. Particular thanks to Don Marshall, Pamela Harmon-Price, Alan Ginns, Jacki Baxter and Michael Glover. Photographs were kindly supplied by the Tourism Commisions of the Northern Territory, Victoria, South Australia and New South Wales, the Tasmanian Department of Tourism, Sport and Recreation, and the Queensland Tourist and Travel Corporation. Thanks to Peter Prineas whose book *Wild Places* was an excellent source of reference.

First published in Australia in 1994 by Reed Books Australia

Second edition published in 2000 by Envirobook

Produced and Published in Australia by
Envirobook
38 Rose Street, Annandale, NSW 2038

Copyright © Leonard Cronin 1994

Key Guide is a registered Trade Mark

National Library of Australia
cataloguing-in-publication data:

Cronin, Leonard

Key Guide to Australia's National Parks.
[2nd ed.]
Includes index
ISBN 0 85881 174X

1. National parks and reserves - Australia - Guidebooks.
2. Australia - guidebooks. 1. Title.

919.40465

Planned and produced by Leonard Cronin Productions

Publisher: Leonard Cronin
Original design: Warren Penny
Original maps: Alan Puckett
Cover design: Robert Taylor
New maps and corrections: Guy Holt
Printer: Kyodo Printing Co, Singapore

CONTENTS

Key Map

Featured Parks

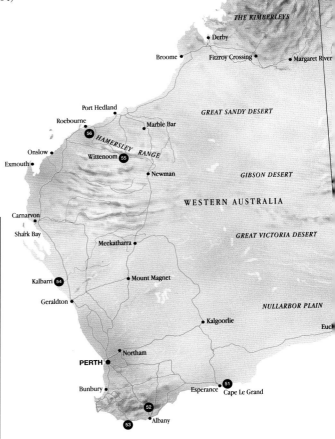

Key to Park Maps

——	Sealed road
——	Unsealed road
- - - -	4WD track
+—+—+	Railway
- - - - -	Walking track
▲	Camping area
⊼	Picnic area
ⓘ	Information
🚐	Caravan site
🛶	Canoeing
✳	Lookout
⊨	Accommodation
Ⓣ	Toilet
🚿	Shower
✆	Telephone
🚤	Boat ramp
✛	Landing strip
⛴	Ferry boat
🚰	Drinking water

Introduction

Australia's national parks are our most priceless assets. They contain the keys to our natural heritage and hold open the door to a journey of discovery that leads beyond the confines of our structured society and into a world shaped and controlled by the primordial forces of nature. This is our world, the world that created, nourished and selected our genetic makeup. Here we take our place in the intricate web of life, the threads of which bind all the lifeforms of planet earth into one complex and self-sustaining ecosystem.

The wilderness should be a part of all our lives, if only for a few days each year, and nowhere else is this easier to realise than in Australia. For here we are fortunate to have one of the greatest national park systems in the world: a network of wilderness areas covering more than 24 million hectares. They range from towering mountain ranges sculpted by the elements to vast plains of rolling red sand dunes and great river systems. Within their borders are uncounted habitats supporting a myriad of organisms filling every available niche, be it a lush rainforest or waterless desert.

The outstanding natural and cultural values of our national parks have led to many of them being proclaimed as World Heritage Areas. Australia has accepted a responsibility to the world community to hold them in trust for the rest of humanity. Hundreds of thousands of visitors are drawn to these parks ever year. They come to experience the wilderness, to stand in awe at the grandeur of the countryside and to enter the Aboriginal Dreamtime world where the beings that created the land and the laws of society are evidenced in the shape of a rock or the curve of a river.

We owe the existence of our national park network to the hard work and dedication of bushwalkers and conservation groups throughout Australia who have lobbied governments and battled with loggers and developers to save ancient forests and pristine habitats. This is an ongoing process, and battles are still being fought to preserve the homes of rare and endangered plants and animals whose last refuges are in our shrinking wilderness areas. Only by expanding the national park system will we be able to ensure the protection of our unique storehouse of genetic material, a heritage we must preserve for future generations.

The parks specially featured in this book have been selected for their scenic and environmental attributes, accessibility, facilities and popularity. They offer a wealth of recreational opportunities from nature study, bushwalking and photography to skiing, white-water rafting, rock climbing, abseiling, diving and surfing.

Minimum Impact

Maintaining the biodiversity of the natural world and encouraging human access can be a delicate balance. Parks such as Kakadu and Kosciuszko attract more than 250,000 visitors every year, and the numbers continue to grow. This puts great pressure on the environment. Walking tracks and unsealed access roads are easily eroded, streams and waterways can become polluted, and the flora and fauna harmed by trampling, introduced diseases and domestic animals.

To ensure the survival of our wilderness areas we must treat them with care and respect. It is important to stay on the formed tracks and to avoid walking on vegetation as this can take years to recover. Camp at existing campsites rather than creating new ones, and take great care with fires. To prevent bush fires and damage to trees many parks only allow the use of fuel stoves.

Wash well away from creeks, even biodegradable soap is alien to the wilderness. Carry out all rubbish, and in areas without toilets bury waste 100 m from camps or waterways. Birds and fish are easily entangled in discarded fishing lines and may suffer an agonising death. Fishermen are therefore asked to retrieve all lines and nets.

All native plants and animals are protected in national parks. They should be observed but not interfered with, and even feeding animals can damage their health and create unnaturally dependent populations. Pets are not allowed in national parks. The smell of a dog will deter many native animals from an area for weeks.

Bushwalking

While many national parks have roads leading to lookouts and scenic drives, to get the most out of your visit you should be prepared to walk. Many features are only seen from the walking trails, and you will experience the full impact of the wilderness, the sights and sounds of the bush and discover fascinating insights into the natural ecosystems by walking quietly through the different habitats.

The Australian climate can be very harsh, and bushwalkers should be well prepared. Wear a hat and loose-fitting protective clothing, particularly in summer when the fierce sun can quickly lead to heat exhaustion. Bring solid footwear with good grip and carry plenty of water. In warm weather the average adult walker needs a minimum of four litres of water per day. This can rise to one litre per hour when walking in hot conditions, and visitors from mild climates may need more. The sensible approach is to undertake long walks in cooler weather and to rest during the hottest part of the day.

Those embarking on full day walks and bushwalkers leaving the walking track system should talk to one of the rangers before departing and let a responsible person know their route and expected time of return. A good topographical map, compass and first aid kit are essential items for wilderness hikers, who should have a minimum of three people in their party.

Animal Bites and Stings

The chances of being bitten by a snake or spider in Australia are minimal, and most visitors to the parks never catch a glimpse of them. Snakes are as keen to avoid us as we are them, and generally keep well out of our way. The few snake bites that do occur nearly always happen when the snake is being attacked. A few sensible precautions will reduce the risk to almost zero: wear long trousers and shoes when walking through dense bush; at night do not walk barefoot, and use a torch. Do not put your hand in rock crevices or holes, and if you do see a snake give it a wide berth and do not attack it.

In the rare event of a snake bite, immediate first aid treatment is essential and will delay the circulation of venom for a few hours. Tie a firm, broad pressure bandage to the bitten area and if possible to the length of the limb. Keep the limb still and immobilised by a splint. Clothing and towels can be used to improvise a bandage, and a newspaper used to make a splint. The victim should remain still to prevent circulation of the venom, and transferred to hospital as quickly as possible. Transport should preferably be brought to the victim, and in remote areas this may require an aerial rescue team. Do not apply a tourniquet or cut the wound as this may increase the amount of venom introduced into the bloodstream.

Tropical coastal waters have their own hidden dangers. Apart from saltwater crocodiles whose disposition is well known, there are a number of venomous marine animals including stonefish, stingrays and box jellyfish (sea wasps). The latter are very dangerous and are found in tropical coastal waters from November to April, effectively ruling out swimming without protective clothing at this time of year. Jellyfish stings should be treated by dousing with vinegar and removing any tentacles carefully with tweezers or a glove. Vinegar deactivates the undischarged venom cells. If this is not available remove the tentacles very carefully, easing them off the skin in one direction only using a plastic credit card or similar to prevent further discharge. Apply mouth-to-mouth resuscitation if required and get the victim to hospital as quickly as possible.

Some venomous fish, such as stonefish and stingrays, lie quietly on the sea bed. To avoid being stung do not walk in shallow coastal waters without strong plastic shoes, and do not touch shells or other marine creatures with bare hands. Treat stings by extracting any spines, washing the area and immersing the wound in hot water (from a car radiator, for example) to relieve the pain.

Overall the Australian bush is friendly and benign, and if treated with respect will reward the visitor with many enriching and enlightening experiences.

New South Wales and ACT

Featured National Parks

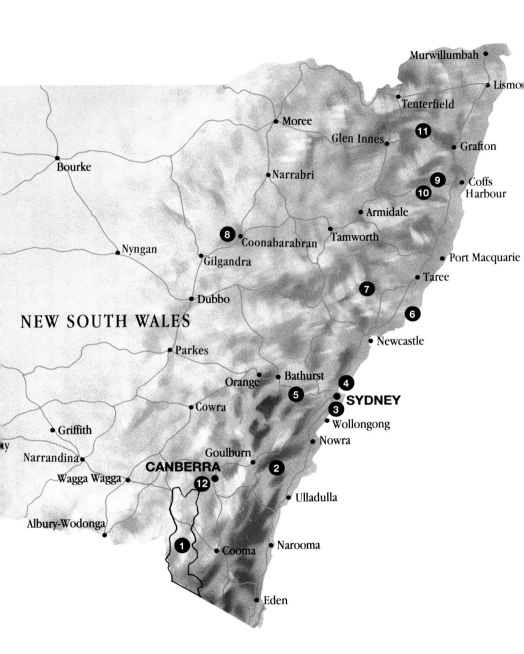

NEW SOUTH WALES

Murwillumbah •

• Lismo

• Tenterfield

• Moree

Glen Innes •   **11**

• Grafton

Bourke

• Narrabri   **9** • Coffs
                         Harbour
             10

• Armidale

8 • Coonabarabran   Tamworth •

Nyngan •   • Gilgandra

• Port Macquarie

7   • Taree

• Dubbo   **6**

• Parkes   • Newcastle

Orange •   • Bathurst   **4**

5   **SYDNEY**

• Cowra   **3**

• Griffith   • Wollongong

• Nowra

Narrandina •   Goulburn •

Wagga Wagga •   **CANBERRA**   **2**

12   • Ulladulla

Albury-Wodonga •

1   • Cooma   • Narooma

• Eden

11

Kosciuszko National Park

Kosciuszko is the largest national park in New South Wales, the centre of the skiing industry and one of Australia's internationally recognised Biosphere Reserves. The 690,000 ha park is a place of glacial lakes, snow gum woodlands, treeless plains and alpine herbfields carpeted with beautiful summer wildflowers.

Kosciuszko National Park has some of the finest and most extensive snowfields in Australia. In summer thousands of visitors come to tour the alpine roads, fish for trout in the clear mountain streams and trek across the high plains. About half of the park is a wilderness area where visitors can experience the area's beauty and solitude.

The eastern slopes ascend in gently undulating hills to a series of rounded peaks rising to 2228 m at Mt Kosciuszko, Australia's highest mountain. Deep gorges and precipitous slopes characterise the western side of the park. The most spectacular is an enormous steep-sided gorge where the land drops 1700 m to the Geehi River. Deep fertile soils have accumulated on the gentle eastern slopes with bare granite rocks protruding on the peaks and ridges.

Formation

Mt Kosciuszko was a plain barely above sea level some 60 million years ago when subterranean forces began pushing up the land to form a high plateau. A major period of uplift about two million years ago tilted the land to the east and created the precipitous western escarpment. The north has been subjected to major volcanic episodes during the past 460 million years, interspersed with periods of uplifting and folding. Rivers have cut gorges into the western edge of the plateau, while the highlands retain their rounded hills and broad valleys. During the last ice age, permanent snow and ice covered some 50 sq km around Mt Kosciuszko. The moraines, cirques and small lakes that dot this area were formed by glaciers piling up rocky debris and gouging into the land.

History

For at least 20,000 years Aborigines have lived in or visited the area to gather food, particularly the bogong moth, a flying delicacy that swarms over the peaks each summer. The bogong feasts were steeped in ritual and tradition, and attracted people from more than 150 km away. Winters were spent in the lowlands where each tribe or clan occupied a different valley.

Squatters moved into the lower valleys in the 1830s, taking Aboriginal land and introducing cattle and sheep. By the end of the 19th century the Aboriginal population had been decimated by diseases and the loss of their land. Some worked as trackers or on farms, but most were forced to live in reserves in Dengate, Tumut, Cann River and Queanbeyan. The squatters felled trees and fired the pastures, causing serious soil erosion and damaging the delicate alpine ecology. Gold was discovered at Kiandra in 1859, starting a gold rush that brought 15,000 people to the area, but the gold seams were quickly worked out. Logging continued until 1944 when Kosciuszko State Park was established. The National Park was declared in 1967, and the final grazing leases were withdrawn in 1972.

The Snowy Mountain Scheme began in 1949, damming and diverting rivers to provide power and irrigate the western plains, but the environmental and economic costs continue to rise along with the water table and salination of the western irrigation areas.

Plants and Animals

The park's size helps to ensure the viability of its wildlife by protecting their habitats and food sources, and in 1977 the park was designated a UNESCO Biosphere Reserve, recognising its international importance.

The range of altitudes creates a range of habitats, from treeless plains to tall forests, alpine heaths and herbfields. The treeless plains of the north are caused by boggy sites and cold air sinking into the valleys limiting tree growth. This has been exacerbated by logging, grazing, and soil compaction by off-road vehicles. Other areas support tall forests of alpine ash and manna gum, and woodlands of snow gums, candlebark, box, stringybark and cypress pines.

Above 1500 m the tall forests give way to sparse woodlands with stunted and gnarled snow gums and black sallees. Above 1800 m only a few dwarf snow gums cling to life in the shelter of bluffs and boulders. Some of the 200 or so alpine plant species are unique to this area. Most are small or low-lying, forming cushions and rounded mats to minimise their exposure to the wind. In summer they create magnificent wildflower displays. Alpine bogs of sphagnum moss soak up water like a sponge, releasing it slowly in summer to feed the streams.

Large mammals such as eastern grey kangaroos, red-necked and swamp wallabies, common wombats and ring-tailed possums prefer the lowlands, leaving the alpine plains to small rodents and marsupials, such as the broad-toothed rat, dusky antechinus and endangered mountain pygmy possum. Only about 2300 mountain pygmy possums survive, feeding on bogong moths, fruits and seeds in summer, and hibernating from May to October. There are 31 reptile species including jacky lizards, Kosciuszko water skinks and venomous snakes such as the red-bellied black snake and tiger snake. The rare corroboree frog can be found in alpine areas.

Falcons, kestrels, ravens and the ground-nesting pipit are often seen at high altitudes, while in the woodlands and forests are gang-gang cockatoos, rosellas, honeyeaters and superb lyrebirds. Introduced rainbow and brown trout have displaced many of the small, slender native galaxias from the mountain streams.

Walks

The park offers many interesting walks, but be prepared for cold and dramatic weather changes at any time of year. You must be well-equipped for long hikes and should register at one of the Ranger Stations before leaving.

One of the most popular walks is the Kosciuszko Walk from the top of the Crackenback chairlift at Thredbo to the summit of Mt Kosciuszko, a 12 km round trip. The walk traverses the treeless alpine area, passing Lake Cootapatamba, a clear blue glacial lake, and along a fairly steep section to the summit.

You can continue along the Main Range Walk, another 12 km from Mt Kosciuszko along the highest line of ridges to Charlotte Pass. This is Australia's highest walking track, with spectacular views over the rugged landscape to the west. The trail ascends Carruthers Peak, heads east towards Blue Lake, the largest of the alpine lakes, and then to Charlotte Pass. This is part of a 20 km circular route from Charlotte Pass via the Summit Walk to Mt Kosciuszko.

There are extensive, spectacular limestone caves and a thermal pool at Yarrangobilly. Canoeing is possible on some of the rivers, and many offer good trout fishing.

Facilities

Sawpit Creek has powered and unpowered sites, fireplaces, toilets, hot showers, a laundry, and furnished cabins. (Bookings: 02-6456 2224.) Camping is permitted at rest areas where there are basic facilities. Bush camping is allowed well away from roads, watercourses and glacial lakes. Above the tree line only portable gas or spirit stoves may be used. Accommodation is available in lodges and hotels in the park and nearby towns.

Access

The park is about 450 km south-west of Sydney via the Snowy Mountains Highway. From Jindabyne access is via the Alpine Way or Kosciuszko Road; and from the west via Khancoban. Snow may close roads from May to October, and snow chains must be carried. The Khancoban road to Kiandra is partially closed in winter.

Climate

The park has alpine weather and conditions can change from hot summer days to freezing nights and heavy snowfalls in a few hours. Visit in summer for wildflower displays, and in winter for downhill and cross-country skiing.

NPWS Snowy Mts Region, PO Box 2228, Jindabyne, NSW 2627. Tel. (02) 6450 5600.

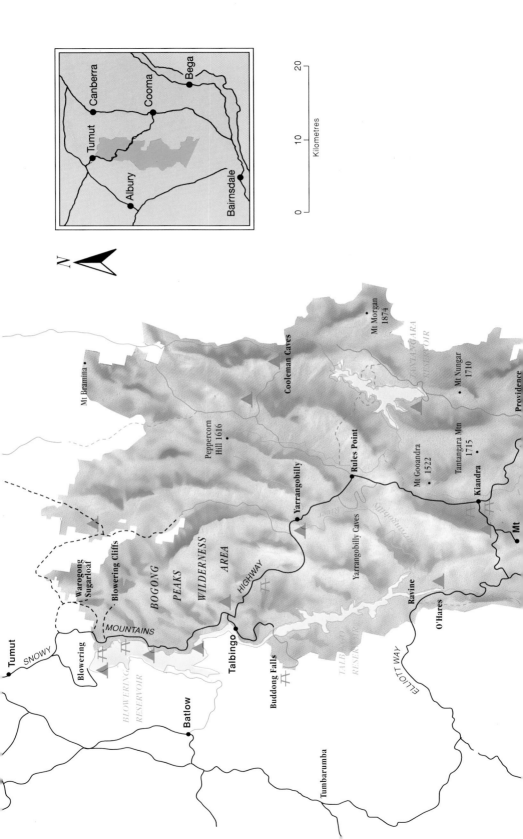

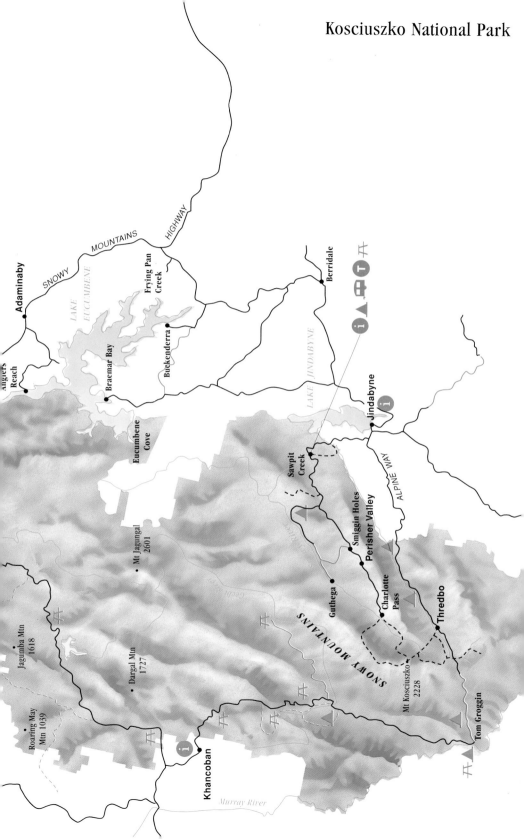

Kosciuszko National Park

Morton National Park

One of the largest national parks in New South Wales, Morton National Park occupies a high sandstone plateau dissected by the deep gorges of the Shoalhaven River. The northern section contains the majestic Fitzroy and Belmore Falls, while the south is a rugged wilderness area with steep-sided valleys, extraordinary monoliths, sandstone cliffs and the famous Pigeon House Mountain.

The park occupies an area of some 172,000 ha, a substantial portion of the Southern Highlands. Shoalhaven River dominates the northern area, cutting a mighty gorge through the sandstone plateau revealing ancient rocks of quartz, slate, siltstone, greywacke and schist. It has been dammed at Tallowa forming Lake Yarrunga which supplements the water supplies to Sydney and Wollongong.

The layers of sandstone were laid down when the land was beneath a shallow sea some 250 million years ago. Subsequent uplifting of the land created the plateau, and the streams and rivers have cut deep into the soft rock to create the present landscape.

Ettrema Plateau forms the central section of the park. About 700 m above sea level, this rocky landscape, softened by sparse woodlands and heaths, has been etched in swirling patterns by ancient rivers and cut through by meandering creeks to form deep, cliff-lined gorges. The most dramatic is Ettrema Gorge, a 400 m deep gash with a lip of precipitous cliffs above its forested slopes.

To the south lies the northern Budawang Range, a strange landscape of flat-topped mountains and rugged cliffs rising above deeply-eroded forested valleys carved by the Clyde River and its tributaries.

Millions of years of weathering has created buttresses, arches and extraordinary monoliths out of the sandstone, notably in The Castle and Monolith Valley area, reached by narrow passes between craggy sandstone mountains. Pigeon House mountain towers above the forested slopes in the south-east corner of the park. This rocky outcrop is actually a volcanic plug, a reminder of the violent forces that helped to form the southern Budawangs.

History

The park area was once part of the territory of the Walbanja and Wandandian tribes, coastal people who lived in the area for more than 20,000 years. The inhospitable nature of the countryside probably discouraged permanent habitation, and the local tribes regarded the gorge country as the likely haunt of mythical creatures. They hunted kangaroos and wallabies here, and evidence of their presence is seen in axe-grinding grooves, rock drawings and hand stencils in the upper Clyde and Endrick valleys. Stone arrangements have been found on Quiltys Mountain and Sturgess Mountain, indicating their use as ceremonial sites. Settlers began arriving in the 1820s, driving the Aborigines from the coast to the mountains, and by the turn of the century they had all but disappeared.

Tourists came to Belmore and Fitzroy Falls, Bundanoon and Kangaroo Valley in the mid 19th century by horse and later by bicycle. Guest houses were built, and the first guide book to the area was published in 1904. The core of the park area was protected in 1938, and Morton National Park was established in 1967. Subsequent additions have increased the park to its present size.

Tianjara Plateau was leased to the Commonwealth Government in the 1940s, and is still being used as an artillery firing range. This inappropriate use has caused considerable damage to the vegetation, and hikers must stick to the vehicle tracks to avoid unexploded bombs.

Plants and Animals

The sandstone plateau supports heaths, swamps, light scrub, woodlands and forests. The major trees are banksias, scribbly gums, Sydney peppermint, red and yellow bloodwood, silver-top ash and thin-leaved stringybark. Shrubs such as broad-leaved hakea, tea trees, sunshine wattle, narrow-leaved conesticks and mountain devil are common in the understorey. In spring the heaths are ablaze with wildflowers. There are red and yellow Christmas bells, mauve trigger plants, flannel flowers, boronias, coral heath, sundews and purple-flowered match heads.

Pockets of cool temperate rainforest grow in the valleys and sheltered gullies of the plateau; these are characterised by black wattle, sassafras, pinkwood, sarsaparilla vines, lawyer vines and many different types of ferns. Dense warm temperate to sub-tropical rainforests cover some of the lower slopes and valley floors. These magnificent forests contain giant red cedar trees, coachwood, turpentine, brown barrel and cabbage tree palms among the lilly pillies and stinging trees. Extensive stands of wet and dry eucalypt forests cover the escarpment slopes. The rare Ettrema mallee tree grows around the cliff edges in the central section of the park.

In the taller forests superb lyrebirds scratch for food among the leaf litter, while small white-throated tree creepers, scrub wrens and shrike tits rustle among the leaves. Satin bower-birds, king parrots, rosellas, gang gang cockatoos, and ground thrushes are all fairly common.

Swamp wallabies, red-necked wallabies, large eastern grey kangaroos, wombats, bandicoots and possums live in the area, and the banks of the Shoalhaven River contain numerous large holes leading into the burrows of the common wombat. Platypuses may be spotted at dawn or dusk when they leave their burrows to feed in some of the streams and pools.

Walks

Scenic walking tracks at Fitzroy and Belmore Falls provide access to numerous lookouts with views of the waterfalls and valleys. Two tracks at Fitzroy Falls, each about 3 km long, provide spectacular views from each side of the escarpment. At Bundanoon there are 14 designated walks, mostly short and easy, leading to lookouts, the abandoned Erith Coal Mine, Fairy Bower Falls, Fern Tree Gully, and into the remarkable Glow Worm Glen.

Although a number of walking trails have been established in the southern section of the park, those leading into the rugged wilderness areas can be difficult to follow, and are only suitable for experienced walkers skilled in the use of a map and compass. Inform a reliable person of your proposed route or complete a Journey Intention Form at the Fitzroy Falls Visitor Centre.

A popular walk leads to the summit of Pigeon House Mountain. This takes about four hours return from the picnic area, passing through eucalypt forest, open woodland, heath and a tall, dense forest before emerging onto the sandstone plateau where steel ladders lead to the summit. Abseiling and rock climbing are not allowed at Pigeon House.

Facilities

The Fitzroy Falls Visitor Centre provides information about the falls and other areas of the park. There is a cafe, shelters, fireplaces, toilets and a camping area here. Bookings are not accepted. The camping area at Gambells Rest has hot showers, barbecues and toilets, but only nine sites. Advance bookings are essential. Bush camping is allowed well away from roads and visitor use areas, but is not permitted in the Valley of the Monoliths, and in other areas indicated at the visitor centre.

Access

The park is approximately 160 km south-west of Sydney via the Hume Highway. Turn off at Mittagong and travel south through Bowral, or take the Princes Highway through Wollongong to Albion Park, and follow the Illawarra Highway through Robertson.

From Nowra you can head north through Kangaroo Valley or travel west towards Braidwood to reach Tianjara Falls and the southern section of the park. Pigeon House Mountain is reached by turning off the Princes Highway 3 km south of Burill Lake. Bundanoon is on the main southern railway line from Sydney.

Climate

The park has a temperate coastal climate with warm summers and mild winters.

Fitzroy Falls Visitor Centre, Nowra Rd, Fitzroy Falls, NSW 2577. Tel. (02) 4887 7270.

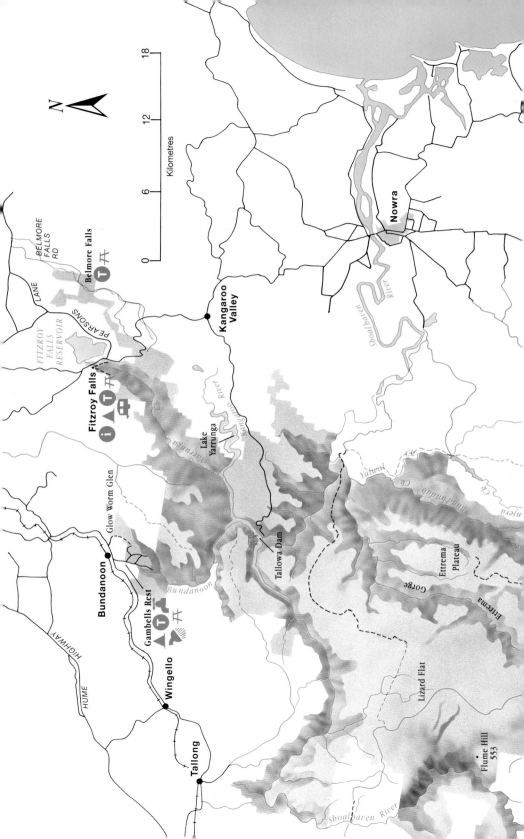

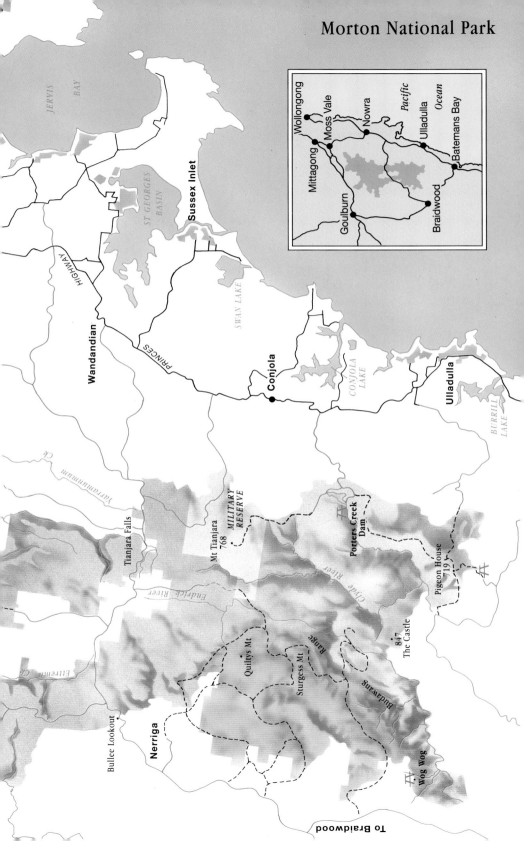

Morton National Park

Wollongong

Mittagong

Moss Vale

Nowra

Pacific

Ulladulla

Ocean

Batemans Bay

Goulburn

Braidwood

JERVIS BAY

ST GEORGES BASIN

Sussex Inlet

HIGHWAY

Wandandian

PRINCES

SWAN LAKE

Conjola

CONJOLA LAKE

Ulladulla

BURRILL LAKE

Yarramunmun CK

Tianjara Falls

MILITARY RESERVE

Mt Tianjara 768

Potters Creek Dam

Pigeon House 719

Endrick River

Clyde River

Ettrema CK

Quiltys Mt

Sturgess Mt

Range

847
The Castle

Budawang

Bullee Lookout

Nerriga

Wog Wog

To Braidwood

Royal National Park

Located on the southern border of Sydney, Royal National Park is one of the city's greatest assets. The area has survived almost unchanged since the arrival of the First Fleet, and the beautiful bays, beaches, cliffs, woodlands and heaths allow us to visualise the Port Jackson area before Australia's largest city was created.

Royal National Park was the first national park to be created in the world. It was first gazetted in 1879 as The National Park, and was renamed in 1954 to commemorate the visit of Queen Elizabeth II. Shaped like a saucer rim descending from 300 m in the south to the tidal estuary of Port Hacking in the north, the park covers 15,014 ha of mostly heath-covered sandstone. Creeks, swamps, waterfalls, clear pools, rugged coastal cliffs of brown and golden sandstone, beautiful isolated beaches, rainforest pockets and woodlands characterise the landscape.

Formation

About 230 million years ago the area was part of a great coastal delta. River systems originating in the New England district carried particles of rock from the folded volcanic hills of the north, building up layer upon layer of sediments above coal deposits from the previous epoch. The sedimentary rocks vary from chocolate-coloured shales to sandstones and conglomerates, capped by the glittering, quartz-rich Hawkesbury sandstone.

A long period of uplift began 100 million years ago. Subterranean forces pushed the land up and tilted it down to the north to form the saucer-shaped Sydney basin. Millions of years of weathering have eaten into the rocks, creating rugged cliffs, gorges, and sea caves where the shales have been washed out from beneath the hard sandstone. Deep rounded potholes like the Figure Eight Pool have been scoured by boulders trapped in depressions and undercut by the surging coastal waters. Layers of different coloured sandstone are visible on the cliff faces with bands of hard red ironstone or ferrocrete nodules running through them. In the southern section of the park dark shale strata and the older sedimentary rocks can be seen at the base of the cliffs.

The Dharawal People

For more than 30,000 years the Dharawal people lived along this coast, moving between the bays, estuaries and inlets of Port Hacking in bark canoes, fishing, collecting shellfish and hunting for game. Middens found beneath the rock overhangs at Curracurrang have revealed discarded tools and the remains of countless meals. The bones of two infants, two juveniles and an adult have been found in a burial site beneath the largest rock overhang here. Bone fishing hooks discovered at Wattamolla indicate that they fished with hand lines from canoes on the lagoon behind the beach.

Rock engravings at Jibbon, Wattamolla and Curracurrang depict human figures, kangaroos, animal tracks, sharks and whales. Axe-grinding grooves have been found on rocks near the water, and hand stencils occur in a number of rock shelters.

Other than these few signs little remains to remind us of an Aboriginal presence in the area. Up against the main body of the occupying forces, the Dharawal were quickly dispossessed of their ancestral lands. The survivors were ravaged by diseases such as smallpox and measles brought here by the early settlers.

Plants and Animals

The poor sandy soils support a surprisingly rich flora and produce beautiful wildflower displays. The vegetation along the coast is mainly heath interspersed with pockets of trees and shrubs around the sheltered creek systems. The more conspicuous species are angophoras, banksias, casuarinas, hakeas, grevilleas, tea trees, the gymea lily, Christmas bells, waratah and pink swamp heath. Behind the dunes encircling Marley are swamplands with paperbarks, tea trees and rushes; while spinifex, pig face, twining guinea flower, wattles, banksias and bloodwoods help to stabilise the dunes.

The richer shale soils support pockets of rainforest, particularly in the south-east section of the park and around the Hacking River. The common rainforest plants here include tree ferns, cabbage tree palms, turpentines, coachwoods and sassafras.

More than 200 species of birds have been identified in the park, including kookaburras, rosellas, cockatoos, ravens, currawongs, superb lyrebirds, green catbirds and satin bowerbirds. The heath communities attract fan-tailed cuckoos, pigeons and quails. Banksia flowers provide food for honeyeaters, spinebills and wattlebirds; and wrens forage in the undergrowth. Along the coast are terns, silver gulls and sea eagles, and the occasional albatross may be seen soaring in the wind.

The majority of mammals are nocturnal, although some may be seen around dawn and dusk. They include the swamp wallaby, ringtail and brushtail possums, bush and swamp rats, the New Holland mouse and antechinuses. Echidnas are common in the grasslands, and deer frequent the coastal woodlands. Whales may be seen offshore at certain times of the year as they migrate to breeding grounds off the Queensland coast.

Venomous snakes such as the tiger, brown, red-bellied black snake and the death adder are occasionally encountered. Like the other reptiles they are protected, and should not be disturbed.

Walks

Numerous well-maintained and signposted walking tracks cross the park. The coast track extends some 26 km from Bundeena south to Otford, and is a leisurely two-day walk, passing through heaths and forests. Magnificent views can be had from cliff tops and headlands, particularly Garie North Head and Marley Headland. The track descends to a number of beaches and bays, including Big and Little Marley, Wattamolla and Burning Palms.

Tracks in the Uloola area meander through heaths, woodlands and forests to the west of the Hacking River, passing waterfalls, freshwater pools and creeks. The Uloola Track begins at Waterfall Station. This 11 km walk takes you through heathlands with beautiful wildflower displays before descending through woodlands and rainforests past Uloola Falls to Audley. A series of crystal clear waterholes at Blue Pools offer a refreshing dip on hot summer days.

Facilities

Caravan and car camping is allowed at Bonnie Vale, where there are showers, toilets and a laundry. Bookings are essential during holidays and long weekends. There are shops at Bundeena, 2 km from the camping area, and kiosks at Audley, Wattamolla and Garie. The bush camping policy is being reviewed, although there are bush camping sites at Uloola Falls near Waterfall and North Era on the coast. Permits must be obtained from the Audley Visitor Centre by each individual camper.

Rowing boats and canoes can be hired at Audley and taken upstream along the Hacking River and Kangaroo Creek.

Access

The park is 32 km south of Sydney and 47 km north of Wollongong via the Princes Highway, turn off past Sutherland for Audley, or enter along McKell Ave from Waterfall. From Wollongong the park is reached via Stanwell Park and Otford.

A regular ferry service links Bundeena with Cronulla Railway Station. There is a good rail service between Sydney and Wollongong, stopping at Loftus, Engadine, Heathcote, Waterfall and Otford. An infrequent tram service links Loftus and the park (call the Sydney Tramway Museum on 02-9542 3646).

Climate

Like Sydney, the park has warm summers and cool winters, with the highest rainfall in summer.

Royal National Park, PO Box 44, Sutherland, NSW 2232. Tel. (02) 9542 0666.

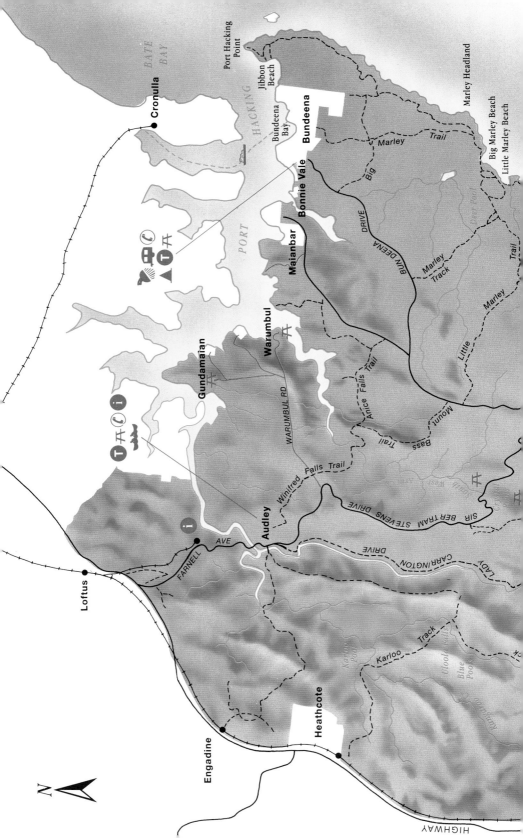

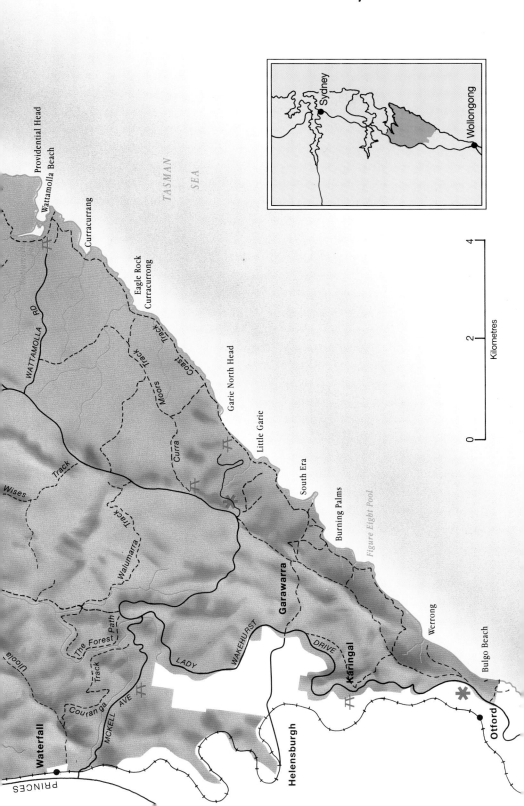

Royal National Park

Ku-ring-gai Chase National Park

One of Australia's oldest and most magnificent National Parks, Ku-ring-gai Chase lies right on the northern boundary of Sydney. Despite its proximity to such a large city this area remains largely untouched, and offers the Sydneysider a wilderness area with secluded beaches and sublime views over the blue waters of Pittwater, Broken Bay and the Hawkesbury River.

The park covers 14,838 ha of rugged sandstone country set around the flooded river valley of Broken Bay. Deep narrow valleys cut through the sandstone by Cowan Creek and other water-courses have formed sheltered waterways long used by sailors and fishermen. There are many beautiful secluded bays, woodlands, heaths and an amazing variety of plants growing on the poor soils of the area.

Formation

The area was once part of a low-lying river delta in which layers of sandstone and shale were deposited over millions of years. The region was uplifted about 100 million years ago. Most of the softer shales have since eroded away exposing the sandstone, which in turn has weathered, leaving high sandstone hills descending steeply to sheltered bays and inlets. Some volcanic activity has occurred around West Head, producing the richer dolerite soils of this district.

History

Guringai (Ku-ring-gai) is the name of the language group of the Aboriginal people who occupied this area before white settlement. Known as the Garigal clan, they lived in the area for at least 20,000 years, using canoes to catch fish and shellfish along the coast. Engravings in the soft sandstone rock are fairly common throughout the park, depicting fish, human figures, clubs and other objects. Charcoal and red and white ochre drawings or paintings can be seen in some of the sandstone caves, while the larger caves were often used for shelter. These sites are important to Aboriginal people and must not be interfered with. The park was established in 1894 to protect the rugged sandstone country on the southern bank of the Hawkesbury River.

Plants and Animals

Despite the poor quality of the park's sandstone soils the area supports open woodlands, eucalypt forests, heaths and rainforest pockets. Wildflower displays colour the landscape in winter and spring. Boronias, eriostemon, pea flowers, yellow wattles, white heath flowers and banksias are all in flower at this time of year, and comprise just a small portion of the 900 plant species recorded.

Common trees include smooth-barked angophoras, casuarinas, banksias (particularly the gnarled and misshapen old man banksia), bloodwood, scribbly gum, stringybark, ironbark, and mangroves. The burrawang palm, which is actually a cycad (*Macrozamia communis*), grows on the richer volcanic soils on West Head. Although poisonous, the seeds of the burrawang were regularly eaten by the Aborigines, who developed a technique of leaching out the poison. Grasstrees and native flax also grow in this area. They were used to make spears, string bags and fishing lines.

More than 180 bird species have been recorded in the park. The nectar-laden banksias attract hundreds of honeyeaters in winter and spring. Lyrebirds are found at West Head and Garigal. The males can be heard during the mating season from May to July performing their territorial displays. Flocks of crimson and eastern rosellas are often seen, particularly around the bird-feeding area at Kalkari Visitor Centre. Black ducks, wood ducks, chestnut teals and grey teals live in the swamps and freshwater pools, feeding on aquatic plants and insects. Superb lyrebirds live in the shady gullies.

Most of the mammals in the area are nocturnal, retreating by day to tree hollows, rocky crevices and burrows, emerging at night to feed on leaves, insects and blossoms. Grey kangaroos live around the Visitor Centre, and can be seen in the early morning and late afternoon. Swamp wallabies and wallaroos live in the park but are rarely seen. Among the other mammals are bats, possums and gliders, koalas, bandicoots, marsupial mice, antechinuses and echidna.

The extensive tidal waterways are breeding and feeding grounds for all manner of aquatic life. Some 40 fish species have been recorded in the area, including sharks, bream, blackfish, mullet, hairtail jewfish and the leatherjacket.

Walking Tracks

The park offers the walker a great choice of tracks, from the short signposted Discovery Track at the Visitor Centre with wheelchair access, to day-long bushwalks following ridge tops and descending to bays and the foreshore. West Head is criss-crossed with walking tracks beginning at West Head Road. Most are easy walks through dry sandstone terrain and forested areas leading to lookouts over Pittwater and Broken Bay. The start of each track is marked by a footprint symbol.

The Garigal Aboriginal Heritage Walk begins at the West Head Picnic Area and introduces the visitor to the lifestyle of the Guringai people. The track is 3.5 km long and passes a rock art site known as Red Hand Cave where there are ochre hand prints, an engraving site with figures, fish and other objects cut into the rock, and a sandstone shelter overlooking Resolute Beach. Other excellent examples of Aboriginal rock art are found close to the beginning of the Basin Track.

Tracks in the Bobbin Head and Cowan Creek area take the walker through various habitats and interesting terrain. The Sphinx Track to Bobbin Head is 6.5 km long and passes through a variety of vegetation types including mangroves along the foreshore of Cowan Creek. Return via the Bobbin Head Track, a one to two hour walk along a fire trail following the ridge past Aboriginal engravings back to the park entrance, a spectacular wildflower walk in spring.

Horse riding is permitted on certain trails. These have been specially selected to minimise erosion and damage to vegetation. Riders must stay on the authorised trails.

Facilities

Camping is only allowed at The Basin camping area on Pittwater, reached by private boat, ferry from Palm Beach, or by walking from West Head Road. There are toilets, cold showers and fireplaces; visitors should bring their own cooking fuel. Fees are charged and booking is essential as the area is very congested during peak holiday periods. A youth hostel on private land at Towlers Bay offers accommodation.

There are kiosks at Bobbin Head, Appletree Bay, Akuna Bay and Cottage Point. The Visitor Centre at Kalkari has an audio-visual display, information sheets and animal exhibits. Guided walks and nature activities are also available. Picnic areas, toilets and fireplaces are found in many locations. Shark nets protect swimmers at The Basin. There are boat ramps at Appletree Bay, Akuna Bay, Brooklyn and Cottage Point. Fuel, bait and provisions are available, and houseboats, cruisers and rowing boats can be hired from private operators.

Access

The park is 30 km north of Sydney via the Pacific Highway, turn off at Pymble or Mount Colah for Bobbin Head, or via Mona Vale Road, turn off at Terrey Hills for West Head. An entrance fee is charged. A regular ferry boat runs from Palm Beach to The Basin. There are railway stations at Turramurra, Mt Ku-ring-gai and Berowra, and a bus service from Turramurra Station to Bobbin Head.

Climate

The park has warm summers and cool winters, with the highest rainfall in the summer months. Visit all year round.

Ku-ring-gai Chase National Park, Bobbin Head, Turramurra, NSW 2074. Tel. (02) 9457 9322 .

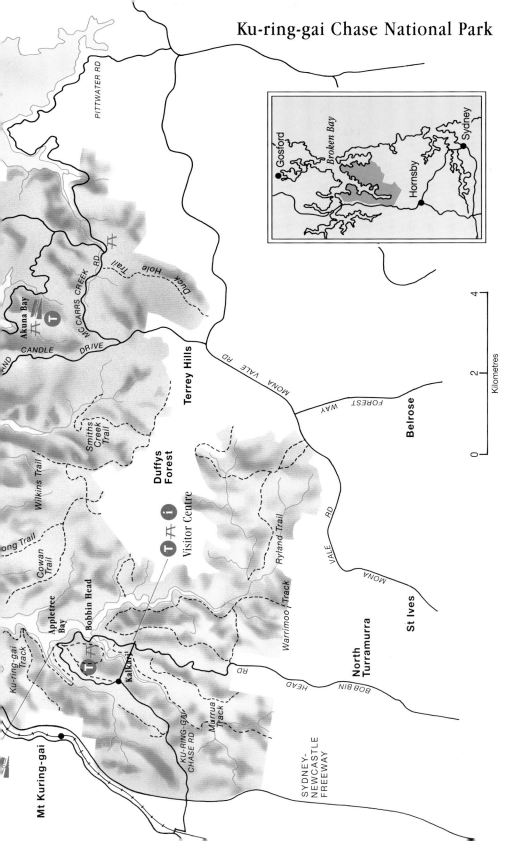

Ku-ring-gai Chase National Park

Blue Mountains National Park

Part of the Great Dividing Range, the Blue Mountains form a rugged barrier between Sydney and the west. The Blue Mountains National Park conserves some of the most spectacular scenery of this region, including vast wilderness areas and a wide diversity of habitats and microclimates.

The park straddles the Great Dividing Range, covering 247,000 ha and comprising three sections. The lower section begins at Glenbrook and incorporates a number of sandstone gorges cut by the Nepean and other rivers. There are swimming holes, lookouts, scenic picnic areas and walking tracks offering a good introduction to the terrain.

The northern section centres around the Grose Valley, a great canyon with sheer-sided walls of coloured sandstone formed by the Grose River and its tributaries. Here are waterfalls, lookouts, walking tracks and magnificent scenery.

The southern section is largely wilderness adjoining Echo Point and the Three Sisters, a popular tourist area where eroded rock pinnacles tower above the Jamison Valley.

Formation

The area was once part of a giant, low-lying river delta filled with sandy sediments. Between 50 and 25 million years ago parts of the east coast were forced upwards to create the Great Dividing Range. Rivers and creeks were etched into the sandstone plateau to form wide valleys and sheer escarpments. Below the sandstone cap are shales, fine sandstones and black coal seams.

The soft sandstone is easily eroded, leaving many precipitous overhangs, particularly in the Grose Valley, where the cliffs are continually undermined by falling rocks.

Settlement

The Blue Mountains were occupied by two Aboriginal clans for at least 20,000 years, and their charcoal and ochre drawings, rock engravings and axe grinding grooves can still be seen in the park. The Gandangara occupied the lowlands around Jamison Valley, leaving the Daruk people to the central core of the Blue Mountains and the Glenbrook area. Like other Aboriginal groups they were in no position to resist European settlement, and most succumbed to introduced diseases and the effects of colonisation.

The Blue Mountains were regarded as an impenetrable barrier by the first settlers, trapping the convicts in Sydney. Towards the end of the 19th century, however, many convicts attempted to escape, lured by rumours of a Utopia beyond the mountains. In 1798 the Governor decided to dispel the Utopian myth and dispatched a convict named Wilson to find a route across the mountains. Wilson had lived with the Aborigines, and used their help to cross the mountains south of Lake Burragorang.

Wilson's journey was apparently unknown to Blaxland who, a decade later, made a number of unsuccessful attempts to find grazing lands beyond the mountains. In 1813 he teamed up with Wentworth and Lawson, and they found a route between the Gross and Coxs Rivers. This journey was recorded as the first European crossing, and became the road via Glenbrook and Katoomba, built by convict gangs and opened in 1815. Tourism developed in 1868 when the Great Western Railway began operating. The Blue Mountains National Park was declared in 1959, with major additions in 1977 and 1987.

Plants and Animals

The low nutrient, sandstone-derived soils on the ridge tops and plateaux support a surprising variety of plant species. The most exposed sites are covered by low heaths, while in dry sheltered areas there are mixed woodlands of eucalypts, smooth-barked apples, banksias, tea trees, wattles and casuarinas, with an understorey of flowering plants such as waratahs, mountain devils, pea flowers and the Christmas bush.

The richer soils of the moist, sheltered lower gullies support rainforest pockets dominated by coachwoods, turpentines and grey-barked sassafras with an understorey of giant ferns, vines, creepers, mosses and lichens.

On the floor of the Grose Valley a forest of giant blue gums, some hundreds of years old with massive, smooth trunks, has survived the forester's axe. Grassy areas, ferns and scattered wattles are the main ground cover beneath the canopy of these mighty trees.

More than 100 bird species have been recorded. Scrub wrens are common in dense shrubs, treecreepers on tree trunks, golden whistlers and yellow thornbills in the upper foliage. Honeyeaters forage among the flowers, while birds of prey, such as the nankeen kestrel hover above searching for mice and lizards. Whip birds, bellbirds, gang gang cockatoos, crimson rosellas and eagles are often seen or heard.

Among the mammals are swamp wallabies, possums, gliders, marsupial mice and wombats. The common reptiles include goannas, jacky lizards, water dragons, skinks and snakes such as the highland copperhead and eastern tiger snake.

Walks

The Grose Valley, Wentworth Falls, Katoomba and Glenbrook are famed for their spectacular scenery, and there are many well maintained and signposted walking tracks, from easy nature walks along the cliff tops to long wilderness trails. For a good introduction to the area take the 1.8 km Fairfax Heritage Track. This trail has disabled access, and winds through typical Blue Mountains ridge top vegetation from the Heritage Centre at Blackheath. The Grand Canyon walk from Evans Lookout is a popular three hour journey through a variety of habitats, following sandstone shelves cut into a narrow chasm by the creek. More strenuous walks in this area lead to the floor of the Grose Valley and the Blue Gum Forest.

Trails in the Glenbrook area will take you to swimming holes, the Nepean River, Warragamba Dam and Red Hands Cave – an Aboriginal site decorated with red ochre hand stencils. The Valley of the Waters nature track at Wentworth Falls takes two to three hours and winds through rainforest, eucalypt forest and woodland, wetland and heath with distant views. Walks along the cliffs offer many scenic lookouts.

Short walks near Katoomba follow the cliff lines around the Three Sisters, leading to waterfalls and rainforests. Harder walks go into the Jamison Valley, out onto the Ruined Castle and Narrow Neck ridges, and deep into the southern section of the park. Long walks into the southern wilderness are for experienced, well-equipped hikers, who must be prepared for bad weather at any time of year. Fill out a trip intention form at a Visitor Centre, or leave details of your route with a responsible person.

Facilities

The District Office is at the Heritage Centre in Blackheath. The small camping area at Perrys Lookdown has toilets and picnic tables. The Visitor Centre at Glenbrook and the Richmond Office issue camping permits and take bookings for Euroka Clearing, which has basic facilities but no drinking water. The Ingar camping area is reached from Wentworth Falls and is fuel stove only with pit toilets and no drinking water. The secluded camp ground at Murphys Glen has basic facilities only.

Bush camping is permitted at least 500 m from roads and facilities, except in the Upper Grose Valley where it is only allowed at Acacia Flat and Burra Korain Flat. Camping is prohibited within 3 km of Lake Burragorang.

Access

The park is approximately 100 km west of Sydney via the Great Western Highway or the Bells Line of Road between Windsor and Lithgow. A train service runs from Sydney to Mount Victoria.

Climate

Summers are warm with cool nights. Winters are very cold, and the weather can change dramatically at any time of year.

Blue Mountains Heritage Centre, Govetts Leap Rd, Blackheath, NSW 2785. Tel. (02) 4787 8877 Richmond Office, 370 Windsor Rd, Richmond, NSW 2753. Tel. (02) 4588 5247

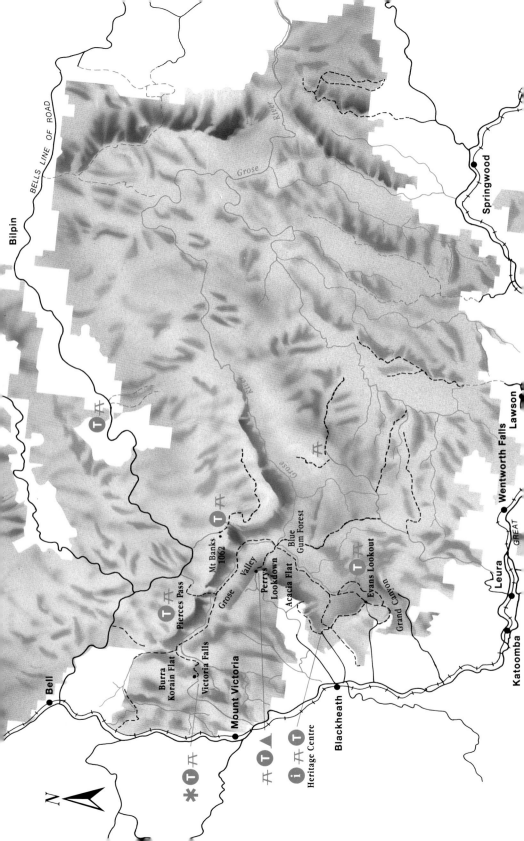

Blue Mountains National Park

Myall Lakes National Park

Of all the coastal parks in New South Wales, Myall Lakes is exceptional both in its popularity and its physical features. The 10,000 ha of tranquil waterways in the park comprise the largest network of coastal lakes in the state. They are separated from the ocean by high sand dunes and are ideal for sailing, canoeing and fishing. Along the coast the Pacific breaks on magnificent beaches, the haunt of surfers and beach fishermen.

The Myall and Boolambayte Lakes and Bombah Broadwater occupy one third of this 31,562 ha park. They are separated by a shallow, winding passage, and their eastern shores are protected from the Pacific Ocean by high, windswept sand dunes. The northern and western shores are fringed with trees interspersed with small, secluded sandy beaches.

Myall River flows through Bombah Broadwater and continues through the park past Tea Gardens before emptying into the ocean at Port Stephens. The lakes are mostly freshwater, increasing in salinity towards the south where seawater flows back into Myall River at high tide. Along the coast are long beaches interrupted by rocky headlands. Broughton Island, 2 km off-shore, is included in the national park, and along with Seal Rocks and Little Gibber is an excellent scuba diving area.

Formation

The Myall Lakes are geologically of very recent origin. They began to form towards the end of the last ice age, about 8000 years ago, when rising sea levels drowned the coastal river valleys leaving rocky hills such as Mungo Brush, Johnsons Hill, Violet Hill and Bombah Point as offshore islands. Sand pushed onshore by tidal currents and the prevailing winds slowly accumulated around some of the islands, and a series of sand dunes began to form between Hawks Nest and Forster. Today these high dunes separate the Myall Lakes from the Pacific Ocean, while Islands such as Broughton Island remain isolated from the mainland, and others are rocky hills rising above the sand plains.

Vegetation

The beach dunes have been colonised by sand-binding grasses and many small flowering shrubs, producing excellent wildflower displays.

Woodlands and eucalypt forests grow in sheltered sites. They are dominated by red bloodwood, blackbutt and swamp mahogany, interspersed with smooth-barked apples, wattles, coast and old man banksias and grasstrees. The lakes are fringed with paperbarks, swamp oaks and other casuarinas.

Mungo Brush is an important littoral rain-forest, and one of the few patches left in Australia. It grows on a carboniferous sandstone hill that was once an offshore island. The surface has weathered to produce soil of greater fertility than the surrounding sandy soils. This type of rain-forest community, growing close to the sea and subjected to salt-laden winds, has a low canopy layer with no tall emergent trees. The species growing at Mungo Brush are generally salt tolerant with small hard leaves, and there are fewer mosses, ferns and epiphytes than in other rainforest types. Common trees include the native olive, coogera, brush bloodwood and shining leaf stinger, cabbage tree palms and the occasional strangler fig. Bright berries of the orange thorn add colour to the understorey.

The Myall River was once bordered with stands of red cedar trees. They were logged in the late 1800s, and today pine plantations grow where these magnificent trees once stood. Sand mining operations have similarly damaged the ecology of areas of the dunes between Tea Gardens and Seal Rocks.

Wildlife

The different habitats attract a wide range of fauna. Among the large mammals are grey kangaroos, swamp and red-necked wallabies, dingos and koalas. Other common mammals are brush-tailed and ring-tailed possums, gliders, bandicoots, echidnas and marsupial mice. Among the reptiles are lace monitors, copper-tailed skinks, geckos, jacky lizards, carpet pythons, red-bellied black snakes and common brown snakes. All native animals, including snakes are protected, and the latter should be given a wide berth.

Numerous waterbirds are attracted to the lakes. Pelicans are common, and make an unforgettable sight as they come in to land like great flying boats. Black swans, ducks, egrets, cranes and herons are abundant. White-breasted sea eagles cruise above the waterways searching for fish, and whistling kites are often seen soaring in the thermals. The forests are home to many species of birds, attracted by the variety of fruits and flowers. In the rainforests are golden whistlers, figbirds, white-headed and flock pigeons, emerald doves, satin bowerbirds, rufous fantails and the spectacular regent bowerbird with gold and black plumage. Olive-backed orioles, king parrots, rufous whistlers, spangled drongos and numerous honeyeaters are among the other forest birds found in the park.

Walks

For spectacular views over the Myall Lakes system and the coastline climb Violet Hill (124 m) a steep, 800 m walk from the carpark. Of the many walking tracks winding through the park one of the most popular is the Mungo Brush Rainforest Track. This is an easy 30 minute stroll through coastal rainforest from Mungo Brush Camping Area, introducing you to this scientifically important community.

Mungo Track follows Mungo Brush Road from Hawks Nest to Mungo Brush, a 21 km walk through many different habitat types. An excellent series of tracks lead from Bombah Broadwater to Johnsons Beach, Tickerabit and Shelly Beach where there are camping areas accessible only by boat or foot.

Facilities

Boats and houseboats can be hired at Bulahdelah and Tea Gardens, south of the park. Boat launching ramps, camping and picnic areas have been developed throughout the park. Bush camping is allowed away from the roads and tracks, except on the ocean beaches and south of Mungo Brush.

Mungo Brush, on the lake shore 21 km north of Tea Gardens, is the most popular camping area, with basic facilities including gas barbecues. The camping ground and picnic area near Yagon Beach has dry composting toilets and a windmill-powered water supply, and can be reached by road from Seal Rocks.

Camping areas with toilets, accessible by boat or on foot, are located at River Mouth, Shelly Beach, Tickerabit, Johnsons Beach and Korsmans Landing. At Bombah Point there is a private camping and caravan park known as Myall Shores. This has powered and unpowered sites, cabins, a kiosk and fuel supplies. Contact (02) 4997 4495 for more information. Fresh water is only available at Mungo Brush, Violet Hill, Bombah Point and Yagon.

Access

The park is 234 km north of Sydney via the Pacific Highway. Turn off to Tea Gardens and Hawks Nest to reach the southern section of the park. Turn off at Bulahdelah along Lakes Road to reach Bombah Point, or turn off along The Lakes Way north of Bulahdelah to Seal Rocks. Side roads lead from The Lakes Way to Korsmans Landing and Violet Hill, although the Clarkes Road access to Korsmans Landing is not recommended for conventional vehicles. The Yagon camping and picnic area can be reached from Seal Rocks. A car ferry operates from Bombah Point to the opposite side of Broadwater giving access to Mungo Brush Road. There are a number of 4WD access routes from Mungo Brush Road to the beach, but vehicles are not allowed on sand dunes or beaches north of Big Gibber Headland.

A regular bus service operates between Newcastle and Bulahdelah, Bungwahl, Hawks Nest and Tea Gardens.

Climate

The park has a temperate coastal climate with warm summers and mild winters.

Myall Lakes National Park, PO Box 270, Raymond Terrace, NSW 2324. Tel. (02) 4987 3108.

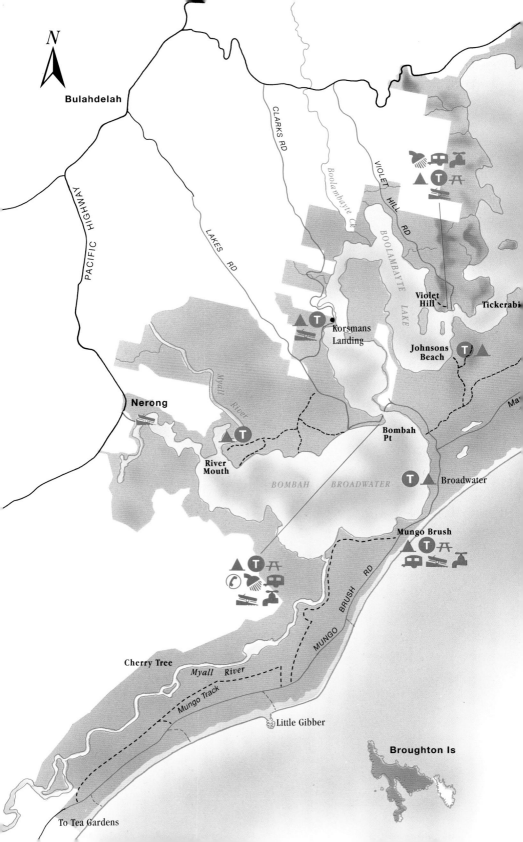

N

Bulahdelah

PACIFIC HIGHWAY

CLARKS RD

LAKES RD

VIOLET HILL RD

Boolambayte Cr

BOOLAMBAYTE LAKE

Korsmans Landing

Violet Hill

Tickerabi

Johnsons Beach

Myall River

Nerong

River Mouth

Bombah Pt

BOMBAH BROADWATER

Broadwater

Mungo Brush

MUNGO BRUSH RD

Cherry Tree

Myall River

Mungo Track

Little Gibber

Broughton Is

To Tea Gardens

Myall Lakes National Park

LAKES WAY

Bungwahl

SMITHS LAKE

SEAL ROCKS RD

MYALL LAKE

Seal Rocks

Sugar Loaf Pt

Ⓣ ▲ Beach

Yagon

Treachery Head

▲ Ⓣ ⌂

ks

Big Gibber Headland

Sands

TASMAN SEA

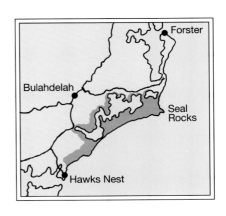

Forster

Bulahdelah

Seal Rocks

Hawks Nest

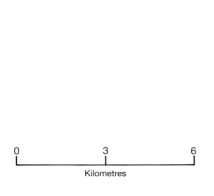

0   3   6
Kilometres

Barrington Tops National Park

World Heritage listed Barrington Tops is the most southerly of the east coast rainforest parks. Six major rivers plunge through magnificent rainforests on their way south to the Hunter or north to the Manning River. In a few hours you can walk from lush sub-tropical rainforests to alpine woodlands and snow grass meadows.

Situated on one of the highest points of the Great Dividing Range, the park covers 40,453 ha on the northern escarpment of the Hunter Valley. It encompasses two linked, high altitude plateaux rising to 1577 m at Polblue Mountain. From here the land drops away in a series of steep valley systems, falling rapidly to 400 m. Careys Peak stands at the head of a spectacular valley with views over the forested ridges as far as the sand dunes of the Newcastle coast. The area has an average rainfall of around 2000 mm a year, and the heavy summer downpours turn the creeks and rivers into torrents, crashing over the plateau from Antarctic beech forests to lowland rainforests.

Formation

The basalt cliff at Careys Peak, the rich dark basalt soils and granite boulders are evidence of volcanic eruptions that occurred in the area millions of years ago. Ancient lava flows piled deep layers of basalt, up to 300 m thick in places, on top of the older sedimentary rocks. A long period of uplift followed, raising the land to form the eastern highlands. As the land rose the creeks and rivers carved their way into the surface to form the valleys and ridges. The sudden drops and steep escarpments are the result of vertical cracks or faults that opened up as the land rose from near sea level to its present height.

History

Little is known about the early history of the region. The territories of four Aboriginal tribes appear to have overlapped here: the Worimi of Port Stephens, the Geawegal of the upper Hunter, the Dainggati of the northern valleys and the Birpai of Taree and the Manning River. The inhospitable climate and topography no doubt discouraged any permanent habitation, and the plateau would have been visited for ceremonial reasons or to gather food and other resources.

This all changed after the appearance of the early settlers, who took control of the foothills, forcing the Aborigines to either accept dispossession or to fight. Those who fought retreated to the unoccupied plateau where they were hunted down in 1835 after the murder of five shepherds.

Apart from the timber-getters who plundered the rainforests for their valuable cedar trees, and the odd bushranger who holed up in the rugged ranges, the mountains were left largely untouched during the 19th century. Increasing scientific interest and recreational use of the area culminated in a proposal to establish a wilderness park, putting a halt to the destructive practices of a few graziers who used the plateau as a summer feedlot. Opposition from the Forestry Commission saw the proposal watered down, and in 1969 about 14,000 ha of non-contentious land were gazetted as a national park. Subsequent additions have increased the park to its present size.

Plants and Animals

Cool temperate rainforests dominated by Antarctic beech trees grow on the sheltered slopes and moist gullies of the plateau. Dripping with ferns and mosses and often shrouded in mist, these ancient trees form circular stands dating back 2000 years or more. Grasslands and swamps characterise the high plains, interspersed with sub-alpine woodlands dominated by snow gums, mountain gums and wattles, with an understorey of snow grass and lomandra. In spring and summer wildflowers colour the area. Lower down the vegetation changes to dry and wet eucalypt forest. The dominant trees here are blue gums, brown barrels, manna gums and messmates, with banksias taking over on the shallow soils.

Sub-tropical rainforests grow in the moist lower gullies. In these you will find giant strangler figs, rosewood trees, pencil cedar, tamarind, corkwood and beautiful stands of palms. Elkhorn and birds-nest ferns grow high in the trees, while fungi, lichens and mosses adorn the forest floor. Watch out for the giant stinging tree, whose broad leaves are covered with stinging hairs.

The damp silence of the rainforest is pierced by screeching yellow-tailed black cockatoos, bell miners, whipbirds, and the superb lyrebird, a great imitator of other birds. With stealth and patience you may see a spotted-tailed quoll, a feathertail glider, or the diggings of bandicoots and the scratchings of native mice. Walk in the sub-alpine woodlands around dawn or dusk and you may see grey kangaroos, swamp wallabies, red-necked wallabies, possums, or wombats.

Walks

The Barrington Tops area is best explored by foot. Sudden and dramatic changes in the weather can occur, and walkers must be well equipped and should inform someone of their planned route. Two major walking tracks provide access to some of the highest areas of the park.

The Link Trail Walk takes six hours, is 22 km one way and climbs slowly through dry eucalypt and magnificent cool temperate rainforests, past a waterfall to sub-alpine woodlands, ending with a magnificent view from Careys Peak. Barrington Tops Walk is less strenuous and takes about five hours over the high level plateau. From Careys Peak the track passes over a grassy plain, crosses the Barrington River, and continues through a wetland area to Bromlow Creek. From here you can go through scrubland to Big Hole camping area, or continue north across Beean Beean Creek, through sub-alpine woodlands to the main road.

Sharpes Creek Walk near the Gloucester River camping area takes one hour return, following the creek through regenerating rainforest. There are a number of short walks from the picnic areas at the end of Gloucester Tops Road. The one hour return River Walk follows the Gloucester River past good trout fishing spots through sub-alpine woodlands with snow gums and mountain gums. The one hour Gloucester Falls Walk leads through similar vegetation to the Falls Lookout where there are fine views of the many waterfalls on the river.

The Antarctic Beech Walk in the same area is a short walk through cool temperate rainforest with stands of ancient Antarctic beech trees and soft tree ferns.

Rocky Crossing Walk from Barrington Guest House takes you into a sub-tropical rainforest environment in the Williams River Valley to scenic cascades and Rocky Crossing Waterfall. The return journey takes four hours. Some areas have been logged, and among the regrowth are stumps of great red cedar trees.

Facilities

There are information bays at Devils Hole, Gloucester River and Williams River. Gloucester River camping area has toilets and BBQs, and campers are asked to pitch their tents in the numbered sites. On the plateau are basic camp-sites with fireplaces at Little Murray and Junction Hole, accessible by 4WD vehicles. Bush camping is permitted anywhere in the park, but must be more than 300 m from roads, tracks, camping and picnic areas. Accommodation is also available at Barrington Guest House on the Dungog Road just outside the park (02-4995 3212).

Access

The park is 321 km north of Sydney and 31 km west of Gloucester. To Gloucester River camping area take Gloucester Tops Rd from the turn off on the Gloucester-Stroud Rd, 10 km south of Gloucester. This road is subject to flooding in very wet weather. The northern area is reached via the mostly unsealed road from Gloucester to Scone. The Salisbury road from Dungog (43 km) is sealed for most of its length and passes the Barrington Guest House before climbing to the southern section of the park.

4WD tracks should not be used in wet weather or between 1 June and 30 September.

Climate

Local conditions vary dramatically from alpine to temperate coastal. Winter snowfalls on the plateau are common, and thick mists may descend at any time of year. The best time to visit the park is from October to April.

Barrington Tops National Park,
PO Box 270, Raymond Terrace, NSW 2324.
Tel. (02) 4987 3108

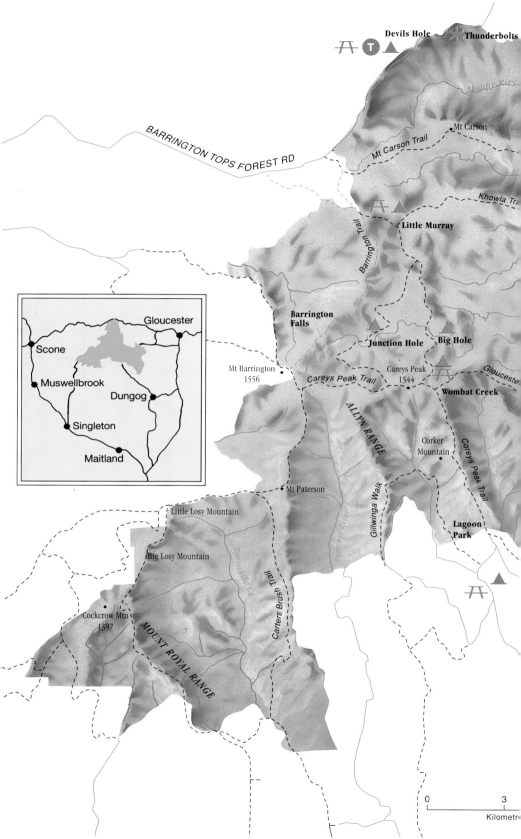

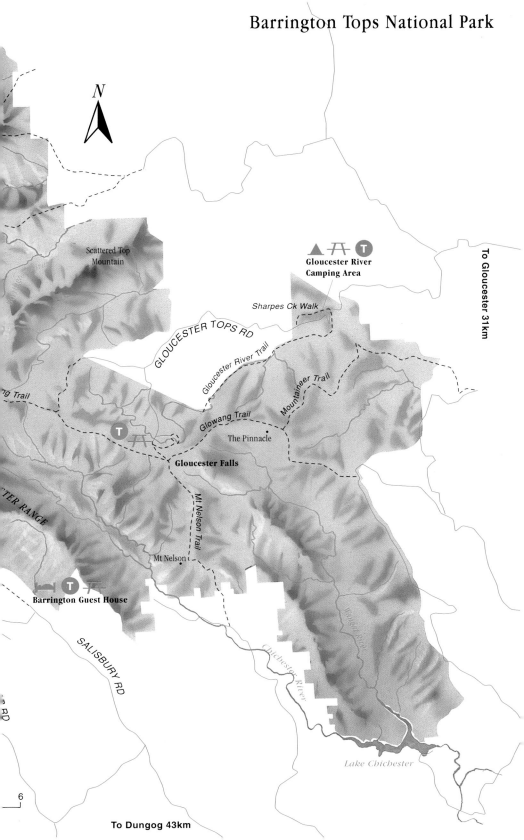

Barrington Tops National Park

Warrumbungle National Park

On the western slopes of the Great Dividing Range where the endless plains begin, the Warrumbungles rise above the flat landscape in a jumble of rock domes, barren spires and forested ridges. The park is a transition zone where plants and animals of the wet eastern side of the Great Divide overlap those of the drier western plains.

The 21,534 ha national park protects part of the Warrumbungle Range, a dramatic area of peaks and spires set among rolling hills, rising to 1206 m at Mount Exmouth. The most spectacular formation is a 90 m high wall of rock known as the Breadknife, that rises precariously from the wooded slopes. All around are tors, bluffs and rock domes: the ragged remnants of ancient volcanoes that once shook this part of Australia.

Formation

Around 13 million years ago the Warrumbungles were at the centre of an active volcanic region. Over a period of 5 million years molten rock and ash poured out of weaknesses in the ancient sedimentary rocks, covering the countryside to a depth of several hundred metres and building a new mountain range. When the volcanoes finally ceased the forces of erosion took over, carving out new shapes from the rock. The tough trachyte that sealed the mouths of the volcanoes after their final burst of activity resisted the weathering process, and remains as the spires of Crater Bluff, Belougery Split Rock and other rocky formations in the park. The Breadknife was once a lava-filled dyke or crack in a volcanic cone that has long-since eroded away.

Beneath the volcanic rock are ancient sandstone beds laid down when the area was submerged beneath the shallow sea that covered much of inland Australia. Rivers and creeks have since cut deep valleys through the volcanic rock and ash, exposing ancient sandstones transformed by the enormous heat and pressure into harder, more resistant quartzite.

History

Before European settlement the Warrumbungle Range provided food and shelter for people of the Kamilaroi, Kawambarai and Weilan language groups. Evidence of the Aboriginal inhabitants can be found in various parts of the park, most commonly in the form of stone flakes used to make cutting, scraping and chopping tools.

The explorer John Oxley and his party were the first Europeans to see the Warrumbungles. They climbed Mount Exmouth in 1818 and named the mountains Arbuthnots Range, after a British civil servant. This was later changed back to Warrumbungle, a Kamilaroi word meaning crooked mountain. Charles Sturt and Thomas Mitchell also explored the district, and white settlers soon followed, seeking pasturelands for their sheep and cattle. The national park was established in 1955.

Plants and Animals

The Warrumbungle Range supports a diverse plant and animal life representative of both sides of the Great Dividing Range. The moist, sheltered southern slopes support plants typical of the higher rainfall areas of the New England Tablelands, while the drier northern slopes are colonised by hardy, water-conserving plants usually found on the dry western plains.

The breakdown of volcanic rocks has created areas with comparatively rich soil supporting woodlands dominated by white box trees, while the low nutrient sandy soils and rocky outcrops support stands of white gum, narrow-leaf ironbark, and black and white cypress pine. In spring and early summer wildflower displays colour the sandstone areas with blooms of wattle, wild irises, pink and purple peas, flannel flowers, boronias, scented sun orchids and pimelias.

The diversity of landform, microclimate and vegetation provides habitats for many animals. Commonly seen are eastern grey kangaroos, swamp and red-necked wallabies, wallaroos, possums and echidnas. The park is home to a breeding population of koalas, and these can sometimes be found in woodlands.

Unfortunately, the once-common brush-tailed rock wallaby has become almost extinct due to predation by foxes and competition by feral goats for food and space.

More than 180 species of birds have been recorded in the park. These include the magnificent wedge-tailed eagle, 19 species of parrots including the brightly-coloured red-winged parrot, cockatoos, and flocks of emus.

Among the reptiles and amphibians are bearded dragons, lace monitors, skinks, blue-tongued lizards, geckos, green tree frogs and brown snakes.

Walks

More than 30 km of walking tracks have been developed, many offering breathtaking views over the park. These range from an easy 1 km self-guiding nature walk to a six hour walk of 16 km. If you become lost, remember that all the creeks in the park flow to Tooraweenah Road or the John Renshaw Parkway.

The track to Fan's Horizon is one of the shortest walks to offer views of the volcanic peaks of the south-east corner of the park. This is a 3.6 km walk with a fairly steep climb with around 1000 steps leading to the lookout. White Gum Lookout Walk is a 1 km return bitumen track suitable for wheelchairs with views over the western plains and volcanic peaks.

One of the most popular tracks and one of Australia's great walks takes you on a spectacular five to six hour journey into the heart of the most scenic area of the park: the Grand High Tops. This well-formed track follows Spirey Creek along an attractive valley, crossing the creek eleven times before rising towards the Breadknife. Steep side tracks can be taken to lookouts at Febar and Macha Tors, Spirey View and Bress Peak. The track zig-zags past the Breadknife with glimpses to Belougery Spire, before ascending to the crest of the Grand High Tops. The views from here are magnificent, revealing a landscape of peaks, domes, streams, forests and valleys.

The park is one of the best places in Australia

for rock climbing, which is allowed anywhere except on the Breadknife and Chalkers Mountain. There are many easy, difficult and classical climbs, although permits must be obtained.

Facilities

There are four campsites with vehicular access: Camps Blackman, Elongery, Wambelong and Pincham (equipment must be carried from the nearby car park). Camp Burbie is walk-in only. Camp Blackman also has powered sites, septic toilets and hot showers, the others have pit toilets and tank water. Camps Wambelong, Elongery and the Woolshed are used by large groups, and bookings are accepted for organised groups only. Backpackers can camp at designated places on the walking trails. Permits must be obtained from the Visitor Centre to prevent overcrowding and protect the fragile ecology. Water must be carried and fuel stoves used.

Balor Hut below the Breadknife can accommodate eight people and may be booked in advance. The Visitor Centre provides park information, souvenirs and a video room. Supplies and accommodation are available in Coonabarabran.

Visitors should bring their own firewood or use a fuel stove for cooking. Electric barbecues, picnic tables and amenities with disabled access are provided at Canyon Picnic Area and the Visitor Centre.

Access

The park is 491 km north-west of Sydney and 33 km west of Coonabarabran. It can be reached from the west via Coonamble, and from the south through Gilgandra via Tooraweenah. Visitors are requested to register at the Visitor Centre. Roads within the park are now sealed.

Climate

The park has hot summers and cold winters, with a low annual rainfall.

Warrumbungle National Park,
PO Box 39, Coonabarabran, NSW 2357.
Tel. (02) 6825 4364.

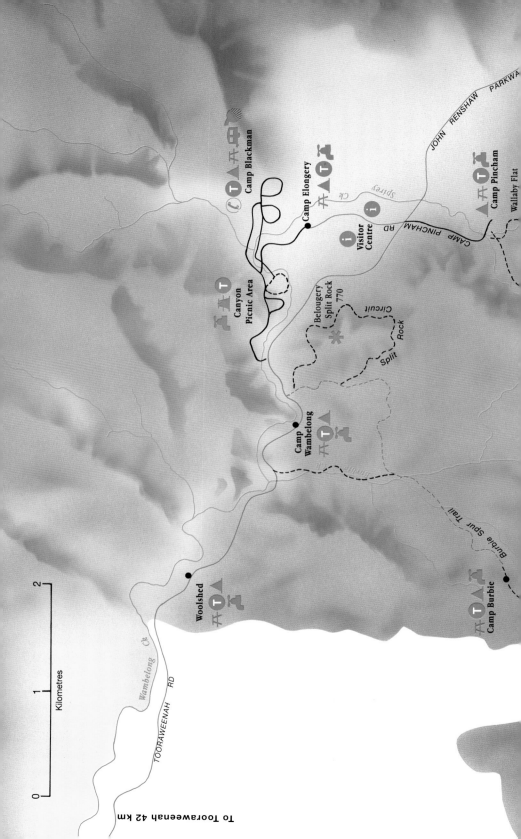

To Tooraweenah 42 km

Kilometres
0 1 2

Wambelong Ck

TOORAWEENAH RD

Woolshed

Camp Wambelong

Canyon Picnic Area

Camp Blackman

Camp Elongery

Belougery Split Rock
770

Split Rock

Circuit

Wambelong

Spirey Ck

Visitor Centre

CAMP PINCHAM RD

Camp Pincham

Wallaby Flat

JOHN RENSHAW PARKWAY

Burbie Spur Trail

Camp Burbie

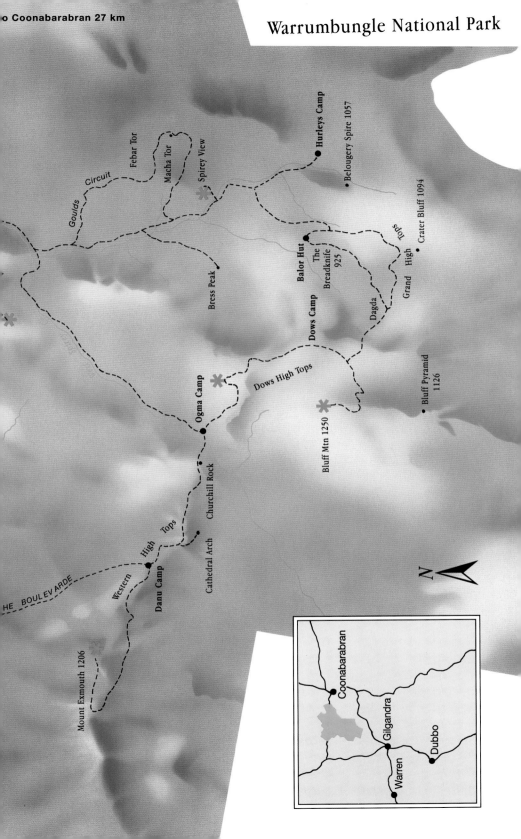

o Coonabarabran 27 km

Warrumbungle National Park

Hurleys Camp

Belougery Spire 1057

Febar Tor

Macha Tor

Spirey View

Goulds Circuit

Crater Bluff 1094

Balor Hut

The Breadknife 925

Bress Peak

Dows Camp

Dagda

Grand High Tops

Ogma Camp

Dows High Tops

Bluff Pyramid 1126

Churchill Rock

Bluff Mtn 1250

High Tops

Cathedral Arch

Western

THE BOULEVARDE

Danu Camp

Mount Exmouth 1206

N

Coonabarabran

Gilgandra

Dubbo

Warren

Dorrigo National Park

The Dorrigo Plateau towers above the lush Bellinger Valley, looking down over the forested ridges and valleys of this rugged scarp country, and out to the Pacific Ocean. Classified as a World Heritage Area, Dorrigo National Park protects the rainforests of the eastern part of the plateau. Visitors find themselves in a timeless world, where great buttressed trees tower above them and thick vines snake down from the high, dense, forest canopy.

This 7885 ha park is on the edge of the escarpment where the land plunges to the Bellinger Valley below, in a series of rugged valleys and ridges stretching out towards the coast. Humid coastal air masses rising from the valley drop their water as they pass up and over the escarpment, giving the area a very high seasonal rainfall. Numerous streams arise in the park and form the headwaters of the North Arm of the Bellinger River. They cascade down the cliffs and valley sides from an altitude of nearly 920 m to the coastal plains. The eastern section embraces the catchment of the Never Never River which drops from the plateau at Gleniffer Falls, the highest waterfalls in the park.

Formation

Some 18 million years ago lava from the Ebor volcano flowed over the plateau, covering the ancient sedimentary and granitic rocks with a deep layer of basalt. The sedimentary rocks were laid down almost 500 million years ago when the land was part of a submerged continental shelf off the east coast. Granite intruded into the layers of sediment, and the whole area was lifted to form the plateau.

Over the past 18 million years the rivers have carved deep gorges into the basalt cap, leaving great fingers of land extending out onto the coastal plain. Weathering has broken down the basalt to form the rich soils of the Dorrigo Plateau, leaving behind some interesting rock formations such as the hexagonal columns at Tristania Falls. In the valleys the basalt has eroded away entirely, exposing the older sedimentary and granitic rocks. These form the less fertile yellow clay soils of the lower gullies.

History

The Dorrigo Plateau was originally within the territory of the coastal Gumbainggirr people, whose land extended from Coffs Harbour to Nambucca Heads. They visited the plateau in summer to take advantage of seasonal food sources, but probably spent most of their time on the drier coastal plains where they hunted for game and fished in the rich waters.

Cedar-getters explored the area in the 1830s, following the rivers in search of valuable red cedar trees. At that time the whole plateau and the valleys were covered by rainforests, known collectively as the Don Dorrigo Scrub. Graziers encroached from the New England Tableland, clearing the forests as they went and driving the Aboriginal people from their lands. There is little doubt that the whole plateau would have been cleared had not parts been set aside in 1902 as flora and fauna reserves. These were added to over the years, and in the early 1980s the park was almost doubled by the addition of 3900 ha in the north-east.

Plants

The rich volcanic soils of the plateau support sub-tropical rainforests. One of the most prominent trees is the strangler fig with its great aerial roots. Other forest giants include red cedars, yellow carabeens and black booyongs with their wing-like buttresses. On the steeper slopes are giant stinging trees. In spring flame trees come alive with a display of vivid red flowers. Vines drape through the trees and birds nest ferns, staghorns, elkhorns and orchids sit high up among the branches. Bangalow palms grow along creeks, and ground orchids thrive in rocky crevices.

Warm temperate rainforests grow on the poorer yellow clay soils in the lower gullies. This type of forest is less complex with an abundance of tree and ground ferns, mosses, orchids and fungi growing beneath coachwood, sassafras, hoop pine, prickly ash and corkwood trees. Some rare trees grow in this forest community, including the Dorrigo waratah, the Dorrigo plum, the Dorrigo laurel and the pink cherry.

In the highlands, particularly in the north-east and around the Never Never picnic area, are small patches of cool temperate rainforest, where ancient Antarctic beech trees grow alongside coachwood, water gum and sassafras trees. Wet sclerophyll forests grow on the ridges sloping down into the Bellinger Valley. They are charac-terised by tall stands of blackbutt, Sydney blue gum and tallow-wood trees with an understorey of blueberry ash and the palm-like burrawang.

Wildlife

More than 120 bird species have been recorded in the park, including pied currawongs, king parrots, honeyeaters and brush-turkeys. The latter often try to take food from visitors' picnic baskets. Deeper in the forest are mimicking superb lyrebirds, satin bower-birds, wonga pigeons, catbirds, small blue-green noisy pittas, and the endangered and highly camouflaged marbled frogmouth.

Most of the mammals are nocturnal, although red-necked and red-legged pademelons feed around the picnic areas in the late after-noon. In the forests are ringtail and brushtail possums, pygmy, sugar and greater gliders, swamp wallabies, echidnas, bandicoots, koalas and carnivorous marsupials such as the cat-size spotted-tailed quoll, and the rat-size brush-tailed phascogale. Platypuses live in some of the creeks; grey kangaroos are common in the grassy areas and open forests, and the rare parma wallaby has been seen in the wet forests.

Walks

The Satinbird Stroll from The Glade picnic area is a 15 minute walk through sub-tropical and warm temperate rainforest, winding round the escarpment along a gently-sloping track with a boardwalk into the canopy. The 5.8 km Wonga Walk branches off this track and leads further into the rainforest, past two waterfalls and along the escarpment with glimpses of the coast through tall eucalypts at Hardwood Lookout.

From the Never Never picnic area a 6.4 km walk leads to Cedar Falls, the most spectacular waterfall in the park. This track descends steeply from the Rosewood Creek Track to the falls. The latter is a 5.5 km loop through warm temperate rainforest along Rosewood Creek past Coach-wood Falls. The Blackbutt track is a one-way 6.4 km walk along the escarpment from the picnic area to the park entrance. Casuarina Falls, 2.4 km along the track, is set among towering black-butts and tallow-wood trees with magnificent views over the rugged countryside.

The north-eastern area can be explored via the old logging roads from Slingsbys Road through Killungoondie Plain. The historic 15 km Syndicate Track leads to Gleniffer in the Bellinger Valley with spectacular views from Lanes Lookout. There is an overnight camping area where the track crosses Wild Cattle Creek.

Facilities

The Glade and Never Never picnic areas have barbecues, tables, toilets and shelter sheds. Dorrigo Rainforest Centre near the park entrance has an exhibition area, theatrette, cafe, rainforest shop, electric barbecues and a skywalk into the rainforest canopy with panoramas over the Bellinger Valley and Pacific Ocean. Rangers conduct guided tours and other activities during the summer holidays.

There are no serviced camp sites, although bush camping is allowed in the Killungoondie-Never Never River area for those taking overnight hikes. Accommodation is available at Bellingen and Dorrigo.

Access

The park is 60 km west of Coffs Harbour, and 4 km east of Dorrigo via the Dorrigo-Bellingen Road.

Climate

The park has a high rainfall with some 2500 mm of rain falling mainly in summer. Winters can be cold. Most of the orchids and the spectacular flame trees bloom in spring.

Dorrigo National Park, PO Box 170, Dorrigo, NSW 2453. Tel. (02) 6657 2309.

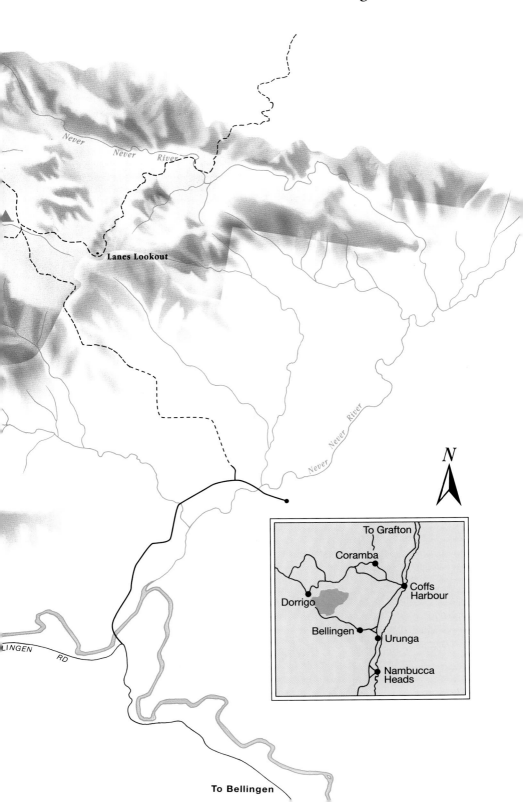

Never Never River

Lanes Lookout

Never Never River

N

LINGEN RD

To Grafton

Coramba

Coffs Harbour

Dorrigo

Bellingen

Urunga

Nambucca Heads

To Bellingen

New England National Park

*New England National Park is a place of swirling mists and breathtaking views.
From the sub-alpine plateau on the precipitous eastern edge of the Great Dividing
Range the land plunges 1500 m into a warm wilderness area of deep folded valleys
clothed in sub-tropical rainforests. The park's exceptional natural beauty and variety
of habitats have led to its inclusion on UNESCO's World Heritage List.*

The park covers an area of some 52,185 ha.
The majority is a wilderness of densely forested
valleys sheltered beneath the cliff walls of the
eastern edge of the New England Plateau. The
escarpment rises to 1562 m at Point Lookout,
one of the highest points north of the Snowy
Mountains, with spectacular views over the
valleys to the Pacific Ocean.

The park's facilities and walking trails are
centred around the top of the plateau, a cool,
breezy and damp region where moist air from
the plains condenses as it rises up the face of the
escarpment. The Bellinger River and a number
of its tributaries rise in the park, and have carved
their way to the coast, forming the virtually
inaccessible complex of valley systems below
the escarpment.

Formation

The processes that have created the present landscape go back 500 million years to a time when
the area was part of the continental shelf and was
submerged beneath a shallow sea. Deposits
washed from coastal mountains by ancient rivers
gradually accumulated on the seabed to form
sedimentary rocks. Subsequent upheavals of the
earth's crust forced the land upwards, folding and
buckling the sedimentary rocks as they emerged
from the ocean. Molten rock intruded into the
old sediments from below, hardening into granite
and converting the surrounding rocks into slate,
phyllite and greywacke.

Some 40 million years ago the New England
Plateau was the centre of violent volcanic activity.
At least five massive lava flows occurred over the
following 22 million years, covering the ancient
sedimentary rocks with a thick cap of basalt and
trachyte rock. The mineral-rich rocks that form
the cliffs at the edge of the plateau come from the
Ebor volcano which was active 18 million years

ago. All that remains of this volcano is a raised
area in the valley where the Bellinger River leaves
the park, known as The Crescent.

Further uplifting of the land has raised the
tableland several hundred metres. The rivers
have carved gorges deeper and deeper into the
plateau, leaving blunt peninsulas, finger-like
projections and a complex system of valleys
below the escarpment. The basalt rock still forms
a thick cap over the plateau, while far below the
cliffs the basalt has completely eroded away to
reveal the ancient folded sedimentary rocks. In
places amazing needle-like outcrops tower from
the shale slopes. These weathered fingers of hard
trachyte rock are the remnants of old volcanic
plugs, sills and dykes.

History

The park crosses the boundaries of the territories
of at least two Aboriginal tribes: the Gumbainggirr and the Thungutti of the coast, and possibly
those of the Dainggati and Bainbai of the plateau
and ranges.

The surveyor Clement Hodgkinson was the
first European to describe the area. He explored
the country north of Macleay Valley in 1841,
eventually coming to the formidable cliffs at the
foot of the escarpment where 'a gigantic range
rose up in perpendicular buttresses'. The land
around the edge of the escarpment and the
rugged valleys below were bypassed by the waves
of settlers and timber-getters who moved into the
area in the 19th century.

The Park was created in 1931 to protect
17,000 ha at the head of the Bellinger Valley.
Additions included a pristine blackbutt forest of
6000 ha, known as the Black Scrub (1983), and
22,000 ha of wilderness in 1996. The park was included on UNESCO's World Heritage List in 1986
as part of the Central Eastern Rainforest Reserves.

Vegetation

The variety of soil types, range of altitude and high rainfall of the area provide suitable conditions for a wide variety of vegetation types.

On the high plateau visitors are drawn to the cool temperate rainforests growing below the edge of the escarpment and in sheltered sites along the creeks. Antarctic beech trees form the canopy layer. These long-lived, ancient trees, dripping with mosses in the misty mountain air, flourished millions of years ago when Australia was part of the super continent of Gondwana. Still quite common in Tasmania, they exist in only a few high, cool places on the mainland. Beneath the canopy are smaller trees such as mountain laurel, southern sassafras, mountain blueberry and prickly ash, with a sprinkling of soft tree ferns, epiphytic orchids and a recently discovered astelia lily that grows in shady sites on the wet cliff faces.

On the drier ridges and slopes the cool temperate rainforest gives way to grassy open forest dominated by brown barrel, common tea tree and coast banksia. On the exposed high plateau are tall, open snow gum forests, interspersed with tall wet eucalypt forests dominated by silvertop, New England messmate, blackbutt, blue gum and tallow-wood trees.

Small heath communities grow on shallow soils in exposed areas such as Wrights Lookout. Here are low shrubs like hill banksia, swamp tea tree, saw sedge, New England baekea, and the rare white eye-bright and pink kunzea.

Along the valley floors and lower slopes the cool temperate rainforest changes to luxuriant sub-tropical rainforest. The dominant trees are towering red cedars, strangler figs, corkwood and small stands of hoop pines. Some, such as the white booyong and yellow carabeen, are stabilised by large buttressed trunks.

Wildlife

The range of habitats from alpine to sub-tropical is reflected in the richness of the park's wildlife. Among the mammals are the platypus and echidna, several gliders, from the tiny feathertail glider to the sugar glider and yellow-bellied glider, possums, a large variety of kangaroos, including the grey kangaroo, the rare parma wallaby, wallaroo, swamp and red-necked wallabies, pademelons and the long-nosed potoroo. Several bat species live in the lowlands, including a large colony of bent-winged bats found in one of the old mine tunnels near Platypus Creek. Dingos may be heard growling at night, but they are seldom seen, and wombats emerge at night from their underground burrows.

Of the 110 bird species recorded in the park 20 are from the sub-tropical rainforest, and many are at the southern limit of their range. The superb lyrebird, scrub turkey and three cockatoo species range widely throughout the park. The mimicking sounds of the lyrebird are often heard echoing up the escarpment around dawn and dusk. In winter you may see flocks of the rare white-headed pigeon and the top-knot pigeon. Around the campsites are pied curra-wongs and Lewin's honeyeater. Wedge-tailed eagles soar in the thermals off Point Lookout searching for prey.

Common reptiles include the blue-tongued lizard, large goanna, leaf-tailed gecko, bearded dragon and water dragon. The strange sphagnum frog was recently discovered in the park, and can be heard calling with a creaking sound from its deep burrow. The female lays its eggs in the burrow where they develop into tadpoles and grow into miniature frogs before emerging.

Walks

Most of the park is a trackless wilderness, and bushwalkers descending from the escarpment must be prepared for very rough walking conditions and slow progress. This area is extremely rugged and demands very good orienteering skills. The ranger will suggest interesting routes through the wilderness area, and should be informed of your plans and estimated time of return.

A number of graded walking tracks have been constructed on the rim of the escarpment in the Point Lookout and Wrights Lookout area. Although mists often obscure the view from the escarpment they enhance the peace and quiet beauty of the rainforest, and on a clear day the tracks offer spectacular views overlooking rainforests, woodlands and waterfalls.

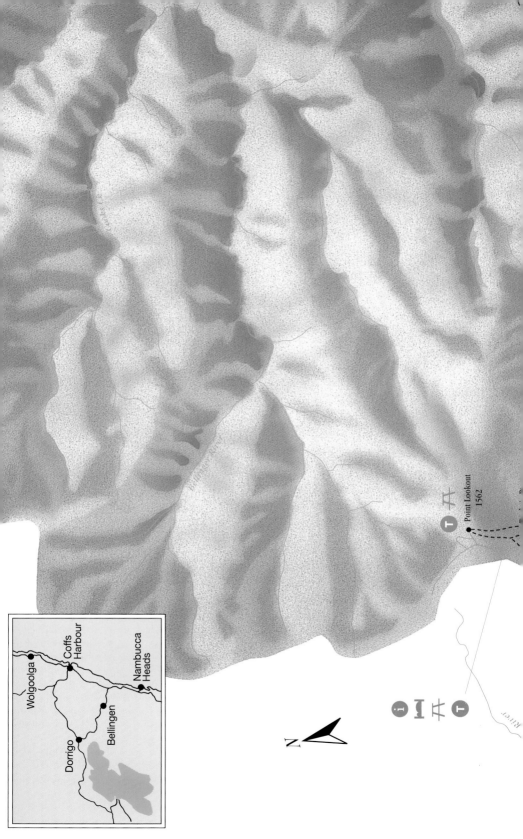

Point Lookout
1562

Bellinger River

Cooks Ck

Wolgoolga

Coffs
Harbour

Nambucca
Heads

Dorrigo

Bellingen

N

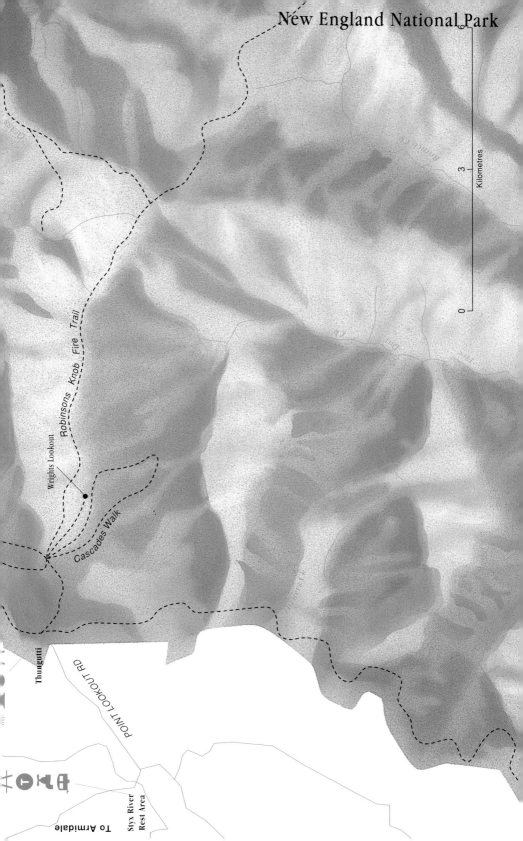

New England National Park

One of the most interesting is the Lyrebird Nature Walk, a 7 km circular walk from Banksia Point. Travelling north the track follows the edge of the escarpment, passing through eucalypt forest, open heath and boulder-strewn areas before descending into cool temperate rainforest below the cliff face. The Eagles Nest Track branches off here and continues north through temperate rainforest under towering basalt cliffs, past the spectacular Weeping Rock to Eagles Nest Lookout.

The Lyrebird Track turns south towards Wrights Lookout past the fern-filled Treefern Valley, through damp beech forests where the trees are draped with hanging mosses and superb lyrebirds may be seen or heard. A short diversion to Wrights Lookout will take you to a small windswept plateau where stunted heath grows on the poor soil, and a few rare plants, such as the purple kunzea and woolly cryptandra grow. From the lookout the track follows the rim of the escarpment through open forest, dense scrub and back to Banksia Point through sclerophyll forests and a small area of temperate rainforest.

The Cascade Walk is a circular track, 7 km long, leading from the fire trail before Wrights Lookout. This follows a leaf-littered path through a magnificent Antarctic beech forest down to Five Day Creek where small waterfalls and cascades tumble over moss-covered rocks as you follow the path upstream. Beech orchids are common in this area, flowering around October, and contrasting with the green of the forest.

For those with limited time a short circular walk from Banksia Point passes through a variety of vegetation types. This 2 km walk takes you into cool temperate rainforest, descends into Tree Fern Valley and returns through open eucalypt forest, passing very dense pockets of hill banksias. The diversity of the vegetation is reflected in the many bird species found along the walk, including lyrebirds, honeyeaters, treecreepers and thrushes.

Facilities

The park is well served with cabin accommodation, camping grounds and picnic areas. Bush camping is permitted, but the ranger should be notified of your intentions. Styx River rest area, 2 km outside the park boundary on the Point Lookout Road, has barbecues, pit toilets and running water. The camping area at Thungutti close to the park entrance has sites tucked away in clearings, a number of walk-in camp sites, barbecues, pit toilets and cold showers.

Cabin accommodation is available at the Chalet for six visitors, Tom's Cabin for eight visitors, and the Residence for ten people. Tom's Cabin is a basic bushwalkers' cabin with bunks, solar lighting, an open fire, gas ring and shower. The others are more comfortable with electricity, fireplace, refrigerator and cooking utensils. They are all located in the Banksia Point area, and may be booked up to six months in advance. Accommodation and supplies are available at Ebor, Dorrigo and Armidale.

Access

The park is 85 km east of Armidale and 140 km from Grafton via the Grafton to Armidale road, turn off 9 km south of Ebor along a good gravel road to the park entrance. Caravans are not permitted on the park access road which is winding, narrow and steep.

Climate

The park has mild wet summers with an annual rainfall of 2200 mm accompanied by frequent mists and fogs. Winters are cold and generally dry, with some heavy snowfalls on the exposed high tops. You should always bring warm clothing and rain-wear.

Dorrigo District Office, PO Box 170, Dorrigo, NSW 2453. Tel. (02) 6657 2309.

Gibraltar Range and Washpool National Parks

The Gibraltar Range rises above the coastal plains to create a landscape of great granite outcrops, steep-sided valleys and magnificent stands of pristine rainforest. These two parks, straddling the Gwydir Highway, are now part of the state's World Heritage Area, but the preservation of the Washpool rainforests was only achieved after a protracted and acrimonious struggle between conservationists and timber workers.

A rugged mountainous region abutting the eastern edge of the New England Tableland, Gibraltar Range National Park was set aside as a reserve in the early 1960s when the highway between Grafton and Glen Innes was first constructed. This part of the Gibraltar Range comprises large areas of granite rock which has weathered into poor quality soils supporting mostly open woodlands and heaths. North of the highway is a pristine wilderness area. Growing on its rich volcanic soils are the largest remaining areas of undisturbed rainforest in New South Wales, and the world's largest coachwood forest.

The 17,273 ha of land comprising Gibraltar Range National Park were of little economic interest to the timber industry, and the area was declared a national park in 1967 to preserve its scenic beauty and great natural diversity. Not so the Washpool. Prior to construction of the Gwydir Highway commercial logging operations were confined to the lower eastern parts of the range where access posed no serious problems. Giant red cedar trees, the 'red gold' of the timber-getters, were felled and carted from the rainforests by hundreds of bullock teams for shipment to Grafton and Sydney. The forests of the interior of the range, protected by the inaccessible nature of the land, were spared the logger's axe.

When the highway was completed, and it became clear that the Forestry Commission planned to allow logging in the Washpool rainforests, the conservation movement sought to have Washpool declared a wilderness area. This proposal met with severe opposition from the timber industry, and the conflict raged for a

number of years until 1982 when the New South Wales Government took the historic decision to protect the remaining rainforests in the state. Washpool National Park was declared in 1983 to preserve 27,715 ha including the Washpool and Coombadjha Valleys, and the Viper and Willowie Scrubs. The forested slopes of the Malara and Desert Creeks were, however, excluded from the park as part of a compromise with the timber industry.

History

Prior to the arrival of European settlers the Gibraltar Range was part of the territory of three Aboriginal tribes: the Bundjalung, the Yokumbal and the Gumbainggirr. There is little evidence to suggest that these people actually lived in this rugged terrain, but they certainly visited the area in search of food and game, and possibly for ceremonial purposes. Stone tools have been found along Coombadjha and Viper Creeks, and stone arrangements recorded in other areas.

Squatters arrived in the Clarence Valley in the 1840s, forcing the Bundjalung people to leave their land along the river and flee to the mountains. Gold prospectors arrived in the 1850s and pushed their way into the western boundary of the park, their hopes fanned by the discovery of gold in the Rocky River. The gold rush was short-lived, however, and apart from a small amount of tin and antimony mined around Main Creek along the northern edge of the park around the turn of the century, the area was left virtually untouched until logging operations began to eat into the accessible margins of the rainforests.

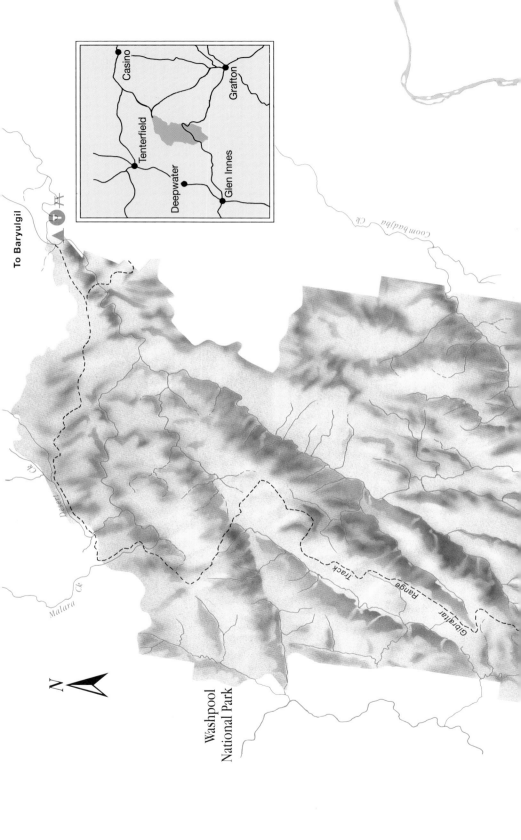

To Baryulgil

Casino

Grafton

Tenterfield

Deepwater

Glen Innes

Coombadjba Ck

Malara Ck

Gibraltar Range Track

N

Washpool
National Park

Gibraltar Range and Washpool National Parks

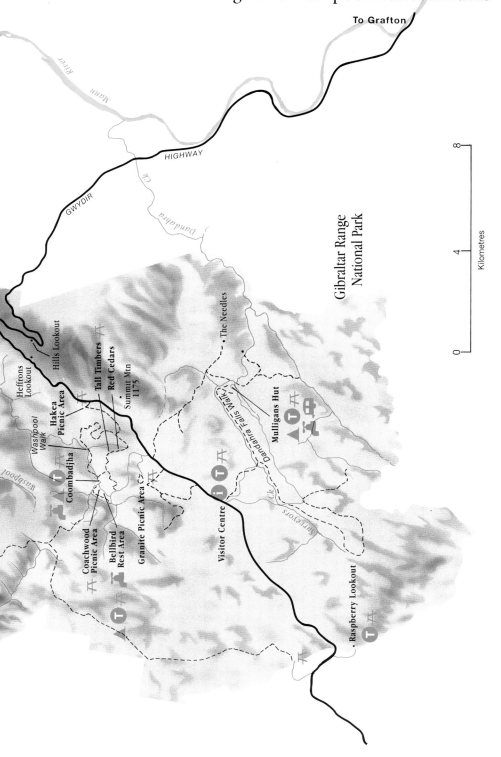

To Grafton

Mann River

HIGHWAY

GWYDIR

Dandahra Ck

Gibraltar Range
National Park

Heffrons Lookout

Hills Lookout

Washpool Walk

Hakea Picnic Area

Tall Timbers

Red Cedars

Summit Mtn 1175

Washpool

Coombadjha

Coachwood Picnic Area

Bellbird Rest Area

Granite Picnic Area

The Needles

Dandahra Falls Walk

Surveyors Ck

Mulligans Hut

Visitor Centre

Raspberry Lookout

8

4

0

Kilometres

To Glen Innes

Formation

The geological origins of the area can be traced back some 500 million years to when sedimentary rocks were being formed on the floor of the ocean that covered this part of Australia. About 400 million years ago massive upheavals of the earth's crust lifted the seabed, tilting and deforming it, and transforming the sedimentary rocks into greywacke, chert and argillite. These ancient rocks are found in outcrops along the eastern edge of the range.

An extended period of volcanic activity began some 25 million years ago. Lava, ash and rock fragments spewed over much of the Washpool area, while a large mass of molten granite intruded into the southern part of the range. Millions of years of erosion have weathered the granite into the present landform of large rocky outcrops, tors and curiously balancing boulders. The volcanic and sedimentary rocks have broken down to form deep, nutrient rich soils in the Washpool area.

Vegetation

The area has a wide diversity of vegetation types ranging from sub-alpine communities on the granite peaks through heaths, swamps and woodlands to eucalypt forests and rainforests. More than 500 plant species have been identified in the area, and the rainforests contain one quarter of all the Australian rainforest species. The poorer soils of the southern areas support an open vegetation of eucalypt forests, woodlands and heaths, with an abundance of wildflowers including Christmas bells, waratahs, golden glory peas and orchids. In spring and early summer the wildflower displays are at their best, and are readily seen from the roads and paths.

The rainforest vegetation reaches its peak in the pure stands of Willowie Scrub. This warm temperate rainforest of some 3000 ha contains the largest coachwood forest in the world. Other rainforest trees growing here include sassafras, corkwood, crabapple, callicoma, scrub beefwood and lilly pilly. Yellow carabeens with their spectacularly buttressed trunks are common at the lower altitudes where the warm temperate rainforest merges with sub-tropical rainforest. The plants here include huge strangler figs, giant stinging trees, brown beech and pigeonberry ash, with an understorey of walking stick palms, bangalow palms, vines, birds nest ferns, staghorns and epiphytic orchids.

There are small areas of dry rainforest in the middle and lower reaches of Washpool Creek. They are characterised by stands of red cedar, shatterwood and the bright red flame tree. Eucalypt forests blend into the rainforest where conditions are suitable, with tallow-woods, Sydney blue gums and brush box growing above a dense rainforest understorey. On the dry, fire-prone ridge tops New England Blackbutts are dominant with a grassy understorey interspersed with forest oaks. Near Redbank Creek dense stands of burrawangs (low-growing cycads) grow beneath a forest of spotted gums.

Wildlife

The area is a sanctuary for many rare and endangered species whose habitats have been infiltrated elsewhere by introduced feral animals. Among them are the parma wallaby, long-nosed potoroo, rufous rat kangaroo and spotted-tailed quoll. These share the area with koalas, pademelons, possums, gliders, common wombats and a vast array of birds.

More than 215 bird species have been recorded in the area. Many, such as the powerful and sooty owls, the red-crowned pigeon and the superb lyrebird reach the limits of their range here. In the dense rainforests are the rare rufous scrub-bird, satin and regent bowerbirds and colourful wompoo fruit doves. Wrens, king parrots, whipbirds, rosellas, bellbirds, honeyeaters and pacific bazas add to the rich array of birdlife found here.

The unusual pouched frog lives in the area. The males of this amphibian carry their tadpoles in pouches until they develop into tiny frogs.

Walks

For the fit and hardy the Washpool area offers wilderness trekking at its best. The country is wild and difficult and any walks must be carefully planned and the route registered with the District Office or placed in the mailbox on Coombadjha Road. Descending to the lower areas following the creeks you will find yourself swimming and scrambling around waterfalls.

The self-guiding Coombadjha Nature Stroll provides an easier introduction to the rainforest. This is a 1.1 km loop from the Coachwood picnic area through warm temperate rainforest similar to the Willowie Scrub to a swimming hole and picnic area in a magnificent setting on Coombadjha Creek.

From Coombadjha rest area the Washpool Walk is a 10 km loop track taking you through different rainforest types to Summit Falls, via superb lookouts. It climbs gently through moist hardwood forests into a dry open eucalypt forest and past Cedar Creek rainforest where some of the finest red cedar trees in the state are to be found, including the famous Twin Cedar trees.

A highlight of Gibraltar Range National Park (south of the highway) is the Dandahra Falls Walk. This is a 5 km return journey from Mulligans Hut passing through tall eucalypt forest into a rainforest with walking stick palms, red cedar and rosewood trees. A turnoff 100 m along the track goes to Dandahra Creek where there are cascades, falls and a series of rock pools ideal for swimming. The main track drops 150 m down a steep section to the spectacular 240 m Dandahra Falls. Rock climbers will find the tors and cliff faces in the area a challenge to their skills. A southern diversion from the track leads to Murrumbooee Cascades, a 2.5 km rainforest walk.

The 3 km walk to The Needles from Mulligans Hut begins by following an old stock route through open forest with abundant wildflowers, and into a diverse warm temperate rainforest, emerging at the six granite outcrops known as The Needles. According to Aboriginal legend they represent six sisters who were turned to stone by an unsuccessful suitor.

From the Needles walk an alternative track turns west along an old logging road across Twin Bridges. It leads to Tree Fern Forest where tall eucalypts tower above a profusion of tree ferns including the common, soft, Coopers and prickly tree ferns. This is a 4 km walk from Mulligans Hut.

Facilities

The Visitor Centre at the entrance to Gibraltar Range National Park has displays and leaflets about several of the walking tracks. Discovery programs are conducted during most school holidays. Camping areas in Gibraltar Range National Park are located near Mulligans Hut where there are tent and caravan sites and a group camping area with basic facilities including cold showers.

Washpool National Park camping areas include Bellbird Rest Area which has secluded sites in the rainforest and on the open grassy flats. At Coombadjha Rest Area there are walkin camp sites across the creek. A small camping area at the far northern end of Washpool has also been developed.

Supplies and accommodation are available at Grafton and Glen Innes.

Access

The parks are located on opposite sides of the Gwydir Highway halfway between Grafton and Glen Innes. Access to the Visitor Centre and the main facilities of Gibraltar Range National Park is via the narrow, unsealed Mulligans Drive. Mulligans Hut is 10 km from the highway. Access to the visitor facilities in Washpool National Park is via Coombadjha Road. The road beyond Bellbird Rest Area leading to Coachwood Picnic Area is steep and slippery in wet weather, and is unsuitable for caravans and buses. The northern section of the park can be reached from Tabulam along the unsealed Ewingar Forest Road, turn off at Baryulgil along the Lionsville Forest Road to the camping area at the junction of Desert and Washpool Creeks. A sealed road to Baryulgil via Coaldale turns off the Grafton to Casino road 11 km north of Grafton.

Climate

Summers are warm and wet, and can turn cold suddenly. Winters are cold and generally dry with snowfalls on the peaks. Spring and early summer are the best times to see the wildflower displays.

Glen Innes District NPWS, 68 Church St, Glen Innes, NSW 2370. Tel. (02) 6732 5133.

Alpine heathlands of the Snowy Mountains, Kosciusko National Park

Left: desert sands of Mungo National Park, south western New South Wales

The eroded sandstone formation of the Three Sisters in the Blue Mountains National Park.

Namadgi National Park

Namadgi protects 106,000 ha of sub-alpine wilderness in the remote and mountainous south-western part of the ACT, just 50 km from Canberra. Rocky peaks contrast with broad grassy valleys and snow gum woodlands, providing breathtaking views, habitats for a wide range of plants and animals, and good cross-country skiing.

The north-eastern section of the Australian Alps was known to the local Aboriginal people as Namadgi, and this large national park occupies almost half of the Australian Capital Territory. Bimberi Peak rises to 1911 m in the west of the park, and is just one of a chain of peaks along the New South Wales border. Below them to the east lies the Cotter River Valley where rainwater and snow melt seep through mountain bogs to feed the Cotter River and fill the Corin and Bendora dams, built in the 1960s as part of Canberra's water supply.

Running north to south are the rugged Tidbinbilla and Namadgi Ranges, part of the Bimberi Wilderness, a remote and undisturbed area surrounding Bimberi Peak. The peaks are usually snow-covered in winter, creating excellent cross-country skiing conditions, although there are no facilities for downhill skiing.

Formation
A shallow sea covered this area more than 400 million years ago. Sediments washed by river systems from the surrounding mountains and hillsides settled on the sea bed and slowly hardened into sandstone, shale and siltstone. These sedimentary rocks are visible to the east of Boboyan Trig, while to the west the surface rocks are granite, formed when molten volcanic rock forced its way up into the sedimentary rocks between 450 and 400 million years ago. Subterranean forces pushed up the land to form a high plateau, and this has slowly eroded, leaving broad valleys and rounded mountains topped by rocky peaks. The soft, overlying sedimentary rocks have worn away to the west of Boboyan Trig, exposing the hard granite, which has weathered into large rounded boulders and rock shelters.

History
The human history of Namadgi goes back at least 21,000 years to the middle of the last ice age when the ranges were snow covered for most of the year. The original inhabitants were the Ngunawal people. They quarried stone for tool making, camped and hunted in the area, conducted ceremonies, made stone arrangements and rock paintings. Bogong moths were collected for food around Mount Kelly where they land in their millions in late spring.

Pastoralists arrived in the 1830s, cleared the land, and built huts, fences and homesteads in this remote area. They took Ngunawal land, destroyed Ngunawal culture and introduced fatal diseases that decimated the population. Space tracking stations operated at Honeysuckle Creek and in the Ororral Valley from the early 1960s to the early 1980s. Bushfires raged through the southern half of the park in 1983, and the following year 94,000 ha was proclaimed as a national park. It was extended to its present size in 1991.

Plants and animals
The alpine and sub-alpine areas provide environments for a wide range of plant communities, from open grasslands to woodlands and alpine heaths. Most of the park is covered with low open woodland dominated by broad-leaved peppermints and candlebarks at the lower altitudes and beautiful snow gums at higher altitudes. Grey kangaroos and red-necked wallabies shelter here during the heat of the day, and are often seen grazing around the forest edges and in the large open grasslands of the Ororral and Boboyan valleys on the eastern side of the park. Introduced grasses were sown in this area by graziers who removed trees to extend the grasslands. Cold air descending from the hills at night causes frequent frosts, inhibiting recolonisation by trees. Smokers Flat is one of many natural treeless flats in the park. They are smaller and often surrounded by tough black sallees, with dense tea trees lining creeks in frost hollows, a habitat

for the rare olive whistler.

Sheltered sites, particularly in the west, support tall wet forests of alpine ash, brown barrels and ribbon gums with dense stands of tree ferns in the gullies. Lyrebirds are often heard here in winter, and the tree hollows provide nests for possums, gliders, owls, kookaburras, pardalotes and crimson rosellas. Patrolling the skies are wedge-tailed eagles and Australian kestrels, the latter are often seen hovering over grassy areas hunting for small animals.

The highest peaks are too cold and windswept for trees. They support alpine herbfields with summer blooms of silver snow daisies and billy buttons. Sphagnum mosses grow in the moist depressions, soaking up water and releasing it slowly throughout the year. Rare and unusual animals like the alpine water skink, broad-toothed rat and corroboree frog live in the alpine heaths and bogs.

The waters of the Cotter River and its tributaries are refuges for native fish such as the mountain galaxia, Macquarie perch and river blackfish. Introduced rainbow and brown trout breed elsewhere, providing sport for anglers.

Walks

There are more than 170 km of marked walking tracks, including the Australian Alps Walking Track which crosses the centre of the park. Short walks include the circuit at Orroral camp ground, a 1 km stroll along the river through open woodlands; the Mount Franklin and the Shanahans Mountain tracks, both moderate 3 km return walks through snow gum woodlands to the summits with magnificent views; and the Yerrabi Track, a 4 km return walk from the car park on Boboyan Rd through sub-alpine forest to Boboyan Trig where there are spectacular views over Bimberi Wilderness.

The Yankee Hat area was occupied by Aboriginal people until the 1860s, and a walking track leads from the car park on Old Boboyan Rd across Bogong Creek to a rock shelter where there are paintings of animals and human-like figures. This is one of the most important Aboriginal sites in the area.

Square Rock walking track begins at Smokers car park and climbs steeply past a maze of rock boulders to Smokers Flat, through snow gums to Orroral Valley Lookout, and on to Square Rock at 1400 m with excellent views of the Brindabella Range and Cotter River Valley.

Longer walks include a 16 km, seven hour return walk from Mount Clear camp ground along Naas Valley to Horse Gully Hut. This easy walk follows the creek through snow gum woodlands. The Orroral Valley circuit is a moderate 19 km day walk from the end of Orroral Rd, joining part of Smokers Trail before returning through the open valley. Bushwalkers should record their trip in a bushwalking register at the Visitor Centre or elsewhere in the park, and be prepared for severe weather at any time of year.

Facilities

The Visitor Centre has displays, an audiovisual presentation and a range of information. There are camp grounds in bushland settings at Mount Clear and Orroral, with basic facilities only, and a three-night limit. Stream water must be boiled before drinking, and total fire bans strictly observed. Firewood must not be collected. Bush camping is allowed along the walking tracks, but is prohibited in the lower and middle catchment area of the Cotter River and by permit only in the upper catchment. Picnic areas have barbecues with wood or gas provided. There are no bins in the park, so rubbish must be taken home. Horse riding is allowed east of the Old Boboyan and Boboyan Roads.

Access

The park is 54 km south-west of Canberra via Brindabella Rd to the north, Corin Rd to Corin Dam, Naas Rd. Unsealed, the roads are narrow and may be closed due to snow, floods or total fire bans. Chains should be carried in winter.

Climate

The park has alpine weather, which can change rapidly from hot summer days to snowfalls and freezing nights. Visit in summer for wildflower displays, and in winter for cross-country skiing.

Namadgi National Park,
PO Box 1065, Tuggeranong, ACT 2901.
Tel. (02) 6237 5222.

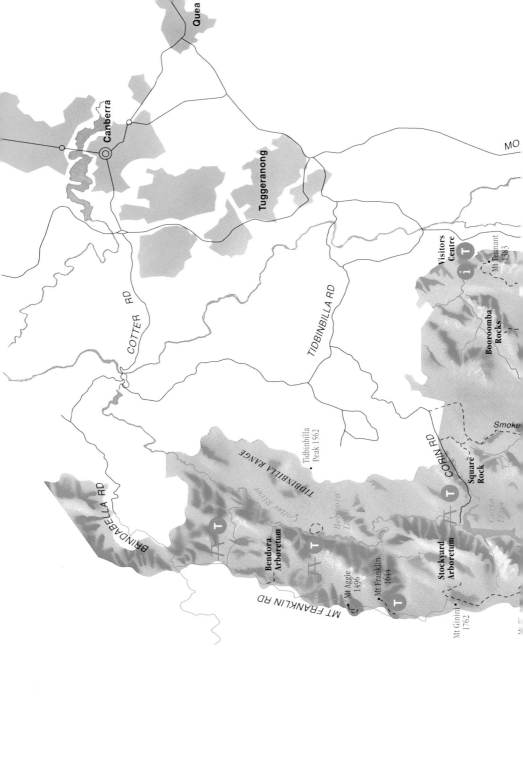

Namadgi National Park

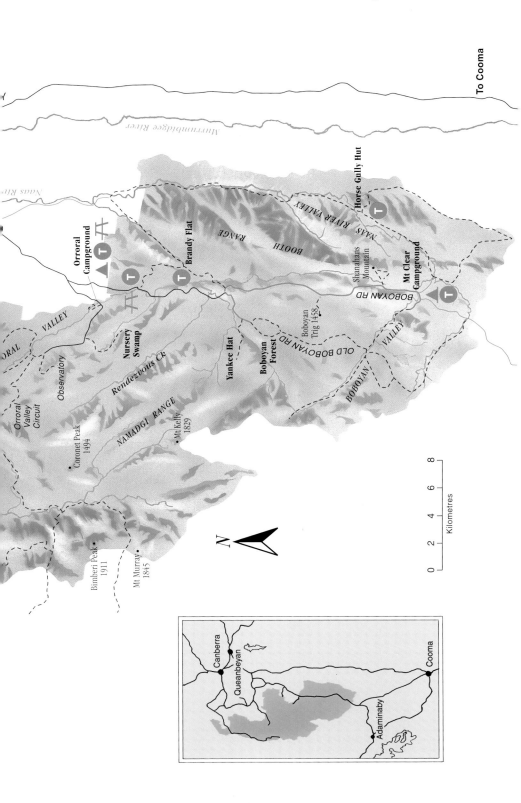

To Cooma

Murrumbidgee River

Naas Riv

Horse Gully Hut

Orroral Campground

Brandy Flat

BOOTH RANGE

NAAS RIVER VALLEY

Shanahans Mountain

Mt Clear Campground

BOBOYAN RD

Nursery Swamp

Boboyan Trig 1458

Yankee Hat

Boboyan Forest

OLD BOBOYAN RD

BOBOYAN VALLEY

VALLEY

Observatory

Rendezvous Ck

Orroral Valley Circuit

NAMADGI RANGE

Coronet Peak 1494

Mt Kelly 1829

Bimberi Peak 1911

Mt Murray 1845

N

Kilometres

0 2 4 6 8

Canberra

Queanbeyan

Cooma

Adaminaby

Abercrombie River National Park (19,000 ha)

In the tablelands between Oberon and Goulburn, this park protects parts of the Abercrombie River, Retreat River and Silent Creek. The river banks are important habitats and movement corridors for the platypus and eastern water rat. The park contains the largest remaining stand of low open forest in the region, and along the Abercrombie River are some of the few remaining river oak forests. There are two major sections: the largest is north of the Abercrombie River, and a separate section is downstream on the south side of the river. Go bushwalking, fishing, canoeing and swimming. Camp at Bummaroo Ford where there are basic facilities. *40 km south-west of Oberon on the Goulburn Rd. (02) 6336 1927.*

Bald Rock National Park (7011 ha)

In the northern tablelands, this park features a huge water-streaked rock dome rising to 1277 m. The largest exposed granite-type rock in Australia, Bald Rock is 750 m long and 500 m wide, and stands 200 m above surrounding bushland. Walk to the summit where there are excellent views to the coast and forested hinterland on the Queensland border. Camp at the picnic area below the rock – basic facilities. *29 km north of Tenterfield, turn off Woodenbong Rd. (02) 6732 5133.*

Bellinger River National Park (2860 ha)

A new park on the edge of the New England Escarpment plunging into the Bellinger River Valley. This scenic area forms a wildlife corridor between Dorrigo and New England National Parks. It protects extensive old growth blackbutt forests, sub-tropical and warm temperate rainforests, and some threatened and rare plants. There are spectacular views from Griffiths Lookout. Most of the park is very steep with limited access. Facilities being developed. *15 km south of Dorrigo on the Thora Rd. (02) 6657 2309.*

Ben Boyd National Park (9490 ha)

Two rocky, beautiful stretches of coastline, 40 km long, to the north and south of Twofold Bay. The park offers excellent surfing, sheltered coves, inlets, caves and the red and white earth formations called the Pinnacles. Flowering heaths, a banksia forest and the remains of the whaling station. Visit the historic Boyds Tower at Red Point. Take the 1.1 km Pinnacles Walk nature trail in the north, and the 9 km walk between camping grounds at Saltwater Creek and Bittangabee Bay on the south side for excellent views. Bookings required for camping. *8 km north and 35 km south of Eden, in two parts off the Princes Hwy. (02) 6495 4130.*

Ben Halls Gap National Park (2500 ha)

Previously a State Forest, this new park lies on the junction of the Liverpool and Mt Royal Ranges in the upper catchment area of the Peel, Barnard and Hunter Rivers. There are undisturbed stands of old growth forests dominated by messmate and mountain gum. Along the creeks are cool temperate rainforest. Greater gliders, spotted-tailed quolls, koalas and powerful owls are protected. Basic facilities are being developed; opportunities for bushwalking, bush camping and nature study. 4WD access only. *60 km south-east of Tamworth via Nundle on Morrisons Rd. (02) 6543 3533.*

Biamanga National Park (4678 ha)

Located on the state's south-east coastal escarpment, this relatively new park protects the steep, forested slopes around Mumbulla Mountain, a sacred site to the Aboriginal people of this area. The eucalypt forests are rich in wildlife. Mumbulla Creek Picnic Area gives easy access to a swimming hole and Mumbulla Falls. An unsealed road leads to Mumbulla Mountain. There are no camping grounds or other facilites. *About 25 km north of Bega via Princes Hwy and Jews Creek Rd. (02) 6495 4130.*

Bongil Bongil National Park (1008 ha)

This new park contains the last major unpolluted estuary in the Coffs Harbour district. There are pristine sandflats, seagrass beds and mangroves along Bonville and Pine Creeks, and one of the few remaining coastal rainforests beside Bundageree Creek. The park protects eight endangered birds including the osprey, black

bittern and rose-crowned fruit dove. Aboriginal middens and stone tools have been discovered near the shore. Go fishing and canoeing, swimming or bushwalking. No facilities.
Just south of Sawtell. Access the southern end via Tuckers Rocks Rd. (02) 6657 2309.

Boonoo Boonoo National Park (2692 ha)

Located on the northern tablelands, the Boonoo Boonoo River winds through high granite country strewn with boulders, supporting open forest, heath, swamp and river habitats. A platform allows stunning views of the 210 m waterfall as it plunges into a rainforest gully. Wildlife includes pretty-faced wallbies, brush-tailed rock wallabies, glossy black cockatos and colourful rosellas. There are many good swimming holes. Basic camping at the Falls or Cypress rest areas.
22 km north of Tenterfield via Woodenbong Rd. (02) 6732 5133.

Booti Booti National Park (1497 ha)

Comprises a beautiful coastline with secluded beaches and coves, a saltwater lake excellent for boating and wind-surfing, and a long surf beach. There are woodlands and rainforest by the coast. There are panoramic vews from Cape Hawke, Booti Hill and Charlotte Head and walking tracks through woodlands and rainforest. Seven Mile Beach is ideal for surfing and fishing, and the western side fronts onto the saltwater Wallis Lake, a popular sailing and fishing spot. There are picnic areas and a good camp ground at The Ruins where the facilities include hot showers. Bookings essential during holidays.
10 km south of Forster, turn off the Pacific Highway onto Lakes Way. (02) 6554 0446.

Border Ranges National Park (31,683 ha)

A World Heritage listed rainforest park on the rim of an ancient volcano centred on Mt Warning. There are sub-tropical and cool temperate rainforests dominated by ancient Antarctic beech trees, numerous waterfalls and breathtaking views from walks on escarpments and ridges. The park is rich in wildlife and protects endangered animals such as Albert's lyre-

bird. Facilities include picnic area and camp grounds at Sheep Station Creek or Forest Tops.
38 km west of Murwillumbah off the Summerland Way or Kyogle Rd. (02) 6628 1177.

Botany Bay National Park (435 ha)

South of Sydney's centre, this park protects cliffs, mangroves, beaches and historic monuments in a narrow strip on both headlands of the entrance to Botany Bay. There is a museum, fort, picnic grounds, walking tracks and an amazing array of native plants. No camping.
Access by bus or car along Anzac Parade or Captain Cook Drive. (02) 9668 9111.

Bouddi National Park (1189 ha)

On the northern entrance to Broken Bay this park is in two sections and includes a marine extension. Steep forested hills descend to cliffs, bays and beautiful small beaches. There are wildflower heathlands, sub-tropical rainforests and a diverse bird population. Camp at Putty Beach where there are basic facilities or walk-in campsites at Tallow Beach and Little Beach.
19 km south-east of Gosford between McMasters Beach and Killcare. (02) 4324 4911.

Bournda National Park (2378 ha)

A coastal park with ocean beaches, creeks, salt and freshwater lakes and an expansive lagoon in an unspoiled part of the far south coast. The 10 km Kangarutha Track is an excellent coastal walk from Tathra South to Wallagoot Lake. Visit sheltered Bournda Lagoon just behind the ocean beach, North Tura lookout and Scotts Bay picnic area beside Wallagoot Lake. Activities include water sports, fishing, bushwalking and bird watching. There is a camp ground at Hobart Beach with good facilities. Booking essential. High Ridge Hut is available for approved groups.
20 km south-east of Bega off Sapphire Coast Drive. (02) 6495 4130.

Brindabella National Park (12,280 ha)

This new park lies at the northern end of the Australian Alps to the north of Namadgi National Park, and protects unique flora and fauna associations. Forests of red stringybark and scribbly gum cover much of the area with brown barrel and ribbon gum on the sheltered slopes. On the higher sites are snow gums and forests of

mountain gum with alpine ash on the southern slopes. The fauna includes rare and vulnerable species such as the peregrine falcon, powerful owl, common bent-wing bat, yellow-bellied glider and koala. The park is popular with bushwalkers. 4WD access only. No facilities.
35 km west of Canberra via Belconnen or Cotter Dam. (02) 6297 6144.

Brisbane Water National Park (11,372 ha)

A rugged sandstone area bordering the Hawkesbury River. There are deep gorges cutting through the plateau and magnificent views over Brisbane Water and Broken Bay. Walk through open woodlands with spectacular spring wildflower displays and pockets of sub-tropical rainforest. Mangroves line the tidal inlets. Wildlife includes the swamp wallaby, echidna, platypus, koala, fawn-footed melomys and more than 150 bird species. Visit Bulgandry Aboriginal site. Picnic facilities at Somersby Falls and Girrakool, and rainforest walks. Bush camping only.
40 km north of Sydney off the Pacific Hwy, by rail to Wondabyne or ferry from Palm Beach. (02) 4324 4911.

Broadwater National Park (3737 ha)

On the far north coast with 8 km of beach and high sand dunes. Much of the park comprises heaths with beautiful spring wildflower displays, undisturbed saltmarsh and swamp forest. Swamp and red-necked wallabies, echidnas and ringtailed possums are common. Koalas feed from eucalypts in the north-west corner, and birdlife is prolific, including the brolga, sea eagle and jabiru. Walk to Salty Lagoon and visit Broadwater Beach picnic area. No camping.
3 km north of Evans Head off the Pacific Hwy. (02) 6628 1177.

Budawang National Park (16,102 ha)

A rugged wilderness area of angular sandstone rocks, spires and cliffs with views over the mountains to the coast. The park abuts the south of Morton National Park, and includes the Budawang Range. There are open eucalypt forests, small rainforest areas and heaths filled with springtime wildflowers. Challenging bushwalking country. Bush camping only. No public roads or facilities in the park. Difficult access.
20 km from Braidwood via Mongarlowe. (02) 4887 7270.

Budderoo National Park (5746 ha)

Famed for its huge trees, fern gullies, rainforests and the spectacular Carrington Falls, this park lies on an undulating sandstone plateau enclosed by the cliffs of Kangaroo Valley and the coastal escarpment. Two rare and endangered birds, the swamp parrot and eastern bristle bird, live here. There are lookouts, an elevated boardwalk into the rainforest and a paved track to the spectacular Minnamurra Falls. Minnamurra Rainforest Centre has picnic areas, shelters and a cafe. Bush camping at Carrington Falls.
110 km south of Sydney via Kiama and Jamberoo or Moss Vale and Robertson. (02) 4236 0469.

Bundjalung National Park (17,679 ha)

A coastal park protecting 38 km of beaches and the unspoiled Esk River on the far north coast. The park contains rainforests, heaths, lagoons, mangroves, swamps and curious rock formations. More than 205 bird, 30 mammal and 38 reptiles species have been recorded. Good fishing, surfing and canoeing. Camp at Woody Head where there are good facilities (02 6646 6134), or at Black Rocks.
55 km south of Ballina off the Pacific Hwy via Iluka Rd or Gap Rd. (02) 6628 1177.

Cathedral Rock National Park (6529 ha)

Features giant granite outcrops and rock sculptures straddling the Snowy Range (1583 m) on the northern tablelands. Explore the formations from the Woolpack Rocks Walk and Cathedral Rock Track. There are eucalypt forests, swamps, and tussocky snow grass and snow gums in the highest areas. Camp at Native Dog Creek or Barokee rest areas where there are basic facilities.
70 km east of Armidale off Armidale-Grafton Rd or Ebor-Guyra Rd. (02) 6657 2309.

Cattai National Park (424 ha)

Beside the Hawkesbury River on the outskirts of Sydney, this small park features forests with stands of rare red cedar trees, an historic homestead, shady picnic areas, a farm animal

enclosure and a number of forest walking tracks. Canoes, paddleboats and bicycles can be hired. The camping area is open at weekends and school holidays. Bookings required.
6 km north of Pitt Town along the Wisemans Ferry Rd. (02) 4572 8404.

Chaelundi National Park (10,314 ha)

This new park is on the eastern slopes of the Great Dividing Range south-west of Grafton, and includes the former Chandlers, Shannon Creek and Sailors Hill Flora Reserves. It protects one of the largest and most diverse stands of dry old growth forest in northern NSW, and is home to important populations of threatened fauna. The beautiful Chandlers Creek flows through the park, and is accessed by a 4WD trail along the southern boundary. No facilities.
80 km south-west of Grafton via Nymboida along Boundary Creek Rd. (02) 6657 2309.

Cocoparra National Park (8358 ha)

The Cocoparra Range is the core of this park. Rising from the western plains, the slopes and ridges are covered with dry eucalypt and cypress pine forests, with many species of flowering wattles. It is a haven for grey kangaroos, peregrine falcons, eagles and other wildlife. Visit Ladysmith Glen and Jacks Creek where a scenic gorge cuts through rich red rocks. There are several picnic areas. Camp at Woolshed Flat which has basic facilities. Bring water.
25 km north-east of Griffith. (02) 6851 4429.

Conimbla National Park (7590 ha)

In the Hervey Range on the central western slopes, this park protects remnants of bushland and the surviving flora and fauna. The park is in two sections surrounded by farming land, and comprises open forests of black pine, mugga ironbark, scribbly gum, red stringybark and box trees, and large areas of heath. Enjoy spectacular views from the Ironbark Walking Trail, birdwatch along the Wallaby Track, and see the springtime wildflower displays. Bush camping only. Bring water.
27 km west of Cowra, off the Midwestern Hwy along Barryrennie Rd. (02) 6331 9777.

Coolah Tops National Park (10,578 ha)

A recently declared park on the Warung Plateau of the Liverpool Ranges, with rich soils and high rainfall supporting tall, old growth forests of stringybarks, mountain gums, black sallees and stands of the largest snow gums in Australia. Wildlife includes greater gliders, wallaroos, wombats, grey kangaroos and swamp wallabies. Visit Lava Rock, Shepherds Peak and Jimmys Creek area. There are waterfalls, a number of picnic areas and basic camping grounds at Cox Creek Falls and Norfolk Falls.
30 km west of Coolah. (02) 6372 3122.

Crowdy Bay National Park (8022 ha)

A coastal park featuring a magnificent beach sweeping from Diamond Head, and a rugged headland rising abruptly to 113 m before dropping away to wetlands and heaths on the coastal plain. It supports grey kangaroos, koalas, wallabies and a diverse bird population. Explore rock formations and tidal pools. A 5 km loop track from Diamond Head gives panoramic views. Basic camping at Diamond Head, Indian Head or Kylies Beach. Bring water.
25 km north-east of Taree off the Pacific Hwy via Coralville or Laurieton. (02) 6584 2203.

Culgoa National Park (15,615 ha)

A recently declared park north of Brewarrina on the Upper Culgoa floodplain in the semi-arid northern border region, adjoining the Culgoa Floodplain National Park in Queensland. Most of the surrounding land has been cleared, and the park protects the state's largest remaining area of coolabah woodlands, and the largest area of native grassland. There is a diverse population of native animals including the koala. Magnificent river red gums line the Culgoa River. Aboriginal sites are common, including scarred trees, clay hearths and stone flakes. Canoeing is possible on the Culgoa River when it is flowing. Basic camping only.
150 km north-west of Walgett via the Castlereagh Hwy and Goodooga. (02) 6836 2692.

Deua National Park (82,926 ha)

Set in the rugged coastal ranges, the park protects extensive wilderness areas with wild and

scenic rivers. Caves, valleys, ridges and spurs have been sculpted into the limestone rock. Enjoy canoeing, rafting, bushwalking, abseiling and adventure caving. Walk to the remarkable 96 m deep Big Hole. Basic camping at Deua River and Bakers Flat on the Araluen Rd, Berlang Rest Area on the Shoalhaven River or secluded Bendethera.
100 km south-east of Canberra via Braidwood. (02) 4476 2888.

Dharug National Park (14,834 ha)

Features spectacular sandstone cliffs, flat-topped ridges and gullies bordering the Hawkesbury River. There are numerous Aboriginal rock engravings, the remains of the convict-built Great North Rd, rainforest pockets, eucalypt forests, mangroves, wildflower heaths and a rich and diverse flora and fauna. Canoeing is popular, walking tracks begin at Mill Creek camping area, where wombats, wallaroos and goannas are often seen. Basic facilities here and at Ten Mile Hollow camping area. Booking advised.
75 km north-west of Sydney via Wisemans Ferry Rd. (02) 4324 4911.

Dunggir National Park (2491 ha)

A recently created park in the coastal hinterland of the mid-north coast preserving some of the region's few remaining old growth forests. Three different rainforest types are protected, and the park's sub-tropical rainforest contains the largest known population of the rare five-leaved Bosistoa. The forests are home to a number of threatened animal species. No facilities.
60 km west of Nambucca Heads via Bowraville and Kosekai Rd. (02) 6657 2309.

Eurobodalla National Park (2180 ha)

This recently created park conserves 30 km of coastline south of Batemans Bay. It is split into three sections between Moruya Heads and Tilba Lake and includes lakes, wetlands, estuaries, headlands, beaches and sandspits. The plant communities of spotted gum forests and littoral scrublands include rare plants and endangered animals such as the long-nosed potoroo, white-footed dunnart, little tern, pied oystercatcher and hooded dotterel. Bingie Bingie Point has complex igneous rock formations, Aboriginal middens

and stone tool workings more than 20,000 years old. Swimming, picnicking, bird watching, bush-walking, canoeing, surfing and scuba diving are popular. Camp at Congo in the northern section where there are basic facilities.
20 km south of Batemans Bay off the Princes Hwy. (02) 4476 2888.

Fortis Creek National Park (7747 ha)

Formerly part of Fortis Creek State Forest, this recently created park lies in the north-east of NSW adjacent to the Banyabba Nature Reserve. It conserves extensive old growth forests including blackbutt, spotted gum, grey gum stringybark and bloodwood. Threatened species include the regent honeyeater, masked owl, powerful owl, bush thick knee, koala, common bent-wing bat and great pipistrelle. No facilities.
20 km north of Grafton via the Summerland Way or Coaldale Rd. (02) 6642 0613.

Gardens of Stone National Park (12,000 ha)

This park adjoins Wollemi National Park and features a varied landscape of limestone outcrops and sandstone escarpments. The Pagoda rock formations are a prominent feature where erosion has sculpted strange domes and other shapes. Banksias, she-oaks and heath plants grow among the rocky outcrops. Eucalypt forests below the cliffs support koalas, yellow-bellied gliders and powerful owls. The Capertree area has deep gullies and habitats for the rare regent honeyeater and turquoise parrot. No facilities.
30 km north of Lithgow off the Mudgee Rd. (02) 4787 8877.

Garigal National Park (2172 ha)

Close to the heart of Sydney this park incorporates Davidson State Recreation Area. The area includes impressive sandstone country and water views. There are walking tracks, excellent boating facilities, and a picnic area near Roseville Bridge. No camping.
12 km north of Sydney city centre, access via boat or public transport. (02) 9451 3479.

Georges River National Park (326 ha)

In the south Sydney metropolitan area, this popular park has spacious riverside picnic areas and

launching ramps at Morgans Creek from where you can explore as far as Botany Bay and Liverpool Weir. Good fishing and a number of short forest trails with good views. No camping.
25 km south-west of Sydney along Henry Lawson Drive. (02) 9722 2159.

Goobang National Park (42,600 ha)
A recently created park in the central west, conserving the largest remnant forest and woodland in the region. The park includes the Herveys, Currumbenya and Bumberry Ranges and valleys. Important plant communities include yellow box, Blakely's red gum, white box and ironbark. Rare and endangered species including koalas, squirrel gliders, brush-tailed rock wallabies, regent honeyeaters, glossy black cockatoos and superb parrots. More than 300 plant species have been recorded including 40 orchids. Bush camping only.
37 km east of Parkes via the Yeoval Rd, or from Tominglay. (02) 6851 4429.

Goulburn River National Park (70,102 ha)
The Goulburn River is the main feature of this park in the Upper Hunter region, flowing sinuously through unspoiled sandstone country, deeply dissected by narrow gorges and orange-coloured cliffs. Wide sandy river banks offer easy walking, the precipitous bluffs and Mt Dangar (670 m) provide excellent views. The area is dry with sparse woodlands and the river attracts wildlife: wombats, grey kangaroos, platypuses, emus, lyrebirds, parrots and glossy black cockatoos. Bush camping only along the river.
300 km north-west of Sydney and 35 km south of Merriwa. Dirt roads. (02) 6372 3122.

Gundabooka National Park (43,592 ha)
Located in the centre of the state, this new park protects part of the rocky Gundabooka Range and the surrounding gently undulating plain. Woodlands of mulga, bimble box, white cypress pine, rosewood and belah grow on the plains, while the shallow soils of the range are dominated by mulga and grey mallee. These plant communities are important habitats for vulnerable species such as the little pied bat, kultarr, brush-tailed rock wallaby, wallaroo and peregrine falcon. Emus, grey and red kangaroos

forage on the grassy plains. 4WD access only. Camping and other facilities are planned.
70 km south-west of Bourke off the Cobar Rd. (02) 6836 2692.

Guy Fawkes River National Park (46,030 ha)
A vast wilderness park on the eastern edge of the New England Plateau in several sections containing the wild Guy Fawkes River and its tributaries, and parts of the Henry River. Gorges, valleys, flats and sandy beaches characterise the river system. The rainforest gullies and open woodlands provide habitats for threatened species such as the glossy black cockatoo, masked owl, squirrel glider, brush-tailed rock wallaby and spotted-tailed quoll. Canoe the Guy Fawkes River after good rain or bushwalking. Visit Ebor Falls where the river plunges from the tablelands, walk to the Guy Fawkes River and camp at Chaelundi rest area where there are basic facilities.
100 km north-east of Armidale. Dirt roads. (02) 6657 2309.

Hat Head National Park (6446 ha)
A coastal park with sweeping beaches protecting a rich coastal ecosystem and one of the largest dune systems in the state. Sandy ridges with low scrub and dry forest in the north give way to paperbark wetlands and freshwater lagoons in the south. There are impenetrable tea-tree thickets and low forests inland. Smoky Cape is the only major granite outcrop along this coast for 400 km. Visit a coastal rainforest and sea caves along the Korogoro Peninsula Walk. Wildlife includes swamp and red-necked wallabies, grey kangaroos, goannas and diverse bird life including black swans, eagles, falcons, fantails and honeyeaters. Basic camping at Smoky Beach or Hungry rest areas. Bring water.
20 km east of Kempsey via Hat Head, South West Rocks or Crescent Head. (02) 6584 2203.

Heathcote National Park (2251 ha)
Adjoining the south-west of Sydney's Royal National Park, this park protects a coastal area of rugged sandstone dissected by steep-sided valleys. Open forests and heaths, swimming holes and small river beaches provide good opportunities for bushwalking, bird watching and bush

camping. Access by foot, the park is popular with scouts and other youth groups.

40 km south of Sydney off the Princes Hwy, walk from Heathcote or Waterfall stations. (02) 9542 0666.

Jervis Bay (Booderee) National Park

Protecting one of the few relatively undisturbed coastal environments left in the state, this park is in two parts, one managed by NSW, the other by the Commonwealth. Rugged cliffs face the ocean, while tranquil beaches line the bay. There are rainforest remnants, eucalypt forests, wetlands and coastal heaths, providing habitats for 43 mammal, 207 bird, 17 amphibian and 29 reptile species, including endangered species such as the ground parrot and eastern bristle-bird. There is a resident pod of dolphins; fur seals visit the area, gannets, white-bellied sea eagles and penguins are often seen; whales pass by on their annual migrations. Visitor facilities include picnic areas, boat launching ramps and walking trails. Camp grounds at Green Patch with good facilities, Caves Beach or Bristol Point (for groups). Book in advance for holiday periods (02-4443 0977). A variety of private accommodation is available nearby.

180 km south of Sydney off the Princes Hwy. (02) 4423 9800 or (02) 4443 0977.

Kanangra–Boyd National Park (68,299 ha)

Sheer sandstone cliffs line the rugged Boyd Plateau, the central feature of this park which is located on the southern boundary of the Blue Mountains National Park. This is a magnificent wilderness area with a labyrinth of canyons, gorges, limestone caves, eucalypt woodlands, isolated rainforest pockets and low heaths. Plateau top tracks lead to Kanangra Falls and lookouts. Bushwalking in the wilderness areas and caving (permits required) are popular. Camp at Boyd River where there are basic facilities.

180 km west of Sydney via Mt Victoria and Jenolan Caves. (02) 6336 1972.

Kinchega National Park (44,180 ha)

The Darling River forms the eastern boundary of this far western dry-country park. Two large permanent lakes attract large numbers of water-birds. Most of the park comprises red sandy plains with a sparse cover of vegetation. Massive river red gums line the river. The park has many Aboriginal sites and relics of European settlers. Camp at Lake Cawndilla Rest Area where there are basic facilities. Along the river, stay in the old shearers' quarters (book in advance).

111 km south-east of Broken Hill. (08) 8088 5933.

Kings Plains National Park (5160 ha)

One of the few protected areas on the north-western tablelands, this little-known park is a trackless wilderness centred around Kings Plain Creek. The poor soils support stunted vegetation of open woodland and heath, rich in wildflowers in spring. There are taller trees along the southern and eastern boundaries. Red-necked wallabies, eastern grey kangaroos and wallaroos are common, with brush-tailed rock wallabies in the gorges and platypuses in the creeks. King and turquoise parrots, rosellas, yellow-tailed and glossy black cockatoos, regent honeyeaters, eagles, falcons and black cormorants are among the 82 bird species. Swim in still pools, rock hop along Kings Plains Creek to the 200 m high waterfall (2.5 hours return). There is a picnic and camping area alongside Kings Plain Creek.

50 km north-west of Glen Innes off Kings Plain Rd via Wellingrove. (02) 6732 5133.

Lane Cove National Park (344 ha)

A small riverside park near the centre of Sydney. There are many picnic grounds set in peaceful bushland settings. Walk along the riverside, visit the wildlife shelter or cruise on the paddle-wheeler Turrumburra. The water is polluted by urban runoff and is not suitable for swimming or paddling. There is a visitor centre, kiosk and wildlife shelter. Camp nearby at the Lane Cove River Van Village (02) 9805 0500.

10 km north-west of Sydney city centre, accessible by public transport. (02) 9412 1811.

Macquarie Pass National Park (1064 ha)

This park protects a small piece of the precipi-tous Illawarra Escarpment. Sandstone cliffs form a huge amphitheatre with steep heavily timbered sides. Macquarie Rivulet tumbles in a series of waterfalls and rapids through a deep gorge lined with sub-tropical rainforests. Lyrebirds, bandicoots, swamp wallabies and wombats may be seen. Walk from the picnic area along the 2 km return Cascades Rainforest Walk or take the Glenview Track from Glenview Rd. A picnic area is located at the foot of Macquarie Pass. Bush camping is allowed away from roads and facilities.

130 km south of Sydney, 7 km east of Robertson, off the Illawarra Hwy. (02) 4887 7270.

Mallee Cliffs National Park (57,969 ha)

In the far south-west of the state, this large park protects a significant area of mallee vegetation in an intensive grazing region. Undulating sand dunes support open mallee woodlands and grasslands, an ideal habitat for the endangered mallee fowl. The park is a wildlife refuge and public access is not allowed at this time.

30 km east of Mildura. (03) 5023 1278.

Marramarra National Park (11,759 ha)

At the Junction of the Hawkesbury River and Berowra Creek, this undeveloped park conserves a large area of the Hornsby Plateau. There are Aboriginal art sites, sandstone ridges, deep gullies, some of the best mangrove communities in the state alongside the Hawkesbury River, tall forests, fern gullies and wildflower heathlands. Little-known waterways such as Marramarra Creek offer good canoeing and the opportunity to see some of the wildlife close up. Pit toilets and barbecues are provided at Marramarra Creek and Gentlemans Halt for picnics and bush camping, both only accessible by boat or foot.

50 km north-west of Sydney via Wisemans Ferry Rd. (02) 9457 9322.

Mimosa Rocks National Park (5335 ha)

A picturesque coastal park featuring Mimosa Rocks, a formation of massive blocks of weathered volcanic rock near Aragunnu Beach. Along the 17 km of coastline are beautiful beaches, lagoons, headlands, offshore stacks and caves. The park supports low woodlands and heaths along the coast and eucalypt forests further inland, with a wide range of animals including swamp wallabies, goannas, wrens, thornbills and seabirds. Snorkelling, fishing, surfing and canoeing are popular activities. There are picnic areas

and basic camping facilities at Aragunnu Beach, Picnic Point, Middle Beach (walk-in only) and Gillards Beach.

22 km north-east of Bega off the Tathra-Bermagui Rd. (02) 4476 2888.

Mootwingee National Park (68,912 ha)

In the far west of the state this park is dominated by the rugged Bynguano Range. It features narrow gorges lined with river red gums, white cypress pines and mulga clinging to bare rocks, waterholes, colourful cliffs, Aboriginal art sites, sandplains and stony gibber plains. The park is a refuge for the rare yellow-footed rock wallaby. Temperatures soar in the summer, and infrequent rains may close the roads. Guides take visitors to see the fine collections of Aboriginal art at Mootwingee Historic Site and Amphitheatre Gorge. Walking tracks lead through gorges and along rugged ridges. Shady camp sites at Homestead Creek. Bring water and ample provisions. Bookings required in holiday periods.

130 km north-east of Broken Hill. (08) 8088 5933.

Mount Imlay National Park (3808 ha)

Dominated by Mt Imlay (886 m), this heavily forested park affords great views of the south coast and East Gippsland across the border. The wide variations in altitude provide many habitats for plants and animals, including a newly-discovered eucalypt (*Eucalyptus imlayensis*). There are rainforest pockets along the gullies, and bird life including superb lyrebirds, wedge-tailed eagles and tree-creepers. A steep, 3 km track leads from the Burrawang Picnic Area to the top of Mt Imlay. Bush camping only. Bring water.

30 km south-west of Eden, turn off the Princes Hwy along Burrawang Forest Rd. (02) 6495 4130.

Mount Jerusalem National Park (970 ha)

In the far north-east of the state, this park incorporates the Blackbutt Plateau, Mt Jerusalem and part of Mt Warning volcano. The park protects the last remaining intact old growth blackbutt stand in the region. There are sub-tropical and warm temperate rainforests, sclerophyll forests, heaths and scrublands. Endangered plants and animals are found here including nightcap

wattle, silverleaf, powerful owl, wompoo fruit dove, Albert's lyrebird and white-eared monarch. No facilities. Limited access.
32 km north-east of Lismore via Coolamon Scenic Drive. (02) 6628 1177.

Mount Kaputar National Park (36,817 ha)

Covering part of the majestic Nandewar Range, this mountainous park features a spectacular array of sharp peaks, rocky ranges, bluffs and spires: the remnants of a chain of volcanoes centred around Mt Kaputar, rising 1524 m above the north-western plains. Open eucalypt forests dominate the landscape with an outlying rainforest community around Pound Mountain.

Kangaroos, gliders, koalas and wedge-tailed eagles are easily seen. Walk from picnic area to Sawn Rocks, a strange organ-pipe basaltic formation. Other trails lead through snow gum woodlands and to rocky peaks with views across the jagged mountains. Camping areas with good facilities at Bark Hut and Dawsons Spring, which also has two self-contained cabins.
35 km north-east of Narrabri via Bingara Rd. (02) 6792 4724.

Mount Royal National Park (3341 ha)

Adjoining the south-western tip of Barrington Tops, this new park conserves the former state forest. There are 11 forest types in the park. Endangered fauna including the Hastings River mouse and parma wallaby and a further 19 threatened species are found here. No facilities.
25 km north of Singleton via Carrow Brook and Main Range Rds. (02) 4987 3108.

Mount Warning National Park (2380 ha)

This World Heritage listed park protects the rainforest-clad Mt Warning, a massive volcano active some 23 million years ago, now eroded to half its original size. An exceptional walking track leads to the summit (1157 m), passing through sub-tropical and temperate rainforest communities as the altitude increases. A final steep climb leads to stunning views over the surrounding peaks. Stay nearby at the caravan park or bush camp along the access road.
12 km south-west of Murwillumbah off the Kyogle Rd. (02) 6628 1177.

Mungo National Park (27,847 ha)

World Heritage listed, the shores of dry Lake Mungo are rich in Aboriginal history going back 40,000 years. The Walls of China, a remarkable 30 km crescent of dunes and earth formations are in the park. Kangaroos, bearded dragons, geckoes, emus and pink cockatoos are common in the saltbush lake bed, belah sand plains and mallee dominated dune country. Stay at the shearers' quarters (bookings required) or at one of two camping areas. Mungo Lodge just outside the park has motel-style accommodation and a restaurant (02-5029 7297).
110 km north-east of Mildura and 150 km north-west of Balranald. (02) 5023 1278.

Murramarang National Park (2169 ha)

A coastal park with beautiful beaches and spotted gum forests. The area includes coastal hills and four offshore islands, featuring cliffs, headlands, offshore rock stacks, rock platforms and Aboriginal sites. Warm temperate rainforest thrives in the gullies on Durras Mountain. Stay at Pebbly Beach, famed for its kangaroos, or Pretty, Depot, South Durras or Merry beaches where there are cabins, caravan and camping sites. Book in advance.
280 km south of Sydney and 10 km north of Batemans Bay off the Princes Hwy. (02) 4423 9800.

Nalbaugh National Park (4106 ha)

Two impressive peaks dominate the park, located on a high forested plateau dissected by precipitous gullies and shadowy ravines. The park protects rare animals such as the powerful owl and spotted-tailed quoll. There are no facilities, established walking tracks or camping areas. Bush camping is allowed.
40 km west of Eden and 20 km south-east of Bombala. (02) 6495 4130.

Nangar National Park (9196 ha)

Includes much of the rugged horseshoe-shaped Nangar-Murga Range, a landmark of the flat central western plains. The forests of black pine, ironbark, stringybark and scribbly gum are rich in flowering shrubs, and an important wildlife refuge in an area largely cleared by pastoralists.

There are interesting walks and excellent views from the escarpment. Bush camping only.
52 km west of Orange. Difficult access, contact Bathurst District Office. (02) 6331 9777.

Nattai National Park (86,000 ha)
A wilderness park abutting the eastern boundary of the Blue Mountains National Park and Lake Burragorang. This is a rugged mountainous region with steep escarpments and sandstone cliffs. There are rainforest gullies, dry ironbark forests and mallee eucalypts growing around the fascinating rock formations of Wild Goat Plateau. Yellow-bellied gliders, platypuses, quolls and kangaroos inhabit the park. There are magnificent mountain and lake views from the picnic areas at Warragamba Dam and Burragorang. Bushwalking and bush camping allowed 3 km away from Lake Burragorang.
110 km south of Sydney between Warragamba Dam and Wombeyan Caves Rd. (02) 9542 0666.

Nightcap National Park (4945 ha)
World Heritage listed, the lush rainforests of the park were defended from logging after almost a decade of protest by conservationists. The park includes the western section of the Nightcap Range, part of the Mt Warning volcanic caldera. Walk among the towering trees and bangalow palms of Terania Creek to Protestors Falls, take the Pholis Walk to the edge of the escarpment, or the 9 km Nightcap Track to Mt Nardi. The rufous scrub-bird and several other rare species are among the park's rich fauna. There is a picnic area at Terania Creek, camping is allowed here for one night only.
35 km north of Lismore. (02) 6628 1177.

North Brother National Park (717 ha)
Located on the mid-north coast, this recently declared park conserves exceptionally diverse coastal forest types including swamp forests, sub-tropical rainforest and old growth blackbutt forests. There are a number of rare and threatened plant populations including *Acacia courtii* and threatened fauna. No facilities.
38 km south-west of Port Macquarie via Kew and West Haven. (02) 6584 2203.

Nungatta National Park (6100 ha)
A high country wilderness park abutting the Victorian border in the south and the Genoa River to the west. The area includes the rugged, forested plateau around Nungatta Mountain. Walk into the park from the Cann River Rd through the spectacular Genoa River gorge where the red sandstone walls glow fiery red in the late afternoon sun. No facilities or vehicle access roads. Bush camping only.
60 km south-west of Eden, 40 km south-east of Bombala. (02) 6495 4130.

Nymboi Binderay National Park (8800 ha)
A recently declared park north of Dorrigo famed for its floristic diversity and spectacular rivers. It comprises dry forest types with patches of rainforest and extensive old growth forests. Stands of the rare Dorrigo white gum are found here. The wild and scenic Nymboida and Little Nymboida Rivers flow through the park. No facilities.
45 km north-west of Coffs Harbour via Coramba. (02) 6657 2309.

Nymboida National Park (18,998 ha)
Two wild rivers, the Nymboida and Mann meet here, providing great opportunities for canoeing and white-water rafting. The scenery is spectacular. There are no established walking tracks, but experienced bushwalkers enjoy the park's challenges. There are no facilities or vehicle access to the park. Camp at Ramornie State Forest camping area at the southern edge of the park. Access is by canoe or on foot.
Off the Old Glen Innes Rd north-west of Grafton. (02) 6642 0613 or (02) 6732 5133.

Oxley Wild Rivers National Park (92,926 ha)
Features a high undulating plateau cut by gorges and valleys, and the highest waterfall in Australia. More than 500 km of wild and scenic rivers flow from the escarpment. There are rainforest pockets, open eucalypt forests and some 755 plant species. A 12 km circular walk from Dangar Falls car park combines gorge views, rock hopping and good swimming holes. Visit Wollomombi Falls, Long Point, Gara Gorge, Dangars Falls, Apsley Falls, Tia Falls and Budds

Mare where there are picnic and camping areas.
*In several sections east of Armidale and
Walcha, check detailed maps for access points.
(02) 6773 7211.*

Popran National Park (3970 ha)

North of the Hawkesbury River this sandstone
park is part of a green belt around Sydney. It
conserves clifflines, gullies, many Aboriginal
sites and an important catchment area with
mangroves, eucalypt forests, rainforests, sedge-
lands and heaths. The park forms a corridor for
the movement of animals between Brisbane
Water and Dharug National Parks. There are
some 18 endangered animal species including
the powerful owl, spotted-tailed quoll, brush-
tailed phascogale, yellow-bellied glider, red-
crowned toadlet and the green and golden bell
frog. Walk to Popran and Ironbark Creeks; take
the 3 km return Mount Olive Track for views
over the Hawkesbury and Glenworth Valley; or
the 248 track through forests of Sydney blue
gums, ironbarks and turpentines to spectacular
views over Ironbark Creek. No facilities.
*25 km west of Gosford via Wisemans Ferry Rd or
Morgans Rd near Mt White. (02) 4324 4911.*

Richmond Range National Park (8325 ha)

A recently created park in far north-eastern NSW
conserving extensive old growth forests, rainforests and rare plants including the Richmond
Range spotted gum. It contains the largest areas
of flooded gum in the state and a very high
diversity of animals. No facilities.
*40 km north-west of Casino via Sextonville
Rd. (02) 6628 1177.*

Scheyville National Park (950 ha)

Located at the north-western edge of Sydney, this
recently created park conserves the largest
remnant of Cumberland Plain vegetation,
comprising mostly open forest of grey box, red
forest gum and narrow-leaved ironbark. The
park includes Longneck Lagoon and most of its
forested catchment. More than 140 bird species
have been identified. There are a number of
cultural heritage sites including the first rural
industries training farm and the remains of the
Scheyville Immigration Hostel. Visit the

Longneck Lagoon Field Studies Centre. A picnic
area and visitor centre have been proposed.
*5 km north-east of Windsor via Pitt Town Rd.
(02) 4572 3100.*

Seven Mile Beach National Park (898 ha)

A small coastal strip comprising beaches, sand
dunes, forests and swamplands. The dune
system is constantly changing and vulnerable to
interference. An interesting variety of plant life
has colonised the dunes, and the park is an
important wildlife refuge. Good fishing, surfing
and walking in the forest. Camp in the northern
section where there are basic facilities.
*140 south of Sydney and 17 km north-east of
Nowra via the Princes Hwy. (02) 4423 9800.*

South-east Forests National Park (90,000 ha)

Adjoining Wadbilliga National Park to the north
and Coopracambra in Victoria, this recently
created park is in several parts and provides a
150 km conservation corridor along the coastal
escarpment. The main section follows the Great
Escarpment some 50 km inland, and protects
some of the country's most important old
growth forests with giant trees hundreds of years
old, some with trunks 3 m across. They provide
essential habitats for endangered species such as
the long-footed potoroo, smoky mouse, white-
footed dunnart, spotted-tailed quoll and powerful owl. At Pipers Lookout there are board walks
and picnic areas. Camp at Six Mile Creek, Big
Jack Rest Area and White Rock Rest Area. Visit
the Merimbula information centre.
*Between Cobargo and the Victorian border via
the Princes or Monaro Hwys. (02) 6495 4130.*

Sturt National Park (310,634 ha)

An enormous desert park in the north-western
corner of the state. Long red sand dunes of the
Strzelecki Desert dominate the western section
where lake beds between the dunes fill after
heavy rain, holding water for several years.
Mesas rise above stony gibber plains in the east.
The dry water courses are lined with river red
gums, but they fill after rain when the desert
becomes green and the wildflowers bloom. A
surprising variety of plants and animals live

here including emus, red kangaroos, bearded dragons, big sand goannas and many colourful birds. Summer temperatures are unbearable. Camp at Dead Horse Gully Fort Grey, Mount Wood or Olive Downs.

330 km north of Broken Hill. Roads may be impassable after rain. (08) 8091 3308.

Sydney Harbour National Park (393 ha)

Created from pockets of bushland encircling Sydney Harbour and three small islands, the park features forts, Aboriginal rock art, heathland-covered sandstone headlands overlooking the harbour entrance, secluded sandy beaches and superb views. The park includes the Quarantine Station at North Head, Nielsen Park at Vaucluse, Gap Bluff at Watsons Bay, Clark, Shark and Rodd Islands. Enjoy a half-day stroll along the Manly scenic walkway, views from the Gap Bluff Track at Watsons Bay or the Hermitage Foreshore Track at Vaucluse, or take a guided tour at Fort Denison, Goat Island or the Quarantine Station. Picnic areas, kiosks and showers on some beaches. No camping.

Access by public or private transport. (02) 9337 5511.

Tarlo River National Park (8074 ha)

Located on the southern tablelands the park includes part of the rugged Cookbundoon Ranges and the deep pools and gravel beds of the winding Tarlo River. The park is a refuge for platypuses, long-necked tortoises, waterbirds, kangaroos and wombats. There are no facilities, although bush camping is allowed.

210 km west of Sydney and 30 km north-east of Goulburn off the Goulburn-Taralga Rd. (02) 4887 7270.

Thirlmere Lakes National Park (630 ha)

Protects five connected freshwater lakes on Blue Gum Creek. The narrow, reed-fringed shallow lakes are among the last undisturbed waterways near Sydney and have great scientific value. They are separated by stands of paperbarks and sedges and surrounded by forested sandstone ridges. The park has a rich bird population, wombats, kangaroos and echidnas. There are

picnic areas but camping is not allowed. Swimming and canoeing are popular.

90 km south of Sydney via the Hume Hwy and Thirlmere. (02) 9542 0666.

Tomaree National Park (3679 ha)

A coastal park at the southern entrance to Port Stephens with numerous beaches separated by rocky headlands and backed by forests and heaths. Wildflowers bloom through winter and spring, dolphins play in the waves and fairy penguins sometimes visit the rocky headlands. There are superb views of the spectacular coastline and offshore islets from Tomaree Headland. Picnic facilities are provided at Anna Bay and Zenith Beach. Camping and other accommodation can be found in nearby towns.

50 km north of Newcastle via the Pacific Hwy and Nelson Bay Rd. (02) 4982 1891.

Toolum National Park (3980 ha)

A World Heritage listed park in the far north-east of the state conserving the Toolum Scrub subtropical and dry rainforests, forest red gum woodlands and moist eucalypt forests. It includes part of the Koorelah Range, Hewetson's Hill and Wallaby Creek catchment. There are more than 10 species of kangaroos and wallabies including the black-striped wallaby, long-nosed potoroo, rufous bettong and red-legged pademelon. Endangered bird species found in the rainforests include the powerful owl, masked owl, red goshawk and Albert's lyrebird. Picnic areas and short walking tracks in the southern section. Bush camping is allowed.

86 km north-west of Kyogle off the Urbenville to Legume Rd. (02) 6628 1177.

Toonumbar National Park (5750 ha)

A World Heritage listed park in the far north-east of the state conserving the Murray Scrub and Dome Mountain sub-tropical and temperate rainforests, old growth moist eucalypt forests and palm forests. Many rare and threatened plants are found here, and the rainforests provide habitats for endangered animals including Albert's lyrebird, the long-nosed potoroo, the yellow-bellied glider and Stephen's banded snake. Camping facilities are proposed at Iron Pot

Creek where there is a walking track to the Murray Scrub rainforests. Difficult access after rain. *35 km west of Kyogle via Toonumbar Forest Drive. (02) 6628 1177.*

Wadbilliga National Park (79,459)

Protects the Brogo wilderness area and the rugged coastal escarpment and plateaux surrounding the Wadbilliga, Tuross and Brogo Rivers. The extensive Wadbilliga Plateau rises to 1337 m at Belowra Mountain. The rivers have carved wide, steep-sided valleys and created the scenic Tuross Falls and Tuross Gorge. There are pockets of temperate rainforest, open forests, heathlands and sub-alpine woodlands with snow gums on the highest sites. The park offers challenging hikes for experienced bushwalkers. Basic camping at Lake Creek or the Cascades (4WD access). 4WD beyond Wadbilliga Crossing. *150 km south-east of Canberra via Narooma and Cobargo. (02) 4476 2888.*

Wallaga Lake National Park (1237 ha)

Wallaga Lake, on the state's south coast, was formed by the drowning of two river valleys some 6000 years ago. The area has great Aboriginal significance. The shores are dotted with Aboriginal shell middens, and Merriman Island within the lake is gazetted as an Aboriginal Place (access is denied). Forested ridges and spurs slope steeply to the lake and the cool, moist gullies support rainforest species. Koalas, potoroos, swamp wallabies and more than 220 bird species are found in the area. Walk in from the Princes Highway or by boat from the lake. Boats can be hired at Regatta Point and Beauty Point. No facilities. *10 km north of Bermagui. (02) 4476 2888.*

Warrabah National Park (3471 ha)

This park features a deep gorge cut by the Namoi River into the granite belt of the northern tablelands creating rapids, cascades and swimming holes along its upper reaches. Woodlands surround the river. Grey kangaroos, wallaroos, possums, some 53 bird species and a variety of reptiles are found here. There is excellent scenery, challenges for canoeists, rock climbers, and fine bushwalks along the river. The rest area has basic camping facilities. *80 km north of Tamworth via Manilla on the Namoi River Rd. (02) 6773 7211.*

Weddin Mountains National Park (8361 ha)

This park protects an undisturbed area of woodlands and heaths surrounded by cleared land, and incorporates the Weddin Range, the hideaway of bushrangers. The rugged range rises steeply above the plains in spectacular orange cliff lines, and falls gently to the west and south. Birds and kangaroos, including the brush-tailed rock wallaby, are plentiful. Take the Peregrine and Eualdrie Lookouts Walk for spectacular views over the rugged cliffs and plains. Basic camping at Seatons or Holy Camp. *19 km south-west of Grenfell. (02) 6331 9777.*

Werrikimbe National Park (35,288 ha)

World Heritage listed park on the eastern escarpment of the Great Dividing Range in the New England Tablelands. Three major rivers have carved deep valleys plummeting more than 700 m down spectacular waterfalls and cascades to the coastal plains. The park features giant rainforest trees, ancient Antarctic beech trees, rare and secretive animals and a great diversity of habitats created by the rugged topography and range of altitudes. Walking tracks lead through the rainforest. Picnic areas provided. Camp at Mooraback, Cobcroft or Brushy Mountain rest areas where there are basic facilities. *450 km north of Sydney and 120 km north-west of Walcha via the Oxley Hwy. (02) 6584 2203 or (02) 6773 7211.*

Willandra National Park (19,386 ha)

A large park in the semi-arid riverine plains country, once one of the most famous sheep stations in the west. The flat red sandy plains support saltbush and grasses, and give way to black box trees and tangled lignum around the temporary wetlands and Willandra Creek. Willandra Billabong is a haven for birds, frogs and other aquatic animals. Red and grey kangaroos and emus are commonly seen on the plains. Camp near the homestead or stay at the

Men's Quarters (02-6967 8159).
64 km north-west of Hillston. Roads are impassable after rain. (02) 6962 7755.

Willi Willi National Park (9620 ha)

This recently created park supports some of the best developed escarpment sedgelands and wet heaths of the district, as well as tall open forests and rainforests, including the last remaining stands of shatterwood dry rainforest in the state. The spotted-tailed quoll, pygmy mouse and mosaic-tailed mouse have been recorded here. Go bushwalking, orienteering, bush camping and rock climbing.

50 km west of Kempsey via Toorumbee Rd. (02) 6584 2203.

Woko National Park (8265 ha)

The steep hills of this park harbour dry sub-tropical and warm temperate rainforest types, untouched by loggers and supporting more than 60 bird species including the brush turkey and rare wompoo pigeon. Swimming, fishing, canoeing and bushwalking are popular. Basic camping beside the Manning River.

30 km north-west of Gloucester off the Gloucester-Walcha Rd. (02) 4987 3108.

Wollemi National Park (492,220 ha)

This is the state's largest wilderness area, extending from the Hunter River to the Blue Mountains National Park. The area is a maze of cliffs, canyons and untouched forests containing the recently-discovered Wollemi pine. Grey kangaroos, wombats, red-necked wallabies and wallaroos are often seen. Follow Bob Turner's Track to the beaches and spectacular gorge of the Colo River. There are Aboriginal art sites, ruins at Newnes and a glow-worm filled railway tunnel. Go canoeing, fishing and swimming at Dunn's Swamp dam. Basic camping at Wheeny Creek, Colo Meroo, Dunn's Swamp and Newnes.

100 km north-west of Sydney off the Putty Rd or via Rylstone. (02) 4588 5247 or (02) 6543 3533.

Wyrrabalong National Park (619 ha)

In an overdeveloped part of the Central Coast on either side of The Entrance, this small park con-serves the last significant stand of coastal rain-forest in the area. Terilbah and Pelican Islands in Tuggerah Lake are important habitats for migrating wading birds. High headlands, cliffs and rock platforms form the coast of the south-ern section, while in the north a large sand bar-rier separates Tuggerah Lake from the ocean. Pelican and Tuggerah beaches are popular swimming and surfing spots, while Bateau Bay is calm and sheltered. Walking tracks follow the coastline. Picnic areas but no camping.

5 km north and south of The Entrance. (02) 4324 4911.

Yengo National Park (139,861 ha)

A wilderness of steep gorges and rocky ridges in rugged sandstone country stretching along the foot of the Great Dividing Range . The area supports a variety of animals including wombats, wallaroos, koalas, the tiger quoll and brush-tailed rock wallaby. Cockatoos, lyrebirds and eagles are often seen. Walk along the Old Great North Rd (an ancient Aboriginal route), enjoy canoeing, bicycling, bushwalking or picnicking. Great views from Finchley Lookout. Basic camping at Mogo (booking advised).

90 km north-west of Sydney via Wisemans Ferry, Putty Rd or George Downes Dr. (02) 6574 5275.

Yuraygir National Park (20,285 ha)

A coastal park in three sections protecting the longest stretch of undeveloped coastline in the state. There are low grassy headlands separating rock platforms and long sandy beaches with low sand dunes. Inland are swamps, lagoons and small lakes in open plains beneath sandstone ridges supporting dry eucalypt forests. Emus are still seen here together with brolgas, storks, kangaroos and lace monitors. Angourie has a famous surfing break, the creeks offer good canoeing, and there is good fishing. Camp at Red Cliff, Sandon River, Illaroo or Station Creek where there are basic facilities.

50 km east of Grafton between Red Rock and Yamba. (02) 6642 0613.

Queensland

Featured National Parks

Mount Isa

Birdsville

CAPE

Weipa •

• Iron range

YORK

• Musgrave

• Cooktown

PENINSULA

Cape Tribulation

GREAT

• Normanton

• Cairns

Atherton •

• Innisfail

Great

11 Hinchinbrook Is

Greenvale •

• Ingham

Barrier

• Townsville
• Ayr

Charters Towers •

• Bowen

Proserpine • **10** Whitsunday Is

9

QUEENSLAND

• Mackay

Reef

Longreach •

Emerald •

• Rockhampton

8

• Gladstone

• Bundaberg

7

Fraser Is **6**

Gympie • **5**

Charleville •

RANGE

Roma •

4

Toowoomba •

BRISBANE
Gold Coast

2 **3**

1

79

Girraween National Park

Set in a landscape of great rounded granite boulders and outcrops, Girraween National Park protects a magnificent section of the New England highlands. Meaning place of flowers, Girraween is like a huge rock garden with crystal pools and beautiful springtime wildflower displays.

Girraween covers an area of 11,700 ha at an average elevation of 900 m, and is set among the farms, orchards and vineyards of the New England Granite Belt. The park comprises steep-sided granite hills dissected by gullies and valleys with numerous waterholes and swimming spots along the clear mountain creeks. Precariously balanced rocks among the angular tors and boulders of the area give the park a Stone Age feel. Across the border in the adjacent Bald Rock National Park is the huge dome of Bald Rock. Said to be the largest exposed granite-type mass in the southern hemisphere, this great rock is 750 m long and 500 m wide, and rises 200 m above the surrounding bushland.

Formation

The rock formations of the area have their origins in a period of geological upheaval some 225 million years ago. A large volume of molten rock welled up from deep beneath the earth's crust, forcing its way into the sedimentary and volcanic rocks near the surface. As the rock slowly cooled it crystallised into a coarse granite and stress cracks began to appear.

The area was slowly uplifted and millions of years of erosion gradually stripped away the softer overlying rocks to expose the hard, cracked granite. Water seeped into the cracks splitting them into great granite blocks with rounded edges. Some of the weaker sections have been severely weathered or completely removed leaving balanced boulders, strangely-shaped tors and sculptured rocks.

Plants

The sandy soils derived from the weathered granite support a diverse array of flowering shrubs. They form low dense heaths, with wattles, pea flowers, rock roses, mint and daisy bushes growing beneath scattered eucalypt and cypress trees.

Swamp communities flourish where drainage is impeded. Sedges, rushes, swamp selaginella and sphagnum mosses grow in these sites alongside beautiful ground orchids. Epiphytic orchids cling to trees and boulders or lodge in crevices in the moist sheltered gullies. Ferns and shrubs such as wild fuchsia, blueberry ash, tableland daisybush, lance beard heath and the large-leaved hop bush share this habitat, and if the soil is deep enough New England blackbutts and round-leaved gum trees thrive.

The well-drained soils on the valley floors, slopes and gullies support eucalypt forests. Many of the 25 species of eucalypt identified here are limited to this area. They include the graceful white-barked Wallangarra whitegum and the bell-fruited mallee. Blackbutt, yellow box, orange gum and the broad-leaved stringybark are common, often mixed with black cypress, rough-barked apple, kurrajong, coast banksia and oleander wattle.

The wildflower displays begin in late July with golden wattle and purple pea flowers, reaching their peak in September and October when the heaths and shrublands are ablaze with colour.

Wildlife

Mammals are best seen at dawn and dusk and by spotlighting at night. Kangaroos frequent grassy areas near the camping ground and Visitor Centre. They include the eastern grey kangaroo which hops with its head held high; the dark brown swamp wallaby and the red-necked wallaby, (both hop with their heads down) and the wallaroo, often seen crouching over to feed.

Brushtail possums search for food around the picnic areas. Ringtail possums, mouse-sized feathertail gliders and the larger sugar gliders inhabit the woodlands, but are rarely seen. Common wombats graze late at night, and you may spot their burrows under fallen logs or at the base of boulders.

Red-bellied black snakes hunt in damp sites for frogs such as Leseur's frog, the eastern banjo frog and the ornate burrowing frog, while common brown snakes bask on rocks. Both species are venomous and should not be disturbed. Among the commonly seen lizards are the copper-tailed skink, bearded dragon and jacky lizard. Geckos often live under sheets of exfoliated granite, among leaves and under bark.

Birdlife is plentiful in the park. Kookaburras, magpies and currawongs frequent the picnic grounds together with brightly-coloured crimson rosellas, blue wrens, eastern yellow robins, eastern spinebills, red-browed firetails, yellow-rumped thornbills and yellow-tufted honeyeaters.

The forests and heaths attract a wide variety of birds. Among the eucalypts are parrots, treecreepers, flycatchers and honeyeaters. In the dense understorey robins, wrens, firetails and thornbills seek shelter and food. The superb lyrebird lives in some of the damp forests at the northern limit of its range. Birds of prey such as the little eagle, wedge-tailed eagle and the Australian goshawk hunt for small animals above the open grassy areas.

Walks

Some of the best wildflower displays are within easy walking distance of the Visitor Centre along the Junction Track. This two and a half hour return walk follows Bald Rock Creek to a large granite outcrop at the junction with Ramsay Creek. Ground orchids are easily seen on the 600 m track to Dr Roberts Waterhole which starts by the road 4 km from the Visitor Centre.

The Pyramid Track takes two hours return, and offers excellent views from the summit of the granite dome of the Pyramid. The walk is easy, but the ascent may prove tiring. Granite Arch is a natural stone archway about 35 min-utes return from the picnic ground. This is an excellent walk full of birdlife, and at night possums feed in the eucalypts.

The track to Castle Rock is an easy two hour return walk with panoramic views from the summit of this great rock slope. Continue to the Sphinx and Turtle Rock, an extra two hour return walk through heathlands to two large rocks resembling the Sphinx and a turtle's back. Experienced rock climbers find Turtle Rock and Mount Norman an interesting diversion.

The track to Mount Norman passes through open forest, heathland and open rock areas, and takes six hours to return to the picnic area. Water should be carried on the longer walks.

Facilities

There is a picnic area and swimming hole near the Visitor Centre on Bald Rock Creek. Tables, water, toilets, fireplaces and firewood are provided. The camping grounds at Bald Rock Creek and Castle Rock have hot showers, toilets, tables and fireplaces with firewood. Caravans are allowed but there are no powered sites. Camping permits are required and bookings should be made, particularly during holiday periods and long weekends.

Access

The park is 260 km west of Brisbane via the New England Highway. A sealed road, 26 km south of Stanthorpe and 11 km north of Wallangarra, leads to the park from the highway.

Climate

The climate is pleasantly cool with dry, cold, frosty nights in winter, and warm days in summer. Most of the rain falls from November to March. Cold changes may occur at any time of year.

Girraween National Park, Wyberba, Via Ballandean, Qld 4382. Tel. (07) 4684 5157.

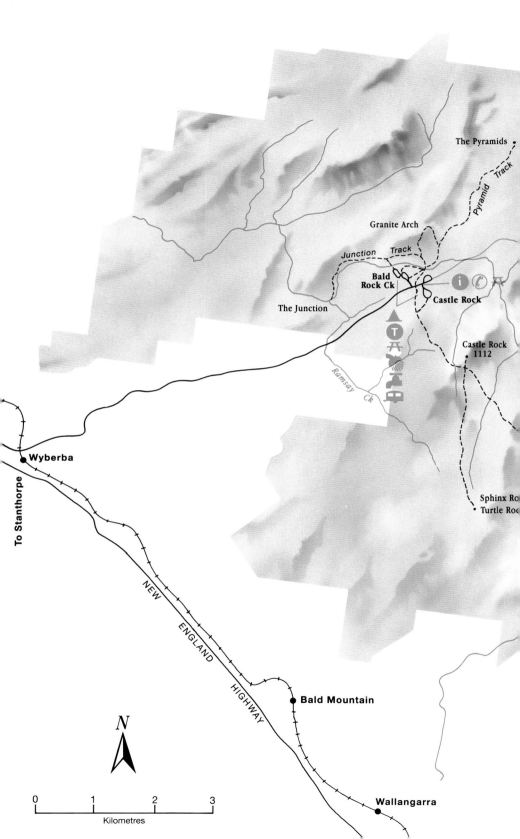

To Eukey

Girraween National Park

Pyramid Ck

Dr Roberts
Waterhole

Rock Ck

Mt Norman
1267

Racecourse Ck

Stanthorpe

Ballandean   Eukey

Wyberba

Wallangarra

Tenterfield

Main Range National Park

Main Range National Park forms part of a spectacular arc of mountains encircling the southern and western sides of Brisbane, known as the Scenic Rim. The park encompasses a succession of impressive peaks, ridges and escarpments, extending 40 km from Kangaroo Mountain in the north to Wilsons Peak on the New South Wales border.

Part of the Central Eastern Rainforest Reserves World Heritage Area, Main Range National Park forms the western limit of an almost continuous belt of national parks and state forests preserving the Scenic Rim from encroaching development. Set in a rugged landscape with breathtaking views, the park encompasses 18,400 ha of dense rainforests, open eucalypt forests and steep rock pavements. An extensive network of walking tracks has been developed, particularly in the Cunninghams Gap area.

Formation

The landform has its origins in an extended period of volcanic activity that came to an end some 20 million years ago. The Main Range volcano was one of a number of volcanoes in the region. Lava, composed principally of basalt with some outpourings of harder acidic rhyolite, flowed over the coastal plain, creating the base for a chain of mountains forming the Scenic Rim. Vigorous erosion by streams flowing from the volcanic peaks has formed the cliffs, escarpments and valleys, and created rich basalt soils.

History

Cunninghams Gap was discovered by Allan Cunningham in 1828 while searching for a pass from the Darling Downs to the coast. Steep grades and rock walls meant that only horse riders could use the track, and it wasn't until a road was constructed in the 1920s that this became a major route to Moreton Bay. Spicers Gap was discovered in 1847 by a stockman, Henry Alphen, and became the first safe route for bullock teams pulling drays laden with wool to the port, returning with supplies for the Darling Downs settlers.

The route was superseded by the Brisbane to Warwick railway line, built in 1871, and the road fell into disuse until car-based tourism became popular in the 1920s and 30s. In 1909

Cunninghams Gap was reserved as a national park, and in the 1960s and 70s a number of other parks, including Queen Mary Falls, Mount Mistake and Mount Roberts were reserved along the range. These were amalgamated into Main Range National Park, which became part of the Central Eastern Rainforest Reserves World Heritage Area in 1994.

Vegetation

The fertile basalt soils are generally restricted to altitudes above 700 m, and support cool subtropical rainforests dominated by tall buttressed trees such as tulip oaks, yellow carabeen and rosewood. Scattered among these are hoop pine, brush box and giant fig trees with a moist understorey of ferns, epiphytes, orchids and lianas. On the sheltered southerly slopes below the cliffs of Wilsons Peak are small stands of warm temperate rainforest with turpentine and lilly pilly. Above the cliffs are heaths of tea trees and mint bushes.

The tall open eucalypt forests on the drier slopes and rocky ridges are dominated by forest red gum, Sydney blue gum and yellow box with a number of stringybarks and other temperate species at higher altitudes. Giant spear lilies grow on the cliffs and rock pavements along Main Range.

Wildlife

The wide range of habitats support one of the most diverse mammal faunas in Australia. One-third of the terrestrial mammal species live here, including both monotremes: the platypus and echidna. Among the 32 marsupial species are the long-nosed potoroo and the rufous bettong. Red-necked and red-legged pademelons are often seen grazing in forest clearings. The spotted-tailed quoll and brush-tailed phascogale, both threatened by logging, are among the carnivorous marsupials. Other endangered species include the Hastings River mouse and the fawn-footed melomys. The park supports 22 bat species including some at the southern limits of their ranges, such as the Queensland blossom bat, black flying fox and little bent-winged bat. The two forest eptesicus bats reach their northern limits in the area.

More than 270 bird species have been recorded. Of particular importance are Albert's lyrebird and the rufous scrub-bird. Both are rare and threatened by clearing of their forest habitat. The males have well-developed vocal courtship displays and are expert mimics. Satin and regent bowerbirds are commonly seen in the forests, and you may spot wonga and topknot pigeons, or the threatened eastern bristlebird.

The area has many frog species including the rare red, black and yellow mountain frog, and the pouched frog whose tadpoles are raised in skin pouches on the hips of the males. Reptiles are well represented, including a number of geckoes and skinks, such as the common blue-tongue lizard. Among the more striking reptiles is the southern angle-headed dragon which changes colour to match its rainforest environment. The aggressive and dangerous rough-scaled snake, and the arboreal pale-headed and Stephen's banded snake occur in the forests.

Walks

Walking tracks in the Cunninghams Gap area begin at The Crest car park. A short rainforest circuit leads to the beginning of the northern track system. The Box Forest Track is an easy one hour walk through rainforest and open forest, following West Gap Creek to the camping area. Gap Creek Falls Track is a demanding 9.4 km walk descending along a ridge from Fassifern Valley Lookout through open forest to the falls.

The cliff face of Mount Cordeaux is spectacular in spring and early summer when the giant spear lilies are blooming. The Mount Cordeaux Track zig-zags through rainforest to a lookout on the southern side, taking about two hours return from The Crest. A 2.4 km detour west of the peak leads to Morgans Lookout where there are magnificent views over the northern section of the

park. The track passes through a beautiful rainforest area where lyrebirds can be heard in the winter. An extension leads to the lookout at Bare Rock.

Palm Grove Circuit is an easy two hour return walk from The Crest. A variety of birdlife can be seen, and the walk terminates in a circuit featuring a dense grove of Bangalow palms. Mount Mitchell, south of the highway, can be reached via a three hour return track through different forest types to a knife-edge ridge on the east peak. From Spicers Gap camping area you can take the rough Mount Matheson Trail, a relatively easy one hour return walk, or continue to the road west of Governors Chair. Koalas are often seen in this area. Bushwalkers heading off the tracks must register at the Park Headquarters before leaving.

Facilities

Cunninghams Gap camping area is opposite the Park Headquarters on the banks of West Gap Creek, and has basic facilities. On the east side of Spicers Gap a small camping area is set in a clearing, with limited firewood and drinking water provided. Camping permits are required and bookings should be made for long weekends and school holidays.

Access

Cunninghams Gap is 116 km south-west of Brisbane via the Cunningham Highway. Spicers Gap can be reached from the east via the unsealed Moogerah Dam Road, which leaves the highway 5 km west of Aratula. The western approach is suitable for 4WD vehicles only, and leaves the highway 1.5 km west of the Park Headquarters. Both approaches to Spicers Gap are unsuitable for caravans and trailers, and may be closed in wet weather.

Climate

Summers are hot with cool nights, while winter days are cool with cold nights. Most rain falls from November to March, but storms and torrential downpours can occur at any time of the year.

Main Range National Park, MS 394, Warwick, Qld 4370. Tel. (07) 4666 1297.

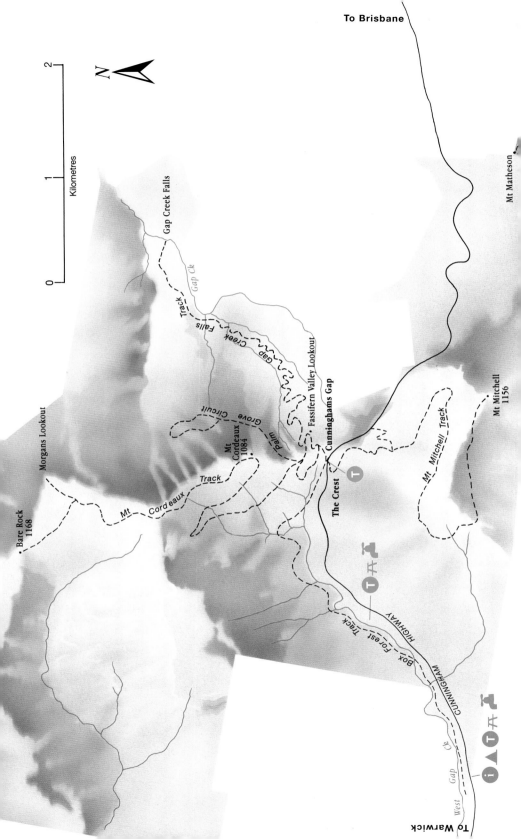

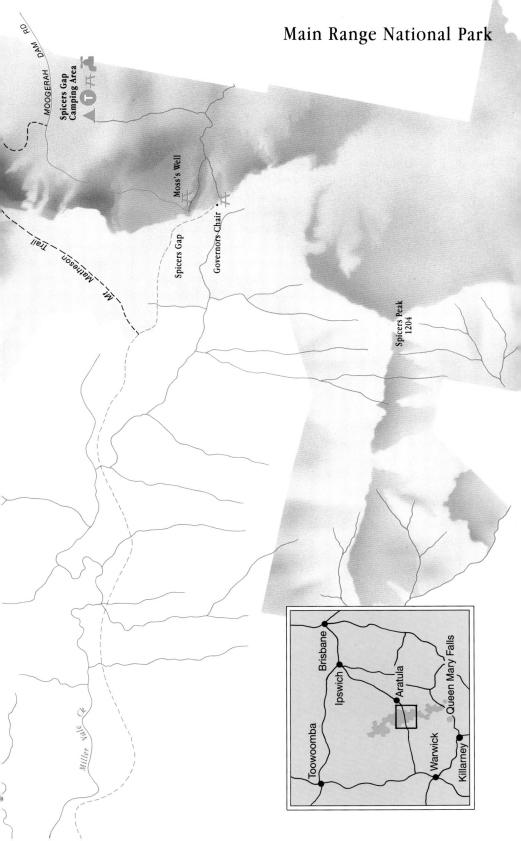

MOOGERAH DAM RD

Spicers Gap
Camping Area

Mt Matheson Trail

Moss's Well

Spicers Gap

Governors Chair

Spicers Peak
1204

Miller Vale Ck

Brisbane

Ipswich

Toowoomba

Aratula

Warwick

Queen Mary Falls

Killarney

Lamington National Park

The cool green rainforest world of Lamington National Park contrasts dramatically with the beachside hustle and hot, humid summer temperatures of the Gold Coast, just 50 km away. Perched on the southern crest of a chain of mountains curving around Brisbane, this major national park is part of the World Heritage Central Eastern Rainforest Reserves and protects the largest area of undisturbed sub-tropical rainforest in south-eastern Queensland.

Within the park's 20,600 ha are hundreds of waterfalls cascading from rugged mountain ridges into densely forested valleys of pristine beauty. The park adjoins the Border Ranges National Park in New South Wales to preserve a variety of vegetation types supported by the area's rich volcanic soils. Sub-tropical rainforests thrive in this high rainfall region, and on the peaks above 1000 m are cool temperate rainforests with magnificent Antarctic beech trees adorned with ferns and mosses. Lamington is the northern-most outpost of these ancient trees, remnants of the last ice age when cool temperate rainforest vegetation dominated this area.

Formation

The mountainous terrain was formed between 20 and 23 million years ago when the area was alive with volcanic activity. Basalt lava flows from Mount Warning spread over the surrounding coastal plain, helping to create a huge dome rising some 2000 m above sea level. During the last stages of eruption a ring of volcanic vents surrounding Mount Warning began pouring out rhyolite, an acidic volcanic rock much more resistant to erosion than basalt. This was over-layed by more basalt from the central vent.

Erosion by streams flowing from the sides of the central vent has broken down the basalt rock to form rich volcanic soils, leaving the harder rhyolite as a mountainous rim around the edge of the bowl-shaped valley (caldera) surrounding Mount Warning. As the layers of basalt beneath the rhyolite erode, great blocks fall away leaving sheer cliff faces often hundreds of metres high. These form the steep escarpments on the edge of the caldera with their panoramic lookouts.

Plants and Animals

The sub-tropical rainforests are dominated by booyong, marara and carabeen trees. Below the canopy orchids, ferns, mosses, vines and fungi flourish in a cool, moist environment. These areas provide numerous habitats for native animals. In the late afternoon red-necked pademelons graze in grassy clearings and forest verges. By spotlighting at night brushtail and ringtail possums, pygmy possums, gliders, bandi-coots, spotted-tailed quolls, marsupial mice, native rats, frogs and geckoes may be revealed. Luminous fungi and glow worms are found on the cuttings and banks along the walking tracks.

The area is famed for its variety of birdlife. Commonly seen around the camping areas are crimson rosellas, satin bowerbirds, pied curra-wongs and brush turkeys. Feeding by visitors has attracted great numbers of these birds to the Binna Burra and Green Mountains areas, to the detriment of the birds' health and the ecosystem.

By walking quietly along the rainforest tracks you will see smaller forest birds such as wrens, warblers and fantails flitting through the under-storey, and you may catch sight of the rare Albert's lyrebird. Common reptiles include the large black land mullets, goannas, geckoes and skinks. Blue Lamington spiny crayfish are easy to spot in the pools and creeks.

On the more exposed slopes the rainforest is drier and species such as hoop pine emerge from the canopy. On the less fertile soils are eucalypt forests and montane heaths.

Walks

Many walking tracks have been constructed in the park. Most radiate out from the two main visitor centres at Green Mountains and Binna Burra. Sudden temperature drops are common and walkers should be prepared for extreme weather conditions.

Do not miss the rainforest circuit at Green Mountains. This 1.3 km track goes through sub-tropical rainforest where the trees are weighed down by giant ferns and orchids. A 120 m boardwalk goes up into the tree canopy 16 m above the ground, with a further 20 m climb to a lookout in the branches of a fig tree. The Python Rock track, sealed for its 2.5 km length, is suitable for wheelchairs, passing through the rainforest to lookouts over the Lost World, Castle Crag and Morans Falls.

Perhaps the best walk for the fit is the 22 km Border Track between Green Mountains and Binna Burra. This is the backbone of the track system with numerous tracks radiating from it. The trail winds along the top of a rock wall with spectacular views of the wilderness area to Mount Warning and the Tweed Range. This is a good day's walk with an overnight stop at the end.

The Mount Merino Track begins halfway along the Border Track and takes you to some large Antarctic beech trees. The rare rufous scrub bird lives in this cool temperate rainforest. The Blue Pool Track branches off the Border Track 250 m from Green Mountains. This is 9.8 km return with a 1.7 km extension to the spectacular Stairway Falls. The track descends through rainforest with large red cedar trees to a popular swimming spot at Blue Pool on West Canungra Creek. You may be lucky enough to see a platypus here.

To see a variety of forest and heath environments take Dave's Creek Circuit, a 12 km round trip branching off the Border Track 2.3 km from Binna Burra. The track passes through rain-forest, tall eucalypt forest and montane heath. A self-guiding brochure is available. From the Binna Burra Lodge a 4 km return trail leads to Kweenbani Cave, an interesting walk through open forest and rainforest. Koalas are often seen in the open forest.

The Senses Trail is a short track for the blind or blindfolded at Binna Burra. This fascinating track follows a circuit through different forest types with a rope guide and braille signs inviting you to touch and smell the plants and rocks, listen to the sounds of the forest and feel the atmospheric changes between the forest types.

Facilities

There are information offices, picnic facilities and kiosks at Green Mountains and Binna Burra. Unleaded petrol is also available at Binna Burra. The small campsite at Green Mountains must be booked well in advance. There are hot showers and toilets, but no barbecues, this area is fuel stove only. Tables and some barbecues are provided at the picnic area. There is a guest-house at O'Reilly's (07-5544 0644). Binna Burra has a range of private accommodation and a private camping ground (bookings: 07-5533 3758).

Bush camping is allowed at specified sites in the park, but not between 1 December and 31 January, and bush campers must contact the ranger for advice and camping permits. Open fires are banned and fuel stoves are recommended for all campers.

Access

Green Mountains is 115 km from Brisbane via Canungra, and 70 km from the Gold Coast via Nerang and Canungra. The sealed road from Canungra is steep, narrow and winding in places, and unsuitable for caravans. Binna Burra is 55 km from Southport via Nerang and 107 km from Brisbane via Canungra. The road is sealed but narrow and winding in places.

Climate

The climate is much cooler than the surrounding plains. Summers are hot with cool nights, while winters are cool with cold nights. Most rain falls from November to March, but storms and torrential downpours can occur at any time of the year.

Lamington National Park, Green Mountains, Via Canungra, Qld 4275.
Tel. (07) 5544 0634.
Binna Burra, Via Nerang, Qld 4211.
Tel. (07) 5533 3584.

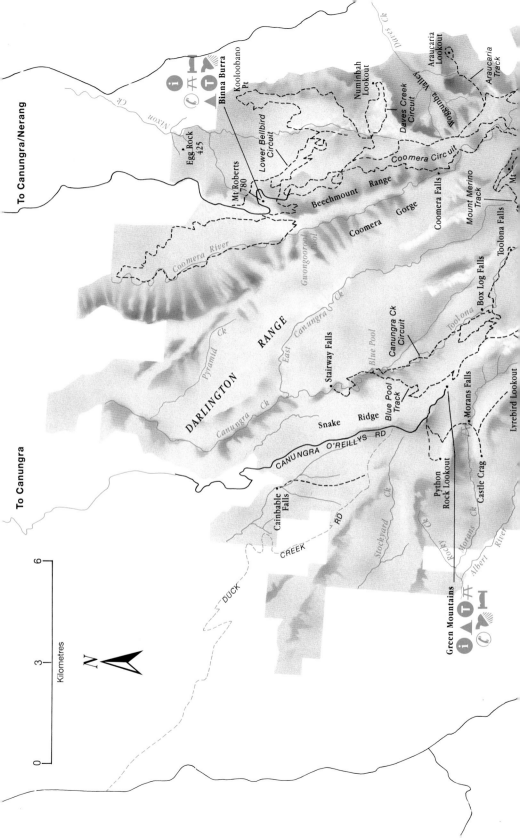

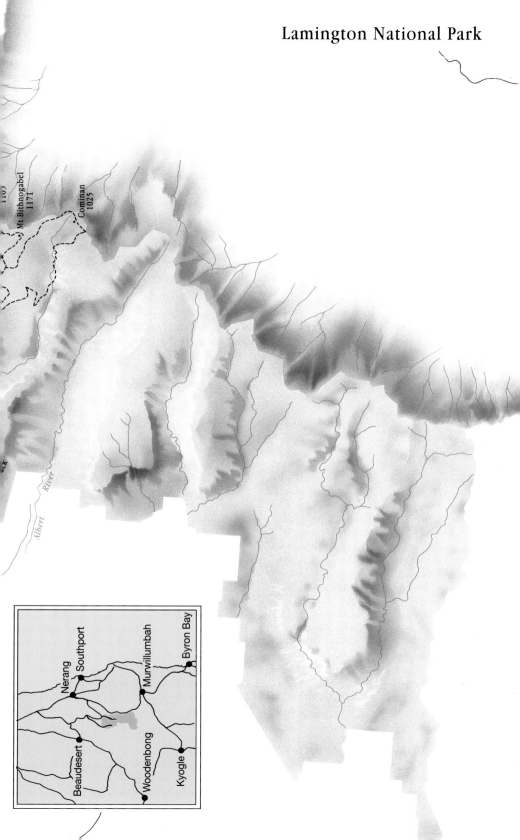

Lamington National Park

Bunya Mountains National Park

*An isolated spur of the Great Dividing Range, the Bunya Mountains rise abruptly
from the flat plains of the Darling Downs. In this cool, moist region are spectacular
waterfalls, brilliantly coloured bird life and the last remaining forests of bunya pines.*

Famed for its magnificent rainforests, Bunya
Mountains National Park straddles a ridge rising
to 1135 m at Mount Kiangarow. The bunya pines
tower above the rainforest canopy, their symmet-
rical crowns standing 50 m above the forest floor.
These stately trees produce enormous cones
weighing 6–7 kg, containing large edible seeds
the size of a small hen's egg, filled with a
delicious milky white flesh.

The park covers 11,700 ha, and at an average
elevation of 975 m it attracts a relatively high
rainfall as the moist coastal air condenses on its
rise from the plains. Consequently the plateau is
the source of a number of creeks which descend
in cascades and waterfalls over cliffs and into valleys filled with magnificent stands of rainforest.

Formation

The Bunya Mountains are the remnant of an
ancient shield volcano that erupted some 30
million years ago creating a massive dome of
solidified basaltic lava. Wind and rain have broken down the basalt into the deep red-brown soils
of the area. Streams have etched into the basalt
leaving behind the harder rhyolite rock that
plugged the volcanic vents. This worn remnant is
today the Bunya Mountains, and the rich soils,
warm temperatures and high rainfall provide
ideal conditions for rainforest plants to flourish.

History

The bunya pines were an important food source
for the Aboriginal people who lived in the area,
and were one of the few tree species they actively
managed. Each clan had a defined territory within the bunya forest, and individual families
claimed ownership of particular trees. They protected them from fire and harvested the nuts,
using loops of liana vines and footholds cut into
the trunk with stone axes to climb the trees.

About every third year the trees produce an

extraordinarily abundant crop, and neighbour-
ing clans were invited to weeks of tribal ceremonies and feasting known as the 'Bonye Bonye'
feast. The guests came from as far south as the
Clarence River in northern NSW, Maranoa River
to the west and Wide Bay to the east. They
camped at the foot of the mountains while the
hosts gathered and distributed the cones amidst
great celebration. The soft young nuts were eaten
raw, while the older nuts were pounded into a
flour and roasted into a cake that could be stored
for several weeks.

Europeans moved into the area in the 1860s,
and in 1878 the whole of the Bunya Mountains
area was opened up to selection. Sawmills were
established and loggers set to work felling the
great red cedar trees and the straight-trunked
pines. Deprived of their traditional lands, the
Aboriginal people were unable to continue their
age-old ceremonies, and the last great Bonye
Bonye feast took place in 1875.

In 1908 the government stepped in to protect
the last remaining stands of bunya pines, and
gazetted 9303 ha as Bunya Mountains National
Park.

Plants and Animals

Cool temperate rainforests feature in the higher
areas of the park. Bunya pines dominate the
canopy with their straight trunks, horizontal
branches and dome-shaped crowns, while vines,
mosses, lichens, epiphytic ferns and orchids grow
among the trees and on the forest floor. At slightly
lower elevations the bunya pines are replaced by
hoop pines.

Woodlands and open eucalypt forests of ironbarks, stringybarks, yellow box, white box and
forest red gums grow alongside the rainforests.
The rainforests of the drier northern and western
areas are dominated by bottle trees, and are

replaced by belah and brigalow woodlands and vine thickets on some of the lower western slopes.

On the western slopes of Mt Kiangarow the rainforest opens out into grasslands, locally known as 'balds', supporting tall grass trees hundreds of years old and over 5 m tall. They are thought to have formed during the last ice age, some 30,000 years ago, when the cold, dry climate forced the rainforests to retreat into small isolated patches, allowing grasses and eucalypt forests to take over. At the end of the ice age, some 10,000 years ago, the warmer, wetter weather allowed the rainforests to expand, a process that continues today.

The colourful birdlife is one of the park's great attractions. Flocks of brilliant green and scarlet king parrots and crimson rosellas come looking for food around the picnic areas. Visitors, however, are asked not to feed the wildlife as this can be detrimental to their health and the area's ecology.

Pythons sun themselves along the tracks and in the clearings, and frogs, such as the great barred frog, may be seen or heard calling around the streams at night.

Small red-necked wallabies congregate in the open grassy areas in the early mornings and evenings, while swamp wallabies and red-necked pademelons feed beside the roads and tracks, hopping into cover if disturbed. Other common mammals include possums, gliders and the yellow-footed antechinus.

Walks

The park has an extensive system of graded walking tracks. Walks from the Dandabah camping area vary from the 500 m self-guiding Bunya Bunya Track, to a 10 km hike to Big Falls Lookout. The 4 km Scenic Circuit is an easy walk through rainforests, past rock pools, water-falls and a huge strangler fig to Pine Gorge Lookout where there are panoramic views over the hills and valleys.

Various tracks lead from the picnic grounds along the Bunya Mountain Road. By arranging a pickup at an exit point you can avoid return-ing along the same route. Barkers Creek Circuit goes past Big Falls where the creek plunges 122 m into a valley filled with hoop pines. The short Westcliff Track follows the cliffs, winding through various forest communities to Westcliff Lookout overlooking the Darling Downs. The 2.5 km Koondaii Lookout Circuit zig-zags down the mountainside, crossing several creeks before emerging at Koondaii Lookout where there are views to the head of the Koondaii Valley.

Westcott Plain Track is a one hour return walk along the cliff edge from the picnic area. Large skinks are often seen along the path, and the trail continues to Mt Kiangarow, winding to the summit where tiny red, white and black mistletoe birds flit through the trees.

The longest of the western trails is the Cherry Plain Track, a three-hour, 6 km walk from Burtons Well to the Cherry Plain picnic area, through forests and grassy plains.

Facilities

The facilities are concentrated at Dandabah where there is a Visitor Centre, a picnic area with electric barbecues and a camping ground with hot showers and fireplaces. The camping areas at Westcott Plain and Burtons Well have toilets and picnic areas. Camping permits are required and bookings should be made in advance. Near the park entrance are motel units, cabins, a kiosk, guest house and private houses for rent.

Access

The park is 109 km from Toowoomba via Jondaryan and a partially sealed road through Quinalow and MacLagan. From Dalby the park is 55 km via Kaimkillenbun and Yamison along partially sealed roads. From Kingaroy it is 56 km via Kumbia along partly sealed roads. The unsealed road from Nanango via Maidenwell has several steep grades and is unsuitable for caravans.

Climate

The climate is mild with an annual rainfall of about 1050 mm. Take warm clothing as the nights can be quite cool, even in summer.

Bunya Mountains National Park, MS 501, Dalby, Qld 4405. Tel. (07) 4668 3127 from 2–4 pm.

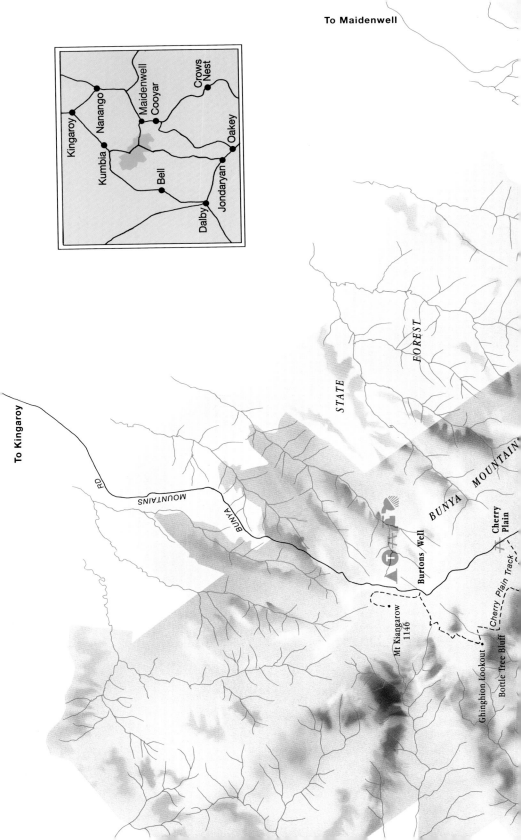

To Maidenwell

To Kingaroy

Kingaroy
Nanango
Kumbia
Maidenwell
Cooyar
Crows Nest
Oakey
Bell
Jondaryan
Dalby

RD
BUNYA MOUNTAINS

STATE FOREST

BUNYA MOUNTAIN

Cherry Plain

Burtons Well

Cherry Plain Track

Mt Kiangarow
1146

Ghinghion Lookout

Bottle Tree Bluff

Bunya Mountains National Park

Cooloola (Great Sandy) National Park

The Cooloola section of Great Sandy National Park protects one of the last remaining areas of undisturbed land along the southern coast of Queensland. Dominated by giant sand dunes supporting towering forests, woodlands and wildflower-covered heaths, this fragile environment is a vital refuge for plants and animals whose habitats have been drastically reduced by coastal development, logging and mining activities.

Coloured sand cliffs and dunes line the long beaches and run like a giant backbone along this 54,700 ha mainland section of Great Sandy National Park. Their inland slopes are densely wooded with tall open forests and rainforests. Large quantities of rainwater are stored in the dunes. This seeps into the ocean, flows into streams, swamps and shallow lakes, or is trapped in elevated lakes above a hard layer of sand cemented together by organic material. Poona is one such lake, its quiet waters stained brown by tannins. Layers of cemented sand prevent water draining freely from low-lying areas behind the dunes. The ground here is waterlogged in the wet season creating large swamplands around the Noosa River and Lake Cootharaba.

Cooloola is part of the Great Sandy Region, a huge sandmass that includes Fraser Island, and in 1996 Cooloola National Park joined Fraser Island to become part of the 140,000 ha Great Sandy National Park.

Formation

The coastal sand dunes owe their existence to the granite and sandstone mountains of northern New South Wales. Millions of years of weathering have worn down the coastal mountains converting much of their rocky substrate into fine sand particles. Rivers have washed the sand into the ocean and the prevailing south-easterly winds combined with the north–south wave action have gradually moved huge volumes of sand north. Over the millennia it has accumulated around volcanic rocks along the coast to create the long sandy beaches of the mainland and islands of sand, such as Fraser Island.

Sand blown from the beaches is trapped by vegetation, slowly building up the coastal sand dunes. Where the coastal vegetation has been destroyed, sand blows further inland, burying forests and piling up to form dunes as high as 240 m.

Aboriginal Inhabitants

Before white settlement the area was occupied by the Dulingbara people. Their lands extended from Noosa along the coast to the southern tip of Fraser Island. The Dulingbara lived in clans comprising between 30 and 160 people. Four clans are believed to have lived in this area, each having a defined territory. Their staple diet was fish and shellfish, supplemented with fruits, vegetables and game. They collected and traded valuable nautilus shells.

Plants and Animals

The vegetation of this sand dune country is rich and varied. Along the windswept coastline grow salt-tolerant and wind-resistant shrubs and trees such as she-oaks, coast banksias and pandans. The shores of Tin Can Bay and parts of Lake Cootharaba are lined with mangroves. Paperbarks, bloodwoods, reeds and ferns grow along the banks of the Noosa River as it winds its way through the park. This lowland area is waterlogged for a good part of the year and supports extensive heaths with scattered banksias and eucalypt trees, and a rich diversity of shrubs and sedges.

Tall open forests of blackbutt, brush box, forest she-oaks and banksias grow on the high dunes. In the sheltered valleys are rainforest pockets with figs, buttressed quandongs, great kauri pines, ferns and orchids. Dense stands of picabeen palms grow in the wetter areas. The lower dunes support open forests and woodlands dominated by bloodwood, scribbly gum and banksias.

Most of the mammals are nocturnal, although swamp wallabies are often seen feeding in grassy areas at dusk. Other kangaroos include the long-nosed potoroo and pademelon. Bandicoots, possums, yellow-bellied gliders, marsupial mice and native rats (including the rare false water rat) are also found here.

The waterways and lakes support a wide variety of birdlife. Chattering honeyeaters are attracted to the flowering banksias and paperbarks, flocks of lorikeets are a common sight, and you may see the glossy black cockatoo or the rare ground parrot. The dune lakes are colonised by four species of frogs adapted to survive in this acidic water. A number of insect species, including the Cooloola monster, a large cricket, have been discovered here.

Walks

The best way to experience Cooloola is to embark on one of the many walking trails. The Cooloola Wilderness trail traverses most of the park from north to south, from Mullens car park to Elanda camping area, passing through open heaths, woodlands, rainforests and wetlands. The 46 km journey can be split into shorter sections by joining the trail as it crosses Cooloola Way, or at Harrys camping and picnic area. Some parts of the track are very wet. Kin Kin Creek between Fig Tree Point and Elanda Point must be crossed by swimming or walking upstream to a log bridge.

In the south a 500 m circuit introduces visitors to the mangrove area near the Visitor Centre at Kinaba. This includes a boardwalk through the mangroves. Teewah Landing track leads from Lake Cootharaba through coastal heaths and across the dunes to the beach. This is 4 km return with views over the area from Mount Seawah.

From Freshwater camping area a track follows Freshwater Creek through scribbly gum forest to Lake Freshwater, and continues through

rainforest and open forest to Bymien picnic area. From Rainbow Beach you can walk to Carlo Sandblow, an expansive natural sand blown dune area, or follow the old telegraph line 7.2 km through open forests, woodlands and rainforest to Bymien.

Facilities

Visitor Centres are located at Rainbow Beach and Kinaba with displays, reference materials and rangers. The main camping area near the beach at Freshwater Creek is equipped with showers, toilets, telephone, picnic tables, barbecues and facilities for the disabled. Harry's camping area is set in open forest by Noosa River and has toilets and picnic facilities. Camping permits are required, and bookings can be made at the Rainbow Beach Visitor Centre or at Elanda for Harry's. A private camping area at Elanda Point has full facilities with a shop, kiosk and boats for hire.

The Noosa River is a beautiful tranquil waterway and an excellent location for a canoeing holiday, stopping at bush campsites along the river. Powerboats must observe the four knot speed limit to avoid damage to the fragile riverside vegetation. Gathering firewood is prohibited.

Access

The park is about 30 km east of Gympie via a sealed road off the Bruce Highway to Rainbow Beach. The unsealed Cooloola Way provides access to the west of the park and Harry's Hut. This road may be impassable after rain. 4WD vehicles are allowed to drive along the beach to Freshwater and Double Island Point. Access is from Rainbow Beach and via a vehicular ferry across the Noosa River from Tewantin. Great care must be taken when driving along the beach. Lower your tyre pressures to 120 kPa and travel as close as possible to low tide times.

Climate

The area enjoys a mild climate, although the summer may be hot and humid.

Queensland NPWS, Rainbow Beach Rd, Rainbow Beach, Qld 4581. Tel. (07) 5486 3160.

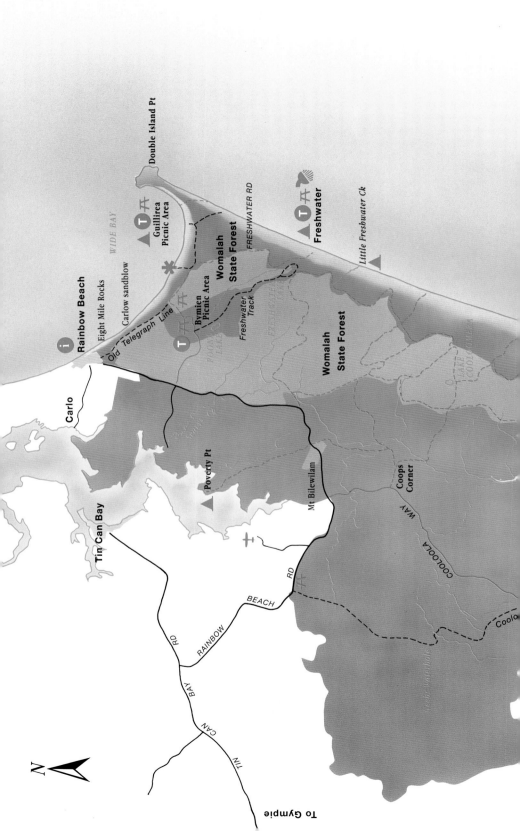

Cooloola (Great Sandy) National Park

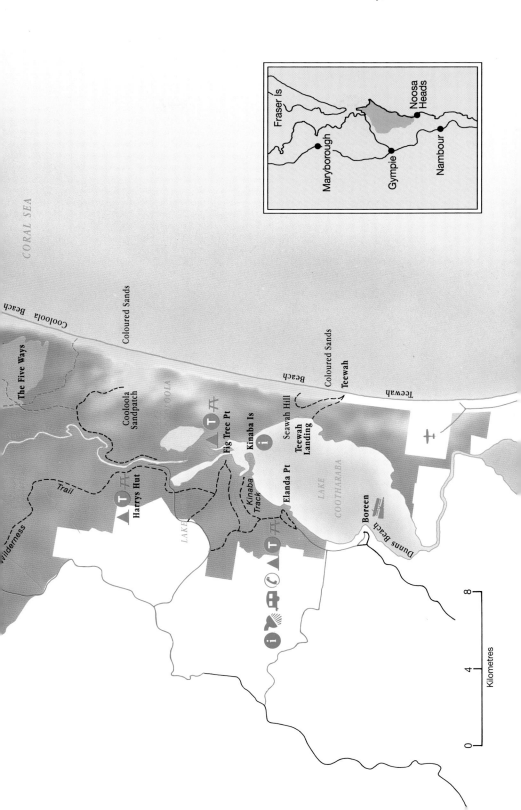

Fraser Is
Noosa Heads
Maryborough
Gympie
Nambour

CORAL SEA

Cooloola Beach
Coloured Sands
The Five Ways
Coloured Sands Beach
Teewah
Teewah
Cooloola Sandpatch
COOLOOLA
Fig Tree Pt
Kinaba Is
Seawah Hill
Teewah Landing
Trail
Harrys Hut
Kinaba Track
Elanda Pt
LAKE
LAKE COOTHARABA
Wilderness
Boreen
Dunns Beach

Kilometres
0   4   8

Fraser Island (Great Sandy) National Park

Fraser Island, the largest sand island in the world, is a fascinating area of shifting sand dunes supporting majestic rainforests, heathlands, crystal creeks and freshwater lakes. Listed as a World Heritage Area, the northern half of the island is part of Great Sandy National Park.

The 166,000 ha island was formed by the northerly drifting of sand eroded from the coastal mountain ranges of northern New South Wales. Over thousands of years of wave action, ocean currents and the predominant south-easterly winds have transported huge volumes of sand along the east coast, creating whole islands and long sandy beaches on the mainland.

The rocks around Indian Head act as an anchor, trapping the shifting sands, creating the long southerly sweep of Seventy-Five Mile Beach and the deep curved bay to the north. The prevailing south-easterly breaking waves shape the beaches and the winds blow the beach sand up into high dunes. The dunes reach 235 m at Burrgum Hill and absorb enormous quantities of rainwater. This either seeps into the sea or runs into streams and swamps. Perched freshwater lakes have formed in depressions on top of some of the sand dunes where mud, sand and peat have bonded into an impermeable layer that traps the rainwater.

The cliffs along Cathedral Beach are famed for their layers of coloured sands. These ancient, mineral-rich Teewah Sands stain the eroded, sculpted cliffs in bright hues of yellow, red and brown. At Lake Wabby a massive sandblow moves steadily westward at a rate of about 3 m a year, filling the lake as it advances.

History

Before the Europeans discovered Fraser Island, which they proceeded to wreck their ships against, mine for its mineral sands and log for its great trees, the island was known as K'gari, which means paradise, and was part of the territory of the Butchulla people. Evidence suggests that people have lived on the island for at least 30,000 years.

The Butchulla visited the island seasonally, living in small clans along the east coast where they collected shellfish, trapped fish and gathered bush foods in the forests. Small molluscs known as eugaries formed a prominent part of their diet, and their shells are piled in middens along the coast.

Captain Cook was apparently the first European to sight Fraser Island in 1770. He estimated the Aboriginal population to be between 2000 and 3000. Europeans began arriving in the 1840s, and in 1860 Fraser Island was proclaimed an Aboriginal reserve. Members of the clan not wanted as labourers or servants on the mainland were banished to the island. Logging operations commenced in earnest in 1863, and the Butchulla were forced into an overcrowded mission settlement. Most succumbed to introduced diseases and malnutrition, and fewer than 200 remained when the settlement closed in 1904. The few survivors were deported to missions around Queensland.

The lighthouse at Sandy Cape was built in 1870, and has stopped many a ship sailing onto the sandbanks. Captain Fraser's brig the Stirling Castle sank 300 km to the north in 1836. He, his wife Eliza and surviving crew members drifted onto the island and were cared for by the Aborigines. Captain Fraser and four crewmen died before a rescue party arrived two months later. Eliza Fraser, on her return to England, spread wild tales of torture and depravity at the hands of the Butchulla. Her fame became so great that the name of the island was changed from Great Sandy to Fraser Island.

Plants and Animals

The accumulation of plant matter, nourished over thousands of years by nutrients derived from sea water spray, has formed a thick mat of humus able to support the growth of tall forests on the sand dunes. Today majestic stands of rainforests grow in sheltered inland areas, with huge kauri pines, tall straight satinay, brush box, figs, ferns, orchids and colourful fungi. Tall blackbutt forests often surround the rainforests on the ridge tops. Along the coastal dunes are salt resistant shrubs and trees such as coastal banksias, she-oaks and pandanus, with vines and grasses growing over the sand.

The water-logged lowlands support paperbark forests and stands of slender picabeen palms. Behind the beach dunes grow low shrubs interspersed with scribbly gums and wallum banksias. This is known as wallum heathland, and is ablaze with wildflowers in spring. Mangroves fringe the sheltered western coastline, creating a rich breeding ground for marine animals and plants. Behind the mangroves cypress pine forests eventually give way to woodlands dominated by gnarled scribbly gums.

There are few large mammals on the island, and only 25 mammalian species have been recorded. Most are small and difficult to spot. Dingos are common, native rats, gliders, possums, bandicoots, the echidna, and fruit bats may be seen here, and in winter humpback whales pass by on their northerly migration. In spring these magnificent sea mammals frequent Hervey Bay on their return to Antarctic waters. Dugongs are commonly seen off the south-west coast, and bottlenose dolphins play in the surf off the headlands.

Lake Bowarrady is well known for tortoises, which, to their detriment, are often hand fed by visitors. A new species of sun fish has been recorded at Lake Boomanjin, and the island has the largest number of acid frog habitats in eastern Australia. More than 240 species of birds have been recorded, including cockatoos, kingfishers, crows, pelicans, pied oyster catchers, ospreys, falcons and the white-bellied sea eagle.

Walks

The best way to experience the range of habitats and beauty of the island is to leave the tourist-thronged beaches and the overused vehicle tracks and go on the walking trails. These are well marked and vary in length from the 700 m Cypress Circuit beginning at the Ocean Lake picnic area, to long hiking trails. Take plenty of fresh water as some of the hiking trails can be quite steep, and walking long distances over sand is very tiring.

Facilities

Camping grounds with toilets, hot showers, barbecues and picnic tables are located at Wathumba Creek, Dundubara and Waddy Point. Sandflies and mosquitoes may be a problem at Wathumba. Bookings must be made during holiday periods and permits are required. Beach camping is allowed at some locations along the west coast, although sites are sometimes closed to allow revegetation. There are a number of commercial camping sites along the beach. Unit, motel and resort-style accommodation is available at Eurong, Happy Valley, Dilli Village and Kingfisher Bay resorts.

Visitors must obtain a permit from the Visitor Centre at Rainbow Beach, other National Parks and Wildlife Service offices, the Hervey Bay City Council office, or at Urungan and River Heads.

Access

Fraser Island is 190 km north of Brisbane via the Bruce Highway. Vehicle access permits are required. Vehicular barges operate daily from Inskip Point near Rainbow Beach to the southern end of the island, and from the Urangan boat harbour and River Heads at Hervey Bay to various points between Ungowa and Moon Point. The sandy forest tracks on the island are only suitable for 4WD vehicles.

There is an airstrip at Toby's Gap, and commercial flights operate from Brisbane, Wide Bay, the Sunshine Coast and Rainbow Beach. Day tours, safaris, backpacking, fishing and combined boat/vehicle tours operate from Rainbow Beach, Hervey Bay, the Sunshine Coast and Brisbane.

Climate

The area enjoys a mild climate, although the summer may be hot and humid.

Queensland NPWS, Rainbow Beach Rd, Rainbow Beach, Qld 4581.
Tel. (07) 5486 3160

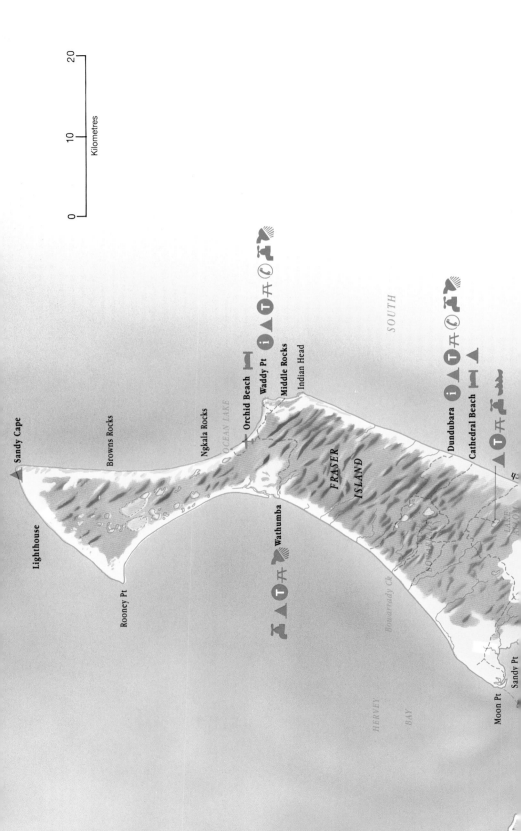

Fraser Island (Great Sandy) National Park

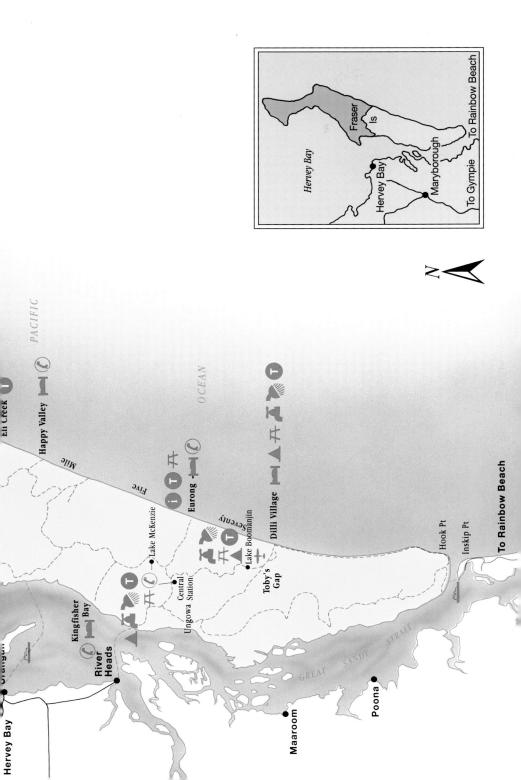

Carnarvon National Park

Sheer white sandstone cliffs rising from the dry inland plains are the visitor's first glimpse of this spectacular park. Like a lost fertile valley, Carnarvon Gorge opens into the plateau, its towering sandstone cliffs sheltering a permanent creek, the lifeblood of a host of plants and animals that make their homes in this cool oasis.

Carnarvon Gorge is only a small part of this 298,000 ha park, the remainder is a largely inaccessible wilderness area protecting some magnificent scenery in the Consuelo Tableland and Great Dividing Range. The gorge winds 30 km between white sandstone walls up to 200 m high and 400 m apart, tinted with yellows and reds, and cracked by side ravines formed by tributaries of Carnarvon Creek.

Although most visitors only see Carnarvon Gorge, the Salvator Rosa and Mount Moffatt sections of the park are well worth visiting. The former for its sandstone formations which reminded the explorer Sir Thomas Mitchell of the dramatic landscape paintings of the painter Salvator Rosa. He described the formations as surpassing any he had ever seen: "Some resembled Gothic cathedrals in ruins, others forts. Other masses were perforated and ... contrasted with the flowing outlines of evergreen woods ... a discovery worthy of the toils of pilgrimage."

Formation

About 160 million years ago the plateau was lower than the surrounding countryside. Great river systems flowed into the depression, depositing massive amounts of sediment, and over millions of years the deposits were compacted to form layers of sedimentary rocks such as sandstone, shale and mudstone. These are visible today as different coloured strata in the gorge areas.

Gradual earth movements tilted the layers of sediment and uplifted the entire region to create a high plateau. A period of volcanic activity followed, and the outpourings of lava left a layer of basalt up to 300 m thick on top of the sandstone. Most of the basalt cap has weathered away, and the underlying sandstone has cracked along vertical fault lines. Over many millions of years

waterways like Carnarvon Creek have widened the faults and gouged deep ravines and gorges into the rock.

History

The beautiful rangeland setting of Mount Moffatt is rich in Aboriginal history. Natural tunnels in the sandstone formations were used as burial chambers, and Kenniff Cave is one of the most important archaeological sites in Queensland. The caves are decorated with stencil paintings and a scattering of faint freehand figures depicting animals, people and objects such as boomerangs, shields and stone axes. Excavations here have revealed evidence of human occupation dating back 19,500 years.

Mitchell's party in 1846 encountered people with red-painted faces carrying mummy-like bundles, presumably preserved human remains to be entombed in burial chambers. They found the remnants of campfires with freshwater mussels, and evidence of systematic burning of the bushland to flush out game and encourage new growth. Two groups are thought to have lived here: the Nuri people on the lowlands, and the Bidjara on the high northern areas. The Maranoa River was said to have been created by Moondungera, the Rainbow Serpent, who caused a large spring to flow from the range.

Extensive rock art sites in Carnarvon Gorge, and the remains of campfires with cooked cycad nutshells show that people occupied the gorge for at least 3600 years. We have no knowledge about the significance of the gorge to these people, who seem to have abandoned the area soon after the arrival of the Europeans in the latter half of the 19th century.

Plants and Animals

Carnarvon Creek flows year round and has allowed the flourishing of a green and fertile valley among the dry ranges. Along the creek grow river she-oaks, weeping red bottlebrushes and native cherry trees. Pelicans, ibises, spoonbills, herons, pied cormorants and other water birds live in this cool oasis. The freshwater keelback snake and the common tree snake hunt around the water's edge for green tree-frogs. The eastern water dragon is a common inhabitant of the area, and patient observers may catch sight of a platypus or a spectacular frilled lizard.

Brush-tailed rock wallabies, grey kangaroos, brush-tailed possums, yellow-bellied and greater gliders and quolls come to drink from the creek, often travelling long distances in search of water. Eastern spinebills and yellow-tufted honeyeaters are commonly seen among the flowering bottlebrushes. In moist sites cabbage tree palms grow alongside clumps of tree ferns, while the dripping rock walls shelter orchids, ferns and mosses. Shrubby open forests of eucalypts such as turpentine, grey gum, Sydney blue gum and spotted gum grow above the creek banks, with an understorey of blady grass and bracken fern, frequented by little fairy wrens hunting for insects.

On the poorer, drier soils of the lower slopes grasstrees and the cycad *Macrozamia moorei* flourish among open eucalypt woodlands. The higher slopes and plateau areas support grassy open eucalypt forests containing black cypress pines and smooth-barked apples.

Walks

The only way to explore the gorge area is on foot. The main track follows the creek to Cathedral Cave, 9.3 km from the Visitor Centre. Aboriginal paintings cover the lower walls of this cave below a large rock overhang. Side tracks lead into smaller gorges and lookouts. A series of stone steps make the 200 m climb to Boolimba Bluff quite easy, and the panoramic view from the top reveals the geological components of the area.

The Amphitheatre is a large chasm carved by water, filled with mosses and ferns, and reached by a steel ladder. It has a still, eerie atmosphere. The Art Gallery is a major Aboriginal site 5.6 km

from the Visitor Centre, with a large collection of rock paintings.

Close to the camping area the short nature trail is a pleasant early morning or evening walk. The Moss Garden in Violet Gorge is a beautiful area where a small waterfall drops into an icy pool surrounded by delicate mosses and ferns. A steep, rough climb from Boowinda Gorge leads to Battleship Spur. The views from the top are worth the effort, but you should consult the ranger before attempting this walk.

Facilities

The main camping area at Carnarvon Gorge must be booked in advance. Permits are required and fees are payable. There are cold showers, a public telephone and Visitor Centre. Campers should bring fuel stoves. The camping area at Big Bend has toilets only. Other campsites in the Mount Moffatt and Salvator Rosa sections are very basic with pit toilets only. Water is usually available, but should be boiled before drinking.

The Oasis Tourist Lodge near the park entrance has cabin accommodation, a general store, petrol, diesel, LP gas and ice.

Access

Carnarvon Gorge can be reached from Roma, 250 km south via Injune and Wyseby along a partially sealed road. From Rolleston the road is only partially sealed. The unsealed roads become impassable after heavy rain, and the creeks are subject to flooding.

The Salvator Rosa section can be reached on unsealed roads from Springsure via Cungelella. Mount Moffatt is 160 km from Injune and 220 km from Mitchell. The roads are mostly unsealed and may become impassable after rain. 4WD vehicles are needed to reach many of the features in these areas.

Climate

Summers are hot, and the winters warm with cold nights. Most rain falls from December to March.

Carnarvon National Park, Via Rolleston, Qld 4702. Tel. (07) 4982 4555.

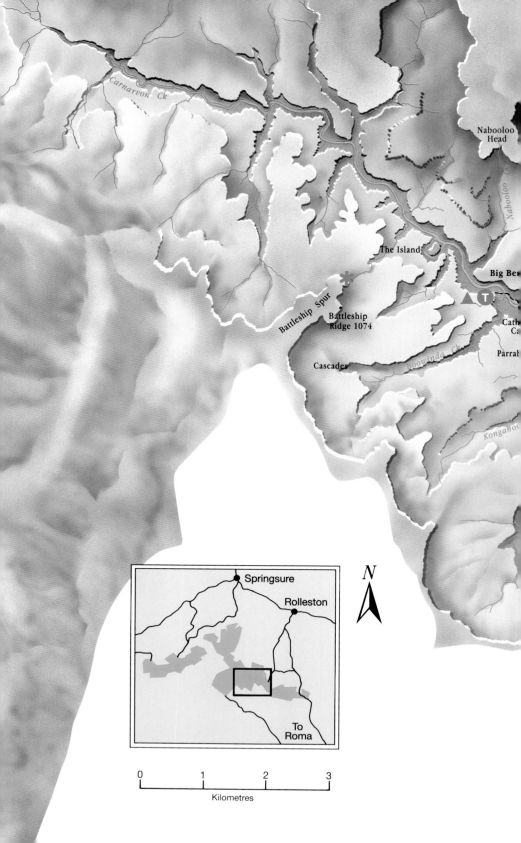

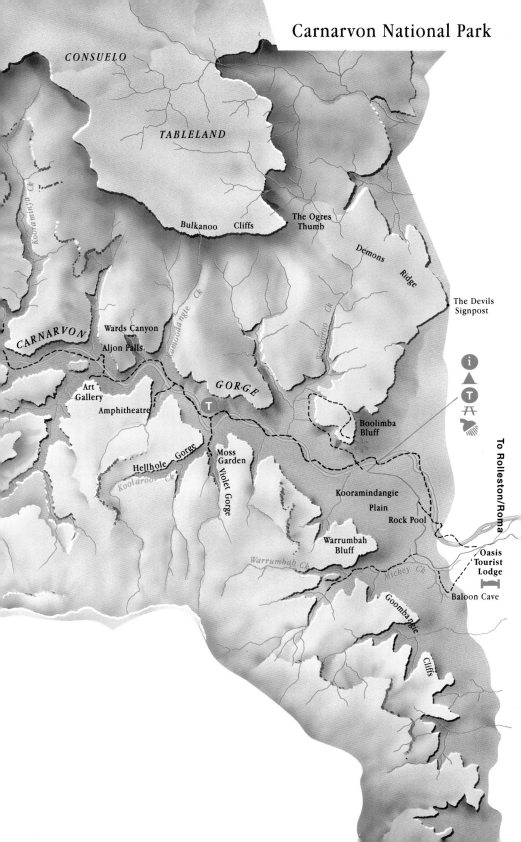

Carnarvon National Park

CONSUELO

TABLELAND

Bulkanoo Cliffs

The Ogres Thumb

Demons Ridge

The Devils Signpost

CARNARVON

Wards Canyon

Aljon Falls

GORGE

Art Gallery

Amphitheatre

Hellhole Gorge

Koolaroo Ck

Moss Garden

Violet Gorge

Boolimba Bluff

Kooramindangie Plain

Rock Pool

Warrumbah Bluff

Warrumbah Ck

Mickey Ck

To Rolleston/Roma

Oasis Tourist Lodge

Baloon Cave

Goombangie

Cliffs

Blackdown Tableland National Park

Rising above the hot dry plains of central Queensland, Blackdown Tableland is an undulating sandstone plateau of tall open forests, woodlands and heaths, where waterfalls cascade over sheer cliffs into deep ferny gorges. At an average altitude of 800 m the park has a moist climate with cooler summers and warmer winters than the plains, and offers a peaceful retreat amidst spectacular sandstone scenery.

Three ranges converge to create the tableland. Expedition Range forms the backbone of the park, rising to 950 m above sea level and supporting tall eucalypt forests. The Dawson Range runs north-west to south-east, with extensive heathlands and abundant wildflowers. Shotover Range to the west receives less rainfall and sparse woodlands grow on its drier soils.

Blackdown Tableland forms the northern extension of the central highlands sandstone belt. The sandstones were created from sediments laid down in lakes and rivers between 145 and 210 million years ago. Subsequent geological upheavals raised the level of the land and caused massive folding and faulting. Weathering has sculpted caves, cliffs and gorges into the rock, creating magnificent scenery and extensive cliff lines.

History

Prior to the arrival of the Europeans the tableland was part of the territory of the Gungaloo, who were said to be a tall, proud and peaceful people. The shortage of large mammals, fish and other game on the tableland probably discouraged permanent habitation. Little remains to tell us much about their culture and lifestyle. They hunted goannas, birds and rock wallabies in the area, and harvested bush foods including palm hearts, yams, figs and macrozamia nuts. Rock art sites near upper Mimosa Creek depict hands, weapons and tools stencilled onto the sandstone overhangs.

Violent conflicts in the 19th century between the European settlers and the Gungaloo reduced the Aboriginal population of the area to a few hundred and destroyed the lifestyle and culture of a people who had lived in the area for many thousands of years. The European settlers established farms and grazing properties on the fertile plains in the latter half of the 19th century.

Clearing of the land severely reduced the habitats of many native animals. The once common bridled nailtail wallaby, which needs the shelter of trees and shrubs to survive, has been reduced to an endangered species, with fewer than 800 of these beautiful animals remaining.

The tablelands, being deficient in soil nutrients, proved to be of little value, and the area was left largely undisturbed until 1971 when a logging road was built by the Department of Forestry.

The park was gazetted in 1982, and covers 32,000 ha. Another 16,000 ha of the tableland are state forest. Logging operations in the state forest have depleted scarce animal habitats and caused soil erosion. Logging was temporarily stopped in 1993.

Plants and Animals

Eucalypt forests cover most of the tableland, with tall dense stands of ironbarks and stringybarks on the deep sandy soils of the higher areas. Glossy black cockatoos feed on the fruits of the rose she-oaks growing beneath the tall eucalypts. The cycad *Macrozamia platyrhachis* grows here among a ground layer of native grasses.

Most phosphates have been leached from the soil, causing bone deficiencies in foraging animals. Thus there are few large mammals. Among those living in the forests are greater gliders and a small transient colony of koalas. Birdlife is quite prolific, however, and more than 120 bird species have been identified. Flycatchers, robins, tree-creepers and brilliant blue forest and azure kingfishers feed in the forests.

Heaths dominate in the drier areas where the soils are shallow. They are ablaze with springtime wildflowers including red grevilleas, ground orchids, and pea flowers such as the purple hardenbergia and yellow dillwynia. Yellow-tufted and white-cheeked honeyeaters are commonly seen in these habitats.

Permanent springs and seepage areas allow mosses, ferns, trigger plants, sundews, tiny sun orchids, bearded orchids, and livistona palms to flourish in the damp, sheltered gullies. Birds feed at the pools, and rainbow lorikeets, currawongs and blue-faced honeyeaters are often seen among the palms.

Wedgetail eagles, peregrine falcons and goshawks soar around the cliffs. Rock wallabies frequent the steep slopes, while the caves and crevices shelter marsupial mice, antechinuses, bats, geckoes, skinks and powerful owls. A number of insect species have been discovered on the tablelands. These include the Blackdown monster, a cricket-like insect that lives underground, two species of cicadas and a Christmas beetle.

Walks

Several gently graded walking tracks lead to lookouts along the cliff line. From the camping area short tracks lead to Officer's Pocket Lookout and to an Aboriginal art site by Mimosa Creek. The 2 km walk to Peregrine Lookout passes through heaths and their springtime wildflower displays. Follow the cliff to Sunset Lookout where the morning and evening light enhances the beautiful sandstone formations.

Steps lead to a series of rocky pools at the foot of Rainbow Falls, a popular 1.3 km walk through open stringybark forest with views over the distant plains and hills. From the top of Stony Creek Falls the view into the 240 m deep sandstone gorge is magnificent, and well worth the 5 km hike through dry open forest. The eastern escarpment offers bushwalkers the chance to explore rugged gorges and untouched wilderness areas. Hikers must be well equipped and should discuss their route with the ranger before leaving.

Facilities

The camping area at South Mimosa Creek has only basic facilities with toilets and picnic tables. Permits are required and sites may be booked in advance. Untreated water only is available at the camp ground, and visitors should bring their own drinking water.

Horseshoe Lookout has a picnic area with toilets, fireplaces and tables. Firewood is limited and visitors should bring fuel stoves for cooking. Rubbish must be taken out of the area. There are no telephones or supplies in the park. The nearest centre with food, fuel and a caravan park is Dingo.

Access

The park is 174 km west of Rockhampton via the sealed Capricorn Highway, and 106 km west of Emerald. Turn off at Umolo along the unsealed road to Horseshoe Lookout. The climb to the tableland is steep and winding and unsuitable for caravans. Roads within the park are unsealed, and access may be restricted in wet weather. Beware of timber trucks and other vehicles on the park roads.

Climate

Summers are warm to hot with cool nights. Winters are cool with some frosts. Most of the rain falls between December and March when dense fogs cloud the tableland and hail storms may cause some damage.

Blackdown Tableland National Park, Via Dingo, Qld 4702. Tel. (07) 4986 1964.

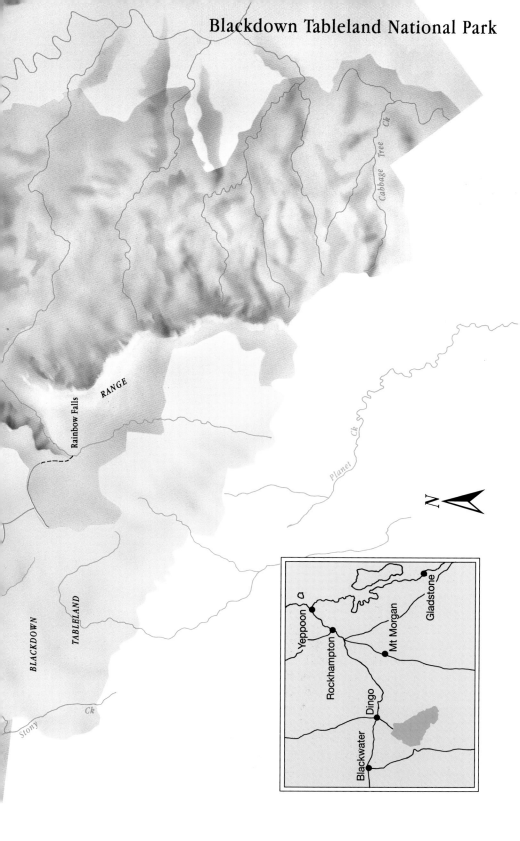

Blackdown Tableland National Park

Cabbage Tree Ck

RANGE

Rainbow Falls

Planet Ck

N

BLACKDOWN TABLELAND

Stony Ck

Yeppoon

Rockhampton

Mt Morgan

Gladstone

Dingo

Blackwater

Eungella National Park

Rising from the sugar cane fields of the coastal plain to the cloudy wilderness world of the Clarke Range. Eungella National Park is a land of luxuriant rainforests and open forests dissected by great gorges between precipitous peaks. This is one of Queensland's largest, wildest and most majestic national parks, a place to experience the primal world beneath the cool rainforest canopy and observe platypuses feeding in crystal pools.

Straddling the Clarke Range, the park protects 51,700 ha of largely inaccessible wilderness rising to 1280 m at Mount Dalrymple. Steep rainforest slopes cut by fast-flowing streams descend to the lowlands of Finch Hatton Gorge to the east, while open forests and woodlands clothe the drier, rugged hillsides of Dicks Tableland to the west.

Eungella is an Aboriginal word meaning Land of Cloud, and aptly describes this cool landscape where the moisture-laden coastal air condenses into mist and rain as it rises from the tropical plains. Most of the visitor facilities and walking tracks are located in a small southern section of the park. The road zig-zags up the range to the small town of Eungella, and follows the southern rim past lookouts to picnic areas and campsites. Finch Hatton Gorge at the base of the range is a beautiful valley where tropical rainforest trees overhang deep rocky pools below the cascading creek.

Rainforests

The rainforests of Eungella are the main visitor attraction. They comprise an unusual mixture of plants and animals more typical of the southern forests than those of a similar latitude.

Before the last ice age this area supported a mixture of tropical and sub-tropical rainforests. Between 30,000 and 10,000 years ago, when the world was gripped in an ice age, the climate of Eungella became cool and dry. The rainforests retreated to wet sheltered areas on the summits of the cloudy mountains and to the deep, moist gorges. Open forests grew in the surrounding areas, isolating the Eungella rainforests from their counterparts to the north and south.

Aborigines regularly burned the open forests to flush out game and stimulate the growth of young green shoots. This technique effectively prevented the expansion of the rainforests as the climate became warmer and wetter.

Today the rainforests of the highlands are dominated by the Mackay tulip oak, a tree found only in this area but related to the tulip oaks of the southern sub-tropical rainforests. Other sub-tropical trees include the silver quandong and the white beech. The lower rainforests are much more tropical in character, and are dominated by trees such as the milky pine and pink toriga, typical of northern tropical rainforests .

The curtain fig, with its mass of aerial roots hanging like a curtain to the forest floor, is a highly visible component of the lower rainforest. Bangalow palms, picabeen palms and fan palms grow at all altitudes, while the alexandra palm is only found in the lowlands. Noticeable among the vines are the climbing pandan and its scarlet fruits, and lawyer cane with its barbed hooks trapping the unwary passer-by. Birds nest and elkhorn ferns, orchids and mosses grow in the trees, while on tree trunks and rotting logs are lichens, mosses and fungi.

Wildlife

Some of the animals of the Eungella rainforests are quite different to those found in similar habitats in Australia. Here are unique subspecies of the brown thornbill and white-throated treecreeper. The Eungella honeyeater lives only in the rainforests of this area, feeding on nectar and insects.

Among the many species of frogs found in the park is the Eungella gastric brooding frog which incubates its eggs in its stomach and spits out the young frog. The Eungella and Liem's day-frogs are also unique and can be seen around the creek beds of Finch Hatton Gorge during daylight hours. The orange-sided skink is another species found only in the rainforests of Eungella.

Among the more than 100 bird species living in the park are magnificent, brightly-coloured rainforest fruit-doves such as the wompoo and rose-crowned fruit-doves, and the white-headed and topknot pigeons. Scratching among the leaf litter you may come across the brush turkey with its red head, yellow neck and black body. This large bird incubates its eggs in a huge mound some 4 m across.

Eungella is one of the few places in Australia where you can nearly always see a platypus in its natural habitat. In the early morning and late afternoon these unusual animals swim and feed in Broken River near the camping area. Sit quietly by the river bank otherwise you will disturb them.

Brushtail possums, sugar gliders and greater gliders emerge at night in the tall open forests. In the thick blady grass understorey the rufous bettong and the native swamp rat are active at night. Currawongs, kookaburras, red-browed finches, blue-faced honeyeaters and colourful rainbow lorikeets are common in this habitat.

Walks

The only way to experience the majestic grandeur of the Eungella rainforests is on foot. Walking tracks begin at the Broken River picnic area and at Finch Hatton Gorge. The rugged northern section offers bushwalkers the chance to explore an extensive wilderness area, but the ranger must be advised before you leave.

A 2.1 km self-guiding circuit from Broken River, the Rainforest Discovery walk, introduces visitors to the sub-tropical rainforest world. Other walks branch off from this track. Turning right across the river onto the Palm Walk track takes you on an 8.3 km journey through ever-changing rainforest habitats with unexpected panoramas of Pioneer Valley far below and into a beautiful area where picabeen palms dominate the rainforest setting.

The Broken River track is a leisurely five-hour 8.4 km walk to Crediton Creek, over rough terrain in places, but well worth the effort. The track meanders through sub-tropical rainforest via quiet pools where platypuses and tortoises feed, and through the habitats of birds such as the whip bird, scrub wren, golden whistler and yellow robin. Return along the road (6.7 km) or have someone drive you to the Crediton Creek entrance and walk back to Broken River.

From Finch Hatton Gorge the Wheel of Fire Falls track is a 2.1 km walk over fairly rough terrain with a side track to a deep pool at Araluen Falls, home of the unique Eungella day frog. The track follows the creek through superb tropical rainforest with clearings revealing cascades and pools, ending at the sheer rock walls and deep pool of the Wheel of Fire Falls.

Branch off this track to Dooloomai Falls, some 3.6 km from the camping ground. The trail passes through rainforest interspersed with flooded gum trees, remnants of the eucalypt forest that once dominated this area. At the falls water plunges 60 m into the gorge below.

Facilities

Camping areas are located at Broken River and Fern Flat, both have showers, toilets and picnic tables. There is a private kiosk, drinking water and information centre at the Broken River picnic area. Gas stoves are preferred for cooking. Camping permits must be obtained from the ranger, and campsites should be booked in advance during holiday periods. Accommodation is also available in Eungella township.

Climate

The climate is sub-tropical to tropical with very warm wet summers and cool dry winters with some frosty nights. Fog and mists are common in summer, and the Pioneer and Broken River systems are liable to flooding.

Access

Eungella is 80 km west of Mackay via a sealed road. Broken River is 6 km from Eungella along the sealed Broken River and Crediton Roads. Finch Hatton Gorge, at the base of the range, is 10 km off the Eungella Road 1 km east of Finch Hatton.

Eungella National Park, C/O Post Office, Dalrymple Heights, Qld 4740. Tel. (07) 4958 4552.

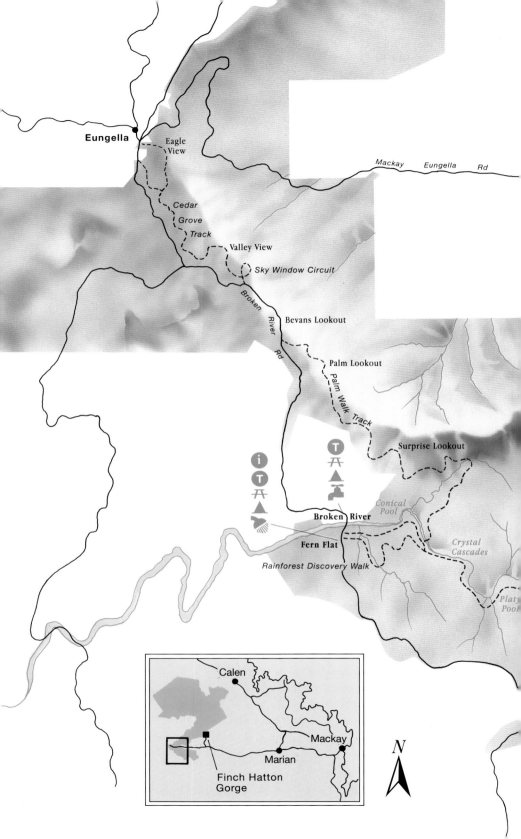

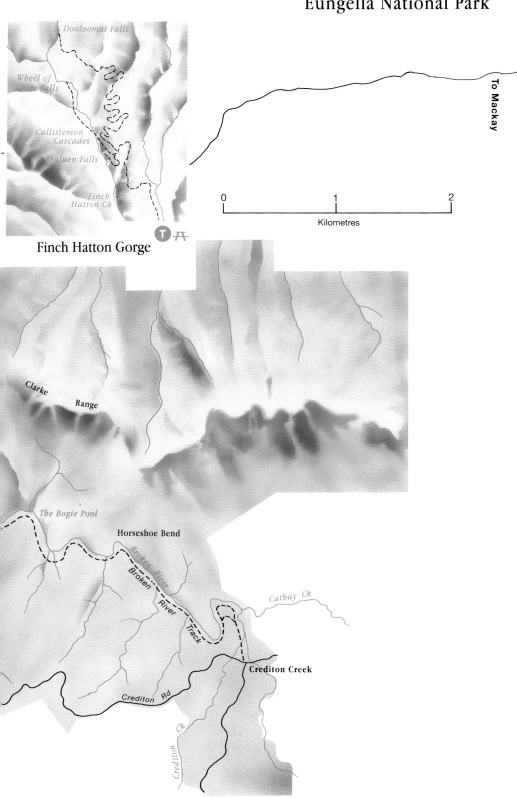

Eungella National Park

To Mackay

Dooloomai Falls

Wheel of Fire Falls

Callistemon Cascades

Araluen Falls

Finch Hatton Ck

Finch Hatton Gorge

0   1   2
Kilometres

Clarke Range

The Bogie Pool

Horseshoe Bend

Broken River

Broken River Track

Cathay Ck

Crediton Creek

Crediton Rd

Crediton Ck

Whitsunday Islands and Conway National Parks

The Whitsunday Islands, set in the vibrant blue tropical seas of eastern Queensland, offer some of Australia's best island-based holiday attractions, from bush camping on deserted islands to sailing cruises and luxury resorts. On the peninsula overlooking the islands Conway National Park protects an area of rugged mountains clad with tropical rainforests, and deep valleys plunging into the Whitsunday Passage.

Protected from the fury of the Pacific Ocean by the outer Barrier Reef islands, the Whitsundays comprise the largest offshore island chain on the east coast of Australia. They are hilly continental islands, rising to 459 m at Hook Peak, densely forested and edged with rocky headlands, precipitous cliffs and sandy beaches. Many are fringed with coral reefs and offer excellent diving and snorkelling. Most of the 74 islands are unoccupied and have been given national park status. Seven have resort complexes located on restricted areas within the national park areas.

Most of the 24,000 ha Conway National Park is a densely-forested wilderness with mangrove-lined shores and fjord-like scenery.

Formation

The underlying granite rock visible on some of the islands was formed by volcanic activity that rocked this part of Australia between 100 and 50 million years ago. Enormous quantities of lava and shattered rock poured over the land, raising the height of the coastal plain by several kilometres. Millions of years of erosion followed, sculpturing the land into a rugged mountain range with long, deep valleys.

During the last ice age, between 10,000 and 30,000 years ago, the sea level was about 100 m lower than today, the Whitsundays were an inland mountain range and the Great Barrier Reef a line of coastal limestone hills. Winds blowing across the coastal plains deposited the pure white silica sands of Whitehaven Beach and built up the sand dunes on Whitsunday Island.

About 6000 years ago the ice caps melted and the low-lying valleys were flooded, forming bays and inlets and isolating the mountains and hills

as offshore islands. Corals and algae created fringing reefs around many of the islands, and their fragmented remains form most of the Whitsunday beaches.

Plants and Animals

The dry slopes of the islands support forests of eucalypts and acacias, dominated by pink bloodwood, poplar gum, Moreton Bay ash and white mahogany. Grasstrees are common in the understorey, attracting flocks of birds and insects to their flowering spikes, while in the moist gullies rainforest plants form dense pockets of vegetation, with hoop pines emerging above a complex understorey of ferns, vines and orchids.

The beaches and rocky shores are home to a wide range of plants and animals. Above the high tide mark sand dunes are stabilised by plants such as the sea bean, goats foot convolvulus and spinifex grasses. Between the beaches and rocky hillsides the orange-footed scrub fowl incubates its eggs in mounds up to 7 m across and 3 m high.

At night the mournful cry of the beach thick-knee may be heard as this bird patrols the beach in search of crabs. Seldom flying, it nests on the sand just above high tide, well away from the feral cats of the mainland. The seas are home to dolphins, sea turtles and hosts of tropical fish.

Rock crabs scuttle about at low tide, scraping algae from the rocks and darting into crevices at any hint of danger, while brahminy kites circle slowly overhead seeking carrion and live prey. White-bellied sea eagles and smaller ospreys join the hunt, looking for fish swimming close to the surface or trapped in rock pools.

Brush-tailed possums and Gould's goannas

visit the camping areas where they are quite adept at stealing foodstuffs. Among the few large mammals is a population of unadorned rock wallabies living on Whitsunday Island, and the recently described Proserpine rock wallaby found on Gloucester Island and in the rainforests of Conway National Park.

Walks

There are short graded walking tracks on South Molle, Lindeman, Long Island and Whitsunday Island. The best way to explore the islands is by walking along the beaches and rocky shorelines, but avoid crushing delicate corals and replace any lifted rocks.

At Shutehaven a 2 km circuit from the picnic area passes through lowland rainforest to an area of mangroves and cottonwoods. Some of the trees are identified, and brush turkeys and scrub hens are commonly seen. Continue another 1.5 km to Hayward Gully, but beware of giant stinging trees. A 6.4 km circuit leads to Mount Rooper where views over the park and islands are magnificent. The track passes through low woodlands with grasstrees and wattles, and continues to Swamp Bay where you can bushcamp, through lowland rainforest to the coral beach with views to the Molle Islands.

Facilities

Information and camping permits can be obtained from the Whitsunday Information Centre near the entrance to Conway National Park. Most island camping areas are small and have no water supplies. The sites must be booked, and you must take sufficient food and water to last three days longer than planned in case bad weather delays your return. Fuel stoves must be used and garbage must be taken back to the mainland.

Whitsunday Island has the most camping areas. Whitehaven Beach is used by larger groups as well as individual campers, and is frequented by commercial tour operators. This beach offers excellent swimming and snorkelling around

giant coral heads. Large private groups can camp at Dugong Beach. Sawmill Beach has a small number of campsites in a clearing divided by a seasonal creek, and at Joes Beach small groups can enjoy the beautiful beach and good snorkelling.

Boat Port on Lindeman Island has a quiet camping area with sandy beaches backed by rainforest. Walking tracks lead through forests and grasslands to spectacular lookouts.

North Molle has a camping area at Cockatoo Beach with about ten campsites around the edge of the forest. On Henning Island moderate sized groups can camp on the northern spit which is accessible at all tides. Tancred Island has a small sheltered camping area with access to a sandy beach and reasonable coral. Small numbers can camp at Sea Eagle Beach on Thomas Island, a fine sandy beach with good snorkelling and accessible at all tides. Hook Island has small campsites at Maureens Cove and Crayfish Beach. Neck Bay Beach on Shaw Island and the western beach on South Repulse Island have small isolated camping areas without facilities.

Some of the resort complexes operate camping areas with more extensive facilities, and Airlie Beach offers a wide range of accommodation.

Access

Conway National Park is 30 km from Proserpine via Shute Harbour Road. Day-cruise sailing boats and power boats, water taxis and aircraft leave from Shutehaven and Airlie Beach. Some of the cruise boats will drop campers on or near their planned route, or if money is no object you can take a water taxi or light aircraft.

Climate

Summers are hot and humid with heavy rain periods. Marine stingers are present from October to May and make swimming dangerous. Winters are warm and dry.

Whitsunday Information Centre, PO Box 332, Airlie Beach, Qld 4802. Tel. (07) 4946 7022.

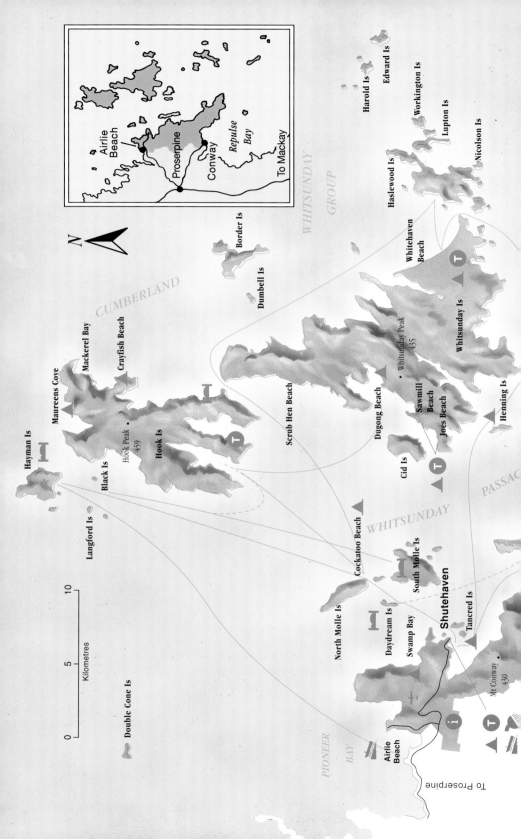

Whitsunday Islands and Conway National Parks

Hinchinbrook Island National Park

The largest island national park in the world, Hinchinbrook Island lies off the wet tropical coast of Queensland, separated from the mainland by a narrow channel fringed with mangroves. Seen from the coast this magnificent island appears as a craggy wall of cloud-covered mountains set amidst a maze of bright green mangrove islands.

Hinchinbrook Island is one of a chain of 15 continental islands between Ingham and Tully, ranging in size from the 39,900 ha Hinchinbrook Island to tiny Tween Island. A series of rugged granite crags rising to 1142 m at Mount Bowen form the southern half of Hinchinbrook Island. Sheer cliffs and forested slopes plunge from the north face of Mount Bowen to a beautiful sandy coastal strip extending 8 km north to Cape Richards. Permanent streams cascade down the mountain side into valleys choked with rainforest.

To the north-west a series of older volcanic peaks forms a more undulating skyline descending to a sandy beach at Hecate Point. The protected western side of the island and Missionary Bay are fringed with great expanses of mangroves, forming an impenetrable forest of stilt-rooted trees broken by a series of wide tidal creeks. These are navigable at high tide and lead into a strange world where an eerie silence descends as the tidal waters drown the cacophony of pops, clicks and slurps emanating from the nutrient-rich mud.

History

The islands were once part of a coastal mountain range. But when the sea level rose at the end of the last ice age (around 10,000 years ago) the low-lying valleys were submerged, creating Hinchinbrook Channel and leaving the mountain peaks as offshore islands. Sediments swept down by the Herbert River have formed the rich coastal plains south of Hinchinbrook Island and built up the mangrove islands in the channel.

The island is a wilderness area virtually untouched since white settlement of Australia.

Early European accounts suggest that there were permanent villages of timber and bark near a complex of fish traps at Missionary Bay and Scraggy Point. The traps covered an area of more than two square kilometres in the form of a series of low walls, creating an elaborate system to trap fish as the tide went out.

Plants and Animals

The mangrove forests are essential breeding and feeding grounds for fish, crustaceans and other marine animals. More than 23 species of mangroves have been identified on the island, their tangled root systems trap nutrients and provide shelter for small aquatic creatures. Crabs, prawns, mudskippers, oysters and snails are among the many animals living here.

Mosquitoes are abundant and make the area uninviting for humans. Mangrove herons are often seen perching on the branches, gerygones, honeyeaters and flycatchers are common birds of the mangroves, and you may spot a beautiful green tree snake moving slowly through the treetops.

Between the mangroves and the mountain peaks grow luxuriant rainforests of palms, vines, figs, quandongs and milky pines, with giant turpentine, red mahogany and pink bloodwood trees soaring up to form a high canopy. The rainforests are largely unexplored and offer exciting opportunities for naturalists. Visitors are often rewarded by the sight of the yellow-bellied sunbird darting around the rainforest clearings. Look out for its nest hanging from branches or foliage at the edge of the forest.

The vegetation becomes sparse nearer the exposed rocky pavements of the central range, with scrublands, heaths and woodlands of black she-oaks and brush box trees growing on the shallow sandy soils. Banksias, wattles and stunted eucalypts grow in the deeper soils between boulders.

The eastern slopes are exposed to strong, salt-laden winds. Eucalypt woodlands with white mahogany and swamp box trees dominate these slopes, with lush vegetation in sheltered gullies and along the creeks. A common sight here is the brilliant blue flash of the azure kingfisher as it flits between perches, or the fluttering flight of a satin flycatcher. Beware of dangerous estuarine crocodiles around the creek mouths.

Walks

A boardwalk has been constructed through the mangrove forest at Missionary Bay, allowing a fascinating walk through an otherwise impenetrable area. A track leads from here over the sand dunes to Ramsay Bay and the beaches and rocky headlands of the eastern shore.

The resort at Cape Richards is linked to Shepherd Bay by a short track, and at the southern end of this beach a 2.2 km track leads to the camping area at Macushla Bay. At Scraggy Point on the western side of the island a 1 km circuit goes from the camping area through an interesting mixed vine forest.

For fit and experienced walkers the East Coast Trail offers an outstanding three to five day walk through tropical rainforests, past mountain creeks and along white sandy beaches. The track is ungraded and rough and slippery in parts, with a number of creek crossings. It is marked with triangular orange markers on trees at irregular intervals. Some of the creeks are dry from August to December, but water should be carried at all times of the year.

The northern section of the East Coast Trail from Ramsay Bay to Little Ramsay Bay is easier walking than the southern section, and makes a pleasant day's walk with an overnight stop at Little Ramsay Bay. The track follows the beach and creek beds behind the rugged headlands to Zoe Bay. You must wade across North Zoe Creek at low tide, or branch off the track to circuit inland around Zoe Bay. Estuarine crocodiles

may be present in the creek mouth, and you should only wade cross when the water level is below 0.5 m. Plan your walk to arrive at low tide, and be aware of the predicted water level.

The southern section of the coastal walk takes you through rainforests, open forests, past mangroves, along beaches and creeks, passing a number of waterfalls and swimming holes. There are campsites at Zoe Bay, Sweetwater Creek, Mulligan Falls, Mulligan Bay and George Point.

Facilities

Camping grounds with toilets, tables and gas fireplaces are provided at Scraggy Point (The Haven) and Macushla Bay. The camping ground at Zoe Bay has toilets and water. A number of bush camping sites have been established along the East Coast Trail. There are no facilities, all rubbish must be taken back to the mainland, open fires are not allowed, and campers should bring fuel stoves and water containers. Camping permits must be obtained from the National Parks office at Cardwell or Ingham. It is advisable to book during holiday periods. There is a private, low-key resort at Cape Richards.

Access

The park is about 120 km north of Townsville via the Bruce Highway or the North Coast Railway. The island can be reached by daily charter boat from Cardwell or Lucinda, or by private boat launched from Cardwell, Fishers Creek (28 km south of Cardwell), Lucinda or Dungeness. There are no safe anchorages on the eastern side of the island.

Climate

Summers are hot and wet with occasional cyclones. Dangerous marine stingers are present from November to May, particularly at George Point, Mulligan Bay and Zoe Bay. Winters are mild and dry.

Dept of the Environment, Bruce Highway, PO Box 74, Cardwell, Qld 4816. Tel. (07) 4066 8115.

Brook Islands

CORAL SEA

Cape Richards

Macushla Bay

SHEPHERD BAY

Cape Sandwich

RAMSAY BAY

Goold Is

Garden Is

N

MISSIONARY BAY

Mt Burnett

Barra Castle Hill

Mt Pitt 722

The Haven

Pt Hecate

Scraggy Point

HINCHINBR

Hinchinbrook Island National Park

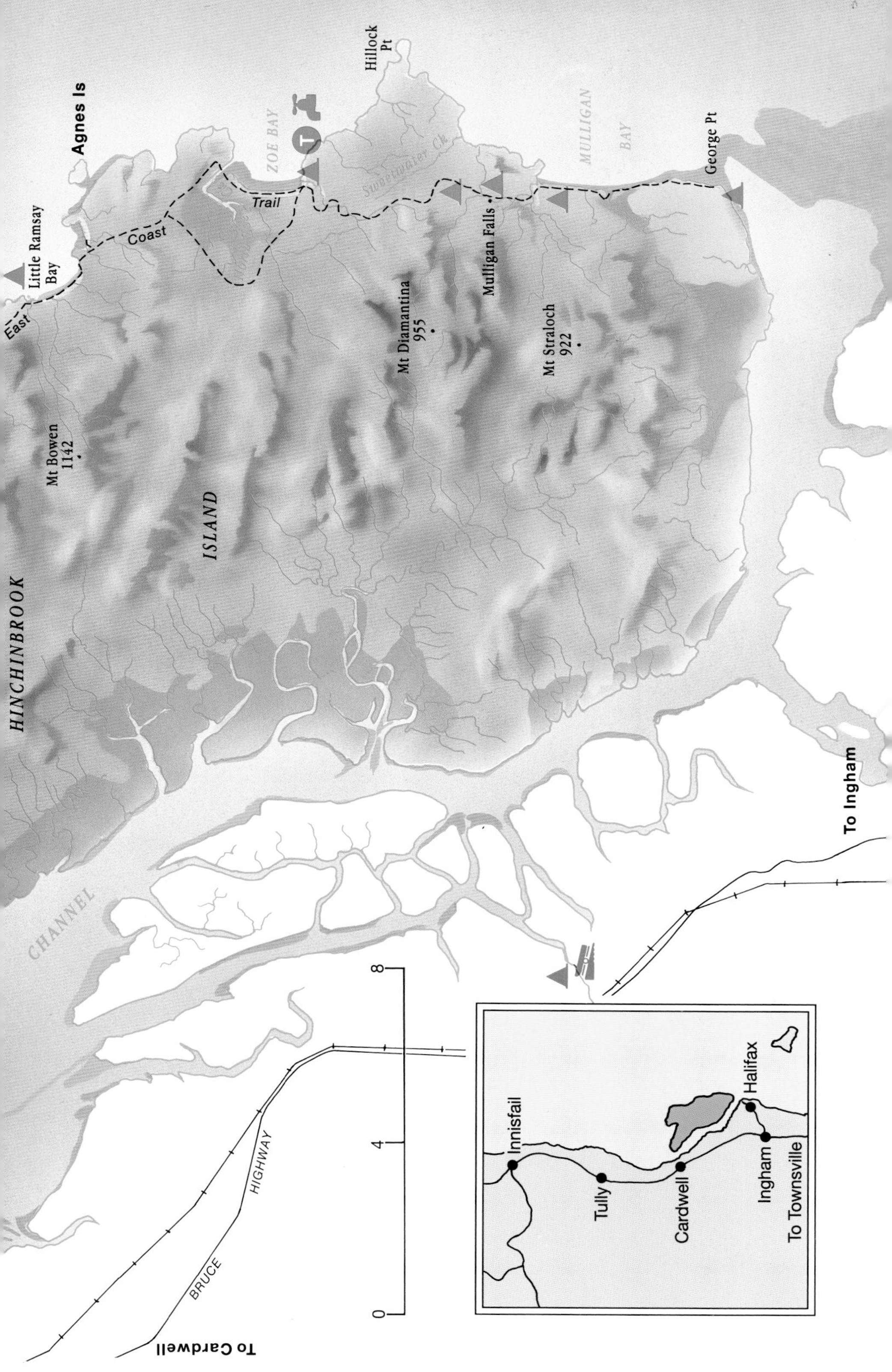

Hillock Pt

Agnes Is

ZOE BAY

Sweetwater Ck.

MULLIGAN BAY

George Pt

Trail

Coast

Little Ramsay Bay

East

Mulligan Falls

Mt Diamantina
955

Mt Straloch
922

Mt Bowen
1142

ISLAND

HINCHINBROOK

CHANNEL

To Ingham

HIGHWAY

BRUCE

To Cardwell

Innisfail

Tully

Cardwell

Halifax

Ingham

To Townsville

To Townsville

Auburn River National Park (390 ha)

On the eastern edge of the Great Dividing Range, inland from Maryborough, this park features the scenic Auburn River Gorge. The river tumbles over pink granite boulders into rock pools, its banks lined with callistemons, tea trees and stunted figs. The open forests in the park are dominated by silver-leaf ironbark and forest red gum. Bottle trees can be found in rainforest pockets. There is a picnic and camping area with basic facilities but no drinking water. Rough bush tracks lead through the park to lookouts.

25 km south-west of Mundubbera via Hawkwood Rd, turn west off Durong Rd after 13 km. (07) 4153 8620 or (07) 4167 8141.

Barron Gorge National Park (2820 ha)

North-west of Cairns on the Kuranda railway line, this park features the deep gorge carved by the Barron River as it drops dramatically from the tablelands to create a 260 m waterfall. (Unfortunately the river has been dammed upstream, and the waterfall now only flows during a flood). Tropical rainforest predominates along the gorge, with small areas of casuarina groves, open woodlands and mountain heath. There are picnic facilities but no camping areas. See the rainforest from the Skyrail cableway.

30 km north of Cairns via Kuranda Hwy. (07) 4052 3096.

Blue Lake National Park (501 ha)

Situated on North Stradbroke Island, this park features a freshwater lake formed in sand dunes and surrounded by eucalypt woodland. The lake is a 2.7 km walk from the car park. No camping.

9 km east of Dunwich off the east coast road. Ferries leave from Cleveland. (07) 3286 9261.

Bowling Green Bay National Park (55,400 ha)

A coastal park just south of Townsville in an area of relatively low rainfall. A long sandspit flanks Bowling Green Bay to the south. Cape Cleveland in the north is a rugged, eucalypt-covered headland. Crocodiles may be seen among the mangrove-lined river mouths.

Freshwater wetlands separate the mangroves from the rugged Mt Elliot area, site of one of the southernmost tropical rainforest communities in Australia. There are walking tracks and popular, well-equipped picnic and camping areas near the cascades on Alligator Creek. The park gates close at night.

25 km south of Townsville off the Bruce Hwy. (07) 4778 8203 or (07) 4721 2399.

Brampton Islands National Park (982 ha)

Continental islands about 40 km offshore between Proserpine and Mackay. Brampton Island is the most popular and is linked to Carlisle Island at low tide. There are white sandy beaches, fringing reefs and coconut palm groves. A resort operates on Brampton Island, and basic camping facilities on Carlisle island.

Access to Brampton Island is by daily launch service or light aircraft from Mackay. (07) 4951 8788.

Bribie Island National Park (4770 ha)

A low sand island forming the north-western edge of Moreton Bay, separated from the mainland by a narrow passage. The centre of the island is outside the park and is covered with pine forests surrounding a large wetland area which attracts large numbers of water birds. The tidal lands and waters around the island are a marine park. Visitors enjoy boating, fishing, swimming, bushwalking and birdwatching. There are picnic areas and camping sites with basic facilities (bookings recommended). Bring your own drinking water. Access by boat or via Bribie Bridge. 4WD within the park.

65 km north of Brisbane off Bruce Hwy. (07) 3408 8451

Burleigh Head National Park (28 ha)

Surrounded by the Gold Coast, this coastal park preserves small areas of rainforest, open forest and heath at the mouth of Tallebudgera Creek. Short nature trails loop through the park. There is a Visitor Centre, picnic facilities and a camping area next to the park.

Off the Gold Coast Hwy at Burleigh Heads. (07) 5535 3032.

Burrum Coast National Park (22,500 ha)

A coastal park opposite Fraser Island, this area features sand dunes, wetlands, mangroves, heaths and eucalypt forests, providing habitats for more than 200 species of birds. To the north is the undeveloped coastal strip of Kinkuna. There are picnic grounds with good facilities and a camping area (4WD access only).

55 km south of Bundaberg and 38 km east of Childers via Woodgate. (07) 4126 8810.

Byfield National Park (8720 ha)

A coastal park north of Yeppoon protecting an extensive windswept dune system covered with heath, bordering Corio Bay. There are sandy beaches and panoramic views from the headlands where ospreys nest. Bush camping only. 4WD access.

20 km north of Yeppoon. (07) 4936 0511.

Camooweal Caves National Park (13,800 ha)

Located in the Barkly Tableland in the arid north-west of the state, this park protects significant areas of Mitchell grass plains, dry woodlands and black soil country. Sinkholes formed by millions of years of water erosion lead to an extensive dolomite cave system stretching several hundred metres underground. Basic camping and picnic facilities. 4WD recommended.

About 190 km north-west of Mt Isa via Camooweal and the Barkly Hwy. (07) 4743 2055.

Cania Gorge National Park (3000 ha)

Located in the Dawes Range north-west of Bundaberg, this park features a beautiful sandstone gorge with pockets of rainforest and open eucalypt forest. Walking tracks lead to the gorge, and hiking trails attract the serious bushwalker. There is a picnic area with facilities but camping is not allowed. A private caravan park and camping ground is located 10 km from the park entrance.

26 km north-west of Monto via the Burnett Hwy and Moonford Rd. (07) 4167 8162.

Cape Hillsborough National Park (818 ha)

A scenic coastal park north of Mackay featuring hoop pine rainforest, open eucalypt forest, mangroves and secluded beaches. The area is rich in wildlife. Scrub turkeys and kangaroos are common and often seen at the picnic area and along the walking tracks. There are basic camping facilities at Smalleys Beach, a resort and council camp ground.

44 km north of Mackay off Seaforth Rd. (07) 4959 0410.

Cape Palmerston National Park (7200 ha)

A scenic coastal park south of Mackay including a long sandy beach, grassy headlands, coastal vine forests, palm stands, wetlands and mangroves. The area attracts a great deal of bird life including the pied imperial pigeon and a number of migrant waders. Basic camping and picnic facilities are provided. 4WD access, carry extra fuel and water.

45 km south of Sarina, turn off the Bruce Hwy at Ilbilbie. (07) 4951 8788.

Cape Upstart National Park (8480 ha)

Preserves the coastal granite headland at the tip of Cape Upstart between Bowen and Ayr. The rugged area is cut by creeks and clothed in a mosaic of vegetation types from heaths to vine thickets. The headland is fringed by sandy beaches. There are no facilities.

Access by boat only. (07) 4946 7022.

Capricorn Coast National Park (114 ha)

Near Rockhampton on the Central Coast, this park comprises mainly rocky outcrops and coastal headlands, the remnants of a period of volcanic activity some 130 million years ago. There are short walks through vine thickets and stunted shrubland to the summits of Double Head and Bluff Point. The views over the coast and Keppel Bay Islands are magnificent, and turtles may be seen feeding in the coastal waters. There are picnic facilities but no camping.

South of Yeppoon. (07) 4933 6595.

Capricornia Cays National Park (178 ha)

Part of the Great Barrier Reef Marine Park, Capricornia Cays includes the islands of the

Lady Musgrave Island National Park, an idyllic coral cay at the southern tip of Queensland's Great Barrier Reef

Right: a cool waterfall in the rainforest of Queensland's Lamington National Park

Fraser Island, the world's largest sand island and one of Queensland's World Heritage Areas

Capricorn and Bunker Group, a chain of coral cays off Gladstone. North-west, the second largest of the Great Barrier Reef islands, is a major nesting site for green turtles, a breeding ground for the common noddy and wedge-tailed shearwater, and supports a major stand of pisonia trees. Lady Musgrave is a forested coral cay on a living reef with a deep lagoon. The beauty and charm of this island attracts many yachts which take advantage of the safe anchorage in the lagoon. Casuarinas line the beach of Masthead Island and loggerhead turtles nest here. This is an ecologically sensitive area and must be treated with respect. Limited bush camping is allowed on Lady Musgrave, Masthead and North-west Islands. Advance booking essential.

Access by charter boat from Gladstone or tourist boat from Burnett Heads and Town of 1770. (07) 4972 6055.

Cedar Bay National Park (5650 ha)

A remote park between Cooktown and Mossman containing some of the best undeveloped coastal scenery in the state. Rainforests predominate on the coast and adjacent mountains, with mangroves and salt marsh along the water. This is an area of great biological diversity. Bush camping allowed. No facilities.

Access by boat or on foot. (07) 4098 0052.

Chillagoe-Mungana Caves National Park (20 ha)

A small national park beyond the Atherton Tableland preserving outstanding examples of a broad limestone belt. The park features jagged limestone outcrops towering above woodlands, and numerous caves, some decorated with coloured stalactites and stalagmites. Regular guided tours are offered through three of the caves. There are picnic facilities but no camping area.

About 240 km west of Cairns via Mareeba and Dimbulah. (07) 4094 7163.

Conondale National Park (6980 ha)

An undeveloped wilderness park on the slopes of the Conondale Range west of Nambour protecting sub-tropical rainforests and wet eucalypt forests. Service roads provide access to bush-

walkers and birdwatchers. No camping.

About 70 km west of Nambour via Maleny and Conondale. (07) 5445 7301.

Cooktown National Parks

Three largely undeveloped parks in the Cooktown area protect areas of great biological significance. Black Mountain National Park (903 ha) features a mountain of massive, black lichen-stained boulders, and preserves the habitat of Goodman's rock wallaby. Endeavour River National Park (2170 ha) encompasses mangroves, mud flats and sand dunes on the northern side of the river, and is the only collecting site of Banks and Solander that remains untouched. Mt Cook National Park (502 ha) features the forested peak of Mt Cook. A walking trail leads to the summit. There are no picnic or camping facilities in these parks.

Access via Cooktown. Endeavour River can only be reached by boat. (07) 4069 5574.

Crater Lakes National Park (959 ha)

Located on the Atherton Tableland, Lake Eacham and Lake Barrine are crater lakes formed in ancient volcanic cones. The lakes are surrounded by tropical rainforest, home to animals such as the musky rat kangaroo, cassowary, rifle-bird and the tooth-billed bowerbird. Walking tracks circuit the lakes. There are picnic facilities but no camping.

19 km east of Atherton off the Gillies Hwy. (07) 4095 3768.

Crows Nest National Park (1020 ha)

A southern inland park on the eastern edge of the Great Dividing Range featuring a large waterfall tumbling into a steep granite gorge. There are walking tracks above and below the gorge, through open eucalypt forests and into the Valley of Diamonds (a deep gorge carved by Crows Nest Creek). The area is popular for picnicking and swimming. Basic camping at the picnic area.

6 km east of Crows Nest via the New England Hwy from Toowoomba. (07) 4639 4599.

Currawinya National Park (151,300 ha)

An oasis of lakes, rivers and wetlands in the semi-arid sandplains and rocky ranges of south-western Queensland. There are two large permanent lakes in the north-west of the park, while temporary lakes and channels of the Paroo River fill after good rain. The sandplains are dominated by mulga woodlands with low shrubs on the dune fields. Coolabahs and river red gums follow the river channels. Red and grey kangaroos and emus are common. Pelicans, the rare freckled duck and many other waterbirds frequent the lakes. This is a remote park. Carry extra fuel, water, food and other supplies. Basic camping only, bring fuel stoves. No power boating on the lakes. Roads may be impassable after rain. 4WD recommended.

170 km south-west of Cunnamulla via Eulo-Hungerford Rd. (07) 4655 4001.

D'Aguilar Range National Park (2050 ha)

This national park in the D'Aguilar Range is managed as part of Brisbane Forest Park. Maiala offers a scenic view of the coastal plain and walks through varied forest communities. A self-guiding nature walk introduces you to the rainforest ecology. Camp and walk in the mist at Manorina, birdwatch at Boombana, or picnic at Jolly's Lookout.

52 km west of Brisbane via Mt Nebo. (07) 3300 4855.

Daintree National Park (76,000 ha)

On the Cape York Peninsula, Daintree is a large tropical rainforest park in the World Heritage Area of the Wet Tropics, characterised by reef-fringed beaches, rugged ranges, forests and woodlands, steep scarps, waterfalls and the many tributaries of the Daintree River. This is one of the few places where tropical rainforest meets coral reef, bringing together two of the world's most complex ecosystems. Wildlife includes the Daintree River ringtail possum, Bennett's tree kangaroo and the Thornton Peak rat. The park includes Snapper Island, a continental island off the mouth of the Daintree River. Grass covers the south-eastern exposed side, while the north-eastern side is rainforested. There are several white beaches of worn coral rubble and an adjacent reef. There are picnic areas and camping grounds at Noah Beach and

Snapper Island. Beware of crocodiles.

80 km north of Cairns via Mossman. (07) 0498 0052. Snapper Is. (07) 4052 3096.

Davies Creek National Park (486 ha)

Located in granite-strewn country north-west of Cairns, this park features a 100 m waterfall plunging over huge granite boulders into a deep valley. Open eucalypt forests dominate and wildflowers bloom in spring. There are small swimming holes, picnic areas and camping area with basic facilities.

About 52 km west of Cairns off the Kennedy Hwy before Mareeba. (07) 4052 3096.

Diamantina National Park (507,000 ha)

A new national park in the south-western plains due west of Longreach, preserving a magnificent example of channel country, semi-arid and arid lands. The park includes part of the usually dry Diamantina River. No facilities, but bush camping is allowed. 4WD access.

About 300 km west of Longreach, access from Winton to the north or Windorah to the south. (07) 4657 3024.

Deepwater National Park (4390 ha)

Between Gladstone and Bundaberg on the central coast this park features a high dune landscape backed by open forest and vine thicket with banksia heath to the west. The park is centred around Wreck Rock with long ocean beaches and rocky outcrops separated by an esplanade. Loggerhead and green turtles nest in the dunes. Deepwater Creek is an undisturbed freshwater stream with dense paperbark forests. Camp at Wreck or Middle Rocks. Picnic areas are provided. 4WD recommended.

About 90 km north of Bundaberg, turn north off Ruhls Beach Rd. (07) 4974 9350.

Edmund Kennedy National Park (6950 ha)

A coastal park set in the lowlands just north of Cardwell with a diverse vegetation of mangroves, dense rainforest, tea tree, sedge, fan palms and sword grass swamps. In 1848 Edmund Kennedy explored this area on his ill-fated journey to Cape York. Nowadays a network of walking tracks and board walks give access to this out-standing park. There are picnic facilities but no camping areas. Beware of crocodiles.

11 km north of Cardwell off the Bruce Hwy. (07) 4066 8115.

Eubenangee Swamp National Park (1720 ha)

This park protects the last remaining wetlands between Townsville and Cairns. Fringed by open eucalypt forest and lowland rainforest, the area is a habitat for many species of birds. No camp-ing. Beware of crocodiles.

16 km north of Innisfail. (07) 4067 6304.

Eurimbula National Park (12,500 ha)

Situated on the central coast between Gladstone and Bundaberg, this is a biologically important area where tropical and sub-tropical habitats overlap. Flowering heaths contrast with rainforests and open eucalypt forests, and emerald doves are common. Bustard Beach is a secluded spot, the sheltered mangrove estuary is a haven for boating and fishing. Picnic facil-ities and camping areas, but take drinking water. 4WD recommended.

110 km south-east of Gladstone via Miriam Vale and 1770 Rd. (07) 4974 9350.

Expedition National Park (108,000 ha)

Located on the central highlands, this park includes the former Lonesome and Robinson Gorge National Parks. It features a plateau with high cliffs overlooking the Arcadia Valley and Dawson River Valley, and the picturesque 30 km Robinson Gorge with its precipitous coloured sandstone cliffs. Open eucalypt forests cover the slopes and pockets of rainforest with cabbage tree palms, ferns and mosses grow in the deep sheltered gorges. A lookout gives panoramic views over Arcadia Valley and a walking track leads to Robinson Gorge. There are Aboriginal art sites, swimming holes and a good range of wildlife. Picnic areas and basic camping facili-ties are provided. 4WD access.

Robinson Gorge is about 100 km north-west of Taroom via Glenhaughton Rd. Lonesome is about 150 km north of Roma via Injune. (07) 4627 3358.

Family Islands National Park (869 ha)

A group of Islands off the coast opposite Tully. The beautiful Dunk Island features golden beaches, coral gardens, fine palms and a resort complex. Broadleaf vine forests give way to open woodlands on the exposed ridges. The wide variety of wildlife includes visiting turtles. There are walking tracks, picnic areas and a camping ground on Dunk Island, and basic camping areas on Wheeler and Coombe Islands.

Access by ferry from Clump Point or by air from Townsville. (07) 4066 8115.

Fitzroy Island National Park (278 ha)

Due east of Cairns, this continental island is part of the coastal granite mountain chain of Bellenden Ker. It has excellent fringing reef, rainforest and woodlands. Walk into the rain-forest and go to the lighthouse where there are spectacular views. Good swimming, diving, snorkelling and bird watching. There are picnic areas, a resort and camp ground.

25 km east of Cairns. Access by boat. (07) 4052 3096.

Flinders Group National Park (2970 ha)

Includes several continental islands in Princess Charlotte Bay off the east coast of Cape York Peninsula. Flinders and Stanley Islands feature magnificent rugged escarpments and cliffs supporting low open eucalypt forests and man-groves lining the sheltered bays. There are small Aboriginal rock art sites on some islands. Bush camping only on Flinders and Stanley Islands.

Access by boat. (07) 4052 3096.

Fort Lytton National Park (6693 ha)

An historic area, built in 1880 to protect Brisbane. It was the state's main military train-ing ground in 1914, but was abandoned in 1945 and maintained by an oil company until it was handed over to the state government in 1988. There are picnic tables, a museum and guided tours of the fort.

On the southern bank of the Brisbane River via Lytton Rd or boat. (07) 3393 4647

Frankland Group National Park (77 ha)

A group of continental islands about 10 km off Russell Heads south of Cairns. These islands support rainforests and casuarina forests, and are fringed with reefs and white sandy beaches. There are camping areas on Russell and High Islands.
45 km south of Cairns, access by boat.
(07) 4052 3096.

Glass House Mountains National Park (883 ha)

Close to the coast north of Brisbane, this park protects four of the massive volcanic plugs that dominate the landscape: Mt Coonoorwin (523 m), Mt Beerwah (556 m), Mt Tibrogargan (393 m) and Mt Ngungun (236 m). Most ascents of these peaks are only suitable for experienced climbers. Picnic facilities but no camping areas.
Off the Bruce Hwy 22 km north of Caboolture via Glasshouse Mountains township.
(07) 5494 6630.

Gloucester Islands National Park (13,400 ha)

A group of inshore islands north of Airlie Beach. Gloucester Island, 20 km east of Bowen, is a rugged rocky island fringed with reefs and sheltered beaches supporting the rare Proserpine rock wallaby. Picnic areas and basic camping sites are provided on Gloucester, Armit, Saddleback and Olden Islands.
Access by boat from Bowen. (07) 4946 7022.

Goold Island National Park (830 ha)

A granite island north of Hinchinbrook Island dominated by eucalypt woodlands with lush broad leaf vine thickets in the moist gullies. There are excellent views of Hinchinbrook Island and the coastal ranges from the western beach. Turtles feed offshore and noisy sulphur crested cockatoos are common. Take drinking water between August and December. There is a small camping and picnic area.
Access by charter boat from Cardwell.
(07) 4066 8115.

Great Basalt Wall National Park (35,200 ha)

A remote, rugged, undeveloped wilderness park west of Charters Tower. The park preserves a basalt lava flow formed during the last major volcanic activity in north-eastern Australia. No facilities. 4WD access in the wet.
100 km west of Charters Towers.
(07) 4787 3388.

Green Island, Michaelmas and Upolu Cay National Parks (11 ha)

Green Island is the most popular Great Barrier Reef destination. This densely-vegetated coral cay has a sprawling resort complex including an underwater observatory and aquarium. Walk through the low forest. Nearby Michaelmas Cay is a sandy coral cay and a nesting site for thousands of ground-nesting seabirds. There is no access beyond the beach. No camping.
Access to Green Island is by regular ferry from Cairns. (07) 4052 3096.

Idalia National Park (144,000 ha)

Located in the Gowan Ranges in semi-arid central western Queensland, this national park conserves the major vegetation types of the area. The park takes in the headwaters of the normally dry Bulloo River and its tributaries. These watercourses are lined with majestic river red gums watered by small springs and waterholes. The ranges comprise many steep escarpments and high peaks with tall shrubs and low mulga woodlands on the escarpment. No facilities. Bush camping only at Monk's Tank with a permit. 4WD access.
100 km south-west of Blackall via the Isisford Rd, turn south at Benlidi railway siding.
(07) 4657 5033.

Iron Range National Park (34,600 ha)

A wilderness area of world-wide significance on the mid-east coast of Cape York Peninsula, containing the largest area of lowland rainforest in Australia. The park features the rugged hills of the Janet and Tozer Ranges. The rainforests, mangroves, heaths and open forests support a wide variety of plant and animal species, many unique to this area, others of New Guinean origin. They include the great palm cockatoo, spotted cuscus, eclectus parrot, nypa palm and more than 50 species of orchid. Camping and picnic facilities are provided. 4WD access in the dry season only. Beware of crocodiles.

About 800 km north of Cairns.
(07) 4060 7170.

Isla Gorge National Park (7850 ha)

Located in the central highlands, this park preserves a complex maze of gorges cut into the sandstone. The ridges support open eucalypt woodlands with a small area of brigalow on the lower flats in the northern section. Isla Gorge is sparsely vegetated. Wildflowers are common in spring. There are walking tracks and a small camp ground and picnic area near the lookout. Bring sufficient water.

About 70 km north-east of Taroom off the
Leichhardt Hwy. (07) 5427 3358.

Jardine River National Park (237,000 ha)

A wilderness park on the east coast at the tip of Cape York Peninsula protecting the catchment of the largest perennial river in the state. The area supports rainforest, open forest, heath and shrub communities, providing habitats for a wide variety of fauna, many of New Guinean origin. Camping and picnic facilities are provided. 4WD access in the dry season only. Beware of crocodiles.

About 850 km north of Cairns.
(07) 4060 3241.

Keppel Bay Islands National Park (720 ha)

A popular group of eight continental islands off Yeppoon. North Keppel is the largest island with casuarinas and pandans lining the beaches. Humpy Island is exposed to the prevailing south-easterlies and has stunted vegetation. Humpy and Halfway Island have good coral reefs. Middle, Miall, North Keppel, Conical and Humpy Islands have good bush camping areas.

Access by boat from Yeppoon, 40 km north-east
of Rockhampton. (07) 4936 0511.

Kondalilla National Park (327 ha)

South-west of Nambour in the Blackall Range this small park protects rainforest remnants and wet eucalypt forest. There is a popular picnic area, walking tracks, a waterfall, and a refreshing rock pool. No camping.

21 km south-west of Nambour between
Mapleton and Montville. (07) 5445 7301.

Lakefield National Park (537,000 ha)

This huge park on the Cape York Peninsula protects examples of the area's vegetation types, including fringing rainforest, open forest, melaleuca woodland, mangroves, mudflats, open grassy plains and swamps. This is a major habitat for a wide variety of birds including black cockatoos, lorikeets, golden-shouldered parrots and water birds. There are picnic areas and numerous bush camping sites along riverbanks and lagoons. Beware of crocodiles. 4WD access.

345 km north of Cairns via Laura.
(07) 4060 3271.

Lawn Hill National Park (282,000 ha)

This large park on the Barkly Tableland in the north-west of the state includes part of the World Heritage listed Riversleigh fossil site. Lawn Hill features an inviting tropical oasis fringed by arid sandstone and limestone terraces. Lawn Hill Gorge is a refuge for rainforest plants and animals, and the emerald green waters of the creek offer good swimming. Rock shelters along the gorge contain Aboriginal art. There are good camping and picnic facilities. 4WD recommended.

436 km north-west of Mt Isa via the Barkly
Hwy. Check road conditions before leaving.
(07) 4748 5572.

Lizard Island National Park (990 ha)

A continental island almost surrounded by fringing reef off the coast north of Cooktown. The island supports woodlands, mangroves, grasslands, heath and rainforest. A track leads to the peak used by Captain Cook to search for a passage through the Great Barrier Reef. There is a tourist resort and camp ground on the island.

Access by boat or plane. (07) 4052 3096.

Lumholtz National Park (140,000 ha)

West of Cardwell in the coastal ranges this large park is part of the Wet Tropics World Heritage Area. It features the magnificent Herbert River Valley with its waterfalls, gorges, rainforests and eucalypt woodlands. Stony Creek plunges 279 m over Wallaman Falls (the highest single drop waterfall in Australia) into a tremendous gorge with vertical walls to join the Herbert River below. There are picnic grounds and a camping area with basic facilities at Stony Creek, upstream from Wallaman falls. Beware of crocodiles. 4WD recommended.

48 km west of Ingham via Lannercost Range Rd. (07) 4776 1700.

Magnetic Island National Park (2790 ha)

The majority of this rugged continental island is a national park. It features hillsides strewn with granite boulders and covered with eucalypt forests. Rainforest pockets can be found in the gullies, and hoop pines grow along the coastal cliffs and headlands. An extensive system of walking tracks leads to scenic lookouts and secluded beaches. A fringing reef offers good snorkelling and reef walking. Private camping and motel-style accommodation is available.

Access by daily ferry service from Townsville. (07) 4778 5378.

Mapleton Falls National Park (26 ha)

West of Nambour in the Blackall Range, this small park protects Mapleton Falls and its surrounding rainforest. There are scenic views from the top of the falls and walking trails leading from the picnic area into the rainforest. No camping.

15 km west of Nambour via Mapleton. (07) 5445 7301.

Millstream Falls National Park (372 ha)

On the western slopes of the Atherton Tableland this park is part of the Wet Tropics World Heritage Area. It is an open woodland area featuring Millstream Falls, reputedly the widest in Australia, flowing over the edge of a columnar basalt lava flow. Swimming, picnicking and walking are popular. No camping.

6 km west of Ravenshoe off the Kennedy Hwy. (07) 4095 3768.

Mission Beach National Parks

A number of parks in the Mission Beach area protect small areas from increasing tourist development on this beautiful part of the north coast.

Kurrimine Beach Conservation Park (6 ha) is an area of coastal rainforest accessible on foot or by boat. Maria Creek National Park (749 ha) preserves a mosaic of lowland swamp vegetation types, and is accessible only by boat. Bicton Hill in Clump Mountain National Park (282 ha) is a rainforested area overlooking Mission Beach and Bingil Bay, and is home to a cassowary population. A 2 km circuit leads from Bingil Bay to a lookout on Bicton Hill. No camping.

About 45 km south of Innisfail off the Bruce Hwy via Mission Beach. (07) 4068 7183.

Moogerah Peaks National Park (927 ha)

In the south-east of the state, this area features rocky cliffs and volcanic peaks surrounding Lake Moogerah, giving spectacular views over Fassifern Valley. Mt Moon, Mt Edwards and Mt Greville are isolated wilderness areas. Mt French is a popular rock climbing area. The area supports open eucalypt forests, dry vine forests in the gullies, and heathlands. Small picnic and camping area at Mt French with basic facilities.

100 km south-west of Brisbane off the Cunningham Hwy near Boonah. (07) 5463 5041.

Mooloolah River National Park (676 ha)

Located on the coastal plain south of Maroochydore, this undeveloped park protects part of the Mooloolah River landscape and wallum vegetation. Canoe and boat access from the river mouth. The area is rich in wildflowers and birdlife. No camping.

105 north of Brisbane and 5 km south of Mooloolaba via Mountain Creek Rd off the Bruce Hwy. (07) 5443 8944.

Moreton Island National Park (16,800 ha)

A large sand island featuring Mt Tempest (284 m) reputedly the world's highest coastal sand dune. There are beach and dune communities, lakes, streams, rocky headlands, sedge and paperbark swamps, banksia heathlands, woodlands, forests, mangroves and salt marshes. There are picnic facilities, camping areas and a resort. 4WD only on the island.

Vehicle permits required.

Access by daily vehicle ferry from Brisbane. (07) 3408 2710.

Mount Archer National Park (1990 ha)

On the eastern fringe of Rockhampton this hilly area protects a variety of vegetation types including rainforest, open eucalypt forest and vine forest. Rock wallabies, bandicoots, kingfishers, lorikeets, whip snakes and blue-tongued lizards are among the animals found here. A walking track leads to Mt Archer and there are a number of shorter walks. Go swimming in the waterholes in summer. Picnic areas are provided. No camping.

In Rockhampton, access via Pilbeam Dve or German St. (07) 4936 9511

Mount Barney National Park (13, 000 ha)

On the Mc Pherson Range south of Beaudesert, this park includes Mt Barney (1360 m), Mt Maroon (965 m) and Mt Lindesay (1191 m), providing challenging bushwalking and rock climbing opportunities. The area supports rainforest, open forest and montane heath. Walk to the Lower Portals on beautiful Barney Creek. Bush camping only.

120 km south-west of Brisbane off the Lindesay Hwy west of Rathdowney via Boonah Rd. (07) 5463 5041.

Mount Coolum National Park (69 ha)

A small undeveloped park on the Sunshine Coast. A rough track leads to the mountain top where there are panoramic views over the ocean and coastline. No facilities or camping.

About 20 km south of Noosa Heads via Tannah St West off David Low Way. (07) 5443 8944.

Mount Etna Caves National Park (390 ha)

In the limestone belt north of Rockhampton, this park is in two parts protecting limestone caves and outcrops essential for the survival of the little bent-wing bat and the rare ghost bat. The cave system is the most dense in Australia and is made up of horizontal caves at various levels connected to the surface by vertical

tunnels. The vegetation ranges from grassland to closed forest. Rock wallabies bound over the rugged slopes, and snakes wait at cave entrances for a meal. More than 75 bird species have been recorded. There are restricted and open access caves. See the bats flying out to feed and visit the karst formations on guided tours to Bat Cleft in summer. No camping.

25 km north of Rockhampton off Bruce Hwy. (07) 4936 0511.

Mount Hypipamee (The Crater) National Park (364 ha)

Located in the Atherton Tableland, this park features a water-filled crater with sheer granite sides. This geological curiosity is a volcanic pipe produced when subterranean gases blasted through the granite rock. Walking tracks lead through rainforest and eucalypt forest surrounding the crater, the habitat of the Herbert River ringtail possum. There are picnic facilities but no camping.

24 km south of Atherton off the Kennedy Hwy. (07) 4095 3768.

Mount Walsh National Park (5270 ha)

Located on the coastal ranges west of Maryborough this park features the rugged peaks of Mt Walsh and the Bluff. Eucalypt forests clothe the slopes, heath communities grow on the exposed rocky faces and palms fill some of the valleys. The peaks offer challenges to experienced rock climbers and bushwalkers. Bush camping only.

90 km west of Maryborough and 7 km south of Biggenden. (07) 4123 7100.

Mungan Kandju National Park (457,000 ha)

Located on the Cape York Peninsula, this huge park extends from the McIlwraith Range to the Archer and Coen River flood plains and preserves a variety of vegetation types typical of the area. They include open eucalypt and melaleuca woodlands characteristic of the drier plains, narrow strips of rainforest bordering the watercourses and deciduous vine thickets. The area provides habitats for rare and beautiful birds. Beware of crocodiles. Bush camping only.

4WD access in the dry season only.
About 520 km north of Cairns near Coen.
(07) 4060 3256.

Newry Islands National Park (464 ha)

Lying a few kilometres offshore between Proserpine and Mackay, these continental islands feature low wooded hills, headlands, beaches and fringing reefs. Picnic areas and camp grounds with water and limited facilities are provided on Rabbit and Outer Newry Islands.
60 km north-west of Mackay. Access by boat from St Helens or Seaforth. (07) 4951 8788.

Noosa National Park (2280 ha)

Between Noosa and Coolum, this coastal park preserves some of the remaining beautiful coastal scenery of this rapidly developing area. Walking tracks at Noosa Heads and Peregian lead through heaths with excellent springtime wildflower displays, open forests and rainforests. The beaches are good for surfing and swimming, and the rock pools at low tide are full of interesting life. There are extensive picnic grounds and a Visitor Centre.
Access from Noosa Heads. (07) 5447 3243.

Orpheus Island National Park (1300 ha)

Part of the Palm Group, this is a continental island 35 km off the Ingham coast. A walking track crosses the island from Hazard Bay, passing through open woodlands, heaths, grasslands and rainforest gullies revealing spectacular views from rocky outcrops. A colourful fringing reef and sandy beaches add to the island's attractions. Bush camp or stay at the tourist resort.
Access by charter boat from Lucinda.
(07) 4066 8115.

Paluma Range National Park (10,600 ha)

Part of the Wet Tropics World Heritage Area, this park incorporates the Mount Spec/Crystal Creek and Jourama Falls sections. It straddles the summit and escarpment of the Paluma Range north-west of Townsville, an area of open eucalypt woodlands on the foothills and magnificent rainforests on the cool moist mountain tops and gullies. There are picnic facilities and walking tracks at McClelland's Lookout on top of the range near Paluma township, and a picnic and camping area at Big Crystal Creek at the foot of the range, good facilities and views of the cascades. The Jourama Falls section features a series of cascades flowing over salmon-coloured granite surrounded by lush green vegetation. A picnic and camping area is nestled at the base of the range by Waterview Creek. A walking track leads along the creek through casuarina and palm groves to two lookouts.
64 km north of Townsville off the Bruce Hwy.
(07) 4770 8526.
Jourama Falls (07) 4777 3112

Porcupine Gorge National Park (5410 ha)

On the western slopes of the Great Dividing Range, this park features a spectacular sandstone gorge deeply etched into the red plains at the head of the Flinders River. Porcupine Creek flows continually at the base of the multicoloured gorge, supporting a surprising variety of plant and animal life and offering visitors a welcome respite from the parched surroundings. There are basic camping and picnic facilities. 4WD recommended in the wet season.
About 450 km south-west of Townsville via Flinders Hwy, north-east of Hughenden.
(07) 4741 1113.

Ravensbourne National Park (100 ha)

On the eastern edge of the Great Dividing Range, Ravensbourne preserves a remnant of the wet sclerophyll and rainforest vegetation that once covered the surrounding area. There are dense groves of piccabeen palms, a rich birdlife, extensive walking tracks and popular picnic areas. No camping.
45 km north-east of Toowoomba via the New England Hwy and Hampton.
(07) 4639 4599.

Simpson Desert National Park (1,012,000 ha)

This is the state's largest park, and adjoins the Simpson Desert Conservation Park in South Australia. It preserves an area of parallel sand dunes interspersed with clay pans, sand drifts and gibber flats, supporting spinifex grasses, open hummock grasslands and shrubs. Its remoteness has saved it from degradation and the area has a surprising wildlife complement including red kangaroos, euros, spinifex hopping mice, wedge-tailed eagles, parrots, finches and many reptiles including Gould's goanna, the thorny devil and desert death adder. Basic camping only. 4WD only. Sand driving experience and good equipment are essential.

About 80 km west of Birdsville. Access via Birdsville. (07) 4658 1761.

Springbrook National Park (2720 ha)

Located on the Gold Coast hinterland, with views over the mountains and coastline. Walking tracks lead into dense rainforest and open forests. Visit Natural Bridge, an unusual geological formation formed by the cascading waters (glow worms illuminate the cave under the arch). You can walk along a rainforest creek in the Mt Cougal area. There are swimming holes and picnic facilities. Camp at Purling Brook Falls.

About 100 km south of Brisbane via Mudgeeraba or Numinbah. (07) 5533 5147.

St Helena Island National Park (75 ha)

This is an historic area in Moreton Bay off the Brisbane River mouth with relics of a penal settlement. There are guided tours and picnic facilities but no camping areas.

Regular boat services operate from Breakfast Creek and Manly. (07) 3396 5113.

Sundown National Park (12,500 ha)

Located on the NSW border, this park protects a rugged area dissected by gorges leading to the Severn River. Dense forests of cypress pine and eucalypts cover the slopes, with dry rainforest scrub in the gorges. There are no tracks, but walking along the river is pleasant and easy. Camp beside the Severn River where there are basic facilities and a nearby swimming hole.

300 km south-west of Brisbane via Stanthorpe. (02) 6737 5235.

Tamborine National Park (1160 ha)

In the hinterland of the Gold Coast, this park is located in the Darlington Range and encompasses a small high plateau edged with cliffs. Most of the area is rainforest and features cool

waterfalls, magnificent views from lookouts, extensive walking tracks and a wide selection of birds, including Albert's lyrebird. There are picnic facilities but no camping areas.

70 km south of Brisbane off the Pacific Hwy between Beenleigh and Nerang, or via Tamborine from Mt Lindesay Hwy. (07) 5445 1171.

Venman Bushland National Park (300 ha)

Conserves the last natural eucalypt forest and paperbark-lined creek in the Redland district south of Brisbane. The park is a haven for koalas, platypuses, possums, red-necked and swamp wallabies. There are walking tracks and picnic areas. No camping.

30 km south-east of Brisbane off West Mt Cotton Rd. (07) 3299 1032.

White Mountains National Park (108,000 ha)

A rugged undeveloped park south-west of Charters Towers. The park features spectacular sandstone gorges and bluffs. No facilities. Walkers must register with the ranger. Bush camping allowed.

About 140 km south-west of Charters Towers via the Flinders Hwy. (07) 4741 1113.

Wooroonooran National Park (79,800 ha)

Part of the Wet Tropics World Heritage Area, this largely undeveloped park is located in the Bellenden Ker Range in north-eastern Queensland, and includes the state's highest mountain, Bartle Frere (1657 m). Most of the park is dense upland rainforest crossed by numerous streams and waterfalls, including the popular Josephine Falls. The area is a sanctuary for rainforest fauna, including tree kangaroos and golden bowerbirds. The North Johnstone River offers good white-water rafting, and a self-guiding trail at Tchupala Falls leads beneath the luxuriant rainforest canopy. There are walking tracks, picnic areas, and basic camping areas.

43 km south of Cairns off the Bruce Hwy for Josephine Falls. (07) 4067 6304.

33 km west of Innisfail via Palmerston Hwy for the Palmerston section. (07) 4064 5115.

Victoria

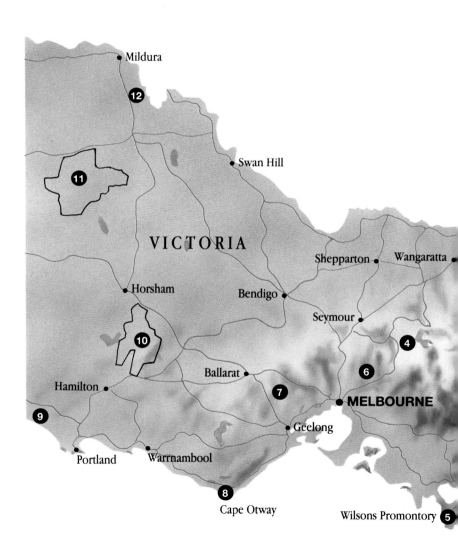

Mildura

12

Swan Hill

11

VICTORIA

Shepparton • Wangaratta

Horsham • Bendigo •

Seymour •

4

10

6

Ballarat •

7

MELBOURNE

Hamilton •

9

Geelong

Portland • Warrnambool

8

Cape Otway

Wilsons Promontory **5**

Featured National Parks

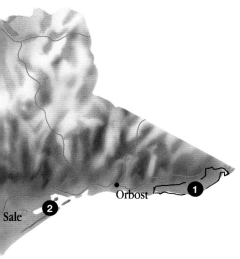

Croajingolong National Park

Extending from the New South Wales border for almost 100 km, Croajingolong National Park protects a magnificent coastline featuring the waters and islands of Mallacoota Inlet, great mobile sand dunes, unspoiled beaches and headlands, and a forested wilderness area where the plants of the north meet those of the south to create unusual and unique communities.

The focal points of this 87,500 ha park are the inlets of Sydenham, Tamboon and Mallacoota, and the river mouth estuaries of the Thurra and Mueller Rivers. Mallacoota Inlet, a favoured haunt of Henry Lawson, has long been a popular holiday destination. It is famed for the beauty of its shoreline, the variety of habitats from sub-tropical rainforests to windswept heathlands, the wildlife, and the recreational opportunities offered by the lakes, forests and beaches.

Many rivers originating in the South Coast Range wind their way through the low tablelands of the park's interior to the coast. Emerging from the sedimentary rocks of the tablelands are bands of hard reddish granite that form the peaks of Howe Hill, Genoa Peak and Mount Everard, and the coastal headlands. Sand dunes link the rocky coastal outcrops to form long sandy beaches. In places these have been stabilised by vegetation and grade into the coastal forest. In other areas, such as Point Hicks and Cape Howe, they are still mobile and provide a good example of the dynamic coastal processes.

Formation

The coastline owes its present form to the changes in sea level associated with the last ice age. About 18,000 years ago global cooling caused a massive expansion of the ice sheets that covered the poles. Vast quantities of water were converted to ice, causing the sea level to fall and exposing the underlying coastal shelf. Sandy sediments washed from the inland mountains formed great river deltas on the new coastal plains. As the ice age came to an end some 6000 years ago, rising seas flooded the coastal plains. The sandy sediments were pushed onto the new shoreline where they were trapped by rocky headlands, forming the coastal sand dunes we see

today. The river valleys were flooded to create the inlets, their indented shorelines reflecting the courses of the original rivers.

History

Captain James Cook sighted the coastline in 1770, naming Point Hicks after the lieutenant who first spotted the Australian mainland. George Bass was forced ashore here during a storm in 1797, and explored Wingan Inlet. During the 1830s explorers surveyed East Gippsland, and the first settler arrived in 1842, a whaler by the name of Captain John Stevenson, who lived near Mallacoota.

This was the beginning of the end for the Aboriginal people who had lived here for at least 17,000 years. They were the Krautungulung, a well-organised nation who hunted for game, fished the rich waters of the inlets, and gathered food from the surrounding bushland. They were also competent warriors and staunchly defended their territory against the new settlers. But they could not hope to combat the weapons and diseases of the Europeans who occupied land around Mallacoota in the mid-19th century.

Transport difficulties saved the area from large-scale agriculture, and the major activities were fishing, logging and a small amount of sand mining, grazing and goldmining. Tourists were attracted to the area in the early 20th century, and Croajingolong National Park was declared in 1979. This new park included the smaller parks of Mallacoota, Wingan Inlet and Captain James Cook.

Plants and Animals

The New South Wales border marks a change in climate, and the plants of the warmer northern districts find themselves gradually displaced by those of the cooler south. The red bloodwood, rough-barked apple and silvertop extend south into this area, replacing the stringybark and box eucalypts usually found in Victorian forests, while southern mahogany is the dominant tree of the coastal woodlands. Patches of sub-tropical rainforest occur in some of the deep sheltered gullies. These are remnants of forests that developed when Gippsland had a much warmer climate. Beneath the dense green canopy of trees such as the lilly pilly, sweet pittosporum, kanooka and yellow wood grow tangled vines, orchids and tree ferns.

Low windswept heathlands cover much of the exposed coastal areas. They are ablaze with wildflowers in spring, including a number of ground orchids. Stunted shrubs such as blunt-leaf heath, prickly tea tree, scented paperbark, pink swamp heath and saw banksia are common here. On the exposed granite cliffs stunted coast banksias, sea box and coast tea trees are able to contend with the harsh winds and salt spray.

Inhabitants of the heaths and woodlands include a number of small mammals and birds such as the white-footed dunnart, long-nosed potoroo, New Holland mouse, and the rare and endangered ground parrot, an elusive inhabitant of the heathlands. Common brushtail and ringtail possums and giant goannas are often seen around the picnic areas, but you will need a spotlight to see the small grey eastern pygmy possums and sugar gliders. The small island group at the entrance to Wingan Inlet is an important habitat for a small colony of Australian fur seals and little penguins.

Some 250 bird species have been recorded in the park. Majestic white-breasted sea eagles are often seen around the shores. Waterbirds such as pelicans, crested terns, gulls and eastern curlews frequent the inlets. The azure kingfisher is often seen in summer as a blue flash streaking along the gullies. In the heathlands are honeyeaters and lorikeets, while the rainforests are home to satin bowerbirds and superb lyrebirds.

Walks

The coastline from Sydenham to Mallacoota is very popular with backpackers who are able to camp overnight at Wingan River, Thurra River and Shipwreck Creek. There are a number of short walking tracks at Mallacoota and from some of the camping grounds.

The Wingan Nature Walk is a good introduction to some of the area's habitats. This self-guiding walk takes about 30 minutes each way and leads from the camping ground to the beach, passing through eucalypt woodlands, across a boardwalk through paperbark wetlands, and over the sand dunes to the beach. Other tracks at Wingan Inlet take you to Lake Elusive, Rame Head for a good coastal panorama, and to Easby Creek. Tracks from Shipwreck Creek lead through the heathlands and to Benedore River, a full day's walk.

Facilities

Visitor Centres are located at Mallacoota and Cann River on the Princes Highway. There are camping grounds with basic facilities at Shipwreck Creek, Wingan Inlet and at the mouths of the Thurra and Mueller Rivers. Sites must be booked for peak holiday periods, and a ballot system operates for Christmas and Easter. Camping facilities are also provided by the local council at Mallacoota, Cann River, Bemm River and Genoa. Motel, hotel and other accommodation is available at Mallacoota and Gipsy Point. There are boat launching ramps at Mallacoota, Gipsy Point, Wingan Inlet, Tamboon Inlet and Bemm River. Canoeing is popular on the inlets and river mouths.

Access

The park is about 450 km east of Melbourne via the Princes Highway. The road from Mallacoota to Genoa is sealed, otherwise the access roads from the Princes Highway are unsealed and unsuitable for caravans. Some of the roads may become impassable after heavy rain.

Climate

The climate is mild with warm summers and cool winters. Visit in spring for the wildflower displays.

Cann River Information Centre, Princes Highway, Cann River, Vic 3890. Tel. (03) 5158 6351.

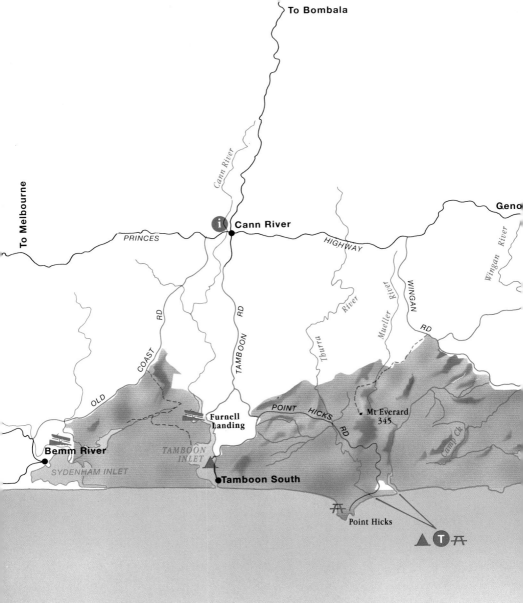

To Bombala

To Melbourne

Cann River

i **Cann River**

PRINCES

HIGHWAY

Geno

Wingan River

OLD

COAST

RD

TAMBOON

RD

Thurra River

Mueller River

WINGAN

RD

Furnell
Landing

POINT   HICKS

RD

• Mt Everard
345

Camp Ck

Bemm River

*TAMBOON
INLET*

SYDENHAM INLET

•**Tamboon South**

Point Hicks

▲T⊼

BASS   *STRAIT*

N

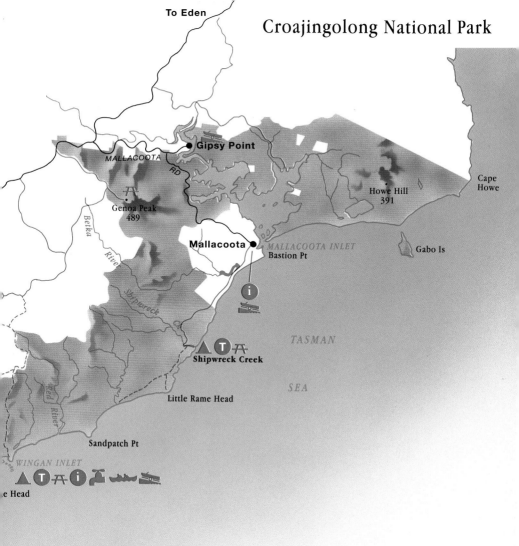

Croajingolong National Park

To Eden

MALLACOOTA

Gipsy Point

Genoa Peak
489

Betka

River

RD

Shipwreck

Mallacoota

MALLACOOTA INLET

Bastion Pt

Howe Hill
391

Cape
Howe

Gabo Is

TASMAN

SEA

Shipwreck Creek

Little Rame Head

Red

River

Sandpatch Pt

WINGAN INLET

e Head

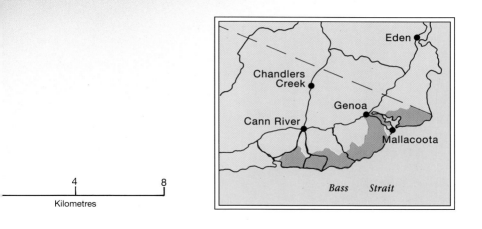

Eden

Chandlers
Creek

Genoa

Cann River

Mallacoota

Bass *Strait*

4   8
Kilometres

The Lakes National Park

The Gippsland Lakes are one of the major inland waterways of Australia. The Lakes National Park conserves the beauty of Sperm Whale Head Peninsula and Rotamah and Little Rotamah Islands; a peaceful bushland retreat fringed by the waters of Lake Victoria and Lake Reeve. The remaining part of the Lakes area is under the protection of the Gippsland Lakes Coastal Park.

The park occupies 2380 ha of low-lying land covered with woodlands and coastal heath, interspersed with freshwater swamps and salt marshes. The area is separated from the seemingly endless unspoiled coastal dunes of Ninety Mile Beach by a narrow channel.

Formation

The coastline was once part of a great sloping coastal plain crossed by river systems draining the hills and mountains of the Great Dividing Range. Rising sea levels at the end of the last ice age, some 6,000 years ago, submerged the plain, and waves lapped against a tortuous coastline at the foothills of the range.

Over thousands of years the breakers piled up sand to form the barriers of Sperm Whale Head, Rotamah Island and Ninety Mile Beach, enclosing the shallow waters of the bay. The sand dunes now rise to 38 m. Rivers deposited sediments behind the barrier, creating the present system of lakes and swamps, and Ninety Mile Beach became a long unbroken sandspit sealing the lakes from the sea.

Human Impact

The explorer Angus McMillan was the first European to set foot on the shores of Lake Victoria in 1840. He found an area rich with wildlife and an unlimited supply of fish and game. He was not alone, however, for the area was occupied by Aboriginal people of the Kurnai nation, who had lived in this area for thousands of generations, taking advantage of the mild climate and abundant food resources.

Angus McMillan spread the word, and soon after graziers descended on the area. They forced the Aborigines from their land, established cattle runs on Sperm Whale Head peninsula and cleared much of Rotamah Island for grazing. Shell middens in the sand dunes along Ninety Mile Beach are all that remains of the Kurnai nation.

In 1890 it was decided to dredge a channel through Ninety Mile Beach to facilitate sea transport to the area. Lakes Entrance was created, freshwater flowed out to sea reducing the water levels in the lakes system by some 450 mm, and salt water flooded in. The increased salinity slowly killed the vegetation binding the sand and silt along the shores of the lakes, allowing the shorelines to be eroded and river sediments to be deposited on the floor of the lakes, gradually decreasing their depth.

Over-grazing, introduced foxes and rabbits and fierce summer fires decimated the wildlife. By 1926 all but one of the original graziers had left, and in 1927 the Field Naturalist Club of Victoria secured 1451 ha of Sperm Whale Head as a nature reserve. The Lakes National Park was proclaimed in 1957, and the two islands were added in 1978. The natural bushland has since regenerated, and much of the wildlife has returned to the area. The Royal Ornithologists Union leases the Rotamah Island homestead to use as a bird observatory. It carries out research programs and runs weekend natural history courses.

Plants and Animals

The park's sandy soils support woodlands of banksia and eucalypts, dominated by peppermints, forest red gums and manna gum, with but-but, yertchuk, saw banksia, coast and silver banksias and coast tea tree. Swamp paperbarks and swamp she-oaks grow in the freshwater swamps.

The coastal heathlands comprise low shrubby species adapted to grow on the poor soils, these include silky tea tree, sweet wattle, prickly moses, common heath and common fringe myrtle. The park has spectacular wildflower displays from August to November, and a great diversity of native orchids.

A large population of native animals live in the park, the most visible being the eastern grey kangaroos, a group of which frequent the picnic area at Point Wilson. Visitors should avoid the temptation to feed them as this can damage their health. Swamp wallabies, wombats, ringtail and pygmy possums, sugar gliders, bats, echidnas, koalas, potoroos, short-nosed bandicoots, the white-faced dunnart and the rare New Holland mouse also inhabit this area. Many favour the heaths where food sources are plentiful. Most are only active at night, and are best seen by spotlighting.

The lakes, woodlands and heaths provide habitats for a wide variety of birdlife, and more than 190 species have been recorded in the park. Hides have been constructed at several sites allowing you to observe many of them in their natural habitats. Among the large birds are emus which roam throughout the park; pelicans and royal spoonbills, often seen on sandbanks in Lake Reeve; black cormorants, black swans, white-faced herons and the rufous night heron.

Birds of prey are often seen wheeling overhead. Wedge-tailed eagles, white-bellied sea eagles, whistling kites and the brown goshawk are known to nest in the area. Kookaburras are common, and the sacred and azure kingfishers may be observed. Colourful parrots, lorikeets, robins and wrens are frequently seen.

Walks

Sandy, gently undulating walking tracks pass through a fascinating variety of landscapes on Sperm Whale Head and Rotamah Island. A self-guided nature walk circuit at Lookout Tower near Lake Reeve introduces visitors to some of the habitats in the park. A number of short tracks in the Point Wilson area lead through kangaroo grazing areas, open woodlands, past swamps where numerous waterbirds can be seen, and through paperbark forests.

The longest walk on Sperm Whale Head is the Dolomite Walking Track. This starts at the picnic area and follows the edge of Dolomite Swamp to Pelican Point and Oil Bore Landing. The track winds through a dense coastal tea tree forest where several types of native orchids grow beneath the canopy. Kangaroos graze around the swamp, and waterbirds congregate here.

Footbridges lead from Rotamah Island to Little Rotamah Island and Ninety Mile Beach. There are a number of walks around Rotamah Island, some with beautiful views from the higher ground over The Lakes area.

Facilities

The Visitor Centre near the entrance to the park has information and displays. Campers must register here. Advance bookings for the small camping ground at Emu Bight should be made for holiday periods. Emu Bight, close to the shore of Lake Victoria, has toilets, fireplaces and picnic tables. Caravans can use this area and the commercial caravan park at Loch Sport.

Camping on Rotamah Island is restricted to groups who book in advance. There are toilets, fireplaces and water, although access is only by boat or on foot. The Observatory on Rotamah Island offers good accommodation facilities and excellent reference material for ornithologists (03-5156 6398).

Point Wilson is a popular picnic area and is the site of the original settler's homestead. A jetty here and on Rotamah Island allows boat access, although there are no boat launching facilities in the park.

Access

The park is 320 km east of Melbourne via the Princes Highway, and 63 km east of Sale. Follow the sealed road to Loch Sport, or take a boat from Paynesville. Roads within the park are unsealed but suitable for conventional vehicles and caravans. Rotamah Island is only accessible by boat, usually via Paynesville (6 km) or Loch Sport (18 km).

Climate

Summers are warm and winters cool. Visit all year round, although the park is at its best from August to November when the wildflowers are in full bloom.

The Lakes National Park, PO Box 40, Loch Sport, Vic 3851. Tel. (03) 5146 0278.

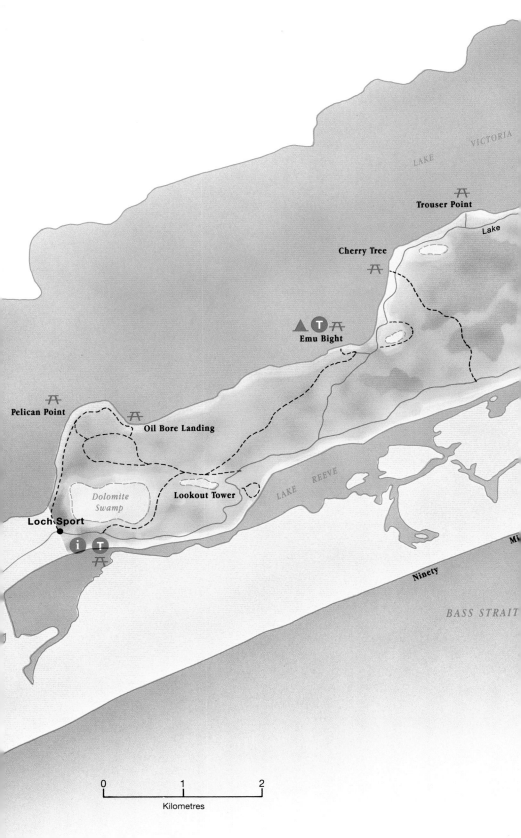

VICTORIA

LAKE

Lake

Trouser Point

Cherry Tree

Emu Bight

Pelican Point

Oil Bore Landing

Dolomite
Swamp

Lookout Tower

LAKE REEVE

Loch Sport

i T

Ninety Mi

BASS STRAIT

0   1   2

Kilometres

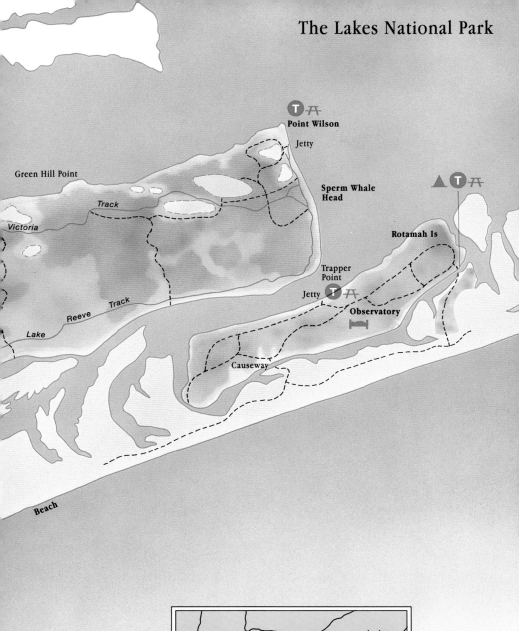

The Lakes National Park

Point Wilson

Jetty

Green Hill Point

Sperm Whale
Head

Track

Rotamah Is

Victoria

Trapper
Point

Reeve   Track

Jetty

Lake

Observatory

Causeway

Beach

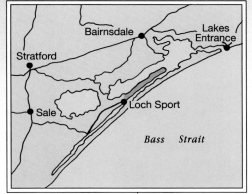

Bairnsdale

Lakes
Entrance

Stratford

Loch Sport

Sale

Bass   Strait

N

Mount Buffalo National Park

Mount Buffalo rises abruptly from the surrounding plains to an undulating plateau dominated by great granite tors and boulders. Crystal clear mountain streams tumbling down sheer-sided gorges, snow gums, colourful wildflowers, spectacular views over river valleys, rock climbing and skiing make this one of the state's most popular national parks.

The park covers 31,000 ha and rises to 1723 m at The Horn. The range is a granite mass in the form of a plateau 11 km long and 7 km wide, towering 1000 m above the plains. Most of the creeks flow north-east, following joints or cracks in the rocks, and Crystal Brook falls 240 m into The Gorge. Mount Buffalo was named by the explorers Hamilton Hume and William Hovell in 1824 on their journey from Sydney to Port Phillip Bay who thought that massive bluff resembled a buffalo. The dark rock walls remained unscaled for another 30 years. Today they are one of the state's most popular rock climbing challenges, and include a sheer 435 m rock face known as the North Wall.

Formation

Ancient seas once covered north-eastern Victoria, laying down deep layers of sedimentary rocks that were subsequently uplifted and folded. Some 300 million years ago subterranean activity forced up a mass of molten granite beneath the sedimentary rock, creating a plateau some 4000 m above sea level.

The softer sedimentary rocks have long since weathered away, exposing the underlying granite. All in all some 3 km of material has washed down from the plateau to create the vast plains through which the Murray and Ovens Rivers flow. Joints in the rock created when the granite cooled have been enlarged by ice and plants, eventually splitting the rock into the large blocks or tors that now dominate the plateau.

History

In the summer months Aboriginal people of the surrounding nations used to climb the plateau to feast on bogong moths, a fat-bodied insect that migrates from the plains in vast swarms to escape the heat. They were a great delicacy, roasted whole or made into cakes. This tradition was brought to an end by the European settlers who drove the Aborigines from the plains, introducing cattle and sheep and felling the trees.

Botanists Ferdinand von Mueller and John Dallachy were the first Europeans to study the natural history of the plateau. They climbed the mountain's southern flank and ascended The Horn in 1853, collecting and naming plants. The area gradually became popular with tourists, and simple accommodation was constructed near the Gorge in the 1880s.

A small part of the plateau was set aside as a national park in 1898, and the remainder of the park was declared in 1908. Limited grazing was, however, permitted on the plateau until 1958, and a number of severe fires were caused by graziers burning-off. The Chalet was built in 1910, and fortunately a proposal to build a multi-storey hotel, an inn and an artificial lake was abandoned after more than ten years of public protest.

Plants and Animals

The plateau is dominated by plants adapted to sub-alpine conditions. Here are beautiful twisted snow gums, tall stately alpine ash trees, mountain gums and other eucalypts such as the Buffalo sallee, a willow-like tree found only in this area. Under the shelter of the trees grow alpine shrubs including the endemic Buffalo sallow wattle and fern-leaf baeckea.

In the valleys on top of the plateau are patches of low heathy grassland. Covered in snow for at least three months of the year, the heaths are a mixture of low grasses, orchids, lilies, daisies, gentians, mosses and other native plants. They grow in clumps and tussocks or low mats for protection against the snow and freezing winds. In boggy areas mosses soak up water so that they can survive the long hot summers. They release water slowly throughout the year, adding to the constantly trickling mountain streams.

At the foot of the plateau are forests of narrow-leaved peppermints, manna gums, silver wattles and blackwood. Higher up the forest is dominated by tall peppermint gums and large candlebarks.

Despite the cold winters the area has a wide variety of animal life. Echidnas and platypuses are found in the lowlands, and the forests are home to ringtail and common brushtail possums and gliders, including the tiny feathertail glider. Among boulders in the snow gum woodlands you will see traces of common wombat diggings, or find these endearing marsupials ambling across the tracks at any time of day. Other mammals include swamp wallabies, marsupial mice including the small carnivorous dusky antechinus and brown antechinus, bush rats, bats and introduced rabbits.

Some 98 reptilian species have been identified. They include four snakes: the white-lipped snake, copperhead, brown snake and tiger snake. Basking on rocky outcrops you may see the short stocky mountain dragon, blue-tongued lizard and numerous skinks.

Among the approximately 130 bird species recorded are superb lyrebirds found in the dense forested gullies and around The Chalet, honeyeaters, robins, crimson rosellas, gang gang cockatoos, sulphur crested cockatoos and yellow-tailed black cockatoos. Rainbow bee-eaters may be seen along the creek banks, while in the grassy and swampy areas masked plovers and quails search for food. Among the larger birds are ravens, currawongs, wattlebirds and nankeen kestrels.

Walks

The park has 100 km of formed walking tracks, varying from nature walks to day-long hikes. The Gorge Heritage Walk is only 2 km long and starts at the Gorge Day Visitor Area opposite The Chalet. This is a beautiful walk through spectacular countryside and introduces visitors to some of the major plant communities in the park and the early days of tourism. Dicksons Falls Nature Walk is an easy 4 km return journey across the plateau through different habitats to the lookout at Dicksons Falls, with views to the Australian Alps in the distance.

Short walks in The Chalet district or on some of the tracks near the main road are recommended for day visitors. Those with more time can embark on any of the tracks that crisscross the plateau, or climb some of the tors like The Monolith.

Facilities

The camping ground at Lake Catani is superb, with toilets, showers and fireplaces. It is only open from November to May, and sites should be booked well in advance during holiday periods (03-5756 2328).

The Visitor Centre at the Park Office has maps, books and other publications, and the rangers conduct walks, talks, nature tours and children's activities in summer and winter peak periods. During the ski season the Visitor Centre moves to Cresta Valley where a 24-hour answering service gives skiing conditions.

Winter motel and lodge accommodation is available at Tatra Inn (03-5755 1988). The Chalet provides guesthouse accommodation all year round (03-5755 1500). Meals are available at these locations, but there are no other supplies in the park and no fuel beyond Porepunkah. The nearest township is Porepunkah, 32 km away. Facilities are provided for downhill, cross country skiing and tobogganing, with ski lifts, ski hire and ski schools.

Access

The park is 320 km from Melbourne via the well-sealed but winding road from Porepunkah. The main roads within the park are sealed, but you must carry snow chains in winter.

Climate

Winters are cold with frequent snowfalls, and apart from skiing the best time to visit is from November to April. Summers are usually warm with cool nights, but can turn suddenly cold, with snow at any time of year.

Mt Buffalo National Park, Mt Buffalo, Vic 3745. Tel. (03) 5755 1466. Cresta Valley, Tel. (03) 5755 1585 or (03) 5755 1216 for skiing conditions.

Mount Buffalo National Park

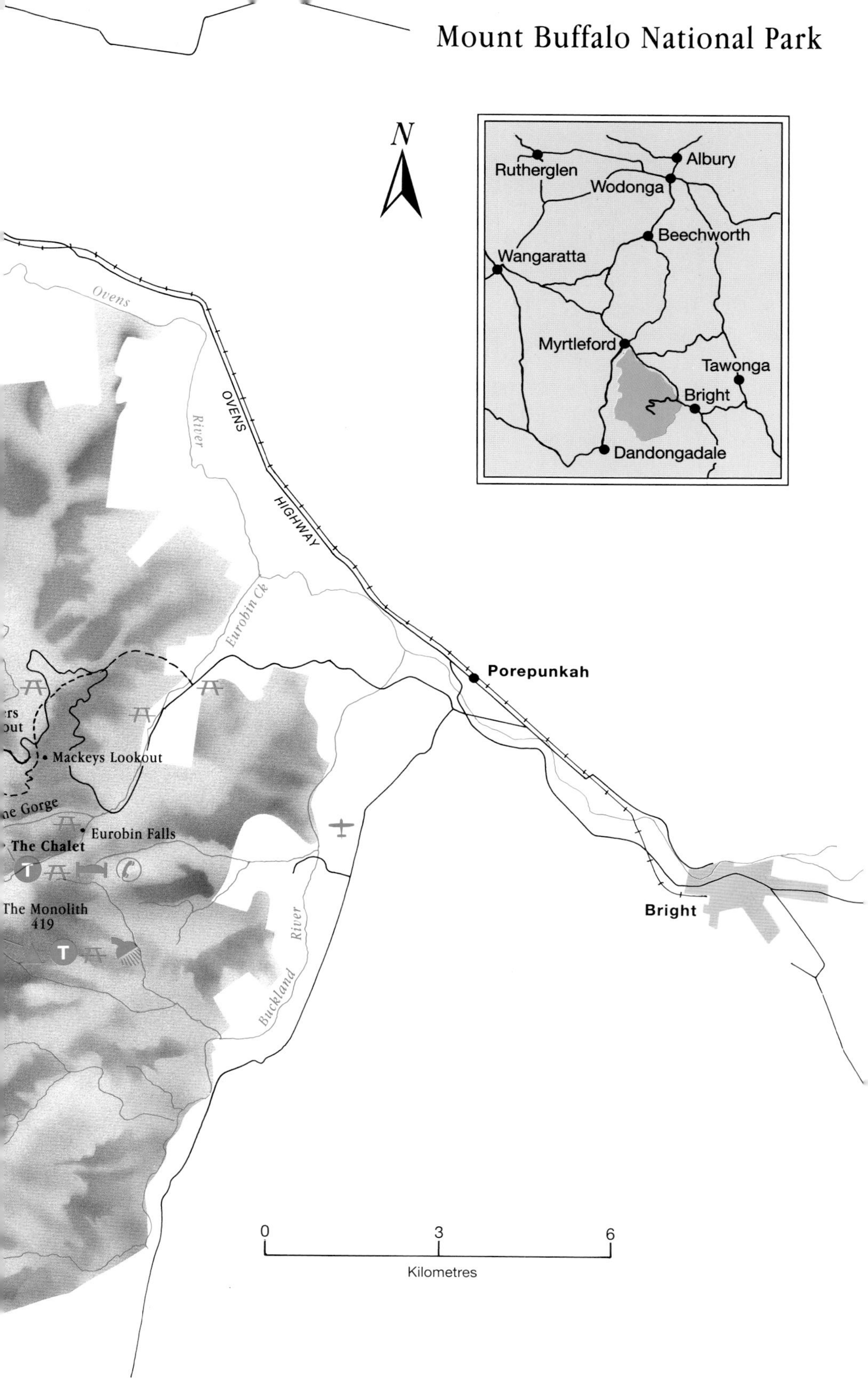

N

Inset map labels:
Rutherglen
Albury
Wodonga
Beechworth
Wangaratta
Myrtleford
Tawonga
Bright
Dandongadale

Ovens

OVENS

River

HIGHWAY

Eurobin Ck

Porepunkah

Mackeys Lookout

ne Gorge

Eurobin Falls

The Chalet

The Monolith
419

Buckland River

Bright

0   3   6

Kilometres

Fraser National Park

Located on the western shores of Lake Eildon, Fraser National Park is a rugged, hilly area once used by graziers and gold-diggers, and now being allowed to return to its original forested state. The lake provides ideal conditions for boating, fishing and water sports in a picturesque setting backed by the grandeur of the Victorian Alps.

This 3750 ha park was declared in 1957, two years after completion of Eildon Dam. The resulting Lake Eildon stores almost four million megalitres of water which generates electricity and helps to irrigate the Goulburn Valley. The original Eildon Dam was built in the 1920s and the lake was known as Sugarloaf Reservoir. When the dam was extended in 1955 the surrounding farmland, forest and buildings gradually disappeared under water, and during periods of prolonged drought the buildings begin to re-emerge as eerie reminders of the past.

The landscape is of hills and ridges with steep spurs of land jutting out into the tranquil waters of the lake. The western boundary follows the sandstone ridge of the lower Puzzle Range, with panoramic views over Coller Bay and the surrounding peaks.

Formation

The sandstone, mudstone and shale rocks of the area were formed some 400 million years ago when this part of Australia was submerged beneath a shallow sea. A period of uplift and folding of the land over subsequent years allowed some of the earth's molten rock to escape through faults, forming plugs of volcanic rock. These igneous rocks are rich in minerals, including gold, and held out the promise of Eldorado to the gold diggers who swarmed to the area in the 1860s. Some struck it rich, but most left as poor as they came.

Evidence of the geological origins of the park can be seen in roadside cuttings where sedimentary strata run in coloured bands, plunging into bowl-shaped synclines or sweeping upwards into dome-shaped anticlines. The fossilised remains of some of Australia's oldest known woody plants have been discovered in these ancient sediments.

History

White settlers began moving into the area in 1839 in search of grazing land to feed the ever-increasing ovine population. They had no interest in the Yauung Illam Baluk people who had lived in the valleys and surrounding hills for thousands of years, regarding them as black devils who performed pagan ceremonies.

Squatters occupied their tribal lands, and these gentle-natured indigenous people were soon decimated by introduced European diseases and robbed of their traditional lands and culture.

Relics of the gold mining days are still to be found in the park in the form of abandoned shafts, trenches and ruined buildings. The miners used timber from the forests for mine props, and the graziers cleared large areas to create grasslands to feed their sheep.

Proposals to dam the Goulburn River were acted upon in the 1920s, and a small dam was built at Eildon to provide extra irrigation water for the Goulburn Valley. This was enlarged in 1955, flooding a large grazing property resumed by the State Government. The house reappeared during the 1968 and 1983 droughts, remarkably intact, with the shingles still attached to the roof.

In 1956 the newly-formed National Parks Authority recommended that the acquired land surrounding the lake be included in a new national park to protect the catchment area and allow the forest to regenerate. The National Park was duly declared in 1957 and named after the chairman of the Authority, A. J. Fraser.

Plants and Animals

Most of the land in the park has been logged and cleared for farming, although small patches of the original forest remain, noticeably around the Lakeside camping area. However, removing the stock and reducing the rabbit population have allowed the seeds of native plants to grow, and forests of red stringybark, narrow and broad-leaved peppermint, candlebark, red box and silver wattle are regenerating well and beginning to clothe the denuded hillsides.

Large numbers of eastern grey kangaroos graze on the grassy slopes, particularly around the camping areas. Swamp wallabies move around singly or in pairs in the more densely timbered areas, coming out to feed in the evening. Koalas can be seen and possums and wombats are commonly encountered at night if you walk along one of the tracks with a torch.

Gang gang cockatoos are often heard in some parts of the park. They make a sound like the creak of rusty door hinges. Crimson rosellas and noisy miners frequent the camping areas looking for free food. The shrubby areas abound with small bush birds, such as wrens, thornbills, fantails, rufous and golden whistlers, yellow and scarlet robins.

In the open forest areas you are likely to see wedge-tailed eagles soaring overhead, red wattlebirds, ravens and pardalotes. Around the lake waterbirds and waders such as the white ibis, black and pied cormorants, pelicans, ducks, black swans and white-faced herons enjoy the tranquillity, while beneath the water brown and rainbow trout swim.

Walks

Walking tracks lead to most parts of the park, the majority beginning in the Devil Cove area. Candlebark Gully Nature Walk should not be missed. This is a 2 km self-guiding walk beginning at Devil Cove and passing through old gold mining areas, various habitat types and an old stand of candlebark trees.

Short but strenuous hikes will take you to lookouts on the spurs and ridges with spectacular vistas over the surrounding countryside.

A challenging full-day hike goes from Devil Cove to Skyline Road. It ascends Keg Spur and follows the Blowhard Spur Track where steep, well-wooded slopes descend on each side of the track. Follow Skyline Road north for 1 km and turn off past the house and shearing shed to the east along the vehicle track that runs along the edge of the park to Aird Inlet.

Take the Blowhard Track back to Keg Spur, or continue around the shore of the lake to Wallaby Bay, a longer route, but flat and pleasantly shaded.

Facilities

Spacious camping areas catering for tents and caravans, with picnic tables, fireplaces, toilets, showers and laundry facilities are located on the southern shore of Coller Bay at Devil Cove, Candlebark and Lakeside.

A number of cabins are also available for rent. Both these and the camp sites are heavily booked during holiday periods, and reservations should be made well in advance.

Accommodation is also available at Alexandra, Eildon and Thornton.

Boat launching ramps are provided on the shore of Coller Bay. Water skiing, wind surfing, power boating, sailing and fishing are all popular activities.

The park is 175 km from Melbourne and 17 km north-east of Alexandra along sealed roads. A daily bus service connects Alexandra to Melbourne.

Climate

The park has warm summers and cold winters. The best times to visit are spring, summer and autumn.

Fraser National Park, Park Rd, Alexandra, Vic 3714. Tel. (03) 5772 1293.

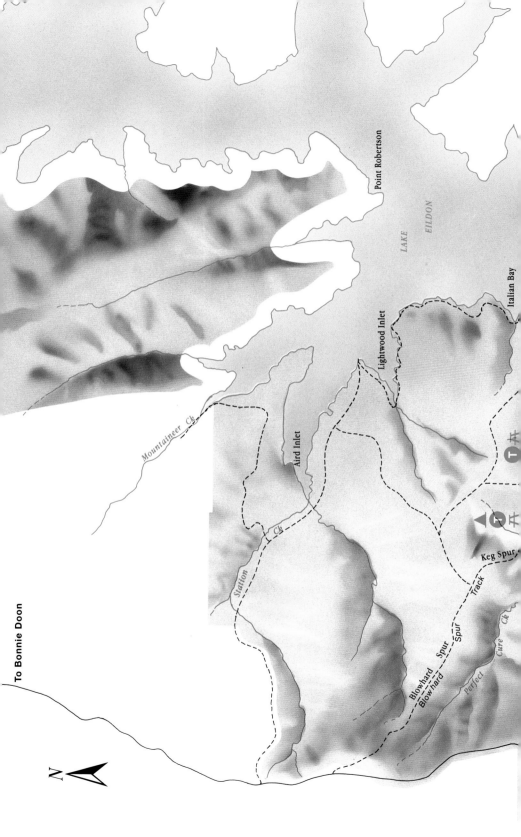

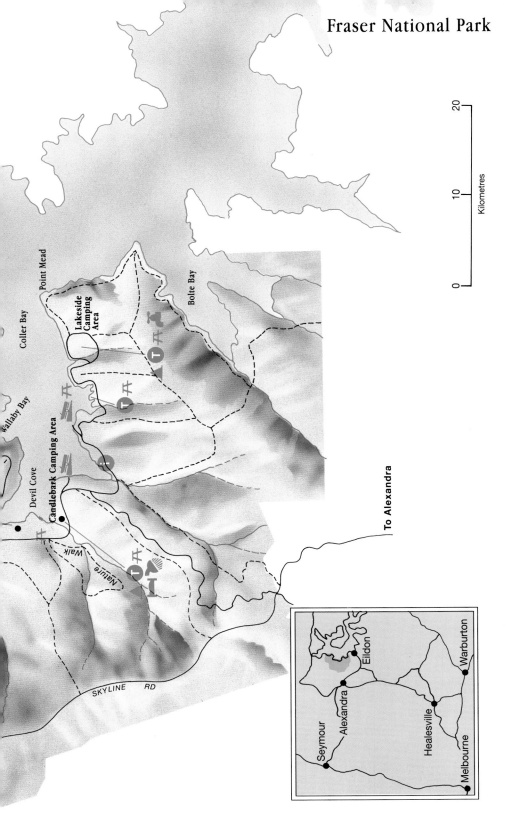

Fraser National Park

Wilsons Promontory National Park

Wilsons Promontory is the most southerly point of the Australian mainland and the site of Victoria's most popular national park. Known locally as the Prom, the park occupies a rugged peninsula jutting out into Bass Strait, with a magnificent coastline of steep granite cliffs and headlands plunging to white beaches and sheltered bays.

The 50,300 ha park is attached to the mainland by a narrow neck of sand known as Yanakie Isthmus. This low-lying area, with long sandy beaches to the west and mangrove flats to the east, creates a stark contrast to the granite outcrops and mountain ranges that form the backbone of the peninsula. Here are luxuriant fern gullies, tall forests on the mountain slopes, heaths, woodlands and spectacular views over coastal headlands, beaches and islands.

Formation

The granite mass that forms the main part of the Promontory was created about 350 million years ago from molten rock that welled up from below the earth's crust. This rock eventually cooled and solidified into granite. Over time the overlying rocks eroded away exposing the granite, which itself has gradually worn down to create the landforms we see today.

Several times in the last million years ice ages have caused the sea level to fall as much as 150 m below its present level. The Promontory would then have been part of a chain of mountains linking mainland Australia to Tasmania. This land bridge was last severed towards the end of the most recent ice age some 12,000 years ago, and the mountain tops became the Bass Strait Islands. Wilsons Promontory was also an island at that time, but the gap between the mainland gradually filled with drifting sands to create Yanakie Isthmus, joining the Promontory to mainland Australia.

Settlement

The Promontory was known as Wamoom to the original inhabitants of the area. They were people of the Brataualung clan, who belonged to the Gippsland Kurnai nation. They harvested fish and shellfish around the coast and collected seabirds and their eggs from the offshore islands. During the winter months they moved inland to sheltered areas to hunt for game and gather edible plants.

George Bass and his crew were the first Europeans to see Wilsons Promontory. They passed by in 1798 on their epic whaleboat voyage from Port Jackson. Sealers and whalers soon followed, operating from safe anchorages at Sealers Cove and Refuge Cove, where they boiled the blubber to extract whale oil. There is little doubt that their interactions with the Brataualung people were far from pleasant.

Timber cutting, tin mining and grazing were important activities on the Promontory, and despite the building of a lighthouse on Southeast Point in 1859, ships still run aground on the hidden reefs and islands.

Naturalists and local conservation groups were instrumental in the Victorian Government's decision to reserve part of the area for public use in 1898. The National Park was declared in 1905, and subsequent additions have expanded the park to its present size.

Plants and Animals

Many different habitats occur in the park, and more than 700 species of native plants have been recorded here. The sandy isthmus supports grasslands and tea-tree scrub, while across the isthmus at Millers Landing the white mangrove reaches its most southerly point, colonising the tidal mud flats that make up much of this area.

In sheltered gullies between the granite peaks are pockets of temperate rainforest with lilly pilly trees growing alongside blackwood, stinkwood and swamp gum. Elsewhere are heathlands interspersed with open woodlands of old man banksias and grasstrees, alongside tea trees, hakeas, swamp she-oaks, guinea flowers and wedding bushes. The heaths are ablaze with wildflowers in spring.

Higher up in the mountain gullies are stands of ancient Antarctic beech trees dripping with mosses and ferns in cool temperate rainforest patches.

There are tall eucalypt forests on the mountain slopes and valleys with stringybarks, messmates, blue gums, peppermints and manna gums. Koalas find these trees much to their liking, and are often seen in the fork of a tree quietly munching away at the leaves.

Other large animals, such as eastern grey kangaroos, swamp wallabies, wombats, possums and emus, are commonly seen in the park, and Australian fur seals live around the offshore islands.

One of the park's special features is the tameness of the birds and animals at Tidal River camp ground. Flocks of beautiful crimson rosellas frequent the area, perching on anyone who proffers food, a practice that is detrimental to the health and biology of the wildlife.

In the heathlands honeyeaters and wattle-birds are active searching among the plants for nectar, pollen and insects. Wrens, robins and other small bush birds are busy foraging in the gullies.

Walks

There are more than 130 km of graded walking tracks in the park, ranging from short nature walks to long overnight hikes.

The Lilly Pilly Gully Nature Walk is a good introduction to the park and its habitats. This self-guiding walk takes less than three hours round trip, and begins on the main road near Tidal River. The track passes through heathland and eucalypt forest where koalas are commonly seen, into the beautiful rainforest at Lilly Pilly Gully, and past granite rock formations where the processes of erosion and soil formation are visibly active. A 4 km track goes from the return leg of this walk to the summit of Mount Bishop.

Many other short walks lead from the main

road to beautiful beaches such as Squeaky Beach, Picnic Bay and Whisky Bay, where there is good swimming, surfing and fishing. The Millers Landing Nature Walk is a 2.5 km walk from the car park on Five Mile Road through banksia woodlands to the most southerly mangroves in the world at Corner Inlet.

Several tracks lead to the scenic eastern and southern areas. Some take more than one day. Permits must be obtained for all overnight hikes.

There are overnight camping areas with pit toilets beside or near the walking tracks. Check with the ranger on water availability and carry a fuel stove as fires are not permitted in the park.

Facilities

The Tidal River area has a large camping ground with sites for both tents and caravans, and a number of fully equipped holiday lodges and cabins. The campsites, cabins and lodges are in great demand during holiday seasons and must be booked well in advance.

The information centre has slide shows, and the rangers organise walks and spotlight tours during peak holiday periods. There is an open-air cinema, laundry, general store, kiosk, petrol station and a resident doctor in the summer.

Many picnic areas are provided, some have electric barbecues. Most of the offshore islands are included in the park, but camping is not permitted on any of them. Bush camping is allowed at designated sites with the ranger's permission. Fuel stoves only.

Access

The park is 200 km south-east of Melbourne via the South Gippsland Highway, turn off at Meeniyan or Foster. Tidal River is 30 km from the park entrance via a sealed road.

Climate

Summers are warm and winters cool. The heaths are particularly beautiful in spring when the wildflowers are in bloom.

Wilsons Promontory National Park,
Tidal River, Via Foster, Vic 3960.
Tel. (03) 5680 9555.

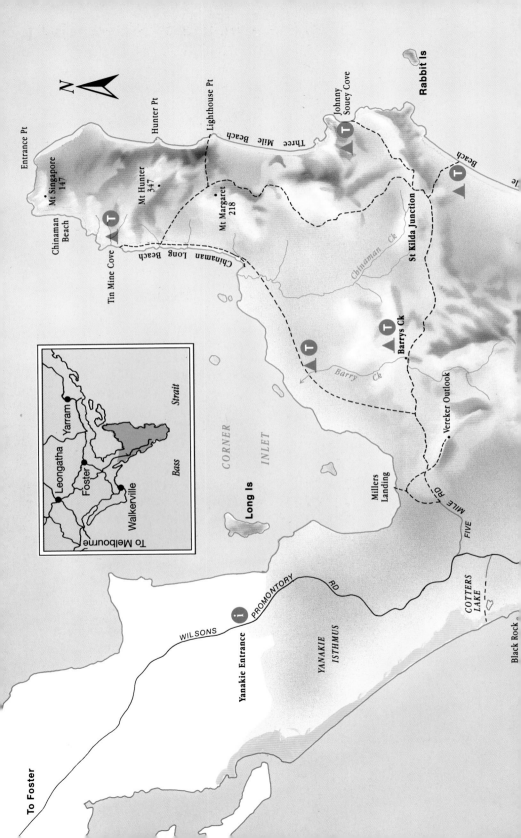

Wilsons Promontory National Park

BASS STRAIT

Refuge Cove

Kersop Peak
223

Cape Wellington

Sealers Cove

Waterloo Bay

South East Pt

Mt La Trobe
754

Mt Wilson
705

Sealers Ck

South Peak
380

Mt Boulder
500

Roaring Meg Ck

Groane Ck

Tidal River

Lilly Pilly Gully

Halfway Hut

Roaring Meg

South Pt

Mt Leonard
560

Mt Bishop
319

Mt Oberon
558

Oberon Bay

Fraser Ck

Mt Norgate
419

Wattle Is

Leonard Bay

Norman Bay

Oberon Pt

South West Pt

Darby River

Whisky Bay

Picnic Bay

Leonard Pt

Squeaky Beach

Pillar Pt

Norman Pt

Anser Is

Darby Bay

Fairy Cove

Tongue Pt

Norman Is

Shellback Is

Five

Tidal River

Glennie Group

0   4   8

Kilometres

Kinglake National Park

Only one hour north of Melbourne, Kinglake National Park is in a low range of hills that form part of the Great Dividing Range. Walking tracks leading through wooded valleys, along forested spurs and into cool, fern-filled gullies make this a favourite area for bushwalkers and a perfect setting for the beautiful Masons and Wombelano waterfalls.

Kinglake National Park is in four sections and covers an area of 21,600 ha, rising to 625 m at Andrews Hill in the northern section. The Kinglake Road runs along a plateau at an elevation of between 450 m and 550 m, effectively separating the northern section from the eastern and western sections on the southern slopes of the range.

The north–south spurs are separated by steep, damp valleys where the creeks plunge from the plateau to the lowlands on their way to the Yarra River. From lookouts visitors can take in the panoramic view of the Yarra Valley, Port Phillip Bay and the You Yangs Range.

The underlying sandstone and mudstone rocks of the area were laid down about 350 million years ago and contain some well-preserved marine fossils, showing that the area was at that time submerged beneath the sea. Subsequent uplifting and folding of the land and millions of years of erosion have created the present elevated landscape of hills and the deeply dissected plateau.

The plateau has a relatively high rainfall of around 1200 mm per year, and is often shrouded in cloud. Rain has eroded the rocks to create the rich red soils of the plateau, now largely cleared for agriculture, while the soils on the slopes have been leached by rain and are much less fertile.

History

Goldminers rushed to the area in the 1850s, and reminders of their toil can still be seen, such as the abandoned mining shafts near Steels Creek picnic area. Timber was cut first by the miners and later by loggers who supplied firewood and building materials to the expanding construction industry in Melbourne.

Local conservationists lobbied hard to have this beautiful area protected from further logging

and clearing for agriculture, and the section south of the Great Dividing Range was declared a national park in 1928. The park soon became a popular tourist destination for Melburnians, and guesthouses and tea rooms were built.

The northern section was greatly extended in 1980, almost doubling the size of the park, and another major extension in 1995 added 10,000 ha of land to the north and west of Kinglake West. The latest addition has high conservation values with stands of old growth mountain ash and temperate rainforest. It is designated a water catchment area for Melbourne and has no visitor access.

This piecemeal approach to conservation has, unfortunately, left the park with four unconnected sections, too many access points and an extensive boundary surrounded by private properties. Domestic pets on adjoining properties use parts of the park as their hunting grounds, seriously affecting the native wildlife, and being so close to a large city the park suffers from some of the problems associated with very high usage.

Plants and Animals

Eucalypt forests are the predominant vegetation type in the park, with a canopy of broad-leaved and narrow-leaved peppermints, red stringybark, messmate stringybark, red box and long-leaved box trees.

The northern section has less rainfall and poorer soils than areas south of the Great Divide, and the trees are more stunted and the forest more open. The understorey here is adapted to the dry, infertile conditions, and includes grasstrees, hairpin banksias, orchids, pea plants, myrtles and heath plants.

In the sheltered southern gullies and valleys numerous ferns, treeferns and mosses grow in profusion alongside shrubs and small trees such as the Austral mulberry, musk daisy bush, Victorian Christmas bush and blanket leaf.

The creeks are an ideal habitat for platypuses and water rats, and the forests are inhabited by swamp wallabies, koalas, echidnas, possums, bandicoots and marsupial mice. Eastern grey kangaroos graze in the open areas in the evenings.

More than 90 species of birds have been identified in the park. These include the superb lyrebird whose calls are often heard in the gullies. These beautiful birds are rarely seen except at the Jehosaphat Gully picnic area, and winter visitors may be rewarded with the sight of a male superb lyrebird displaying on his mound.

The sound of a creaking door in the forest is likely to be the call of a gang gang cockatoo. Currawongs, crimson rosellas and kookaburras are regular visitors to the picnic areas, while in the moist gullies grey shrike thrushes, superb fairy wrens, scrub wrens, eastern yellow robins and white-throated tree creepers are common. White-eared honeyeaters and eastern spinebills are often seen foraging among the banksias and heath plants.

Walks

Bushwalking is one of the most popular activities, and the park has many well-graded tracks. Two tracks have been specially constructed for people with limited mobility. The 500 m Cicada Circuit Track from The Gums camping area meanders along Island Creek where koalas are often seen, and the Lyrebird Walk at the Masons Falls picnic area is a short and very interesting nature trail.

At the other end of the spectrum is the 20 km, full-day Everard Circuit Walk. This begins at Jehosaphat Gully picnic area and takes you through the different park habitats, winding up to Mount Jerusalem and Mount Everard where the views over the park and the city are superb.

Short tracks lead to the beautiful Wombelano Falls in the northern section, where lyrebirds are often heard calling around the slopes of the gully, and to Masons Falls in the western section through a forest of messmate trees with lush ferns in the gully.

An interesting half-day walk takes you from the park office through a messmate forest to Running Creek. The track follows the creek through different vegetation types before climbing up to Mount Sugarloaf where there are good views over Melbourne and the surrounding ranges. The trail continues along the ridge before heading back to the park office.

Facilities

There is an excellent camping area set among tall eucalypts and ferns close to a meandering mountain stream at The Gums in the northern section of the park. Advance booking is essential as only 12 sites are provided, four of these are suitable for caravans, and two are for overnight walkers. Pit toilets, wood barbecues and tank water are provided.

The picnic areas at Masons Falls and Jehosaphat Gully have gas or electric barbecues, water and toilets. Wood fires are prohibited at these picnic areas, although visitors may bring their own gas barbecues. There is a park office and information centre near Masons Falls.

Horse riding and mountain bike riding is permitted in some sections of the park, and only on designated trails. Contact the park office for details.

Access

The park is 65 km north-east of Melbourne via the Melba Highway from Yarra Glen. From Whittlesea take the Whittlesea to Kinglake Road; or take the Heidelberg to Kinglake Road via Eltham.

Climate

The park has warm summers and cool winters and is particularly beautiful in springtime when the wildflowers are at their best. In winter superb lyrebirds may be seen doing their courtship display.

Kinglake National Park, National Park Rd, Pheasant Creek, Vic 3757.
Tel. (03) 5786 5351.

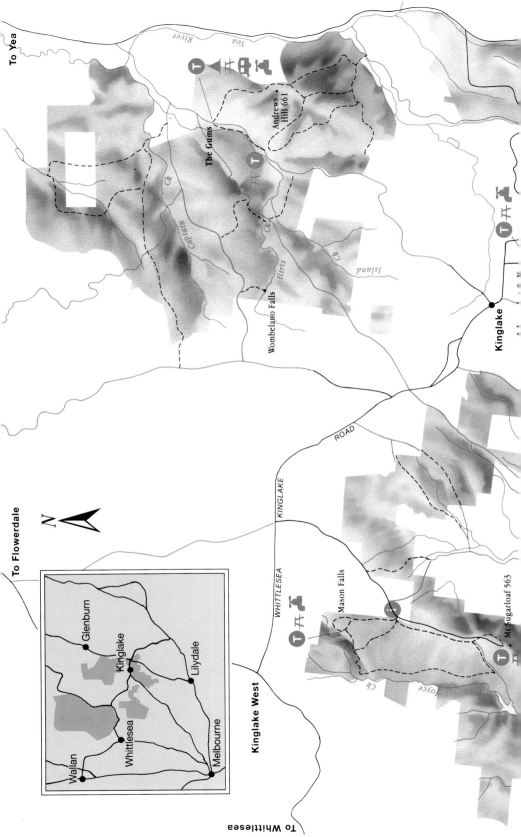

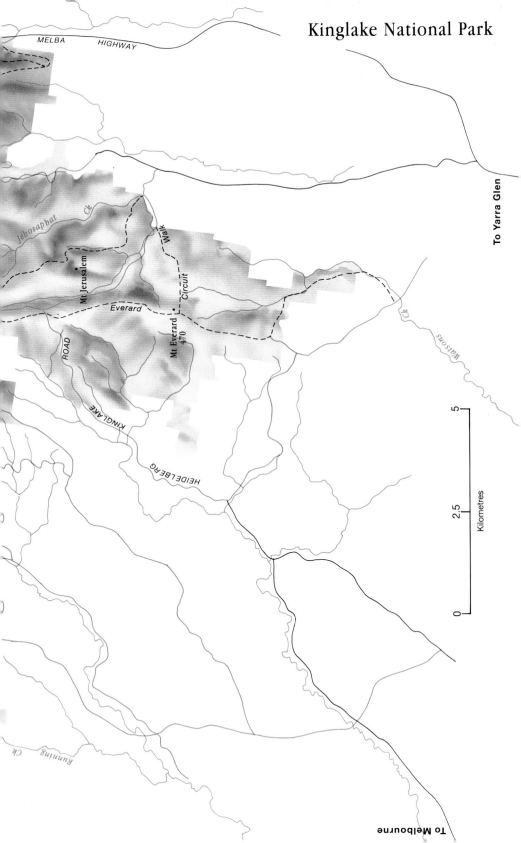

Kinglake National Park

Brisbane Ranges National Park

Little more than an hour's drive from Melbourne takes you to the state's richest wildflower habitat. Set in a low range of mountains dissected by rocky gullies, Brisbane Ranges National Park provides a refuge for plants and animals displaced by agricultural activities in the surrounding districts. The area's unusual geology has preserved plants that have long since vanished from other parts of the region, together with a correspondingly diverse bird population and the greatest density of koalas in Victoria.

Rowsley Fault marks the eastern boundary of the Brisbane Ranges. Along this line the land falls abruptly to the low-lying Port Phillip Basin. Deep gullies such as Anakie Gorge cut into the eastern scarp, while the western area is a gently undulating plateau rising to 400 m.

The area is in a rain shadow and has a low annual rainfall of only 680 mm. The dry-looking hills and infertile soils of the park have protected it from the farmers and graziers, who have cleared the more fertile lands to the east and south. These harsh conditions nurture some of the most magnificent wildflower displays in the country, and the diversity of habitats found in the hills, valleys and gullies provide ideal conditions for some 475 plant species, about one-sixth of Victoria's total flora.

Formation

The oldest rocks in the region are slates and sandstones deposited on the bed of an ancient shallow sea more than 500 million years ago. Subterranean activity 100 million years later forced molten magma into the deeper rock layers. In some places cracks in the bedrock allowed the molten rock to penetrate into the upper sedimentary rocks, forming vertical dykes. These granitic rock intrusions are rich in quartz and minerals, including gold.

Millions of years of erosion subsequently cut deep into the sedimentary rocks, followed by global cooling when sheets of ice covered the land. The melting ice left piles of broken rock that eventually consolidated into tillite, a multi-coloured rock found in local quarries.

Erosion continued, wearing down the mountains until most of Victoria became a featureless plain with winding rivers flowing into great coastal deltas. Thick layers of sandstone were laid down along the coast, and these were overlaid in places by basaltic lava from volcanoes that began erupting in the area some 70 million years ago.

This period of volcanic activity finally ceased about one million years ago when the area was uplifted along the Rowsley Fault, leaving the low-lying Port Phillip Basin to the east. Rivers and streams have since carved their way deep into the layers of rock, creating gorges and valleys, and exposing seams of gold-bearing rock.

History

Before the arrival of the Europeans the Brisbane Ranges were within the territory of the Kurung, an Aboriginal nation controlling 3400 sq km of land to the west of Port Phillip Bay. The Wathaurog clan occupied the Brisbane Ranges, and a number of archaeological sites have been discovered, including quarries by the Moorabool River, workshop areas, and a shallow cave containing various artefacts.

Squatters arrived in the 1830s, concentrating their farming activities on the fertile land to the east and south along the Moorabool River. The Kurung were forced from their lands and either worked for the squatters or fled to the hills where those who survived were decimated by introduced diseases and the arrival of thousands of gold-hungry prospectors.

The goldrush began in 1851. Prospectors scoured the ranges, cutting trees for mine props, building timber and firewood. The town of Steiglitz was built on the fortunes of the gold miners. But this was short lived, and apart from a brief revival in the early 1900s the town began to decline in the 1870s as the gold seams petered out. Today Steiglitz is a ghost town maintained for the benefit of tourists.

The Upper and Lower Stony Creek Dams were completed in 1873, creating a reservoir to supply Geelong's growing population, and 3000 ha of the Brisbane Ranges were reserved as a catchment area.

The flora, fauna and beauty of the Brisbane Ranges have long attracted naturalists, and 1132 ha were declared a national park in 1973. The park was enlarged to 7470 ha in 1979, and to 7718 ha in 1995 by incorporating the adjacent Steiglitz Historic Park.

Plants and Animals

The leached and infertile soils of the higher areas support eucalypt woodlands of peppermints, white sallee and brown stringybark with a heath understorey. Acacias, grasstrees and some of the area's more unusual and endemic plants grow on these poor soils. They include the Brisbane Ranges grevillea, the rusty pomaderris and golden grevillea, normally found in Gippsland, and plants like the scented bush-pea and velvet daisy-bush, typical of western Victoria. Insectivorous plants such as sundews and bladderworts are common in damp areas, and a great array of ground orchids like the blue caladenia and rare brittle greenhood can be seen. In the gullies and sheltered sites along the creeks are stands of eucalypts such as manna and swamp gums, host trees for koalas, with an understorey of shrubs such as the woolly tea-tree, dense mint bush and sticky boronia.

Among the mammals are grey kangaroos, swamp wallabies, echidnas, possums and gliders. Koalas are common, and their numbers have increased over the years by introductions from Phillip and French Islands. Small mammals are not well represented.

More than 180 bird species have been recorded in the park. Of these, three species are of particular interest: the brightly coloured yellow-tufted honeyeater, the white-throated nightjar and the rainbow bee-eater. Nesting high in the cliffs are magnificent peregrine falcons and wedge-tailed eagles.

Walks

One of the most popular and interesting walks is the Anakie Gorge Walk, most of which is suitable for wheelchairs. This 3 km track leads through the gorge between the picnic areas at Anakie Gorge and Stony Creek. Koalas are often seen in the manna gums alongside the creek. Nelsons Track (3 km one way) intersects the Anakie Gorge Walk some 2 km from Stony Creek Picnic Area and climbs to the ridge top to Nelsons Lookout with views over the gorge and reservoir.

There are panoramic views over the Stony Creek catchment from the Outlook, reached from Stony Creek Picnic Area via the Outlook Track, a 2 km walk climbing over the saddle. A circuit from here reveals a diverse display of wildflowers in spring. An easy 2.5 km return track, the Kurung Walk, climbs steadily from Stony Creek Picnic Area north to join Switch Road, where there are views over the You Yangs and Anakie Gorge.

Tracks lead from the picnic areas to various lookouts and through heathy forests where there are magnificent spring wildflower displays. A three day walk through the park has been developed; notes available from the park office.

Facilities

The camping area at Boar Gully is equipped with basic facilities, and advance booking should be made, particularly during holiday periods. Collecting firewood is not allowed; campers should bring a fuel stove. Accommodation and supplies are available at Bacchus Marsh.

Access

The park is 80 km west of Melbourne via Princes Highway, turn onto the Ballan Road from Geelong; or take the Western Freeway to Bacchus Marsh and follow the Geelong Road, turning off to Boar Gully.

Climate

The park has a fairly low rainfall with warm to hot summers and cool winters. Visit in spring for the wildflower displays.

Brisbane Ranges National Park, Ballan Rd, Anakie, Vic 3221. Tel. (03) 5284 1230.

To Bacchus Marsh

Sapling Gully
Picnic Area

Spring Ck

AEROPLANE RD

Brisbane Track

Sheoak Hill

THOMPSONS RD

Boar Gully

To Ballan

Mount Wallace

Reilly Ck

Bacchus Marsh

Mt Wallace

Melbourne

Anakie

Inverleigh

Geelong

Kilometres

0   2   4

Brisbane Ranges National Park

To Bacchus Marsh

To Werribee

Staughton Vale

Little River

Stony Ck

GRANITE RD

Anakie Gorge
Picnic Area

STAUGHTON VALE RD

To Geelong

Griffin Hill

Stony Creek
Picnic Area

Anakie Gorge
Walk

Nelsons
Track

Nelsons
Lookout

Kurung
Walk

SWITCH RD

LOWER
RESERVOIR

Track

Outlook

Outlook

UPPER
RESERVOIR

Yankee Gully

Steiglitz

To Maude

To Meredith

To Meredith

N

Otway National Park

The Otway Ranges plunge in forest-clad slopes to the deserted beaches and sandstone cliffs of the southern Victorian coast, creating a landscape of rare beauty and ecological diversity. Luxuriant eucalypt forests, fern gullies, cool temperate rainforests, heathlands and a spectacular coastline characterise Otway National Park, a major scenic attraction on the Great Ocean Road.

The 12,750 ha park protects the catchment area of the Calder, Parker and Elliott Rivers, and includes a narrow coastal strip from Cape Otway to Princetown. This is a varied and dramatic area of worn sandstone cliffs, sand dunes and excellent surfing beaches between rugged headlands.

The Otway Range runs in a south-westerly direction for some 80 km branching south to Cape Otway and west to Lavers Hill. The park preserves the southern branch of the range, where the rainfall is high and the soils are rich in nutrients, supporting tall eucalypt forests.

Much of the remainder is state forest and suffers from logging activities and pine plantations. Strong arguments have been raised to include other areas such as the West Barham Valley and its ancient forests in the park, the boundaries of which appear to have been drawn along economic rather than ecological lines.

Formation

The area was an inland depression some 150 million years ago when the Gondwanan landmass was being torn apart. Rivers flowing from the eroding hills and mountains deposited deep layers of sediments in the Otway Basin, eventually compressing to form the sandstones, mudstones and shales of the area. The coastal sediments have proved to be a rich source of plant and animal fossils, including dinosaur fossils and the earliest known fossils of the acacias.

As the continents drifted apart the land south of a faultline running from Cape Otway northeast to Airey's Inlet subsided, allowing the sea to flood into the area, creating the southern coastline. The rocks along the faultline are tilted up and form the steep cliffs along this section of the coast. To the north the land was lifted about 700 m in a complex domed structure to form the Otway Range.

History

Bass and Flinders proved the existence of Bass Strait in 1798, and Lieutenant James Grant aboard the Lady Nelson named Cape Otway in 1800. The Strait cut the sea journey around the southern coast by up to five days, but many ships floundered on the treacherous coastline before the lighthouse was built in 1848.

Timber cutters quickly moved into the area, felling the huge trees around Apollo Bay and Lorne, dragging the logs to the shore by bullock teams where they were floated out to ships. The first sawmill opened in 1852 at Apollo Bay, and a tramway was constructed from a mill at Elliott River to Apollo Bay, 6 km away. Part of the tramway can still be seen.

Selectors arrived at the Otways in the 1880s and began ringbarking, felling and burning magnificent trees in their bid to clear the land for farming. Fortunately the poor access and the immensity of the task left many allotments only partially cleared or untouched. The Otways became the major supplier of timber to the gold mines in the Ballarat region, and timber production peaked in the 1920s and again in the 1940s with the housing boom.

Otway National Park was created to protect the area's biological, historical and landscape values. The nearby Melba Gully State Park, sometimes called the Jewel of the Otways, was donated to the people of Victoria in 1975. This beautiful park preserves a cathedral-like gully crowded with Antarctic beech trees and tree ferns above an understorey of low ferns and mosses.

Plants and Animals

Forests of towering mountain ash and lush fern gullies greet the visitor to the Otways. These magnificent trees are second only to the

Californian redwoods in height. They form a dense canopy together with mountain grey gum, southern blue gum, messmate and manna gum, blocking out most of the sunlight and creating an open understorey.

The sheltered mountain gullies support pockets of cool temperate rainforest where the dark green leaves of ancient Antarctic beech trees contrast with the grey-green foliage of the eucalypts. Mosses and lichens cover the trunks, and among the buttresses grow bright orange fungi.

Dry open forests with a dense understorey grow on the more exposed slopes, and along the coast are grasslands and low shrubs. The skirted tree fern and forest boronia reach their western-most limits here, while the southern sassafras, common in the mountain forests of Victoria and Tasmania, is surprisingly absent from the forests of the Otways. Other absentees are the greater glider, the superb lyrebird, the pilot bird and the wombat, all found in similar habitats in Victoria.

Some 45 native mammal species have been recorded. They include the southern potoroo, the rare tiger cat, the platypus, yellow-bellied glider swamp wallaby, red-necked wallaby, echidna, and ten species of bat.

Of the 250 bird species more than half breed in the park, others, such as the wandering albatross from the Antarctic, the Japanese snipe, and the fluttering shearwater from Eurasia, are regular visitors. The forests are home to numer-ous species of honeyeaters and the magnificent grey goshawk, and are the westernmost limit of the satin bowerbird. The king parrot, powerful owl and rufous bristlebird are among the other notable birds of the park.

A rare carnivorous snail, the Otways black-snail, is often seen in the wet forests, and a fascinating inhabitant of Melba Gully is the larva of the fungus gnat, a tiny glow worm that hangs by sticky threads, attracting insects with its pale blue light.

Walks

A short walk through the rainforest of Melba Gully is a highlight of a visit to the Otways.

Indulge in some beachcombing on some of Victoria's best beaches, or head off into the forests where you will find magnificent trees, creeks and rainforest gullies. A short rainforest walk has been developed at Maits Rest, introduc-ing visitors to the cool temperate rainforests of the Otways.

From Shelly Beach Picnic Area a track leads downhill to the mouth of the Elliott River from where you can explore the rugged coastline. A track follows the ridge west of the river to Elliott Road, looping back to the picnic area, a fairly hard two hour walk.

From the Aire River Camping Area you can follow the coast to Cape Otway lighthouse and return via the inland route, a fairly easy eight hour round trip.

A stroll from Johanna Beach Camping Area leads along the coast to Rotten Point, passing the mouth of the Johanna River, along one of the State's best known surf beaches.

Facilities

There are three camping areas in the park with basic facilities, and fresh water is available from Parker River or Blanket Bay Creek. Blanket Bay is sheltered and close to a fine sandy beach. Sites should be booked in advance during peak holiday periods.

Apollo Beach has a full range of accommodation, and there are caravan parks along Lighthouse Road and at Princetown.

Access

The park is about 200 km south-west of Melbourne via the Princes Highway, turn off at Colac towards Lavers Hill and follow the Great Ocean Road into the park, or take the winding, scenic, Great Ocean Road from Geelong. Parker Road is frequently closed in wet weather.

Climate

The climate is temperate with sudden changes. Most of the rain falls in winter, when it can be very wet and cold.

Otway National Park, Cartwright St, Apollo Bay, Vic 3233. Tel. (03) 5237 6889. Lavers Hill: tel. (03) 5237 3243.

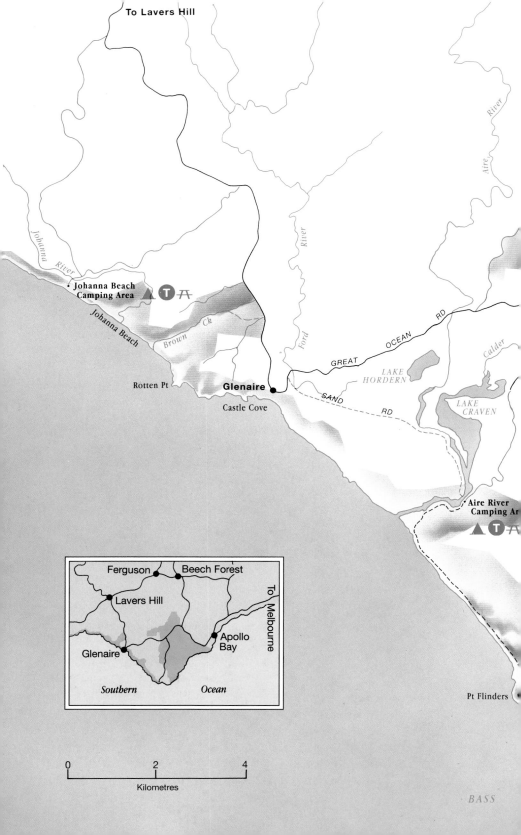

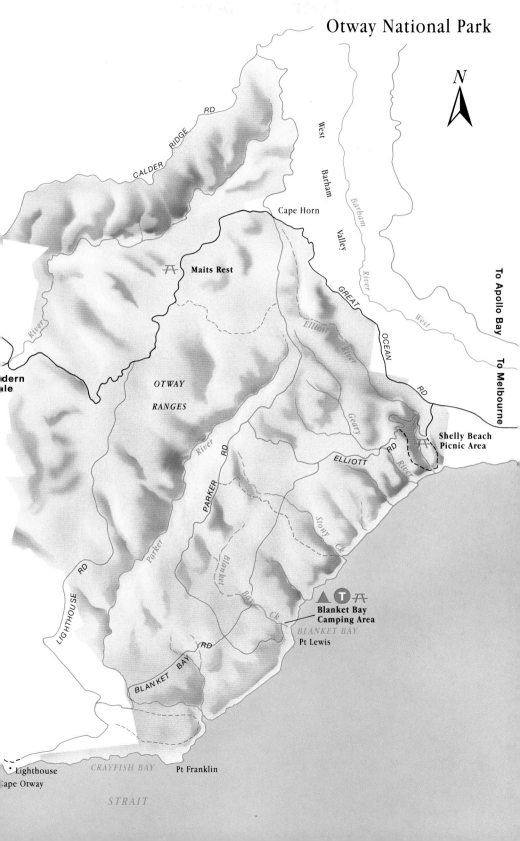

Otway National Park

N

CALDER RIDGE RD

West Barham Valley

Cape Horn

⊼ **Maits Rest**

Elliott River

GREAT OCEAN RD

Barham River

West

To Apollo Bay

To Melbourne

River

dern le

OTWAY
RANGES

River

PARKER RD

Geary

River

ELLIOTT RD

⊼ **Shelly Beach Picnic Area**

Parker

Stony Ck

LIGHTHOUSE RD

Blanket Bay

Ck

▲ T ⊼
Blanket Bay Camping Area

BLANKET BAY

Pt Lewis

RD

BLANKET BAY

• Lighthouse
ape Otway

CRAYFISH BAY

Pt Franklin

STRAIT

Lower Glenelg National Park

Lower Glenelg National Park was created to preserve the lower reaches of the magnificent Glenelg River and the plant and animal communities it supports. Rising in the Grampians, the Glenelg winds some 400 km through western Victoria on its way to the ocean at Nelson. The most spectacular feature of the park is the gorge through which the river flows for the last 35 km of its journey.

The 27,300 ha park is located on the extensive coastal plains of south-western Victoria. The Glenelg River meanders across the plain, cutting deep into the limestone to form a spectacular gorge more than 50 m deep in places. Rainwater has also eaten into the soft rock, creating large limestone caverns. Some have vertical shafts and contain the fossilised remains of animals that have fallen to their deaths or been carried there by an underground stream. The remains of long extinct marsupials such as the giant kangaroo and marsupial lion have been found in the caves, together with bones of the Tasmanian tiger and Tasmanian devil, both extinct on the mainland.

Only one of the 60 known caves in the park is open to the public: the Princess Margaret Rose Cave. This contains excellent examples of actively growing stalactites, stalagmites, helictites and other spectacular limestone formations.

Formation

Between 40 and 25 million years ago this area was submerged beneath a shallow sea. Over time marine deposits and other sediments accumulated on the sea bed and were slowly compressed to form limestone rock. Subsequent uplifting of the land combined with lowering sea levels have exposed the sea bed, forming the present plain.

The formation of Princess Margaret Rose Cave began some 800,000 years ago when the Glenelg River was 15 m above its present height. Water from the river worked its way along a fault-line for 300 m scalloping the walls of the cave and levelling the floor. Rainwater seeping down through cracks and fissures from above dissolves the limestone which reforms as calcite crystals in the air of the cave. These crystals create the beautiful limestone formations, coloured by minerals washed down from the overlying soil.

Settlement

Major Thomas Mitchell, the Surveyor General of New South Wales, was the first European to visit this area, naming the Glenelg River in 1836. The poor soils deterred farmers and other settlers until 1947 when surrounding districts were being cleared and planted with pine trees. Pressure from local conservation groups over many years saved the lower reaches of the Glenelg, and in 1968 a park was finally declared. It was enlarged to its present size in 1975.

Princess Margaret Rose Cave was discovered in 1936 by Keith McEachern, who helped to develop it as a tourist attraction, cutting steps into the limestone and installing electricity. The first guided tours were conducted in 1941, and the cave was incorporated in the park in 1980.

Plants and Animals

Although much of the soil in the park is infertile and poorly drained, it supports an impressive array of native plants. This is due to the wide range of habitats and its geographical location. The park is in an area where plants from eastern Australia overlap those from the west. More than 700 species have been recorded here, representing plants of the woodlands, heaths, swamps, rivers and dunes. They include more than 50 orchid species found in the heaths and fringing forests. The gullies associated with Moleside Creek support the most westerly stands of treeferns in Australia.

Much of the park is covered by eucalypt woodlands dominated by brown stringybarks and messmates on the drier sites, and manna gums along the watercourses. Kentbruck Heath in the eastern section of the park is well known for its brilliant springtime wildflower displays. The poor soils and swampy sites of this area encourage the prolific flowering of heath plants such as wattles, swamp boronias, correas, pea flowers and ground orchids.

The park is a refuge for many animals displaced by clearing of the surrounding land. Among the 30 species of mammals are the rare blunt-faced rat, which needs the diversity of plants found in fire-prone heathlands, and the southern potoroo, a small shy member of the kangaroo family, once thought to be extinct in Victoria. Brush-tailed possums and echidnas are often seen, and the large eastern grey kangaroo and red-necked wallaby graze in grassy areas. The park has one of the few remaining wombat colonies in south-western Victoria, and the once common yellow-bellied glider is now confined to the park and the few bushland areas left in the south-west.

Four species of bats have been recorded. The common bent-wing bat congregates in large colonies in some of the caves, hanging from the roof in closely-massed clusters. These tiny mammals are extremely sensitive to human interference, and their caves must not be disturbed. Platypuses and eastern water rats live in burrows along the river banks.

The reedbeds growing in the quiet shallow sections of the river provide shelter and food for many water birds such as the dusky moorhen, black duck and chestnut teal. Bright orange and blue azure kingfishers may be seen darting along the river searching for fish. Other birds include the emu, painted quail, ground thrush, yellow-tailed black cockatoo, honeyeaters, fantails, flycatchers and the rare rufous bristle bird.

Activities

The park is on the route of the Great South-west Walk, a 250 km loop between Portland and the western boundary of Lower Glenelg National Park, through forests, along rivers and coastal dunes. A combination of walking trails and vehicle tracks allow you to walk along the river as it journeys through the park. The short, self-guiding River View Nature Walk takes in some of the surface features of the Princess Margaret Rose Cave area. A 4.5 km loop walk follows the river to Lasletts Picnic Area, passing close to limestone cliffs and through gently undulating woodland.

Canoeing on the Glenelg River is very popular. There are no rapids or fast currents, and a number of excellent overnight camping areas have been established along the river. It takes about four days to canoe from Nelson to Dartmoor. Canoes can be hired in Nelson. Water skiing is permitted in designated zones east of the Princess Margaret Rose Cave area and west of Simsons Landing, and a number of boat launching ramps are provided. The Glenelg is also famed for its fishing. Bass, southern black bream, mulloway, yellow-eye mullet and Australian salmon are all found in the river.

Facilities

The Visitor Centre and park office is located 2 km from Nelson on Glenelg Drive. Information is also available at the Princess Margaret Rose Cave Visitor Centre where there is a comprehensive display and an audiovisual presentation about the caves. Guided cave tours lasting about half a day are conducted on most days.

Camping grounds with toilets and drinking water and picnic areas have been established along the river. Caravans are allowed at the Princess Margaret Rose Cave area, and three cabins are available for overnight accommodation here. Permits are required and bookings should be made in advance. There are caravan parks and a range of other accommodation at Nelson, Mount Gambier and Portland.

Access

The park is 400 km west of Melbourne via the Princes Highway, turn off along the sealed road from Portland to Nelson, or take the unsealed road from Dartmoor. Roads within the park are generally unsealed. Commercial boat tours operate from Nelson to Princess Margaret Rose Cave.

Climate

The park has warm summers and cool winters. Visit in spring for the wildflower displays.

Lower Glenelg National Park, Forest Rd, Nelson, Vic 3292. Tel. (08) 8738 4051.

CAVES RD

To Mt Gambier

Sandy Waterholes

Princess Margaret
Rose Caves

Hutchessons

RIVER

WANWIN

Donovans

RD

McLennans Punt

Glenelg

River

Wilso

Simsons
Landing

Sapling Ck

Nelson

Wilso

PORTLAN

DISCOVERY

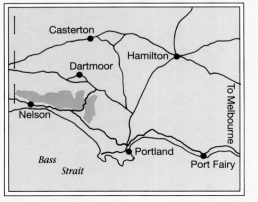

Casterton

Hamilton

Dartmoor

To Melbourne

Nelson

Bass
Strait

Portland

Port Fairy

N

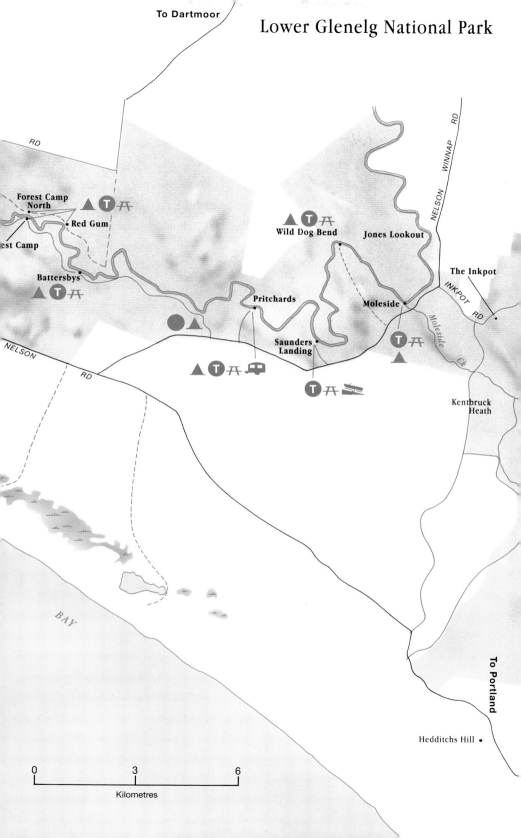

Lower Glenelg National Park

To Dartmoor

RD

Forest Camp
North

Red Gum

est Camp

Wild Dog Bend

Jones Lookout

The Inkpot

Battersbys

Pritchards

Moleside

NELSON

RD

Saunders
Landing

Kentbruck
Heath

BAY

To Portland

Hedditchs Hill

NELSON WINNAP RD

INKPOT RD

Moleside Ck

0   3   6

Kilometres

Grampians National Park

Grampians National Park is a huge botanical garden where plants and animals that have become extinct in other regions flourish among the sandstone ranges. More than one-third of the state's animal species live in this area, and in spring more than 1000 species of wildflowers, some found nowhere else on earth, cover the peaks and valleys.

The Grampians are a series of rugged sandstone ranges forming the westernmost heights of the Great Dividing Range. The 167,000 ha national park was declared in 1984 and protects some of the most magnificent parts of the Grampians, with its strange rock formations such as the Balconies, waterfalls, lakes, gorges and mountain peaks rising to 1168 m at Mount William.

Formation

The landscape has its origins in a period of geological activity some 400 million years ago when the land rose up to form a great island of mountains. The sandy sediments of the area were tilted to form parallel ridges, while slow folding of the rocks created the basin now filled by the waters of Lake Wartook, and the horseshoe-shaped Mount Difficult Range.

Rising sea levels saw the foothills pounded by the Southern Ocean for millions of years, leaving deep limestone deposits. These were buried beneath 60 m of lava, the result of a prolonged period of volcanic activity that began 5 million years ago and finally ceased a mere 6000 years ago. The seas have long since retreated, but the wind, rain and river systems have continued to create the fantastic rock formations and rugged slopes that tower above the surrounding plains.

History

The plains surrounding the Grampians were occupied by a number of Aboriginal nations who created a complex drainage system at the foot of Mount William. This controlled the waters flowing from the mountain streams, creating an ideal environment for eels, which they trapped at various outlets.

The physical features of the Grampians were woven into the creation mythologies of the local people, and more than 100 Aboriginal rock art sites have been found in the area. Some depict animal tracks or simple human figures, others are in the form of linear designs, hand stencils or hand prints in red ochre. There is little evidence to suggest that the area was permanently occupied, and it is thought that the rock art sites were used mostly for ceremonial purposes. The Billimina and Wab Manja art sites near Buandik camping area are among the most extensive.

Thomas Mitchell was the first European to visit the Grampians in 1836. Graziers settled in the district soon after, followed by gold miners and loggers. The indigenous people were forced from their land, their food sources were depleted by grazing, and those who survived disease and the other effects of colonisation were obliged to adopt the ways of the European invaders.

Plants and Animals

The rugged hills, ranges and valleys of the Grampians provide one of the most beautiful and diverse habitats for native plants in Victoria. The plant communities range from stunted heaths on the Major Mitchell Plateau to stringybark forests, red gum woodlands and luxuriant fern gullies. The wildflower displays are most colourful between August and November, with boronias, wattles, grevilleas and more than 100 orchid species coming into bloom. Some plants are only found here, such as the spectral duck orchid, the skeleton fork fern and long fork fern. The slopes are mostly covered by woodlands and dry eucalypt forests. The most common trees on the rocky hillsides are messmate and brown stringybarks, mountain grey gums and Oyster Bay pines.

On the valley floors the poorly drained soils are suitable habitats for swamp gums, silver banksias and prickly tea trees. River red gums grow along the banks of the rivers. Many of these magnificent trees were unfortunately logged, and many of the old trees were ringbarked. The tree hollows in their gnarled and twisted limbs provide homes for animals such as possums, owls, parrots and bats.

More than 200 bird species have been recorded in the Grampians. Kookaburras, pied currawongs, striated thornbills and yellow-tailed black cockatoos are numerous. Crimson rosellas, honeyeaters and golden whistlers feed in the stringybark forests. Emus move in mobs among the heath plants and grasstrees, while wedge-tailed eagles soar high above the escarpments searching for small animals. Aquatic birds such as egrets, ducks, ibises, cormorants, spoonbills and herons live along the watercourses. White-breasted sea-eagles, kites and swamp harriers hunt for fish, small birds and other animals in these areas. Among the forest birds are kingfishers, wrens, rainbow bee-eaters, treecreepers, robins, owls and galahs.

Many mammals are found here. Members of the kangaroo family include the commonly seen swamp wallaby, red-necked wallaby, grey kangaroo and long-nosed potoroo. Possums, gliders and southern brown bandicoots shelter in tree hollows and logs. Platypuses may be found in some of the creeks, but great patience is needed to spot them. Among the small mammals are the rare smoky mouse, the heath mouse, the fat-tailed dunnart and the yellow-footed antechinus.

Walks

There are more than 160 km of walking tracks in the park, ranging from short strolls to overnight expeditions for experienced bushwalkers. The Wonderland area near Halls Gap is one of the most popular parts of the park. There are well-signed walking tracks leading to waterfalls, spectacular views and unusual rock formations. Short walks go to lookouts at Lake View (1 km), Sundial Peak (4 km) and Boronia Lookout (7 km). A very popular lookout is the Pinnacle. The easiest track to this magnificent viewpoint is a 4 km walk from the Sundial Picnic Area; or you can go via the Grand Canyon, a strenuous 5 km walk past fascinating rock formations; or take the Wonderland Loop from Halls Gap camp ground, a long but rewarding 11 km hike. Do not miss the short

walk to the rock formation known as the Balconies. This is a 2 km track through lichen-covered tea-trees from the car park at Reed Lookout. The impressive MacKenzie Falls are one of the most spectacular waterfalls in Victoria, and are only one hour return walk from the car park. The track follows the river.

Facilities

The Visitor Centre, 2.5 km south of Halls Gap shopping centre, should not be missed. It has extensive information, displays, a book and gift shop and an audiovisual presentation of the natural and cultural history of the Grampians. Next to the Visitor Centre the Brambuk Living Cultural Centre provides visitors with information about the Aboriginal cultural heritage. It incorporates a restaurant, souvenir shop and auditorium. There is a kiosk near MacKenzie Falls and numerous picnic areas in the park with fireplaces, tables and toilets.

Camping areas accessible by car are located at many sites in the park. They have pit toilets, fireplaces and picnic tables. Fees are payable and bookings are not accepted. Bush camping is permitted except in the Wonderland Range, around Lake Wartook and other signposted areas. Caravan parks, motels, guest houses, host farms and cottages for rent are located at Halls Gap and in towns around the park. Zumstein Recreation Area is very popular with day visitors, and has toilets, electric barbecues and fireplaces. Kangaroos also congregate here, but visitors are requested not to feed them as this can damage their health.

Access

The park is 260 km from Melbourne and 460 km from Adelaide. Main roads in the park are sealed, secondary roads are unsealed and may become slippery after rain. The vehicular tracks are generally rough and may be closed at times. They are best suited to 4WD vehicles.

Climate

Summer temperatures are often high, and winters cold. Best times to visit are spring, when the wildflowers are in full bloom, and autumn.

Grampians National Park, Halls Gap, Vic 3381. Tel. (03) 5556 4381.

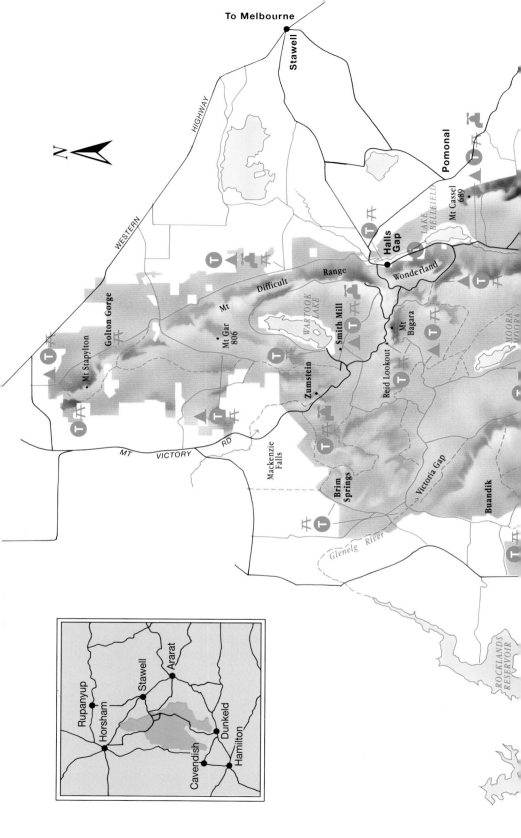

Grampians (Gariwerd) National Park

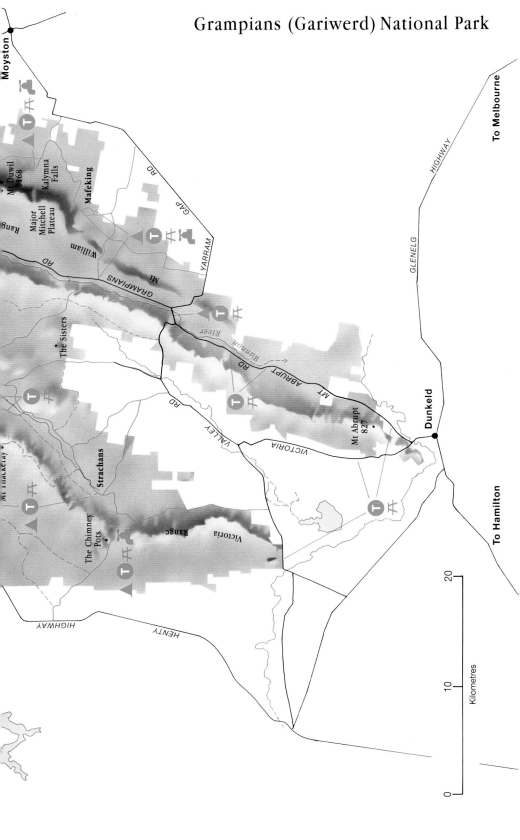

Wyperfeld National Park

Located in the flat, semi-arid north-western corner of Victoria, Wyperfeld is one of Australia's most fascinating national parks. This is mallee country where dry watercourses flanked by large trees wind through undulating sand dunes covered with a sea of low, grey-green vegetation. Although many of the watercourses are now permanently dry the area is rich in plant and animal life.

The central feature of this huge, 356,800 ha park, is a chain of lake beds connected by Outlet Creek, the northern extension of the Wimmera River. The lakes only fill when the Wimmera River over-supplies Lake Hindmarsh to the south of Lake Albacutya. This happened in 1918, 1956 and 1976.

When it rains the semi-arid landscape is transformed by tiny ephemeral desert plants that sprout from long-dormant seeds, carpeting the ground with clusters of flowers.

Wyperfeld protects one of the last great tracts of mallee left in Australia. Vast areas were cleared by farmers to grow wheat, a long and exhausting struggle against this highly resistant vegetation that grows back as fast as its stems are cut or burned.

Fires from lightning strikes are common in mallee country. The low leafy vegetation is rich in oils, and burns fiercely leaving the ground bare, but the underground rootstocks send out new stems almost immediately.

Formation

Some 25 million years ago the whole of north-west Victoria was submerged beneath a shallow sea. As the seas slowly retreated westerly winds blew sand over the exposed inland areas, building a complex of rolling dunes.

The dunes we see today were formed between 40,000 and 15,000 years ago, and were blown into crescent-shaped jumbled complexes, or into linear dunes forming long ridges trending from east to west. Over the years they have been stabilised by vegetation, but the combined effects of grazing, fire, rabbits and increased human activities have caused some of the dunes to lose their plant cover and become mobile.

Settlement

Before the arrival of the Europeans Aboriginal people regularly moved north along Outlet Creek in search of food. Evidence shows that they occupied the area for at least 6000 years, but because of the low and unreliable water supply they rarely stayed in one place for long. This nomadic lifestyle took them through the area in times of plenty when Outlet Creek was flowing, and they would travel north to Wirrengren Plain to trade with people from the Murray River.

James Clow was the first European to venture along Outlet Creek north of Lake Hindmarsh in 1847. He followed the creek to Wirrengren Plain where he established the first pastoral run. Other settlers followed and set about clearing the mallee for grazing and wheat growing. In 1909 a number of naturalists persuaded the government to temporarily reserve 3900 ha of this fast-disappearing habitat. Wyperfeld National Park was declared in 1921, and has been considerably enlarged in recent years.

Plants and Animals

More than 450 plant species have been recorded. They occur in distinct communities, and most can be seen close to the camping area.

Open woodlands grow along the dry water-ways and lake beds, with heathlands on the rolling sand plains to the west and south-west, and mallees covering the eastern section of the park. The open woodlands comprise mostly black box and river red gums with a variety of grasses and herbs among scattered shrubs such as wattle, moonah and oondoroo.

A few of the lunettes support dense stands of slender cypress pines on their acidic soils, but the large areas once covered by this distinctive conifer have been decimated by bushfires and rabbits, which eat the pine seedlings.

The heathlands comprise a large variety of low shrubby plants dominated by desert banksias, tea trees and shrubby she-oaks. In spring the heaths are ablaze with wildflowers such as heath myrtle, mint bushes, daisy bushes, orchids, guinea flowers and wattles. Most of the heath plants are well adapted to fire. Some have woody cones or capsules that only release the seeds after being burnt. Others regenerate from underground rhizomes.

The mallees are shrubby eucalypts with numerous stems arising from an underground rootstock called a lignotuber. This stores food and sends up new stems if those above ground die. The dominant mallee species are the grey-leaved Christmas mallee with a dense ground layer of porcupine grass; the yellow mallee growing above tea trees and heath-myrtles; and dense stands of red and dumosa mallees with a ground layer of annual herbs.

Animals living in the mallee are adapted to an arid, sandy habitat with a pattern of irregular rainfall. Mitchell's hopping mouse and the desert silky mouse live here, together with a large variety of reptiles such as the sand goanna, dragons, skinks and geckoes. Snakes, however, are rarely encountered at Wyperfeld.

Emus, red kangaroos and western grey kangaroos are often seen feeding around the dry lake beds and woodlands. Common brushtail possums and bats make their homes in the mallee, and are quite easy to spot, together with the prolific birdlife.

More than 200 bird species have been recorded, and are one of the park's great attractions. Some of the most conspicuous include sulphur-crested cockatoos, mallee ringneck parrots, red-rumped parrots, galahs, eagles, and smaller birds such as variegated fairy-wrens and red-capped robins. Of particular interest is the mallee fowl. This rare bird incubates its eggs in a large mound of earth and leaf litter.

Walks

Two self-guiding nature walks, one at Lake Brambruk, the other at Black Flat, give a close-up look at the plant and animal life of the park. They are each 6 km long, and leaflets are available from the Visitor Centre.

Many birds and animals can be seen on the Lignum Track to Eastern Lookout. This 10 km walk starting at the Visitor Centre passes several dry lake beds and may be muddy after rain.

The Desert Walk Circuit is a 6 km hike along a sandy track through typical mallee vegetation and stands of native pine, with excellent views over Big Desert and Outlet Creek.

There are many other signposted tracks passing through the different vegetation types. Contact the ranger before embarking on longer walks and take plenty of water.

Facilities

The Visitor Centre has displays and information. The large wooded camping and picnic area has tables, toilets and water. Casuarina camp ground in the northern part of the park has basic facilities, and is a good base for exploring this area.

Water is scarce and should be used sparingly. Showers and flush toilets have been removed to conserve water. A variety of accommodation is available at Rainbow and Hopetoun. The nearest supplies are sold at Yaapeet, 22 km away.

Access

The park is 450 km north-west of Melbourne, and can be reached via sealed roads from Hopetoun or Rainbow. Access to the western areas of the park is via the 4WD Nhill to Murrayville Road, but this may be impassable during wet weather.

Climate

Summer is very hot and dry with a high fire danger and bees can be a nuisance at this time of year. Winter days are pleasant, but the nights are often below freezing.

Wyperfeld National Park, RMB 1465, Yaapeet, Vic 3424. Tel. (03) 5395 7221.

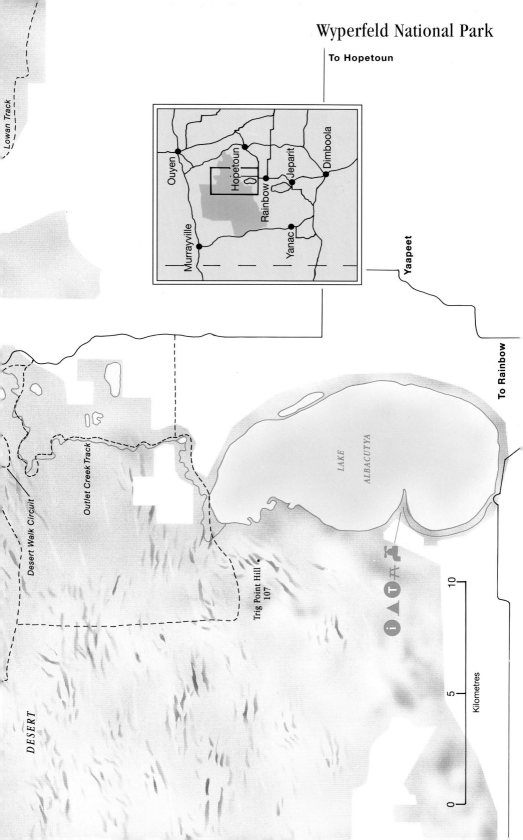

Wyperfeld National Park

To Hopetoun

Lowan Track

Ouyen
Hopetoun
Jeparit
Dimboola
Murrayville
Rainbow
Yanac

Yaapeet

To Rainbow

LAKE
ALBACUTYA

Desert Walk Circuit

Outlet Creek Track

Trig Point Hill
107

DESERT

0   5   10
Kilometres

Hattah-Kulkyne National Park

*In the semi-arid far north-west of Victoria, bordered by the snaking Murray River,
Hattah-Kulkyne National Park is an oasis of mallee woodlands surrounding a system
of tranquil lakes set among rolling sandhills. The ecological significance of this area is
recognised by naturalists throughout the world, and in 1982 the park was listed by
UNESCO as a World Biosphere Reserve.*

The lakes are not always filled. Their existence depends on the flooding of the Murray River. When the water level rises enough it spills over a natural rockbar into Chalka Creek, filling each of the lakes before looping back into the Murray.

In a very wet year the lakes themselves overflow, flooding the surrounding countryside and attracting great flocks of waterbirds to the park. The Murray does not flood every year, however, and although the inflows may be frequent enough to keep water in some of the lakes for a number of years, from time to time they dry up completely.

The area is only slightly above sea level, and was submerged many times between two and four million years ago as the ancient seas rose and fell. The sand ridges we see today are built upon coastal sand dunes formed around two million years ago when the ocean finally relinquished its dominance over the Murray Basin. They are overlaid in many places by yellow sand blown from the deserts of South Australia.

The mallee vegetation began establishing itself some 16,000 years ago and has largely stabilised the sand dunes, allowing the flourishing of a complex, semi-arid ecosystem.

History

Before the arrival of the Europeans the area was inhabited by the Latjilatji people, who had lived here for at least 5000 years, occupying the land from Chalka Creek to Mildura. Evidence suggests that they established permanent settlements in the area, probably moving to richer sites during long, dry periods. They constructed barriers across the water channels of Chalka Creek to trap fish when the floodwaters receded, hunted for game, and collected fruits and vegetables from the surrounding bush.

Large sheets of bark were stripped from river red gums to construct canoes. These fragile craft were punted using wooden poles, and fish were speared or netted. A few scarred trees remain as evidence of the traditional canoe building industry of the Latjilatji.

European settlers began arriving in the 1840s to take up grazing leases. Records from the 1860s put the numbers of the Latjilatji at about 50. Deprived of their land and traditional food sources, and smitten by diseases introduced by the new settlers, they were doomed to extinction, and the last survivor died in 1942.

Grazing animals and rabbits radically altered the original vegetation, and the whole ecosystem was beginning to show signs of serious degradation by the mid-20th century. In 1960 community pressure led to 17,800 ha being permanently set aside as Hattah Lakes National Park, and in 1980 Kulkyne Forest was added to form the present 48,000 ha Hattah-Kulkyne National Park.

Removal of grazing animals and control of the rabbit population has allowed the natural vegetation to regenerate.

Plants and Animals

Graceful river red gums grow around the shores of the lakes and creeks. Further from the lakes where there is less chance of flooding are woodlands of black box and shrubs like the prickly bottlebrush and the long-leaved wattle, eumong. Cypress pine and buloke grow on some of the rolling sand plains, while mallee vegetation flourishes on the higher, dry and infertile sand ridges.

Mallee eucalypts are low, multi-stemmed trees that grow from an underground rootstock called a lignotuber. Destruction by fire or other damage to the above-ground part of the tree encourages the lignotuber to send out new shoots. This adaptation and their ability to withstand long periods of drought allow mallee eucalypts to colonise fire-prone arid environments.

Beneath the mallee grow shrubs such as the desert grevillea, hop bush, desert cassia and large hummocks of porcupine grass. Small animals use the spines of porcupine grass for protection from larger predators and for shelter from the sun. Rufous-crowned emu wrens and striated grass wrens are usually found here. They build nests in the grassy clumps and hide between the spines if threatened.

More than 200 bird species have been recorded in the park, and many can be seen by taking a leisurely stroll around the lakes. Majestic white-bellied sea eagles follow the rivers from the ocean and fly over the lakes searching for fish. Regent parrots, yellow rosellas, sulphur-crested cockatoos, mallee ringneck parrots and the mound-building mallee fowl are all found in this area. Noisy miners are responsible for the incessant chattering around the camping ground.

The best time to see mallee wildlife is at dusk and dawn when the animals are most active. Red and western grey kangaroos and emus graze around the lakes during the twilight hours. Red kangaroos can be distinguished from the greys by their whitish limbs and under-belly and the reddish fur of the males. Many animals live underground to escape the heat and conserve water. Some, such as Mitchell's hopping mouse emerge from their deep under-ground burrow systems to feed at night. Blind snakes, which feed on ants and termites, often leave their subterranean nests at night, and may be seen moving silently on the surface. They are quite harmless and like all other snakes should be left alone.

Walks

The distant horizons and sheer isolation of this area evoke a sense of peace and solitude in all who come here, and the best way to begin to understand the nature of this remarkable land is to walk quietly through the bush.

A short, self-guided nature walk starting near the park entrance takes you through a fascinating variety of mallee vegetation. The track meanders for 1.2 km through different habitats, and an explanatory leaflet introduces you to some of the semi-arid ecosystems of the park. From the camping ground a track circuits the series of southern lakes. Lake Hattah retains water for some three years after a flood. The other lakes in this part of the park are more ephemeral, but teem with life in the wet seasons.

Hattah Nature Drive is designed for vehicles, but is an easy and very rewarding two hour walk, particularly in the early morning or evening when the kangaroos and emus are feeding.

Facilities

Camping is allowed in most areas along the Murray River, and camping grounds with basic facilities including pit toilets, tables and fire-places have been established at Lake Hattah and Lake Mournpall.

Water is scarce, and only a limited supply of drinking water is available at the Visitor Centre and Lake Mournpall camping ground. Visitors should use portable stoves rather than collect fallen timber which is an important habitat for insects and reptiles.

Hotel, motel and lodge accommodation is available at Red Cliffs, Colignan, Robinvale and Ouyen. Petrol and other supplies are available at Hattah and Colignan.

The park tracks are good for cycling. Canoeing, fishing and swimming are popular pastimes.

Access

The park is 500 km north-west of Melbourne via the sealed Murray Valley Highway. Turn off at Hattah to the park.

Climate

The summer heat is harsh. Autumn, winter and spring are the best seasons to visit. Bring warm clothing as the nights can be cold.

Hattah-Kulkyne National Park, RSD Hattah, Vic 3501. Tel. (03) 5029 3253.

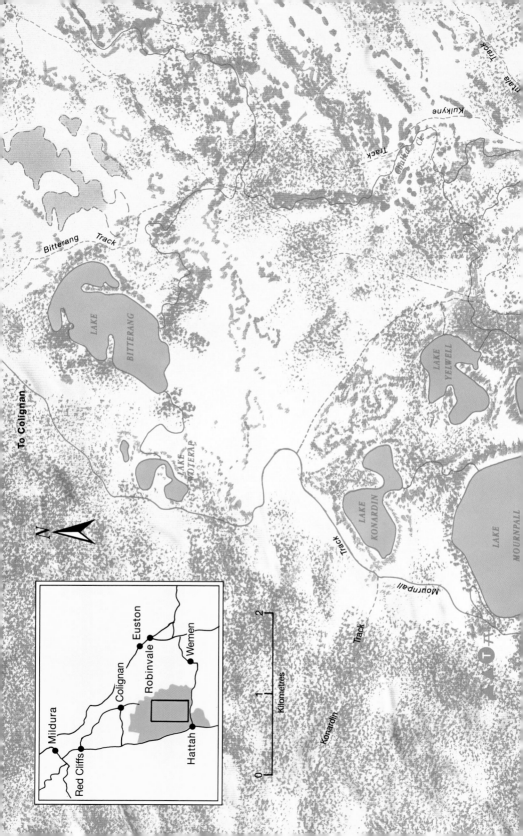

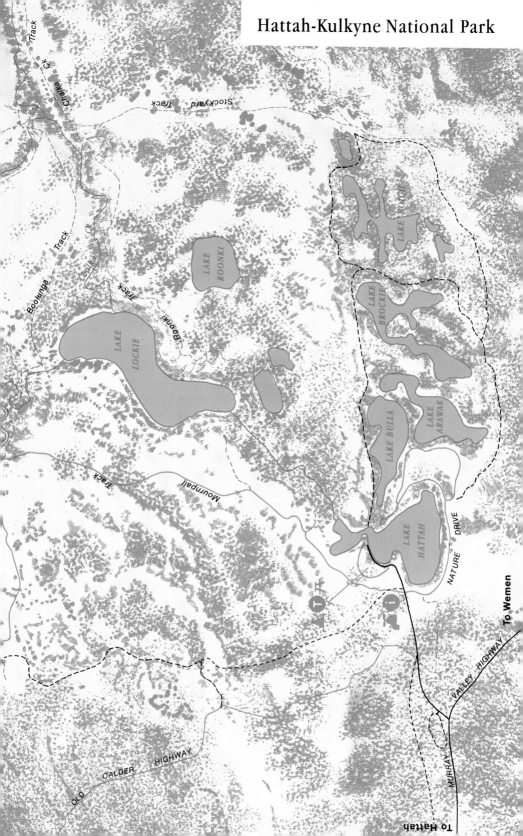

Hattah-Kulkyne National Park

Track

Chalka Ck

Chalka Ck

Stockyard Track

Boolunga Track

Track

ROONKI Track

LAKE ROONKI

LAKE LOCKIE

LAKE MOURNPALL

LAKE BROCKIE

LAKE BULLA

LAKE ARAWAK

Mournpall Track

LAKE HATTAH

NATURE DRIVE

To Wemen

MURRAY VALLEY HIGHWAY

OLD CALDER HIGHWAY

To Hattah

Alpine National Park (646,000 ha)

This huge, magnificent park extends from central Gippsland to the NSW border, and includes the state's highest peaks and most spectacular mountain scenery. Much of the area is declared wilderness, and together with the adjoining Kosciuszko National Park protects almost the entire alpine region of south-east Australia.

The forests, heaths, snow gum woodlands and alpine grasslands support a variety of wildlife including the rare and endangered mountain pygmy possum, and springtime wildflowers.

Vehicle access is limited, and bushwalkers regard this area as one of the most scenic and challenging walking country in the state. Cross-country skiing on the high plains, horse riding, fishing and canoeing are popular activities. There are short walks to scenic lookouts and long trails including part of the 655 km Australian Alps Walking Track. Be prepared for sudden, dramatic weather changes at any time of year.

There are camping areas in the park and lodge and motel accommodation in the adjacent ski resorts at Mt Hotham, Falls Creek, Mt Buller and Dinner Plain.

350 km north-east of Melbourne via Bright, Mansfield, Traralgon or Bairnsdale. (03) 5755 1577.

Alfred National Park (3050 ha)

Straddling the Princes Hwy in east Gippsland, this park protects some of the most southerly occurrences of warm temperate to sub-tropical rainforest. This is a mountainous area with outstanding scenery. The rich flora of the park includes many epiphytic orchids, vines and ferns in the forests. Bushwalking is popular although much of the park was burnt in 1983, but the vegetation is regenerating. No facilities.

470 km east of Melbourne between Cann River and Genoa. (03) 5158 6351.

Baw Baw National Park (13,300 ha)

The granite Baw Baw plateau supports an extensive area of sub-alpine vegetation and magnificent stands of ancient Antarctic beech trees found in cool temperate rainforest pockets in the gullies of the Thompson and Aberfeldy River valleys. The park includes the steep slopes of Mt Erica and deep valleys. There are snow gum woodlands and snow grass plains on the Baw Baw Plateau.

Take the self-guiding rainforest walk near Mt Erica car park and the track to the plateau past the strange Mushroom Rocks. Bushwalking, cross-country skiing, canoeing and fishing are popular activities. There are camping and picnic areas at Aberfeldy River and Eastern Tyers River.

200 km east of Melbourne via Moe and Erica or Baw Baw Alpine Resort via Powelltown or Drouin. (03) 5165 3204.

Burrowa-Pine Mountain National Park (18,400 ha)

Located in the north-east corner of the state, Burrowa-Pine Mountain National Park consists of two linked mountainous blocks featuring a number of massive granite outcrops and scenic waterfalls with extensive views from the ranges.

The volcanic Mt Burrowa rises to 1300 m in the south, while the northern block is dominated by the granitic Pine Mountain (1062 m). The two blocks have different soils and different vegetation. There are rare species of grevillea, tea-tree, dampiera and acacia. Climbing, hiking and nature study are popular. Take the Bluff Falls Nature Walk. Picnic or camp near Cudgewa and Bluff Falls.

430 km north-east of Melbourne between Cudgewa and Walwa. (02) 6055 6111.

Churchill National Park (271 ha)

Churchill National Park is a popular recreation area just east of Melbourne. The park features good views from the numerous walking tracks over the Dandenong ranges and the city suburbs. Open eucalypt forests support kangaroos, swamp wallabies and more than 100 species of birds, including bell-birds. There are good picnic areas but no camping facilities

32 km east of Melbourne via Churchill Park Drive, Rowville. (03) 9796 8763.

Coopracambra National Park (38,800 ha)

A rugged park in east Gippsland on the NSW border between Cape Howe and the headwaters of the Murray River, featuring the spectacular sandstone gorge of the Genoa River, the striking granite outcrops of the Mt Kaye area and a very rich flora. This is a wilderness area and offers many challenges to experienced bushwalkers. There are no facilities in the park. Access by conventional vehicle to Beehive Falls on the eastern edge and Mealing Rd through the southern part only.

500 km east of Melbourne, east of Cann Valley Hwy. (03) 5158 6351.

Dandenong Ranges National Park (1920 ha)

Within easy reach of Melbourne, the popular Dandenong Ranges National Park protects magnificent mountain ash forests with waterfalls, fern gullies and panoramic views. There are many walking tracks, picnic areas and scenic lookouts, but camping is not allowed in the park.

50 km east of Melbourne via Burwood or Maroondah Hwys, or by train.
(03) 9758 1342.

Errinundra National Park (25,600 ha)

In the high country of East Gippsland near the NSW border, this park is mostly above 1000 m. It protects the state's largest stand of cool temperate rainforest and some beautiful untouched wet sclerophyll forests of shining gum and cut-tail, with giant trees hundreds of years old. A self-guiding walk at the heart of the park takes you into the ancient forest at Errinundra Saddle where you are likely to find swamp wallabies and lyrebirds.

Call in at the Orbost Rainforest Centre for a full range of information about the area. Camping and picnic areas are provided. Winter rain and snow often make the unsealed roads into the park impassable.

90 km north-east of Orbost. (03) 5161 1375.

Lind National Park (1365 ha)

Located in east Gippsland, this park is set in mountainous terrain and protects some of the few remaining pockets of warm temperate rainforest in the state. The wildlife includes lyrebirds, cockatoos, wallabies, dingos possums and wombats. There are beautiful springtime wildflower displays in the dry sclerophyll forests. Visit the picnic area beside the Euchre Valley Nature Drive. No camping facilities.

430 km east of Melbourne on the Princes Hwy between Orbost and Cann River.
(03) 5158 6351.

Little Desert National Park (132,000 ha)

Located on the state's western border, this large park is desert in name only. The sandy soils support heaths and scrubby mallee woodlands, and are full of life. There are brilliant spring wildflower displays among the heaths and abundant birdlife including the remarkable mound-building mallee fowl. Kangaroos, emus and reptiles are common.

Several walks begin at the camping area south of Kiata, and there are three excellent nature walks. Kiata, Horseshoe Bend and Ackle Bend have picnic areas and camp sites with basic facilities. Summers are very hot. The central and western blocks are accessible by 4WD only.

36 km north of Horsham via Dimboola or Mitre. (03) 5389 1204.

Mitchell River National Park (11,900 ha)

This Gippsland park surrounds the spectacular Mitchell River as it passes through high cliffs. There are a number of gorges including the Den of Nargun. The park preserves remnant stands of luxuriant rainforest in some of the gorges. Take the Mitchell River walking track downstream to the Den of Nargun. Canoeing and rafting are popular activities. There are camping and picnic areas.

300 km east of Melbourne via the Princes Hwy and Fernbank. (03) 5152 0400.

Wilpena Pound, a strange geological formation in Flinders Ranges National Park, South Australia

Rawnsley's Bluff in the Flinders Ranges National Park, South Australia

One of the offshore stacks featured in Victoria's Port Campbell National Park

The Grampians on the south coast of Victoria, one of the state's great botanical repositories

Mornington Peninsula National Park (2686 ha)

Mornington Peninsula National Park takes in Point Nepean, Greens Bush and the magnificent coastal scenery and bushland between Portsea and Flinders. The walk from Portsea to Bushrangers Bay and along Main Creek is one of the best coastal walks in the state. There are long sandy surf beaches, picnic areas and a kiosk. Bookings are required to visit the Point Nepean section, which has historic fortifications, a quarantine station, interpretive displays, soundscapes and spectacular views of Port Phillip Heads.

95 km south of Melbourne via the Peninsula Freeway and Point Nepean Rd.
(03) 5984 4276.

Morwell National Park (396 ha)

This Gippsland park protects some of the magnificent forests growing on the steep slopes and ridges of the Strzelecki Ranges. There are stands of blue and grey gums, blackwoods, lush fern gullies and prolific birdlife. There is a self-guiding nature trail, picnic facilities, but no camping grounds in the park.

170 km east of Melbourne and 16 km south of Morwell. (03) 5122 1478.

Mount Eccles National Park (5470 ha)

Located in the south-west of the state, Mount Eccles is part of a volcanic region that last erupted about 7000 years ago. Mount Eccles itself is a scoria hill created about 20,000 years ago when a volcanic eruption sent out a huge lava flow 15 km beyond the present coastline. The three main craters hold the tranquil waters of Lake Surprise. There are lava canals, caves, craters, stony rises and a variety of plant and bird life. Follow the nature trail around the rim of the crater. A picnic area and a camp ground with caravan access and basic facilities is located near the entrance.

40 km south of Hamilton via Macarthur.
(03) 5576 1338.

Mount Richmond National Park (1733 ha)

Mount Richmond is an extinct volcano in the south-western corner of the state covered by a layer of sand. The park is noted for its spring-time wildflower displays, including more than 50 orchid species, and its wildlife. A sealed road leads to a lookout tower with scenic views overlooking the coastline. There are walking tracks through the forest and heathland. A picnic area is provided but camping is not allowed.

32 km west of Portland. (03) 5523 3232.

Organ Pipes National Park (85 ha)

This is a small park close to Melbourne, centred around a dramatic group of 20 m high basalt columns formed when the lava from an ancient volcano cooled in the valley of a river that flowed through the area. The natural vegetation has been successfully restored to this ex-pastoral property. There are picnic areas but no camping facilities in the park.

25 km north-west of Melbourne via the Calder Hwy. (03) 9390 1082.

Murray-Sunset National Park (633,000 ha)

In the semi-arid north-western corner of the state, this huge park protects a large area of mallee, pine buloke woodlands, salt plains and a wide range of dry-country plants and animals. The diverse habitats include Murray River wetlands, flood plains, billabongs and surrounding undulating plains supporting grasslands, native pine woodlands, mallee-covered dunes and salt-bush flats.

There are brilliant sunsets, kangaroos, emus and spring wildflowers to be seen. Historic sites relate to Aboriginal occupation, pastoral settlement, salt and gypsum mining. Pink Lakes has gas barbecues, picnic areas and camp sites. Rocket Lake, Mopoke, Pheenys Tk and Mt Crozier have picnic and basic camping. Or stay at the Shearers Quarters where accommodation is basic (03-5028 1218). Summers are very hot and drinking water is limited.

Conventional vehicles can access Pink Lakes, Settlement Rd and seasonally the Murray River/Lindsay Island area.

20 km north-west of Ouyen via Mallee or Calder Hwys. (03) 5092 1322.

Port Campbell National Park (1750 ha)

This long narrow coastal park protects the spectacular limestone formations around Port Campbell, including the Twelve Apostles, London Bridge and Loch Ard Gorge. Walking tracks lead to lookouts over the cliffs and off-shore stacks. A number of shipwrecks can be seen from cliff-top vantage points. Discovery Walk gives insights into the ecology of the area. Watch the mutton birds flying home on summer evenings to their nesting sites. There is a small colony of little penguins.

Surfing, snorkelling, swimming and short walks are popular activities. Visit the excellent Information Centre and Camp at Port Campbell where there are caravan sites and full facilities (bookings are essential in holiday periods: 03-5598 6369).

250 km west of Melbourne via Colac. (03) 5598 6382.

Snowy River National Park (98,700 ha)

Located in eastern Victoria along the Snowy River, this park is famed for its mighty gorge. The park lies in a remote area with magnificent river scenery, spectacular deep gorges and forests of grey gum, alpine ash, messmate and native pine. The rare brush-tailed rock wallaby lives in the rugged mountain ranges of the area.

Canoeing, rafting, bushwalking and swimming in the river pools are popular activities.

The self-guiding Silvermine Walking Track is a good 15 km hike, although there are other shorter walks.

The main access to the river is at McKillops Bridge where there are camp sites with basic facilities and a picnic area. 4WD only in the park along Deddick River Trail. Access by conventional vehicle to Raymond Falls in the south.

450 km east of Melbourne via Buchan, Bonang or Orbost. (03) 5154 6222.

Tarra-Bulga National Park (1522 ha)

Located in the Strzelecki Ranges of south Gippsland, this park features some of the state's finest tree fern gullies. There are giant mountain ash, Antarctic beech trees and many superb lyrebirds in the forests. Call in at the Balook Information Centre adjoining the park, take the enchanting nature walk to Cyathea Falls on Tarra River, see the forest canopy from the suspension bridge near Balook on one of two self-guided nature walks, and stop at one of the picnic areas. No camping facilities are provided.

220 km east of Melbourne near Balook along Grand Ridge Rd. (03) 5196 6166.

Yarra Ranges National Park (76,000 ha)

This new National Park protects the headwaters of the Yarra River and pristine old growth mountain ash forests, rainforests and fern gullies. Among the rich wildlife is the endangered Leadbeaters possum. There are waterfalls, scenic lookouts, including spectacular views from Mt Donna Buang, scenic drives, walking tracks and picnic areas. No camping.

60 km east of Melbourne via Healesville or Warburton. (03) 5964 7088.

Tasmania

Featured National Parks

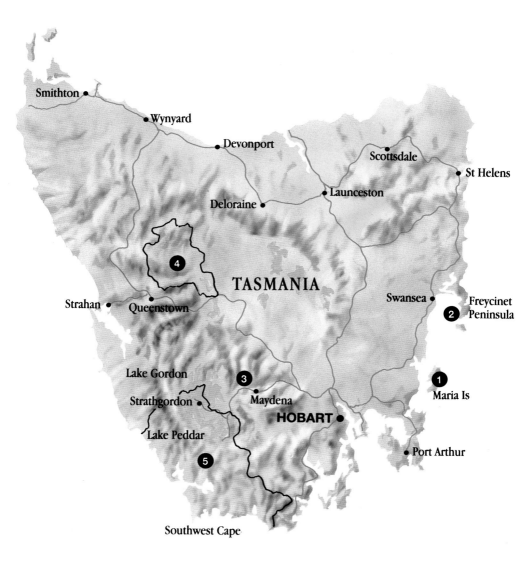

Smithton

Wynyard

Devonport

Scottsdale

St Helens

Launceston

Deloraine

4

TASMANIA

Strahan   Queenstown

Swansea   Freycinet
Peninsula
2

Lake Gordon

3

1

Strathgordon   Maydena   Maria Is

HOBART

Lake Peddar

5

Port Arthur

Southwest Cape

Maria Island National Park

Off the east coast of Tasmania, only ninety minutes' drive from Hobart, lies the secluded and scenic Maria Island. Rich in colonial history, this beautiful island is a wildlife refuge and a peaceful haven away from the trappings of civilisation.

Shaped like an hourglass more than 20 km long and up to 13 km wide, Maria Island is essentially two islands linked by a narrow sandy isthmus. The 11,550 ha park includes sparkling white sandy beaches, spectacular limestone and sandstone cliffs and a coastal mountain range with lush rainforest gullies. The western coast slopes gently to the sea. Swamps and lagoons have formed behind the beaches, while further inland are gently sloping hills and valleys, and numerous creeks draining the eastern mountain range.

By contrast the east coast has sheer cliffs plunging into the ocean. A marine section protects a variety of marine habitats around the northern and western coastlines including reefs with large underwater caverns, seagrass beds and forests of giant kelp.

Formation

Around 375 million years ago Maria Island was part of a huge mountain chain extending along the east coast of present-day Tasmania. Erosion gradually wore down the mountains leaving only a ridge rising a few hundred metres above plains to the west. Rising sea levels eventually flooded the plains, and the ridge became an island around which were deposited beach gravels, shell banks, mud and sand.

A period of subterranean activity some 165 million years ago forced hard crystalline dolerite rock to come close to the surface. Erosion gradually removed the softer rocks on the surface, exposing the dolerite. A period of intense earthquake activity 50 million years ago raised the eastern side of Maria Island along a fault line, and as the land lifted the older, softer rocks were exposed below the dolerite cap. Erosion has cut deep into the softer rocks on the eastern uplifted part, leaving the dolerite-capped ridge of the present-day Maria Range.

About 10,000 years ago the sea levels rose again, drowning the valleys to leave two islands surrounded by a shallow sea. Sand has accumulated between them forming an isthmus of sand dunes and lagoons connecting the two islands.

Storm waves and the sea swell continue to eat into the east coast, creating steep cliffs and isolated formations like The Pyramid on the island's southern tip. On the sheltered west coast the sand deposits have formed fine, white beaches.

Convicts, Wine and Silk

Before the arrival of the Europeans, Maria Island was home to a group of Aboriginal people who called themselves the Tierremairremerlow. They spent the winter months on the mainland coast, living mainly on shellfish and sea vegetables. Using simple canoes and rafts they made the 15 km journey to the island across the Mercury Passage, stopping halfway at a small island now called Lachlan Island. The British arrived in 1825 with 50 convicts, and set up a penal colony at Darlington. The colony was disbanded in 1832, and over the next decade whalers, pastoralists and smugglers lived on the island until it was resumed as a convict station from 1842 to 1850.

Various enterprises were established, including wine-making, silk production and a cement works. All eventually failed, and in the late 1960s the Tasmanian Government established a wildlife reserve to protect mainland birds and mammals whose habitats were being destroyed by land clearing. The Government gradually bought up the island properties and transported selected species from the mainland. In 1972 it was proclaimed a National Park.

Plants and Animals

Much of the island is covered with dry open eucalypt forests and woodlands, interspersed with dry coastal heath. Manna gums grow on sand dunes and the central mudstone slopes. Black peppermint and black gum are found on the swampy alluvial flats north of the isthmus, while the gum top stringybark and urn gum populate the eastern slopes. On the drier western side the woodlands have an understorey of she-oaks, prickly box, silver and black wattles and the native cherry. Blue gum and messmate stringybarks grow into tall trees in the higher areas with an understorey of tree ferns. Along the creeks and in damp gullies are pockets of rainforest with sassafras and celery top pine.

When the Europeans first arrived on the island the only large land mammals they found were the pademelon, potoroo, common wombat, ringtail possum and echidna. Forester kangaroos, Bennett's wallabies, Tasmanian bettongs and brown and barred bandicoots were introduced in the late 1960s, and they graze on the grasslands created by the early pastoralists. Other native mammals include water and swamp rats and the eastern pygmy possum. All three Tasmanian land snakes are found here: the tiger snake, copperhead and white-lipped whip snake. Other reptiles include the blue-tongued lizard, and six skink species.

The island has a variety of habitats exploited by more than 130 bird species. Along the shore are albatrosses, gannets, cormorants, mutton birds, crested terns, silver and Pacific gulls. The lagoons and swamps attract black ducks and chestnut teals, Japanese snipe and white-faced herons. Brown falcons are often seen circling over the grasslands, and white-breasted sea eagles patrol the coast. Parrots, cuckoos, honeyeaters, pardalotes and flycatchers are common around the forested areas. Approximately half the known population of the endangered forty-spotted pardalote is found here. The Tasmanian native hen and the rare Cape Barren goose were introduced and thrive on the island.

Walks

Short walks from Darlington lead to the Fossil Cliffs where large fossilised shells are embedded in the limestone, and to the intricately-patterned Painted Cliffs, passing mobs of grazing forester kangaroos and Cape Barren Geese.
A four hour return walk leads to the summit of Bishop and Clerk, from where there are magnificent views over the mainland and sheer-faced cliff walls to challenge rock climbers. A moderately easy track taking about three hours one way extends to the summit of Mount Maria. The 13 km journey to Point Lesueur takes about three hours one way. A few ruins remain to mark the site of the convict station built here in 1847.

Those embarking on long walks should register their intentions in the Ranger Station or Commissariat Store log books, and must sign out on their return.

Facilities

There is an interpretation centre at the historic Coffee Palace with displays and artefacts. Visitors must wash all dirt from boots, tent pegs and trowels before coming to the island to prevent the introduction of phytophera fungus. There are no shops, no power, and only limited accommodation in the Penitentiary. The units here are in high demand and can be booked six months in advance. They have mattresses and a wood stove for heating. Bring a fuel stove and lamp.

The main camping area at Darlington is frequented by kangaroos, trumpeting Cape Barren geese and possums. Water is limited; use it sparingly. There are small camping areas at Frenchs Farm and Encampment Cove with tank water. Walkers can stay at the restored farmhouse at Frenchs Farm; take a fuel stove.

Access

Maria Island is 15 km from the mainland and 88 km north-east of Hobart. A daily ferry service operates from the Eastcoaster Resort at Louiseville, just north of Ortford (03-6257 3264). There is a landing strip at the northern tip of the island, and light aircraft can be chartered at Triabunna or Hobart. Boats can be chartered from Ortford and Triabunna for fishing, diving and trips around the island. Cycling is the best way of travelling to the southern end of the island. Cyclists should ride on the formed roads only and must wash dirt from their tyres before coming to the island.

Climate

Although Maria Island has a pleasant and mild climate, the weather can change dramatically, becoming cold and wet even in summer.

Maria Island National Park, via Triabunna, Tas 7190. Tel. (03) 6257 1420.

Maria Island National Park

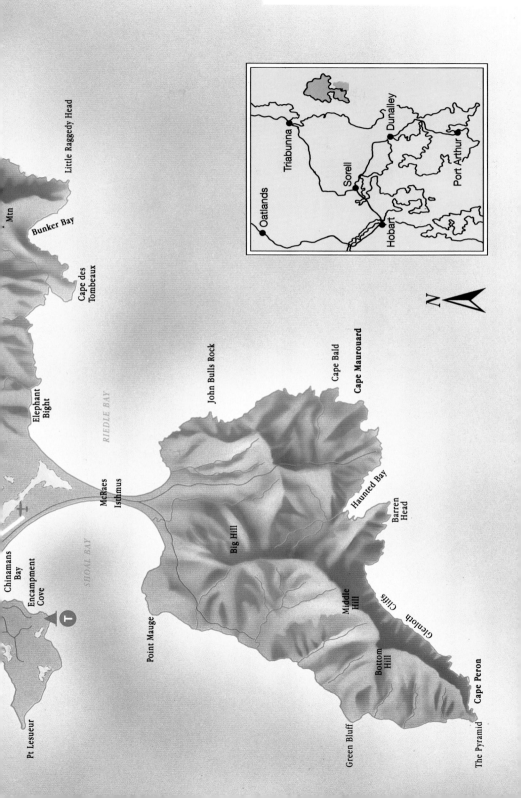

Freycinet National Park

*The rugged red granite peaks and magnificent coastal scenery of the Freycinet
Peninsula and Schouten Island make up one of Tasmania's oldest national parks. The
mountains, wetlands, lagoons, beaches and rocky shores provide a great diversity of
habitats and opportunities for bushwalkers, rock climbers, skin divers, boating
enthusiasts and naturalists.*

The park covers 13,000 ha of coastal heaths,
dry open woodlands and forests. The steep, four-
peaked ridge of the Hazards to the north is
separated from the rest of the peninsula by a low-
lying marshy isthmus bordered by Wineglass Bay
and Hazards Beach.

A mountain range rising to 620 m at
Mount Freycinet extends the length of Freycinet
Peninsula, with high rocky cliffs falling away to
the Tasman Sea to the east, and sandy beaches
interspersed with low headlands to the west.

Formation

The present landform is the result of major earth
movements that took place between 60 and
50 million years ago. During this period the area
was rocked by earthquakes. Fault lines opened up
and huge blocks of the earth's crust gradually
rose above the surrounding land. One of these
was to become Freycinet Peninsula and another
the eastern highlands of the mainland. The low-
lying area between the two is now Great Oyster
Bay and the lowlands.

Millions of years of erosion have worn down
the rocks to leave the present series of mountain
peaks. Rising sea levels at the end of the last ice
age about 10,000 years ago submerged the
low-lying land bridge joining Schouten Island to
the peninsula. The more exposed areas of the
coastline have been undercut by waves, causing
the granite to collapse and leaving steep cliffs. In
more sheltered sites or where there are softer
rocks, beaches, rock platforms and low
headlands have been formed.

History

Large shell middens along the beach at Coles Bay
are the most obvious signs of the area's original
inhabitants: a clan of Aboriginal people who
called themselves the Toornomair. Part of the
Oyster Bay nation, they were hunter-gatherers
who spent the winter months on the coast living
on shellfish and marine vegetables.

British settlers arrived on the east coast in
1821. At that time whales were a common sight
around the coastline, and in 1824 a whaling
station was set up at Parsons Cove to exploit this
rich resource. Other stations soon followed. The
whalers hunted their quarry, the southern right
whale, to the brink of extinction, and by the
mid-1840s the whalers had departed. Coal and
tin mining ventures operated for a number of
years, but were hampered by the difficulties and
expense of sea transportation.

In 1916 Freycinet Peninsula was declared a
national park, Schouten Island was added in
1967 and the Friendly Beaches to the north were
added in 1992.

Plants and Animals

The park has surprisingly rich plant communities, and almost one-third of Tasmania's flowering plant species are found here.

Most of the park is covered by shrublands, dry
eucalypt forests and woodlands with a heathy
understorey of hakeas, fringe myrtle, common
heath and manuka. Blue gum dominates on the
western side of Schouten Island, with patches of
black and white peppermint trees and a grassy
ground cover.

The wetter gullies support yellow-flowering
silver banksia, Oyster Bay pine and stinkwood.
She-oaks are the most noticeable trees along
much of the coastline. Succulents, such as the
round-leaved pigface, ice plant and bearded
glasswort grow in the most exposed sites.

Orchids are a great feature of the peninsula,
with several species in flower at any time of year.
Apart from Tasmania's only rock orchid,
Dendrobium striolatum, which forms large
mats over some of the granite slabs, most are

found in the heathlands and on poor sandy soils. Common species include the wax-lip orchid, spider orchid, spotted sun orchid, potato orchid, helmet orchids and greenhoods.

The varied habitats provide homes for a wide variety of mammals. Red-necked wallabies and brush-tailed possums are seen around campsites and picnic areas. In the forests are pademelons, bettongs, the long-nosed potoroo, spotted-tailed and eastern quolls, Tasmanian devils, sugar gliders and ringtail possums. These are nocturnal and best seen by spotlighting at night.

Echidnas forage by day for ants among the leaf litter. Native rodents include the New Holland mouse, swamp rat and the carnivorous water rat, occasionally seen at dawn around lagoons and estuaries.

Several species of insectivorous bats live in the park, roosting in trees or tree hollows. The lesser long-eared bat and the small forest eptesicus are the most common.

One of the most noticeable reptiles is the large, fast-moving White's skink that lives in burrows under rock ledges. The large blue-tongued lizard may be seen in the drier east coast areas, and the long-legged southern dragon lives in heathlands on sandy soil. The three species of Tasmanian snake are found here: the tiger snake, copperhead and white-lipped whipsnake. All are venomous and should be left alone.

More than 145 bird species have been recorded. The flowering plants attract several honeyeaters including the beautiful eastern spinebill and the bright green yellow-throated honeyeater. Yellow wattlebirds and the flightless Tasmanian native hen forage around the camp ground.

Walks

All the walking tracks begin at the car park at Parsons Cove. The ascent of Mount Amos is a popular three hour return journey. This is a steep climb, but rewards the walker with magnificent views.

A self-guided nature walk leads to the lookout on the Wineglass Bay Track. Continue to Wineglass Bay and return via the Isthmus Track, a four hour journey encompassing various habitats and magnificent scenery.

A circuit of the peninsula is a comfortable two day walk, camping at Hazards Beach (two hours from the car park), Cooks Beach (a further two hour walk) or Bryans Beach (another hour).

The Peninsula Track at the northern end of Cooks Beach climbs to Mount Graham where the views are spectacular. This takes about five hours, with another hour to the car park. Water should be carried.

Rock climbers may test their skills on the granite faces of the Hazards and nearby cliffs.

Facilities

The main camping area is by the beach at Coles Bay, and should be booked in advance during the main holiday periods. There are powered sites, toilets, fireplaces and fresh water. General stores at Coles Bay sell fuel, food and gas, and there is a post office, restaurants and a tavern. There are barbecues and toilets at Honeymoon Bay and Ranger Creek.

The campsites at Hazards Beach, Cooks Beach, Bryans Beach and Wineglass Bay have pit toilets and limited water supplies. Campers should bring fuel stoves.

The privately-owned Freycinet Lodge inside the park at Coles Bay provides fully-catered accommodation. There is a youth hostel and a variety of other accommodation at Coles Bay.

Access

The park is 60 km from Swansea, turn into Coles Bay Road from the Tasman Highway. Roads within the park are mostly unsealed.

Climate

Winter is generally mild, but the weather can change dramatically at any time of year.

Freycinet National Park, Via Coles Bay, Tas 7215. Tel. (03) 6257 0107.

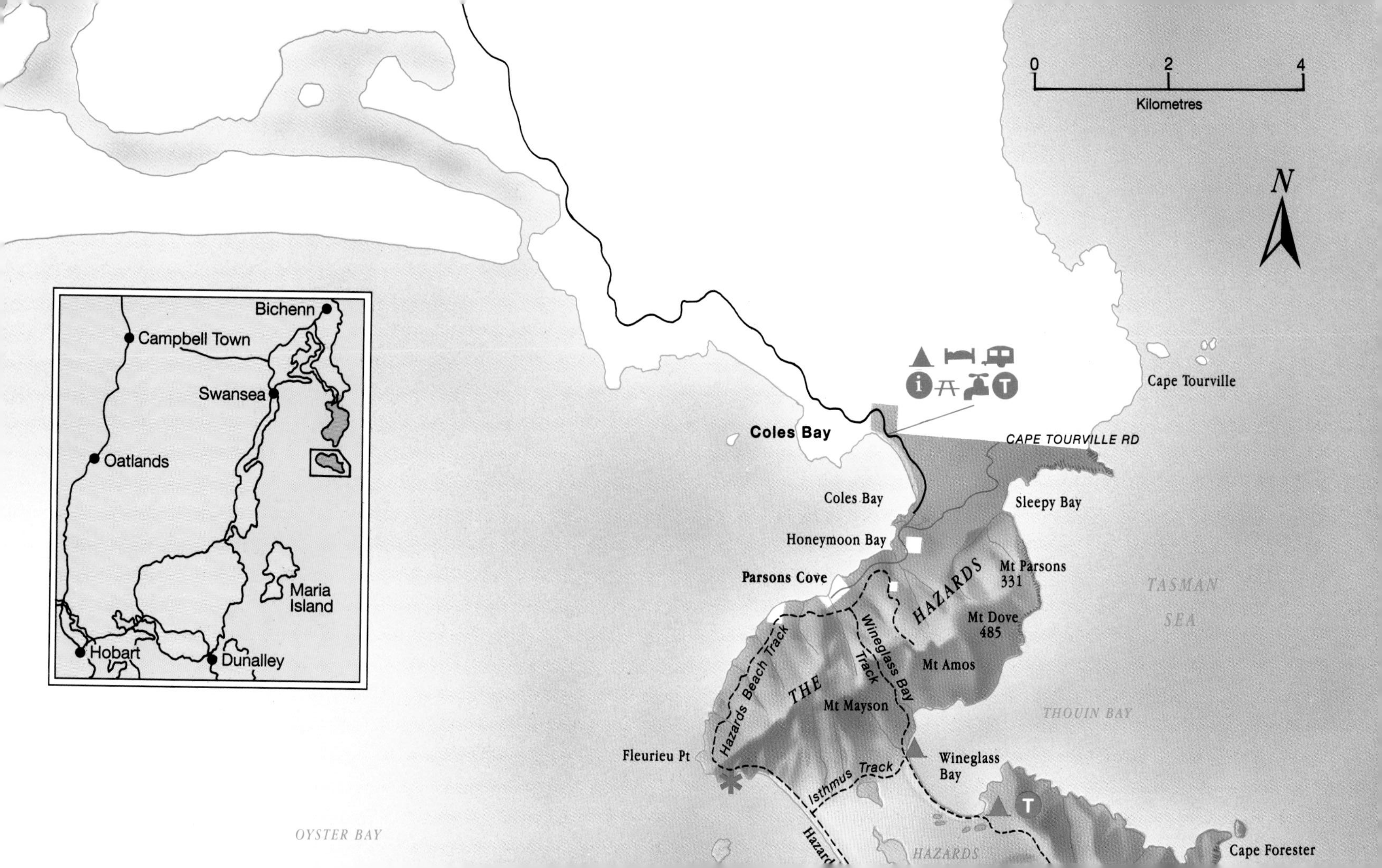
0
2
4
Kilometres
N
Cape Tourville
CAPE TOURVILLE RD
Coles Bay
Coles Bay
Sleepy Bay
Honeymoon Bay
Parsons Cove
THE HAZARDS
Mt Parsons 331
Mt Dove 485
Mt Amos
Mt Mayson
Wineglass Bay Track
Hazards Beach Track
Isthmus Track
Fleurieu Pt
Wineglass Bay
TASMAN SEA
THOUIN BAY
OYSTER BAY
HAZARDS
Hazard
Cape Forester
Bichenn
Campbell Town
Swansea
Oatlands
Maria Island
Hobart
Dunalley

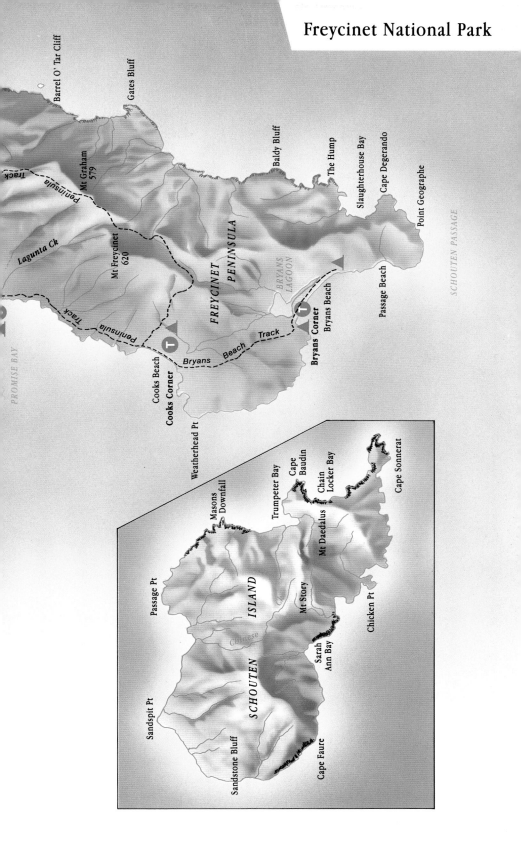

Freycinet National Park

Barrel O' Tar Cliff

Gates Bluff

Baldy Bluff

The Hump

Slaughterhouse Bay

Cape Degerando

Point Geographe

Mt Graham 579

Peninsula Track

Lagunta Ck

Mt Freycinet 620

FREYCINET PENINSULA

BRYANS LAGOON

SCHOUTEN PASSAGE

Peninsula Track

Bryans Beach

Passage Beach

PROMISE BAY

Bryans Corner
Bryans Beach

Bryans Beach Track

T

Cooks Beach
Cooks Corner

T

Weatherhead Pt

Masons Downfall

Trumpeter Bay

Cape Baudin

Chain Locker Bay

Cape Sonnerat

Passage Pt

Mt Daedalus

Mt Story

SCHOUTEN ISLAND

Chinese

Chicken Pt

Sandspit Pt

Sarah Ann Bay

Cape Faure

Sandstone Bluff

Mount Field National Park

Rugged mountains, strings of glacial lakes, alpine moorlands, rainforests and the magnificent Russell Falls await the visitor to Mount Field, one of Tasmania's oldest national parks. Winter visitors can take advantage of cross-country and downhill skiing in the Lake Dobson area.

Most of the park is at an altitude of 800 m or more, rising to 1434 m at Mount Field West, and falling to 150 m in the Russell Falls area. The central area of this 16,977 ha park is a high plateau of moorlands dotted with numerous lakes and rocky tarns, crossed by ridges and rugged mountain peaks.

Much of this magnificent landscape was created by the movement of glaciers during the last ice age, between 20,000 and 10,000 years ago. At its peak an ice cap covered the highest area of the park and glaciers flowed out, gouging out valleys as they moved across the landscape. Shattered rocks, soil and boulders were picked up and dumped as the glaciers melted, leaving piles of rubble known as moraines. The moraines dammed many of the creeks, forming lakes and tarns.

Mount Field National Park was declared in 1916 following the efforts of surveyors and dedicated naturalists. Unfortunately, in 1949 a forested section of the park occupying some 1500 ha, including magnificent stands of giant swamp gums, was excised from the park and logged for woodchips. In exchange an equivalent-sized area of mixed forest was added to the park.

Vegetation

The dense forests of the lower areas of the park contrast with the alpine moors, bogs and shrublands of the plateaux. The forests around the park entrance contain stands of swamp gums, the tallest hardwood trees in the world. Some specimens grow to more than 100 m, with ribbons of bark peeling from their huge trunks. Other forest trees include white gums, stringy-barks and yellow gums.

Soft tree ferns form canopies in the creek gullies, while in the wetter valleys and on sheltered slopes are pockets of cool temperate rainforest dominated by myrtle beech, sassafras and leatherwood. White sprays of the native laurel can be seen in the understorey during November and December.

The world's tallest heath plant, *Richea pandanifolia*, thrives on the side of the valley below Mount Monash. This remarkable plant with palm-like leaves, may grow to 12 m. It shares this habitat with King Billy pines and the deciduous fagus or tanglefoot beech.

The peaks and plateaux are covered in shrublands, bogs and moorlands, with varieties of cushion plants forming soft mounds. Dwarf mountain pines and pencil pines grow around the lakes and tarns.

Wildlife

The different habitats provided by the variety of plant communities are home to a wide range of animals. Pademelons and red-necked wallabies are often seen grazing around the picnic areas in the late afternoons and evenings. Barred bandicoots share these areas at night, digging for insects and earthworms. Long-nosed potoroos live in dense undergrowth. These shy, squat, rabbit-sized kangaroo-like marsupials also dig for their food, but are seldom seen.

Brushtail, ringtail and pygmy possums make their homes in the park. They rest by day in tree hollows or nests, and may be seen feeding after dark. Three large flesh-eating marsupials live in the area: the scavenging Tasmanian devil may be heard growling at night, or you may catch a glimpse of the cat-size spotted-tailed or eastern quoll. Australia's two monotremes, the platypus and echidna are both found here, and a quiet, patient observer may catch a glimpse of a platypus in the early morning swimming in one of the lakes or creeks.

Among the reptiles are the three venomous

Tasmanian snakes: the copperhead, tiger and white-lipped whipsnake. They are protected and should not be disturbed. Lizards are commonly seen, and include the small-scaled and spotted skinks, and the squat southern blue-tongued lizard.

Frogs are more likely to be heard than seen. Around Lake Dobson the quacking duck sound is probably Burrows' tree frog, and the bleating lamb call that of the Tasmanian froglet.

The forests provide habitats for numerous bird species. In the eucalypt forests commonly observed birds include green rosellas, yellow-tailed black cockatoos, crescent honeyeaters, currawongs, grey fantails and the golden whistler. In the rainforests you may encounter the superb lyrebird, pink robin, swift parrot, brush bronzewing and the ground thrush. Fewer birds live in the alpine areas. The most common are eastern spinebills, pipits and high-flying wedge-tailed eagles.

Brown trout were introduced and provide good fishing in some of the lakes. Unfortunately they feed on Tasmania's native trout and the mountain shrimp, a species that has remained unaltered for at least 200 million years.

Walks

A ten-minute sealed nature walk leads to Russell Falls, one of Tasmania's most spectacular water-falls. The track passes through magnificent forest with giant eucalypts and myrtles towering above. You can continue to the top of Russell Falls and to Lady Barron Falls via Horseshoe Falls and Tall Trees Walk, through a forest dominated by mas-sive swamp gums, returning via Lady Baron Creek and Tyenna River to the park entrance, a two hour journey.

The Lyrebird Nature Walk, 7 km along the Lake Dobson Road, is a 15 minute self-guided walk through temperate rainforest.

The Pandani Grove Nature Walk around Lake Dobson takes about one hour and provides a good introduction to the plants and animals of this sub-alpine area, but be prepared for cold and wet weather in the high country.

Seagers Lookout is a short, steep climb from Lake Fenton, offering magnificent views over the park. The round trip track to Mount Field East takes about four hours via Beatties Tarn and Lake Nicholls and across the aptly-named Windy Moor.

Those taking longer walks should be equipped with compass and map in case fog or mist descends. One of the most interesting walks circles the Rodway Range via a series of lakes and tarns, with magnificent views over the whole park. The track to Lakes Belcher and Belton in the south crosses open moorlands and has muddy sections, but there are good views over the south-west as the track descends into the Humboldt Valley.

Facilities

Most facilities are located at the entrance to the park. There is a kiosk in the old Visitor Centre with displays. Huts 1 km from the Lake Dobson Road car park have very basic accommodation and must be booked in advance. There are bush-walker huts at Lakes Belcher, Newdegate and Nicholls, Twilight Tarn and K Col.

The camping ground has powered sites, hot water, showers and laundry. Campers should bring their own stoves, bookings are no longer accepted and the area is usually very busy during holiday periods (03 6288 1477 for camp ground information).

Ski tows, ski hire and instruction are available at Mount Mawson in winter. Accomm-odation is restricted to club lodge members and guests.

Access

The park is 75 km west of Hobart via Westerway on sealed roads. Wheel chains should be carried in winter to negotiate the Lake Dobson Road.

Climate

The weather is often wet and cold, and can change dramatically. Winters can be bitterly cold. Bring warm and waterproof clothing and good walking boots.

Mt Field National Park, PO Box 41, Westerway, Tas 7140. Tel. (03) 6288 1149.

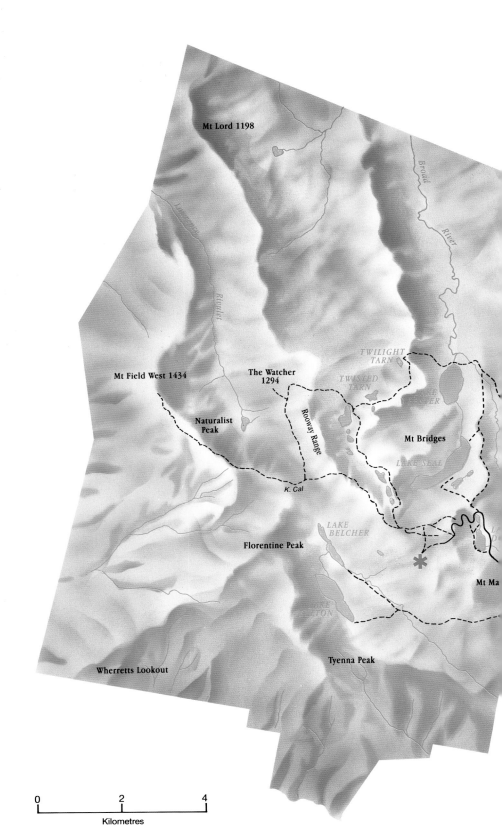

Mt Lord 1198

Broad

River

TWILIGHT
TARN

TWISTED
TARN

Mt Field West 1434

The Watcher
1294

Rooway Range

Mt Bridges

LAKE SEAL

Naturalist
Peak

K. Cal

LAKE
BELCHER

Florentine Peak

LAKE
D

LA
D

*

Mt Ma

Wherretts Lookout

LAKE
TON

Tyenna Peak

0   2   4
Kilometres

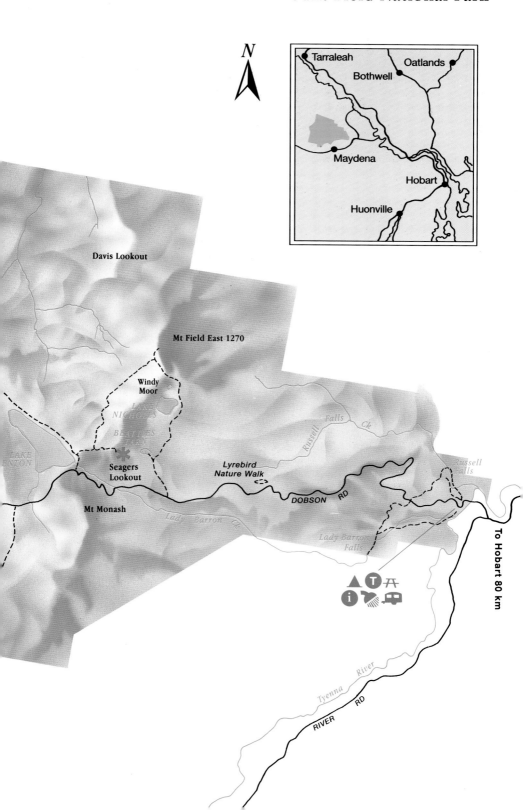

Mount Field National Park

Cradle Mountain–Lake St Clair National Park

Set in one of the finest mountain landscapes in Australia, Cradle Mountain – Lake St Clair National Park is the most famous national park in Tasmania. Part of the Tasmanian Wilderness World Heritage Area, it is a place of rugged mountains, glacial lakes, wild open alpine moorlands, deep gorges and forested valleys.

The park covers 161,000 ha and includes Tasmania's highest mountain, Mount Ossa, which at 1616 m is just one of the many rugged, dolerite-capped mountain peaks in the area.

The Cradle Mountain region in the north rises to a high, treeless plateau with crystal clear rocky pools and gently undulating contours. The plateau is broken by rocky gorges and steep-sided valleys with numerous lakes and tarns, and dominated by the jagged ridge of Cradle Mountain to the north and Barn Bluff to the south.

The centre of the park comprises a plain at an altitude of around 900 m, dotted with lakes and surrounded by Mount Oakleigh, Mount Pelion East, Mount Ossa, Mount Thetis, Mount Achilles and Mount Pelion West. The Forth River rises here and flows out through a beautiful forested gorge.

Further south the skyline is cracked by the rugged peaks of the Du Cane Range. These average around 1500 m and give rise to a number of creeks flowing into the Narcissus River and thence to Lake St Clair. This is a deep, glacial lake with the rainforest-clad slopes of Mount Olympus and Mount Rufus forming its western shores.

Formation

The jagged peaks and undulating plains were shaped during the last ice age, which held Tasmania in its grip some 20,000 years ago. A huge ice cap, some 65 km across, covered the area around the Du Cane Range and Cradle Mountain Plateau, with only the highest mountain tops rising above a sea of ice.

As the temperatures rose and the ice began to recede, great slices of rock were torn from the mountain sides to create the rugged peaks that today dominate the landscape. The moving ice smoothed out the lower ridges and peaks to produce the gently rounded contours of the plateaux. Glaciers in the valleys gouged into the rock to deepen the valleys by up to 35 m. Several glaciers converged on the area occupied by Lake St Clair, where they carved a rock basin 200 m deep, creating Tasmania's deepest lake.

Plants and Animals

The vegetation of the park varies from alpine moorlands to eucalypt forests and cool temperate rainforests.

The fragile soils of the alpine moors are bound together by five species of cushion plant. Each plant grows in the form of a soft cushion up to 1 m across.

On the windswept mountain tops grow stunted shrubs and trees, richeas, alpine daisies and mountain rocket with its pale yellow flowers and red fruit. Christmas bells are common around Lake Dove, while lemon-scented boronia occurs around Cradle Valley and the slopes of most peaks.

Native Tasmanian conifers such as the King Billy pine, growing to 40 m and living for a staggering 1200 years, are found in fairly exposed positions. The smaller pencil pine grows around the edges of tarns, while the creeping pine forms dense mats of branches near the summit of most peaks.

On the slopes of Cradle Mountain and other sites protected from the weather, such as the Labyrinth, grows Tasmania's only deciduous native tree – fagus or tanglefoot beech. In the river valleys are forests of tall eucalypts, such as messmate stringybark and gum-topped stringy-bark, with yellow gum and stunted snow gum at higher altitudes.

On the lower slopes, sheltered from the freez-ing winds and blizzards, the wet misty weather provides an ideal environment for cool temperate rainforest plants. Myrtle beech dominates these rainforest pockets forming a damp, peaceful, green world with ferns, mosses and lichens hang-ing from their branches and covering the fallen logs. Sassafras shares the forest canopy, but on poorer soils and where the canopy is broken grow leatherwood, native laurel and celery top pine. Pandani, a giant heath plant growing to 12 m, appears in the high altitude wet forests.

More than 20 species of mammals have been recorded in the park. The most likely to be seen are the beautiful Bennett's wallaby that frequents the huts looking for food scraps, the pademelon and the brush and ringtail possums. At night eastern and spotted-tailed quolls come searching for food, and if you are lucky you may spot the pink muzzle and red eyes of the Tasmanian devil, or hear it growling in the dark.

The rare broad-toothed rat lives in the sedge-lands, and the long-tailed rat may be found in the rainforests. Elsewhere Australia's two egg-laying monotremes, the echidna and platypus are common.

Among the 80 or more species of birds recorded in the park are black cockatoos, green rosellas, yellow wattlebirds, scrubtits, scrubwrens, thornbills, small honeyeaters and robins. Cuckoos, martins and a number of other species migrate to the mainland during the winter.

All three species of Tasmanian snakes are found here: the tiger, copperhead and white-lipped whipsnake. There are many skinks including the common metallic skink and the snow skink, which lives at higher altitudes.

More than half of Tasmania's ten species of frogs inhabit the park, and at dusk the frog chorus reverberates across the swamps and lakes.

The waterways contain native trout, crayfish and mountain shrimp. The tubular burrows of the land crayfish are commonly seen in boggy ground in the buttongrass plains.

Walks

Walking tracks within the park vary from short nature walks in the Cradle Valley area to the 80 km Overland Track. Walkers should register at the Visitor Centre or at the booths at Lake Dove and Waldheim before and after taking any walk lasting more than 10 minutes.

The tracks following the shores of Lake Dove offer easy family walking with good views, passing through rainforests and past beautiful quartzite beaches. A circuit takes you around the magnificent Crater Lake, surrounded by high cliffs covered with deciduous beech trees.

Full day walks include a trek to the summit of Cradle Mountain. The track is fairly steep and should not be attempted in bad weather. Views from the summit are superb, and there are sever-al return routes to Lake Dove. The western track passes a beautiful hanging glacial lake before descending through rainforest to Lake Dove.

The Overland Track

The Overland Track traverses the park from Cradle Valley to Cynthia Bay on the shores of Lake St Clair. This 80 km walk takes five to six days, and is perhaps the most famous in Australia. The route is easy and safe for anyone of average fitness, but a tent, food, a fuel stove, sleeping bag, waterproof and warm clothing must be carried.

There are unattended huts at convenient intervals along the track, but these are often full in summer months when hundreds of people are using the track, and it is often preferable to sleep in a tent. The weather can change dramatically, and snow has been known to fall in mid-summer.

From Cradle Valley there is a choice of tracks, all of which join the main Overland Track, ascending to the plateau at 1300 m. The journey to Waterfall Valley is very exposed, and care must be taken in bad weather. The mesa-like dolerite mass of Barn Bluff may be climbed, giving panoramic views over the northern half of the park. This side track takes two and a half hours return.

The track descends steeply into Waterfall Valley where, as the name implies, waterfalls

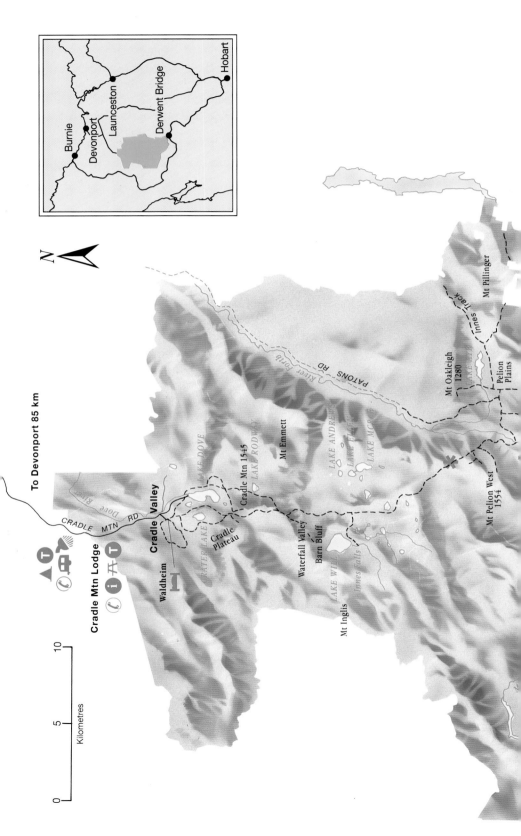

Cradle Mtn Lake St Clair National Park

To Hobart 167 km

Derwent Bridge

Derwent Basin

LAKE LAURA

Mt Ida 1253

LAKE ST CLAIR

Cynthia Bay

LAKE ST CLAIR RD

Narcissus Bay

Overland Track

Mt Olympus 1447

Cuvier Valley Track

Little Hugel

FORGOTTEN LAKE

Mersey River

Falling Mtn

Du Cane Gap

The Acropolis 1471

Mt Massif 1470

The Guardians

Walled Mtn 1410

Mt Gould 1491

Mt Byron 1378

LAKE PETRARCH

Mt Ossa 1617

Mt Cuvier 1380

Mt Manfred 1402

High Dome 1320

Mt Nereus 1180

LYELL HIGHWAY

cascade from the numerous creeks along the sides of the valley. This is the first overnight stop, with good camping areas and a hut. The track climbs gradually to the moor with views of many small tarns surrounded by pencil pines. A side track leads to Lake Will where the view of Barn Bluff is magnificent.

Lake Windermere is the next stop, with good camp sites and a hut. The track passes through open woodland, opening out onto a ridge called Pine Forest Moor, where there are panoramic views of the surrounding mountain peaks.

The track meets the slopes of Mount Pelion West at Pelion Creek where the camping area has been closed for rehabilitation, and then descends to Frog Flats on the headwaters of the Forth River. There are good campsites on the edge of the forest in a vast amphitheatre surrounded by mountain peaks.

A steady rise takes you to Pelion Plains where there are two huts, good campsites and a swimming hole. The track continues through rainforest and wet eucalypt forest to Pelion Gap between Mount Ossa and Mount Pelion East, both of which can be climbed from here.

The track descends to Kia Ora Creek with its beautiful falls, swimming hole and hut. A further 45 minute walk takes you up to Du Cane Hut where the camping is good. From there the track descends through a dense forest of King Billy pines, sassafras and myrtle beech trees to the Mersey River.

The next 2 km are a steady ascent to Du Cane Gap. Here are impressive views over the peaks of the Du Cane Range to the right, with The Acropolis, Mount Geryon and Mount Massif forming the western wall of the valley.

The track passes Windy Ridge Hut and continues through eucalypt forest to a buttongrass plain crossed by duckboards to Narcissus Hut at the tip of Lake St Clair where there is good camping. A track leads from here to Lake Marion, while the Overland Track follows the edge of Lake St Clair through rainforest to Cynthia Bay, about five hours away.

Facilities

The Cradle Mountain Visitor Centre has exhibitions, information, a shop and Ranger Station. Electric barbecues, picnic shelters and toilets are nearby. Cradle Mountain Lodge just outside the park provides accommodation, meals, basic food supplies and petrol (03-6493 1303). Cabins are available for rent at Waldheim, and the Cradle Mountain Camp Ground (03-6492 1395) has camping and caravan sites, a bunkhouse, electric barbecues, shelters, hot showers, laundry and toilets. A shuttle bus operates between the camp ground and Lake Dove seasonally or by demand.

Camping supplies, fuel, food and clothing cannot be bought in the area, although you can hire bushwalking equipment in Devonport and Launceston.

A new Visitor Centre has been built on the shores of Lake St Clair with displays, ranger offices, a kiosk and restaurant. There are picnic facilities, powered and unpowered campsites, cabin and bunkhouse accommodation at Cynthia Bay (03-6289 1137). Accommodation and fuel are available at Derwent Bridge.

Access

Cradle Valley is 85 km south of Devonport via Sheffield or Forth. The last 7 km are unsealed. From the west coast take the Cradle Mountain Link Road from the Murchison Highway north of Que River. Lake St Claire is 167 km northwest of Hobart and 88 km east of Queenstown via the Lyell Highway, which may be closed by snow in winter. Coaches leave from Devonport, Launceston and Hobart.

Climate

With a rainfall of more than 2000 mm a year, the park is generally wet. Weather conditions can alter dramatically and quickly from burning sun to freezing cold, and blizzards can occur in mid-summer. Visit in summer and autumn.

Cradle Mountain–Lake St Clair National Park, Cradle Mountain, Via Sheffield, Tas 7306. Tel. (03) 6492 1133.

Southwest National Park

Southwest National Park is the largest and one of the most remote national parks in Tasmania. This is a vast wilderness area of majestic mountain ranges, thickly forested valleys interspersed with extensive buttongrass plains, and a wild rugged coastline with magnificent beaches and bays. The park is a significant part of Tasmania's World Heritage Area, one of only three large temperate wilderness areas remaining in the southern hemisphere.

Encompassing 605,000 ha and traversed only by walking tracks, this park offers wilderness adventures in a landscape of dramatic contrasts and wild weather. In the north the rugged folds of the Frankland Range rise up from the shores of the artificially created Lake Pedder. To the south and west, flat broad plains between jagged ridges follow the river systems flowing to the coast, and to the beautiful complex of bays and estuaries of Port Davey and Bathurst Harbour.

Perched high in the ranges numerous cold, clear glacial lakes and tarns feed the creeks and rivers. Much of the coast comprises rocky headlands and steep cliffs between the white, untouched sands of wave-swept beaches.

Formation

The dramatic landscape owes much of its formation to a succession of ice ages over the last half-million years. Up to six separate glaciations occurred. The ice caps on the mountains sculpted rock basins, plucked out rounded amphitheatres in the mountain sides, and left narrow razorback ridges between the valley snowfields.

Sea levels were up to 100 m lower during the peak of the last ice age, some 20,000 years ago, and the coast was much further out to sea than today. Tasmania was still attached to the mainland via a land bridge linking the Furneaux Islands.

About 18,000 years ago global temperatures began to increase, melting the ice caps and raising the sea level until its present level was reached some 6000 years ago. The low-lying coastal valleys and plains were flooded, creating a new coastline and bays and inlets such as Port Davey and Bathurst Harbour.

The barren rock faces of the rugged mountain ranges in the north and west are mostly hard quartzite left behind after the water and ice eroded the softer overlying rock. In the south-east are block-like dolerite-capped peaks with vertical columnar cliffs ideal for rock climbers.

History

South-west Tasmania has been occupied for at least 30,000 years, despite the cold conditions during the last ice age. While the high country would have been covered with ice and snow, food resources at lower altitudes were probably far more abundant than today, with extensive grasslands providing a good habitat for game animals.

Many of the caves and rock shelters in the area show signs of human habitation, and a number contain red hand stencils or smears of red pigment. Some date back at least 10,000 years, making them among the earliest known rock art sites in the world.

Until around 1500 years ago the south coast was probably only visited on a seasonal basis to exploit the seals, sea birds and land mammals. Year round occupation was facilitated by the construction of huts erected along the coast, and the use of canoes and rafts enabled the residents to fish and visit nearby islands for game. Important Aboriginal archaeological sites have been discovered in the park at Port Davey, Louisa Bay and Prion Beach.

At the time of the European invasion the coast was the territory of two Aboriginal groups separated by the Ironbound Range. They lived in villages of dome-shaped huts built of sticks, lined with bark or feathers and thatched with grass. At its height the population of the south coast would probably have been no more than 300 people. In 1833 the remaining free Aborigines of the south-

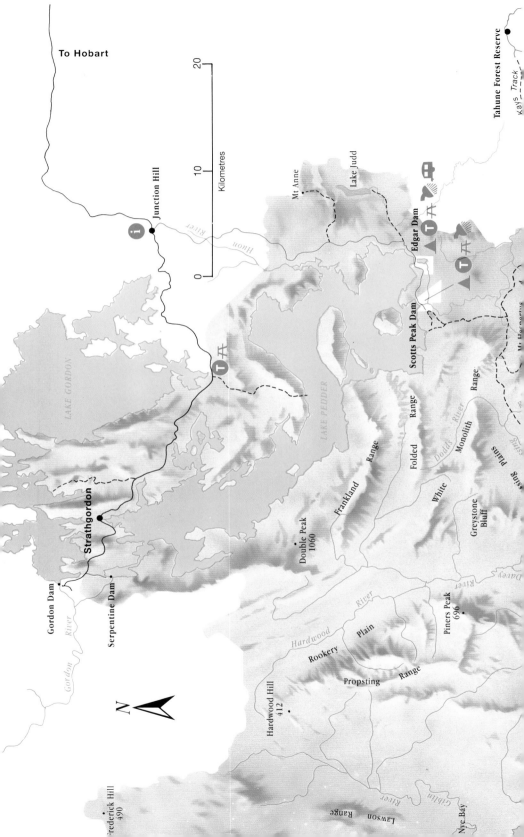

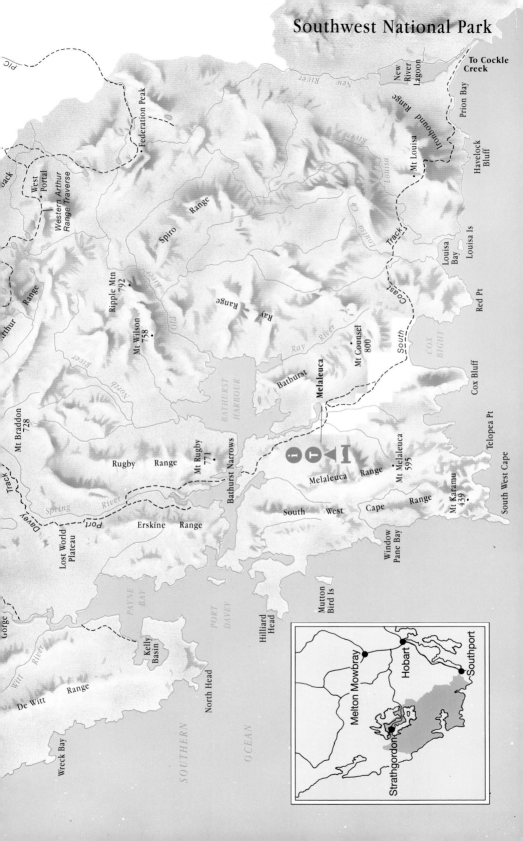

west were rounded up. Of the 49 people captured, only 35 survived to be transported to Flinders Island.

A temporary settlement was formed at Port Davey around 1817, and was occupied by whalers and loggers who, over the next 60 years, hunted the whales to the verge of extinction and stripped the area of its precious huon pine. Tin was mined at Cox Bight intermittently from the 1890s to 1941, but other than this the area received little attention until it was mapped in the 1950s.

In 1955 Lake Pedder National Park was declared in response to proposals by the Hobart Walking Club to protect its wilderness value. The park was extended in 1968, and again in 1976 when it was renamed Southwest National Park.

Amidst great controversy and with no concern for its environmental impact, much of the park was flooded by damming the upper Huon and Gordon Rivers in 1972. Lake Pedder thus became the first part of a grand hydro electric power scheme that included a proposal to dam the Franklin River.

The controversy was fuelled by the Supreme Court's decision in 1975 to uphold an application to mine extensive limestone deposits on the slopes of Precipitous Bluff. These two major conservation issues were the subject of heated nationwide debate, and the following year Precipitous Bluff was included in the park. Further additions were made in 1981 and 1990. The Franklin-Gordon Wild Rivers National Park was proclaimed in 1981, and the 1.38 million ha Tasmanian Wilderness World Heritage Area was declared in 1989.

Vegetation

Sweeping buttongrass moors cover large areas in the west and south-west where the soils are infertile. These sedge plants bear globular seed heads on long stalks, and form clumps amidst tea trees, paperbarks and heath plants. The thin, poor soils of the peaks and ranges support hardy, dwarf shrubs such as the prickly richea, and a dense carpet of green cushion plants.

Extensive cool temperate rainforests grow on the sheltered slopes and valleys, particularly in the east and south-east where there are fewer bush fires and better soils. Even the thin and infertile soils at the heads of valleys can support patches of rainforest, obtaining nutrients from traces of sea salt in the rain. The mature rainforest communities are dominated by myrtle beech and sassafras trees, forming a dense canopy with an open understorey of ferns and mosses. On the poorer soils leatherwood trees and celery top pine become common, with a denser understorey of shrubs such as native laurel, dogwood, musk daisy bush and honeywood.

In fire-prone areas eucalypts take over the forests, with messmate stringybark, gum-topped stringybark and Smithton peppermint dominant. Often there are sudden transitions from open plains to dense forests.

Wildlife

Birdlife is varied and interesting, and the most visible component of the area's wildlife. Overhead soar wedge-tailed eagles and peregrine falcons. Green rosellas and black currawongs are common in forest and alpine regions. The endangered orange-bellied parrot, one of the rarest parrots in the world, and the vulnerable ground parrot breed in the moorland communities. Fringing scrub and forest communities are frequented by the dusky robin, striated fieldwren and the beautiful firetail.

Among the mammals Bennett's wallabies, Tasmanian pademelons, Tasmanian devils, eastern and spotted-tailed quolls and wombats are common in most of the park's habitats. The rare swamp antechinus inhabits the buttongrass moorlands. The eucalypt forests provide tree hollows for five species of arboreal mammals: the common ringtail, brushtail, little pygmy and eastern pygmy possums, and the sugar glider. The Tasmanian and Ewing's tree frogs live in alpine habitats together with numerous lizards including the rare southern snow skink.

The red-headed velvet worm is only known to occur in the park, living in rotting logs and capturing its prey with a jet of sticky fluid fired from projections on its head. The common tiger snake inhabits wet sites in the moorlands hunting for frogs and tadpoles. Burrowing beneath the buttongrass tussocks are freshwater crayfish.

Walks

This vast and remote area is traversed by a number of walking tracks, and experienced walkers will find the rugged terrain and wild climate matched by the beauty and grandeur of the area. However, this is a fragile environment, and the increasing number of people visiting the park are putting pressure on the track system which is showing signs of considerable damage in places. Walkers are therefore asked to stay on the major formed tracks, to use fuel stoves and observe the rules of minimal impact bushwalking. Walkers should record their journey at the registration booths at the track heads.

The most popular walk is the South Coast Track beginning at Cockle Creek, meandering mainly through the lowlands, past pristine beaches and crossing the Ironbound Range (800 m) to Melaleuca. This is a 75 km, five to nine day journey, depending on the number of side trips, and the track has deep muddy sections.

The other main track is the Port Davey Track from Melaleuca to Scotts Peak Road, a 60 km, four to five day hike along a well graded, although often muddy lowland track. Rowing boats are provided at Bathurst Narrows and New River Lagoon for the crossing, and one boat must be left at each side for the next party. If you are on your own this will involve three journeys, the second one towing the second boat back.

The Western Arthur Range Traverse leads from the Port Davey Track or McKays Track beginning at Tahune Forest Reserve. This is a very rugged trail for fit and experienced bushwalkers with good equipment and some climbing skills. A rope is required for pack hauling. The full traverse is 20 km long and takes six to ten days round trip from Scotts Peak.

The Eastern Arthurs, dominated by the spectacular Federation Peak, is accessed from McKays Track from Tahune Forest Reserve, or from the southern end of the Picton Road. Trips take from three to seven days, and like the Western Arthurs this is a rugged track for experienced, well-equipped bushwalkers with some climbing skills.

Shorter tracks lead to Mount Anne (6 km), Lake Judd (7 km), and to Mt Wedge with good views of the area. The Creepy Crawly Nature Trail is a self-guiding 20 minute walk along a duckboard through a beautiful rainforest area some 2 km along Scotts Peak Road from Frodshams Pass.

Facilities

Camping areas accessible by car are located at Edgar Dam and the Huon River. The facilities include toilets, picnic and cooking shelters and barbecues. Very basic accommodation is provided for 20 people in two huts at Melaleuca. Bush camping is permitted at Melaleuca and at designated sites along the walking tracks.

Cockle Creek in the south-east corner of the park has a large camping area around Rocky Bay with basic facilities only.

Access

The park is 120 km from Hobart via Maydena. Turn off at Frodshams Pass to Scotts Peak Dam. Light aircraft fly from Hobart to Melaleuca. Scenic flights, boat tours and a number of organised wilderness tours are available. Small coaches run from Hobart to Scotts Peak and Cockle Creek (03-6334 4442).

Climate

The area has a high rainfall and dramatic changes in weather conditions from hot sun to snow and blizzards. Snowfalls may occur at any time of the year, although they are most common in winter and spring. Snow may remain on the higher peaks until well into December.

Southwest National Park, PO Box 41, Westerway, Tas 7140. Tel. (03) 6288 1283 for the Port Davey Track and the Western Arthurs.

Station Rd, Dover, Tas 7117.
Tel (03) 6298 1241 for the South Coast Track, Eastern Arthurs and Southern Ranges.

The tranquil waters of Wineglass Bay in Freycinet National Park, Tasmania

Sir John Falls on the Gordon River in Tasmania's Franklin-Gordon Wild Rivers National Park

The Walls of Jerusalem National Park, part of the Tasmanian Wilderness World Heritage Area

Asbestos Range National Park (4281 ha)

A northern coastal park with rocky headlands, beautiful sandy beaches and freshwater lagoons. The vegetation includes open forests, heaths with excellent wildflower displays in late spring, and grassy plains: an important grazing area for the large populations of forester kangaroos, wombats and wallabies living in the park.

A boardwalk leads through wetlands and a freshwater lagoon to the ocean. More than 80 bird species live here, and a bird hide has been constructed. Activities include good swimming and boating at Bakers Beach, water skiing near Port Sorell, horse riding and bushwalking. The 90 minute Springlawn Walk visits a tea tree forest and lagoon, or walk to Archers Knob for sweeping ocean views. A five hour return walk goes from West Head to Badger Head along the picturesque Badger Beach.

There are picnic areas and a camping and caravan site with basic camping facilities in an idyllic setting. Bring your own water.

65 km north-west of Launceston via West Tamar Hwy. (03) 6428 6277.

Ben Lomond National Park (16,527 ha)

Located on the high plateau formed by Ben Lomond Range, this alpine park is best known for its excellent winter skiing. The scenery is dramatic with views from the heights over north-east Tasmania. The vegetation includes alpine wildflowers and wet sclerophyll forests on the slopes.

Climbing and bushwalking are very popular in the summer, and in winter a kiosk, tavern, restaurant and accommodation huts service the skiers. A public shelter is open year round. Basic camping only.

48 km south-east of Launceston via a steep, winding road. (03) 6390 6279.

Douglas-Apsley National Park (16,080 ha)

This east coast park protects the largest undis-turbed area of dry sclerophyll forest in Tasmania and provides a haven for a number of rare plants and animals including the Tasmanian

grayling (a small fish found only in the park).

The Apsley and Douglas Rivers have cut dramatic gorges through the forested ridges. Rainforest pockets, waterfalls and spectacular views of the coast add to the grandeur of the area. The two and a half day Leeaberra Track traverses the park from north to south across a plateau dissected by the Douglas and Apsley Rivers, through forest, past lookouts and into the gorges. A ten minute walk from the car park through eucalypt forest goes to a viewing platform where there are vistas over the park and river. A two hour return walk leads to Apsley Gorge. Visit the deep Apsley Waterhole, a five minute walk.

There are picnic areas and basic camping facilities.

185 km north-west of Hobart via the Tasman Hwy. (03) 6257 0107.

Franklin-Gordon Wild Rivers National Park (440,000 ha)

World Heritage listed, the Franklin River is one of the most challenging rafting rivers in Australia. This glacier-worn, remote and rugged landscape is one of deep gorges, impressive peaks, including the glistening white quartzite dome of Frenchmans Cap, rainforested valleys and the calm waters of Macquarie Harbour.

There are dramatic views from the Lyell Hwy, the access route to a number of walks. The Franklin River Nature Trail is wheelchair-friendly and takes you to the confluence of the Franklin and Surprise Rivers. Cruise boats travel across Macquarie Harbour and up the Gordon River.

There are picnic areas and a camp ground at Collingwood River with basic facilities.

180 km west of Hobart via Derwent Bridge or Strathgordon. (03) 6471 251 or (03) 6471 7122.

Hartz Mountains National Park (7140 ha)

World Heritage listed, this glacier-carved area comprises a high moorland plateau sprinkled with lakes surrounding Hartz Peak. Alpine vege-tation grows on the heights while cool temperate rainforests and wet sclerophyll forests cover the slopes. Climb Hartz Peak, a three hour return walk, where there are magnificent views of Federation Peak and the South-west Wilderness. Short walks lead to Koeghs Falls, Arve Falls viewing platform and Lake Osborne, one of the park's finest glacial lakes with the imposing backdrop of Devils Backbone Ridge.

There are picnic facilities and shelter huts for protection. Bush camping is allowed in the western end of the park, fuel stoves only. Summer is the best season to visit, but bring warm clothing and register before going on a walk.

80 km south-west of Hobart via Geeveston on an unsealed road. (03) 6298 1577.

Mount William National Park (13,899 ha)

Located on the north-east corner of Tasmania, this coastal park is an important habitat for forester kangaroos, observed in large numbers along the scenic drive. The mountain range slopes down to a beautiful rocky coastline with pristine white beaches. Climb Mt William for excellent views from the 216 m summit.

A coastal trail leads to Cobblers Rocks past swampland and she-oaks. Visit Stumpys Bay for privacy and good swimming. Horse riding is permitted on special trails.

There are picnic areas and beachfront camp sites with basic facilities.

147 km north-east of Launceston via Gladstone. (03) 6357 2108.

Rocky Cape National Park (3064 ha)

A small coastal park encompassing a deserted, spectacular, rugged coastline of rocky outcrops jutting into Bass Strait with small sheltered beaches. Inland are hills covered with heaths and woodlands. The park is known for its sea eagles and other bird life, and rock shelters used by Aboriginal people 8000 years ago.

Walking tracks lead through the park to beaches and bays. The three hour Inland Track from the western end of the park to Sisters Beach offers superb coastal views from lookouts at

Tinkers Hill and Broadview Hill, and good wildflowers in spring. Organise a car shuttle. Sisters Beach is one of the island's most attractive beaches. It is set in a shallow protected bay backed by hillsides of tea trees and saw banksias.

There are picnic areas but no camp sites.

100 km west of Devonport. (03) 6458 1415.

Strzelecki National Park (4215 ha)

Located on south-western tip of Flinders Island in the Bass Strait, this park features rugged granite mountain peaks rising dramtically from the coastline, beautiful beaches and fern gullies. Climb to the summit of Mt Strzelecki (756 m) and enjoy exhilarating views over the island and coastline. Bennett's wallabies, pademelons, wombats possums, rosellas, black cockatoos, tiger, copperhead and whip snakes are common.

Go canoeing, swimming, fishing, rock climbing or take the overnight walking track to Badgers Corner. Camp or picnic among the she-oaks at Trousers Point where bays of white sand are lapped by aquamarine waters.

Fly from Launceston to Flinders Island. (03) 6359 2217.

Walls of Jerusalem National Park (51,800 ha)

World Heritage listed, this is a spectacular sub-alpine wilderness park. Five steep mountain peaks form a natural amphitheatre surrounding a high central basin where ancient forests of pencil pines border glacially formed lakes. This high and exposed park is very popular with bushwalkers all year round.

Be prepared for extreme weather conditions at any time of year, bring a good map and compass. Bush camping only. No vehicle access.

Visit the nearby Marapooka and King Solomons Caves. Take the 15 minute walk at Devils Gullet on the northern boundary for breathtaking views of the Walls of Jerusalem and Cradle Mt.

130 km south-west of Launceston. Walk in from Lake Rowallan (03) 6363 5182.

South Australia

Featured National Parks

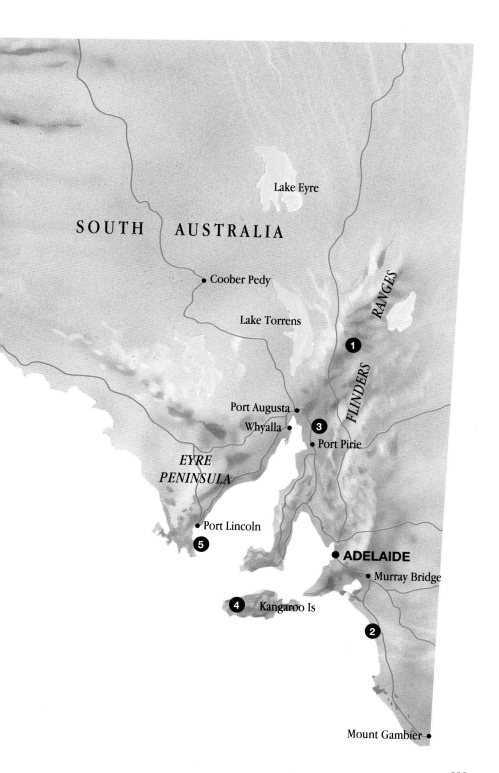

Lake Eyre

SOUTH AUSTRALIA

● Coober Pedy

Lake Torrens

FLINDERS RANGES

❶

Port Augusta ●
Whyalla ●
❸
● Port Pirie

EYRE PENINSULA

● Port Lincoln
❺

● ADELAIDE
● Murray Bridge

❹ Kangaroo Is

❷

Mount Gambier ●

Flinders Ranges National Park

Set in one of the most ancient landscapes on earth, Flinders Ranges National Park lies in a rugged mountain range dissected by deep, tree-lined gorges leading to rolling hills and plains. Included in this magnificent park is the extraordinary geological formation known as Wilpena Pound, a great oval basin seemingly suspended above the plains by mighty ramparts of rock.

This 96,746 ha park protects a large area of the Central Flinders Ranges: a dry, convoluted landscape where sparse vegetation covers the red and brown earth and bright green ribbons mark the courses of winding rivers.

Formation

Between 500 and 1000 million years ago the area was part of a long undersea trough known as the Adelaide Geosyncline. Rivers flowing to the sea carried sediments from the surrounding hills and mountains. They accumulated in layers on the sea bed, gradually compacting into rocks such as sandstone, quartzite, limestone, siltstone and mudstone.

Some 500 million years ago underlying forces began pushing the land upwards, folding and fracturing the rock strata into domes and valleys. Exposed to the elements the softer rocks weathered away, leaving the harder sandstones and quartzites protruding as long ridges above the valleys and plains. Streams have cut through the ridges to form deep gorges between hard quartzite rocks, or V-shaped valleys where the rocks are softer.

Wilpena Pound is a basin encircled by craggy sandstone ridges. Inside these ramparts the erosion from softer rocks has been trapped, while those outside have washed into the low-lying Lakes Torrens, Eyre, Callabonna and Frome, leaving the Pound suspended above the plains.

History

Aboriginal artefacts found in the area date back at least 10,000 years. Before white settlement the area belonged to the Kyuani, Pangkala and Wailpi tribes, who were part of the larger Adnyamathanha group. They travelled within defined territories according to the availability of food and water, meeting for ceremonial and other social occasions. Springs attracted game, and red ochre used throughout Australia for medicine and painting was mined on the plains at Parachilna. People travelled from as far as southern Queensland for this fine quality ochre, trading the narcotic pituri plant, shell ornaments, spear shafts and beanwood shields.

The first European to visit the area was Edward John Eyre, who trekked from Adelaide to Lake Torrens in 1840. The search for water led to the discovery of Wilpena Pound in 1850, and pastoralists began arriving soon after. Their stock contaminated the water supplies, ate the food plants and competed with native animals. Faced with starvation the Adnyamathanha began killing introduced animals. The white settlers regarded this as theft and retaliated with violence and poisoned flour. A protracted guerilla war followed. Hundreds of people were killed, many Aborigines died from introduced diseases and others were forced by starvation to work for the pastoralists. Ironically a succession of poor seasons eventually forced most of the settlers to abandon their properties.

Plants and Animals

River red gums and South Australian blue gums follow the larger watercourses, extracting enough subterranean moisture to survive the long dry seasons. Introduced wild hops cover whole hillsides with a display of striking red flowers in spring. Salvation Jane, or Paterson's curse, adds a magnificent mauve springtime carpet to the land.

On the higher slopes and in Wilpena Pound grow gum-barked coolabahs, drooping she-oaks, wattles and grasstrees. Cypress pine woodlands are common on the slopes, their pollen falling in smoky clouds on still spring mornings. Mallees, native box, grasstrees, porcupine grasses and low fuchsia bushes grow at the foot of the range.

At dawn and dusk emus and red kangaroos frequent the grassy plains, and the euro may be seen browsing on spinifex and leaping up the steep slopes. There are small colonies of yellow-footed rock wallabies high up in the gorges, and a number of bat species have been recorded including the white-tailed mastiff-bat, the western little mastiff-bat, the little brown bat and Goulds wattled bat.

Flinders Ranges froglets are often heard calling from reed clumps beside waterholes, a habitat they share with the spotted grass frog that burrows into the banks. Reptiles commonly seen include wood and Bynoes geckos, tawny and central bearded dragons, tree skinks, eastern blue-tongued lizards, carpet and childrens pythons and brown snakes.

Flocks of galahs and little corellas fly screeching through the gorges in clouds of pink, grey and white, contrasting the lime green of low-flying mallee ringneck parrots. Birds of prey, such as the Australian kestrel and wedge-tailed eagle hover over the plains. Around the rock pools are parrots, honeyeaters, wrens, warblers, butcher birds and wagtails.

Walks

This is some of the best bushwalking country in Australia. Temperatures are mild from May to October, and the clear desert air allows you to see far out to the distant plains. The terrain is rugged and bushwalkers must be well prepared. Those embarking on long walks should complete a log sheet at the Wilpena park office before leaving.

From Wilpena a short walk leads through the gorge into the Pound. An easy track climbs to Wangarra Lookout with a panoramic view of the area. A strenuous climb to Mount Ohlssen Bagge is rewarded with excellent views of the Pound and country to the east.

A track crosses the Pound through woodlands and grassy areas to Edeowie Gorge where the creek flows over falls and through a gorge with steep red cliffs. This is a good day's walk, but well worth the effort. The best views of the Pound are from St Mary Peak, a tiring, seven hour walk from Wilpena.

Arkaroo Rock is an important archaeological site. A track from the car park takes about two hours return along a moderately graded trail. The rock walls are adorned with red ochre images of emu tracks, snake lines, barred circles and leaves.

In the north the Trezona Track is a four hour journey from the camping ground following the ridge through native pines before winding west across the ABC Range to Aroona Ruins. A trail leads through Wilkawillana Gorge following Mount Billy Creek past low undulating hills and the steep rocky face of the gorge. Small cone-shaped fossilized shells more than 500 million years old can be found in the walls of the gorge, showing that the area was once a sea-bed.

Facilities

The park headquarters are at Wilpena. The main camping ground at Wilpena is managed by the Flinders Ranges Tourist Service, which also runs the Wilpena Pound Motel (08-8648 0004). There are 200 unpowered sites, 48 powered sites and full facilities including a kiosk and general store with fuel and ice.

The camping grounds at Dingley Dell and Slippery Dip are used by tour groups. Visitors should bring fuel stoves as firewood is scarce and trees must not be damaged.

Access

The park is approximately 430 km north of Adelaide and 35 km from Hawker via sealed roads to Wilpena. Regular coach services run to the park, and many tours include the park on their itinerary. Coach tours, 4WD tours and scenic flights can be arranged in the park.

Climate

Rain is rare, but when it rains there may be flash floods. Summers are hot with temperatures exceeding 40 degrees Celsius. Winters are mild with cold nights, often near freezing.

Flinders Ranges National Park, Wilpena, SA 5730. Tel. (08) 8648 0048.

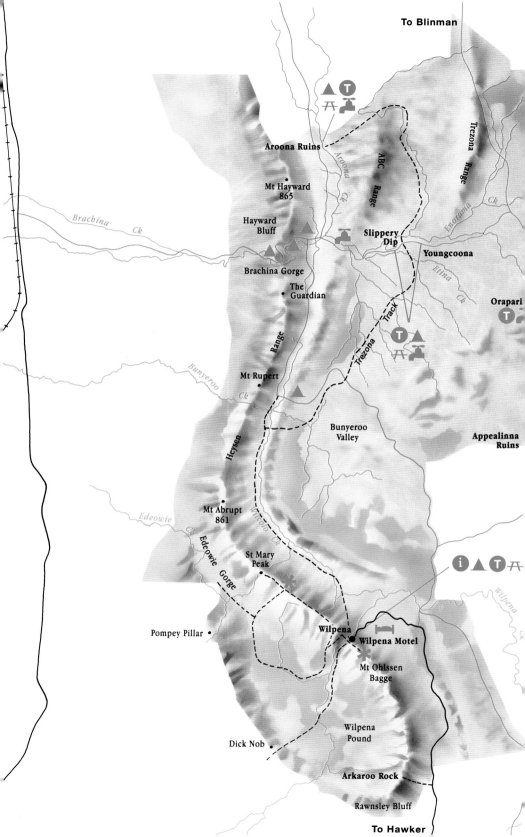

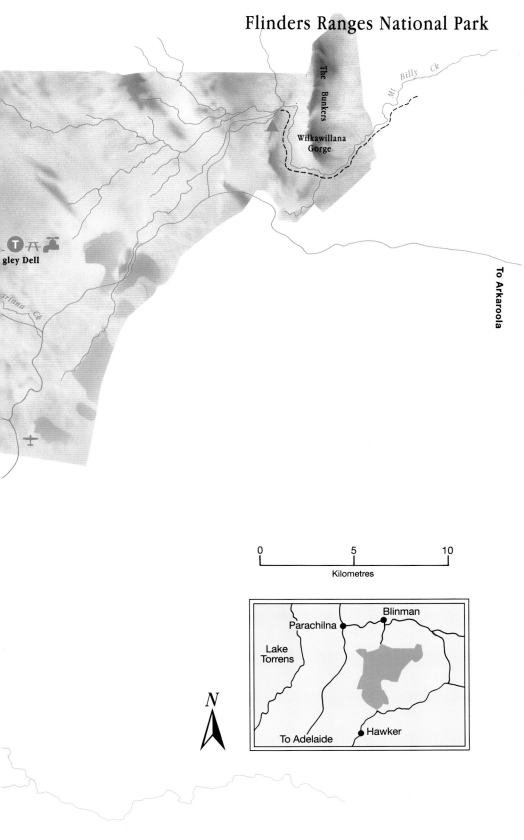

Flinders Ranges National Park

The
Bunkers

Mt Billy Ck

Wilkawillana
Gorge

gley Dell

rinna Ck

To Arkaroola

0   5   10
Kilometres

N

Lake
Torrens

Parachilna

Blinman

Hawker

To Adelaide

Coorong National Park

The Coorong is a narrow ribbon of water isolated from the Southern Ocean by the Younghusband Peninsula: a long narrow sandspit that curves in a misty haze southwards from the mouth of the Murray River. The national park protects most of the peninsula and the Coorong itself, a fascinating area rich in birdlife and a favourite haunt of fishermen.

Coorong National Park is one of the state's most important wetland areas and of world-wide biological significance. Established in 1966 the park occupies 46,745 ha in the flat, low-lying Murray Basin. It comprises a long narrow coastal strip and a series of shallow lagoons behind the Younghusband Peninsula. The average depth of the lagoons is less than 3 m, and in the south they are three times as salty as the ocean. The Younghusband Peninsula is a constantly-changing sand barrier about 100 km long and 2 km wide, pounded by the surf and buffeted by the wind into Saharan-like ridges and valleys.

Formation

For many millions of years the low-lying coastal plains of the Murray Basin were submerged beneath a shallow sea, and rivers flowing from the Mount Lofty Ranges deposited their sandy sediments on the sea bed.

A series of ice ages began around two million years ago, locking up much of the planet's water in the polar ice caps. The sea level fell and the Murray Basin became part of a vast plain that stretched to the south of Kangaroo Island. As the ocean receded it left behind parallel lines of sand dunes, each line representing a period when the sea level remained constant and the waves had time to build up a coastal dune system.

When the last ice age came to an end some 10,000 years ago the sea level had risen by at least 100 m. Kangaroo Island was again isolated from the mainland and the wind and waves piled sand on top of one of the previous dune systems, creating the sand barrier that was to become Younghusband Peninsula. A lagoon formed behind the barrier, and the sand continued to build up, closing the southern entrance to the lagoon about 2000 years ago.

History

The name Coorong comes from the Aboriginal word Karangk, meaning long neck, referring to the Younghusband Peninsula.

For more than 40,000 years Aboriginal people have lived in this area. The lagoons and ocean provided a plentiful supply of fish and shellfish, the inland forests and plains were full of game, and there were fruits, vegetables, fungi, bulbs, roots and honey to be collected.

These people were the Ngarrindjeri, a nation of some 22 clans with defined territories related to each other by kinship, trade and ceremonial rites. Each clan had an organised system of government with democratically elected leaders and a president (known as the Rupulle).

The Coorong belonged to the Tanganekald clan, who at the time of European settlement were a group of about 600 people occupying some 2000 square kilometres of coastline. They lived in villages, trading basketware, nets and skin cloaks for spears, ochre and stone tools. They fished from bark canoes and reed rafts, and ate large numbers of cockles. The only signs of their habitation today are shell middens, campsites, burial sites and stone ovens.

The first Europeans the Ngarrindjeri came into contact with were sealers and whalers who lived at Encounter Bay in the 1780s. Captain Charles Sturt landed at Rufus River in 1829 and returned with reports of a rich and fertile land.

Pastoralists descended on the area and came into violent conflict with the Ngarrindjeri who fought hard to keep their land. They were shot and poisoned by the settlers, decimated by a smallpox epidemic, and were finally driven out by an army of police who embarked on a ruthless massacre in 1841.

Plants and Animals

Although the Aborigines modified the ecology of the Coorong, they achieved a balance with nature, taking only what they needed to sustain life. Not so the Europeans, who introduced grazing animals, rabbits and foxes, cleared the land, and erected barrages at the mouth of the Murray to hold water in Lakes Alexandrina and Albert. The Younghusband Peninsula has largely escaped this human onslaught, although damage to the dune vegetation by vehicles is causing large sand drifts that may eventually threaten the vegetation cover and structure of the Coorong lagoon, swamps and lakes.

The foredunes are partially stabilised by sand-binding grasses such as spring rolling grass and marram grass, with coastal daisy, cushion bush and angular pigface. The sheltered sites behind the foredunes support coastal wattles, large shrubs and paperbark trees, interspersed with freshwater pools where water is trapped by hard sheets of sediment and fed by the water table.

More than 238 bird species inhabit the park, and the waterways abound with fish, including mullet, bream, mulloway and trout. The fringes of the Coorong support reeds, sedges and salt meadows providing habitats for waterfowl, crabs, water rats and snakes.

More than 10 species of ducks and some 80 species of other aquatic, swamp and shore-feeding birds have been recorded here. Waterfowl migrate to the area in spring and summer, and in times of drought the Coorong is a natural refuge for inland waterfowl. Pelicans breed on some of the islands, and long flights are often seen in the Coorong. Spoonbills, ibises, cormorants, grebes, black swans, gannets, plovers and terns are commonly seen. In the dunes are singing honeyeaters, bronze-winged pigeons and the rare and endangered orange-bellied parrot.

The area supports a diverse animal population, and you are likely to see echidnas, grey kangaroos, red-necked wallabies and emus.

Walks

Much of the area can be seen by driving along the coast road and following short tracks across the dunes. The self-guiding Lakes Nature Trail begins at the car park 2 km from the Salt Creek entrance. This 3 km circuit is an easy walk through the park's different habitats. It follows the shoreline of a carbonate lake before crossing sand dunes and ponding levees from old salt works, where the drying water has a pink colour.

A ten-minute walk across the dunes 3 km north of Policemans Point leads to a viewing area overlooking a series of islands, which form South Australia's largest permanent pelican breeding colony. During the breeding season up to 1000 pelican pairs and their young congregate here.

Facilities

Camping is allowed almost anywhere in the park except on the bird-nesting islands. Camp sites are usually off a designated road or track, and have basic facilities. Good camping areas can be found off the Old Melbourne Road, particularly in the pink gum forest near Salt Creek and in the tea tree areas to the south. There are camping areas at all the beach crossings. Permits are required and campers should bring their own firewood or a fuel stove, and observe seasonal fire bans.

There are private camping and caravan parks at Meningie, Woods Well, Policemans Point and Kingston S.E., with facilities, supplies and petrol.

Access

The park is about 180 km south-east of Adelaide via the Princes Highway. 4WD vehicles are allowed on the beach, although they must stay on designated tracks when driving to camping areas between the dunes. The tracks are marked by posts on the foredune, and a green post marks the camping area behind the dunes. Drive at falling and low tide only, and just above the water line. The 42 Mile Crossing is the only all-weather year-round track. The ocean beach is closed to vehicles from 24 October to 24 December between Tea Tree Crossing and the Murray River mouth to protect the hooded plover during its nesting season.

Climate

The area has warm summers and cool, wet winters.

Coorong District Office, 32–34 Princes Highway, Meningie, SA 5264. Tel. (08) 8575 1200.

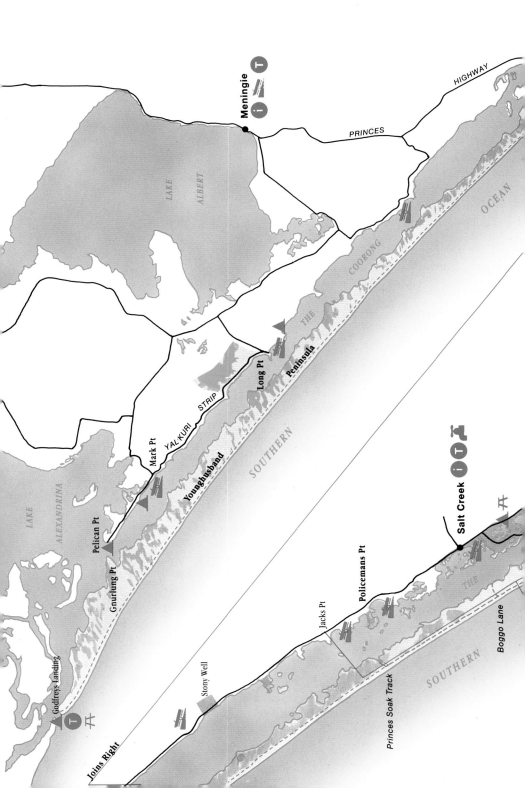

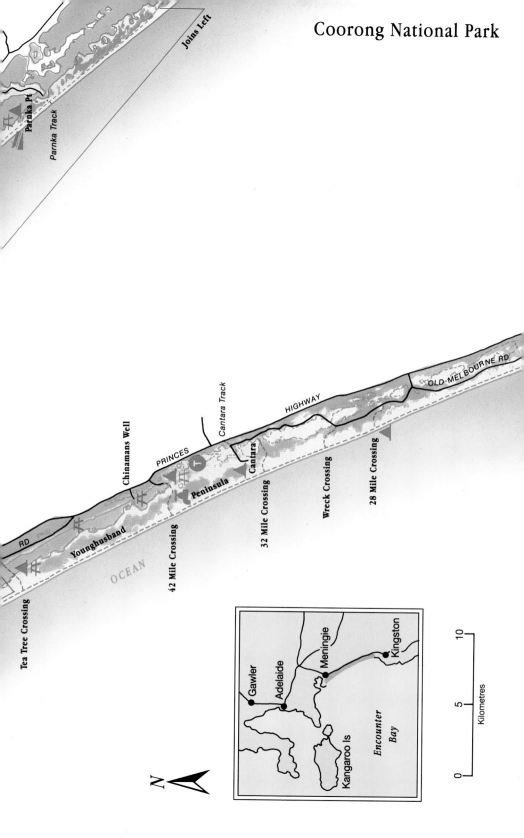

Coorong National Park

Mount Remarkable National Park

Mount Remarkable National Park is located in the southern Flinders Ranges between the flat lowlands of Spencer Gulf and the high undulating wheat country. This is an area of dramatic scenery where creeks flow between deep, narrow, tree-lined gorges of red-brown sandstone. Reliable rainfall in the area supports dense woodlands and a diverse collection of plants and animals.

The 15,632 ha park is in two sections and incorporates the former Mambray Creek and Alligator Gorge parks. Mount Remarkable, at 960 m, stands as a precipitous backdrop to the small historic town of Melrose on the south-western corner of the park, and is chiefly responsible for the high rainfall in the area.

The centre of the park is a large fertile oval basin rimmed with sharp ridges. The Mambray and Alligator Creeks rise here and wind their way through the basin, cutting through the ridges as they flow to the Gulf. Alligator Gorge is the most striking of the gorges in the park, its sheer red-brown quartzite walls form a deep canyon carved through the range. Mambray Creek winds through a tree-lined gorge, emerging onto the open plains where emus and red kangaroos roam.

Much of the park was used to graze sheep, and old fence lines can still be seen in the steep and rugged terrain. Magnificent river red gums were taken from Mowbray and Alligator Creeks late in the 19th century and used for jetty piers and railway sleepers. Some clearing took place in the centre of the park near Kingfisher Flat in the 1950s, but has since regenerated.

History

The Flinders Ranges were formed some 500 million years ago when the area was subjected to massive underground forces that forced up the land in a series of folds and faults. Many of the faults are still geologically active and some parts commonly experience earth tremors and rock falls. The softer strata have eroded away to form the valleys while the more resistant rocks remain as ridges. Streams have opened up fault lines in the ridges and cut their way through the resistant quartzites and sandstones creating steep-sided gorges.

Pastoral runs were established in the Mount Remarkable region in the 1840s, and the Alligator Gorge area was leased in 1882. The Aboriginal inhabitants found their food sources depleted and native animals replaced by sheep, some of which they killed for food. The European settlers regarded this as stealing and the ensuing conflict caused the death of a number of settlers and Aborigines. The outcome was inevitable, and the Aboriginal people were forced to abandon their traditional homelands or work for the pastoralists.

Plants and Animals

Most of the park is woodland. Large old river red gums line the creek beds mixed with tall sugar gums and white cypress pines. Sugar gums were once widespread but are now confined to the southern Flinders Ranges, the Eyre Peninsula and Kangaroo Island. In some areas they are mixed with long-leaved and narrow-leaved box trees and South Australian blue gums. A wide variety of shrubs and small trees grow below them, including the fringe myrtle with its dense pink or white blossoms, red bottlebrushes and numerous wattles. They produce magnificent wildflower displays in spring and early summer.

On the upper slopes grasstrees and porcupine grass grow, and drooping she-oaks cling to the precarious rocky hillsides. Some mallee eucalypts are found in the Mount Remarkable area including the peppermint box, red mallee and mallee box.

The rocky slopes are home to the rare yellow-footed rock wallaby and the more common euro. The latter have coarse shaggy fur and are often seen around dawn and dusk feeding on native grasses and shrubs. A few small colonies of yellow-footed rock wallabies live high up in the gorges, but their populations have been much reduced over the years and their shy nature makes them difficult to spot. Western grey and red kangaroos inhabit the woodlands and plains, and are often seen near Mambray Creek.

Among the most commonly seen birds in the park are striking green rosellas, noisy sulphur-crested cockatoos, galahs, budgerigars, laughing kookaburras, wattlebirds, magpies, small fairy wrens and robins. Birds of prey such as wedge-tailed eagles, nankeen kestrels, falcons and black-shouldered kites hover over the plains looking for small animals.

Walks

A number of signposted walking trails in the park lead to panoramic views of the ranges and secluded gorges. Most visitors take the Alligator Gorge Trail, a 2 km walk from the parking area down a series of steps into the gorge where the sheer red quartzite cliffs close in around you. Follow the creek upstream to an area known as The Terraces where large patterned rocks form steps through the creek; or downstream to the confines of The Narrows where the gorge becomes a close-walled vertical crevice.

A track leads from Alligator Gorge to Mambray Creek. This 13 km walk descends to the floor of the pound beneath the tree canopy and follows the creek through dense stands of river red gums with magnificent wildflower displays in spring. To avoid returning along the same route leave a vehicle at one end of the walk, or arrange a pick-up.

From Mambray Creek the popular 15 km Hidden Gorge and Battery Ridge circuit through leads along narrow valleys and gorges deep inside the park, and returns along Battery Ridge with views over Spencer Gulf. The Mount Cavern Trail is a more strenuous 11 km walk across the high ridges of the Black Range to the summit of Mount Cavern, descending to the cool Mambray Creek Gorge. The shorter Sugar Gum Lookout

Trail takes about two hours and involves an easy walk along a deep valley of river red gums before ascending to a lookout with splendid views of the stark red cliffs of Alligator Creek and Mount Cavern to the south-east.

A walking trail from Melrose leads to the top of Mount Remarkable for excellent views over the surrounding countryside. This walk takes about four hours return and begins at the Diocesan Centre just north of the town.

Facilities

A camping ground, school camp area and picnic area are located near the park headquarters in the Mambray Creek section of the park. The camp sites should be booked during holiday periods, and permits are required to camp in the park. The park and camping ground are closed on days of extreme fire danger. Bush camping is allowed except during the fire danger season, and the ranger should be consulted about suitable sites. There are private camping grounds at Port Germein, Wilmington and Melrose.

The Alligator Gorge section has toilets, picnic areas and a Ranger Station. The rangers conduct seasonal activity programmes during school holidays and long weekends, including slide shows, walks, campfire nights and rock wallaby watches. Wood fires are banned from 1 November to 30 April, and visitors are requested to bring portable stoves and should not collect firewood.

Access

The park has three major access points. The Mambray Creek area is accessible from an unsealed road off Highway 1, 45 km north of Port Pirie. Alligator Gorge can be reached via an unsealed road from Wilmington. The Mount Remarkable section lies directly behind Melrose.

Climate

Summers are hot and dry with temperatures often exceeding 40 degrees Celsius and a high fire danger. Winters are mild with cold nights, often near freezing.

Mount Remarkable National Park, PMB 7, Mambray Creek via Port Pirie, SA 5540. Tel. (08) 8634 7068.

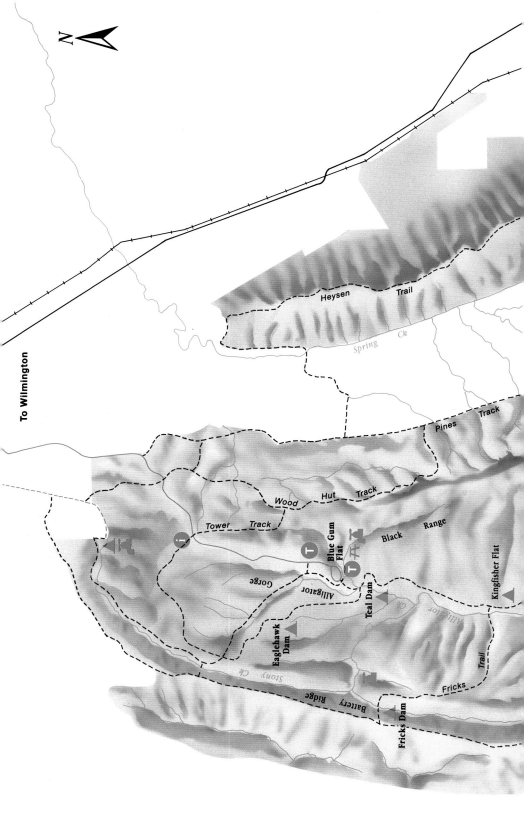

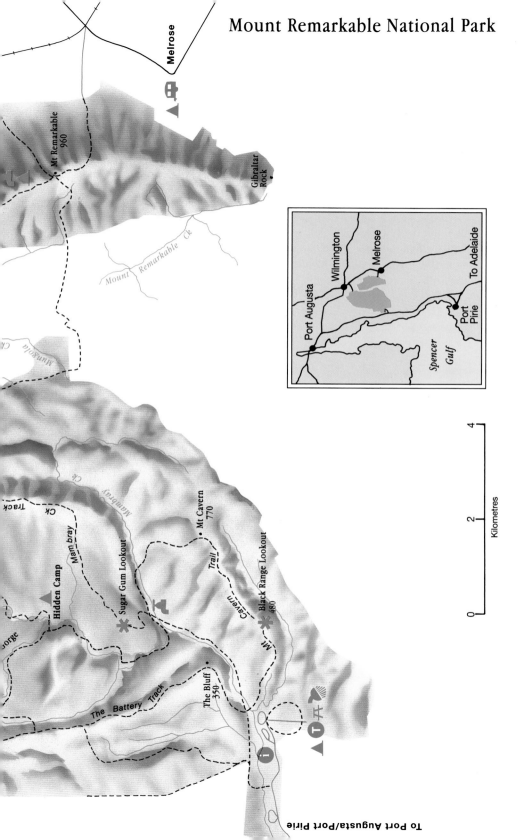

Mount Remarkable National Park

Melrose

Mt Remarkable
960

Gibraltar
Rock

Mount Remarkable Ck

Mangola Ck

Wilmington

Port Augusta

Melrose

To Adelaide

Port
Pirie

Spencer
Gulf

Track

Mambray Ck

Mam bray Ck

Hidden Camp

Sugar Gum Lookout

Mt Cavern
770

Cavern Trail

Black Range Lookout
480

Mt

The Bluff
350

The Battery Track

Gorge

0   2   4
Kilometres

To Port Augusta/Port Pirie

Flinders Chase National Park

Separated from the mainland by the narrow Backstairs Passage, Kangaroo Island is Australia's third largest island and the site of one of the most important national parks in South Australia. Its rocky southern coastline is the home of seals, sea lions and penguins. Most of Flinders Chase National Park is a wilderness area of dense and divergent vegetation that provides a refuge for a wide range of animals, some of which have long since vanished from the mainland.

The park occupies the entire western part of the island, protecting 73,662 ha of mallee-covered low sand hills in the south, a forested plateau in the north, and a rugged coastline of sheer cliff faces, arches and hollowed boulders.

On the southern tip of the park Remarkable Rocks is a cluster of enormous granite boulders weathered into shell-like caverns and precariously balanced on top of a smooth granite dome.

At Cape du Couedic the sea has pounded its way through the promontory to form the magnificent Admirals Arch, a tunnel in the limestone rock where New Zealand fur seals play in the surging waters.

Much of the park is a trackless wilderness where native animals live undisturbed by people and untainted by introduced predators and diseases. The most interesting areas are accessible from the roads and walking tracks.

History

Kangaroo Island is in effect an isolated extension of the Fleurieu Peninsula and part of the Mount Lofty Range. It was possible to walk from the mainland to the island just 12,000 years ago before the sea levels rose at the end of the last ice age, drowning the coastal lowlands.

The Island became completely isolated between 6000 and 10,000 years ago, and the Aboriginal population mysteriously disappeared at the same time, possibly succumbing to disease or migrating to the mainland.

Matthew Flinders landed on the island in 1802 to stock up on provisions for the crew of his ship The Investigator. The large kangaroo population inspired him to give the island its present name. Whalers, sealers, sailors and escaped convicts visited the island in the early 19th century.

The whalers set up whaling stations at Point Tinline and Hog Bay, leaving when they had killed virtually every whale in the surrounding ocean, while the sealers hunted the fur seals to the verge of extinction. Whales are rarely seen anywhere near the island today. The seal population is slowly recovering, however, and some of the colonies are re-establishing themselves.

By 1826 the island's human population had reached the notable figure of 200 males and a number of Aboriginal women kidnapped from Encounter Bay. The graziers and farmers who followed removed most of the natural vegetation in the central and eastern districts. Fortunately the western area was declared a national park in 1919, protecting this last wilderness area and providing a sanctuary for the island's wildlife and for animals whose habitats are threatened on the mainland.

Plants and Animals

The vegetation is similar to that of Western Australia and Tasmania, and some of the plants growing on the island, such as Tepper's trigger plant, *Pomaderris halmanturina* and *Adenanthos sericea*, do not exist on the South Australian mainland. Some 450 plant species, including more than 50 orchids and 23 eucalypts have been recorded in the park.

The north-western plateau, at an altitude of about 300 m, is dominated by mallee and stringybark woodland. Permanent creeks flow in the valleys, lined with tall eucalypt forests of sugar gums, pink gums and swamp gums interspersed with tea trees, banksias and wattles. Ferns and mosses clothe their banks. Dense mallee scrub and heaths grow in the coastal districts.

This rich habitat supports more than 20 species of reptiles and frogs, 200 bird species and 12 species of mammals. There are no rabbits, foxes or dingos on the island, and the largest native predator is Rosenberg's sand goanna. This huge lizard grows to about 1 m long and ranges over large areas foraging for insects, frogs, reptiles, small birds and mammals.

Around the Visitor Centre native mammals gather to feed. They include the Kangaroo Island kangaroo (a subspecies of the western grey kangaroo), the small tammar wallaby, parrots, and the introduced emu and Cape Barren goose. The koala, ringtail possum, platypus and brush turkey were also introduced in the 1920s and 30s when it was thought they may become extinct on the mainland.

New Zealand fur seals and sea lions live in colonies along the southern coastline. Sea lions come ashore to breed at Seal Bay (a reserve outside the park), and are used to humans, allowing people to walk among them. Guided tours take visitors close to these large mammals.

There are rich pickings for water birds in the coastal waters. These include little penguins, waders, pelicans, oystercatchers, ospreys, avocets, stilts, reef herons, albatrosses and white-breasted sea eagles. Among the many land birds are the tawny crowned honeyeater, brush bronzewing, glossy black cockatoo, western whipbird, robins and wrens.

Walks

A number of walking trails wind their way through sugar gum forests, coastal dunes, heaths and mallee scrubs.

The Rocky River Trail is an easy 3 km walk to the headland at the mouth of Rocky River with a panorama of the coastline. The track descends through dense coastal mallee to a small sandy beach where the river tumbles over a waterfall.

The Sandy Creek Trail is the same length, but meanders along the creek through a sugar gum forest to more stunted coastal vegetation and dense coastal heath.

The Breakneck River Track is 6 km long and follows the Breakneck River through sugar gum forest where ferns and orchids grow on the river bank. Nearer the coast the forest gives way to dense coastal mallee scrub, and the track leads past deep waterholes to a broad sandy beach.

The longest walk is the 8 km Ravine des Casoars Trail. This is moderately hard, descending steeply to the beach where large limestone caverns can be entered at low tide (take a torch).

Facilities

Most of the park's facilities are located at the Rocky River Park Headquarters in a small clearing at the heart of the forest. There is an information centre, kiosk, picnic areas and a caravan and camping area with toilets and hot showers. Bush camping areas are located at Harveys Return, West Bay and Snake Lagoon. Camping permits must be obtained from the Park Headquarters.

Access

Kangaroo Island can be reached by air from Adelaide and by car ferry from Cape Jervis to Penneshaw. The park is 113 km from Penneshaw and 62 km from Kingscote via the sealed Playford Highway. Roads within the park are unsealed.

There is no public transport on the island, but bus tours operate from Kingscote, and cars can be hired.

Climate

The island has warm summers and cool wet winters.

Flinders Chase National Park, PMB 246, Kingscote, SA 5223. Tel. (08) 8553 7235.

To Kingscote 62 km

N

Cape Borda
Lighthouse

Harveys Return

HIGHWAY

WEST
END
HIGHWAY

PLAYFORD

SHACKLE TRACK

Ravine des Casoars

Ravine des Casoars Trail

Vennachar Pt

West Bay

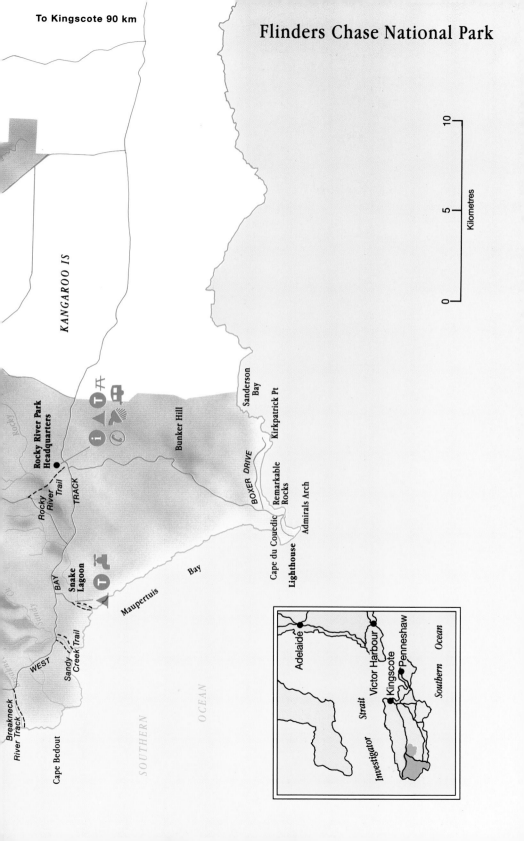

Flinders Chase National Park

To Kingscote 90 km

KANGAROO IS

Rocky River Park
Headquarters

Rocky
River
Trail

TRACK

Snake
Lagoon

BAY

WEST

Sandy
Creek Trail

Breakneck
River Track

Cape Bedout

Maupertuis

Bay

SOUTHERN

OCEAN

Bunker Hill

BOXER DRIVE

Remarkable
Rocks

Cape du Couedic

Lighthouse

Admirals Arch

Kirkpatrick Pt

Sanderson
Bay

Kilometres

0   5   10

Adelaide

Victor Harbour

Kingscote

Penneshaw

Investigator   Strait

Southern   Ocean

Lincoln National Park

Separated from the Eyre Peninsula by a narrow neck of land, Lincoln National Park is a rugged, picturesque headland of cliffs and sheltered beaches surrounded by a host of small islands. The park preserves an area noted for its dramatic coastline and variety of bird and animal life, including the distinctive Port Lincoln Parrot and breeding colonies of little penguins and Australian sea lions.

The 28,000 ha park occupies the whole of the Jussieu Peninsula, a south-eastern arm of the Eyre Peninsula jutting out into the Spencer Gulf, and a number of small offshore islands. The islands are important conservation reserves with large breeding colonies of Australian sea lions and sea birds, and permission must be obtained before visiting them.

A low range of granite hills and cliffs form the eastern side of the peninsula. High cliffs take the brunt of the Southern Ocean in the south, while large sand dunes are formed by the gale force winds that batter the south-western coast. The sheltered northern coastline of wide beaches and granite outcrops looks out onto the calm waters of Boston Bay, a harbour three times the size of Sydney Harbour. Tall mallees grow almost to the water's edge along the northern shores, providing sheltered campsites and safe moorings.

Formation

The Jussieu Peninsula owes its present landform to the accumulation of massive amounts of sand deposited around the granite headlands over the past two million years. The high lime content of the dunes has in many places cemented the sand together to form coastal limestone hills. Erosion by the wind and rising sea levels has gradually eaten into the hills to create the spectacular high cliffs we see today.

History

Aboriginal people of the Nauo tribe occupied the peninsula for thousands of years before the arrival of the Europeans. Semi-circular limestone fish traps have been found in the Sheltered Horse Peninsula area. A gap in the centre of the wall was blocked with stones, a net or bushes to trap fish swept or herded into the enclosure at high tide. They fashioned spears from mallee saplings, heating the wood in hot ashes to harden and straighten it, then drilling it with a stone tool.

Many of the features of the peninsula and the islands owe their present names to Captain Matthew Flinders who explored this coastline in 1802. Some refer to his English homeland of Lincolnshire, including Port Lincoln itself. Cape Catastrophe was the site of the wreck of a small cutter manned by eight sailors who lost their lives in heavy surf while searching for fresh water along the coast. Flinders named eight offshore islands in their honour, and erected a memorial tablet at Memory Cove.

Settlers arrived at Port Lincoln in 1839. Large areas on the national park, particularly around Cape Donington were cleared for farming in the 1870s, wood was harvested for pit props and to supply the building industry in Adelaide, and guano (bird excrement) was mined from the offshore islands for fertiliser. The area was first set aside as a flora and fauna reserve in 1957.

Plants and Animals

The shallow soils of the park support low coastal heaths, dense melaleuca thickets, patches of she-oaks and woodlands dominated by coastal white mallee and yorrell, with an understorey of wattles, guinea flowers, native cherry and velvet bush. In the most protected coves tall mallee grows right to the water's edge.

The areas cleared for farming are now grassy plains where western grey kangaroos and emus graze in the early morning and evening. Other mammals in the park are difficult to see, although you may catch sight of whales, dolphins, fur seals or sea lions in the surrounding waters. Western pygmy possums, dunnarts, hopping mice and bush rats live in the area, but their numbers have been sadly depleted by introduced predators and farming activities.

The offshore islands are home to breeding

colonies of Australian sea lions, short-tailed and fleshy-footed shearwaters, white-faced storm petrels and little penguins.

Hopkins Island has a large breeding colony of short-tailed shearwaters, and more than 70,000 birds live here in summer, travelling all the way from the North Pacific to this small island. The sight, sound and smell of these birds is an unforgettable experience.

If you get permission to visit the islands be sure to wear protective clothing as black tiger snakes are common. Other reptiles in the area include sand monitors, bearded dragons, jacky lizards, peninsula brown snakes and the peninsula dragon, often seen basking on rocky outcrops.

More than 100 bird species have been recorded in the park. The limestone cliffs are nesting sites for two beautiful birds of prey: the osprey and white-breasted sea eagle. Sooty oystercatchers, terns, cormorants, herons, pelicans, gulls and dotterels are common along the coast, while the mallee scrubs and heaths provide food and shelter for the brilliantly-coloured Port Lincoln parrot, common bronzewing, tawny-crowned honeyeater, babblers, robins, scrub wrens and the rare western whipbird. Butcherbirds, shrike-thrushes and golden whistlers forage among she-oaks. Small birds of the heathlands include the southern emu wren and rufous field wren. The rock parrot is common on many of the islands and foredunes, and can be approached while it is feeding.

Walks

Most walking tracks are located in the northern section around Stamford Hill and Surfleet Point. The capes and promontories provide spectacular views across the park and bays. A climb to Flinders Monument on the top of Stamford Hill will reward you with views over the rugged coastline, islands and bays, or follow the coastal tracks along the sandy beaches and rocky outcrops from Woodcutters Beach to Spalding Cove.

Memory Cove and Cape Catastrophe can be reached by a 4WD track through coastal mallee and disused farming areas. Near the southern tip of the peninsula the track passes steep limestone cliffs before descending to the sheltered beach of Memory Cove. This remote area is ideal walking country for experienced bushwalkers, but you must carry plenty of food and water.

Taylors Landing is a sandy cove between two limestone headlands used by boats and barges plying between Taylors Island and the mainland. You can walk along the cliffs and discover small secluded coves. The clifftop walk at Wanna is an exhilarating experience on a stormy day, but take great care.

Facilities

There are a number of good sheltered camping areas in the northern area, although camping is only permitted at the areas shown on the map. Basic facilities are provided at Surfleet Cove and Taylors Landing where there are toilets and water but no powered sites or showers. Firewood collecting is not allowed and visitors should bring fuel stoves. Camping permits must be obtained from the District Office at Port Lincoln.

Donington Cottage on Cape Donington is fully furnished, has five rooms and can be booked in advance. All types of accommodation are available at Port Lincoln.

Access

The park is 10 km south of Port Lincoln along a sealed road. Some of the tracks in the park are rough and may be unsuitable for conventional vehicles. Advice should be obtained from the District Office at Port Lincoln.

Access to Memory Cove Wilderness Area is by permit only, and only 15 4WD vehicles per day are allowed into the area. Tourist boats visit the park from Port Lincoln.

Climate

The area has warm summers and mild winters. Most of the rain falls between June and August.

NPWS Eyre District Office, 75 Liverpool St, Port Lincoln, SA 5606. Tel. (08) 8688 3111.

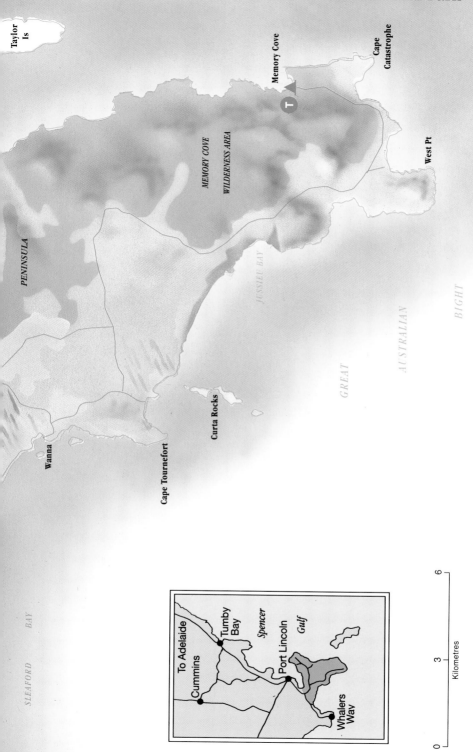

Lincoln National Park

Taylor Is

Memory Cove

Cape Catastrophe

West Pt

MEMORY COVE
WILDERNESS AREA

PENINSULA

JUSSIEU BAY

GREAT

AUSTRALIAN

BIGHT

Curta Rocks

Cape Tournefort

Wanna

SLEAFORD

BAY

To Adelaide

Cummins

Tumby Bay

Spencer

Gulf

Port Lincoln

Whalers Way

0   3   6

Kilometres

Canunda National Park (9086 ha)

A long, narrow coastal park west of Mount Gambier with rugged limestone cliffs in the north and massive mobile sand dune systems along dangerous surf beaches in the south.

Low coastal vegetation of wattle, tea tree and grasses dominate the landscape between the dunes and Lake Bonney. Wildlife includes the rare rufous bristle-bird and endangered orange-bellied parrot. Cliff top walks from 1.6 km to 4 km long in the northern section give spect acular coastal views of islands, sea stacks and offshore reefs.

From the car park on the Bevilaqua Ford Track a short walk leads to spectacular sand dunes known as the Khyber Pass.

Camp at Boozy Gully where there are basic facilities. 4WD access along the beach.

Conventional vehicle access to Cape Buffon and Boozy Gully.

13 km south of Millicent. (08) 8735 6053.

Coffin Bay National Park (30,380 ha)

Covering the entire Coffin Bay Peninsula, this park protects a beautiful coastal wilderness area with a great variety of wildlife including the unique Coffin Bay brumbies. White-bellied sea eagles, ospreys, albatrosses and petrels are commonly seen.

There are several scenic drives. Almonta Beach is one of the state's finest surfing beaches. Basic camping only.

49 km west of Port Lincoln. (08) 8685 4047.

Gammon Ranges National Park (128,228 ha)

Located in the northern part of the Flinders Ranges, this wilderness park encompasses a landscape of deep colourful gorges and rugged mountains set in an arid isolated area. Italowie Gorge and Weetoola Gorge are popular picnic and bushwalking areas. The park is rich in wildlife, but only experienced bushwalkers should venture off the beaten track.

The main camping areas are at Italowie

Gorge (on the access road to Weetoola Gorge), Wooturpa Spring (near Mainwater Well) and Arcoona Well, or stay at the nearby Arkaroola resort. 4WD recommended off the main road. Summers can be very hot.

95 km west of Leigh Creek. (08) 8648 4829.

Innes National Park (9100 ha)

Covering the toe of Yorke Peninsula, this park has spectacular coastal scenery with weathered cliffs and beaches backed by sand dunes, salt lake flats and low undulating scrub inland.

Kangaroos and emus are often seen. Fishing, surfing, diving and camping are popular. Camp at Pondalowie Bay where there are good facilities.

6 km south of Marion Bay. (08) 8854 4040.

Lake Eyre National Park (1,228,000 ha)

This remote and arid park includes all of Lake Eyre North and the adjoining Tirari Desert, and preserves an important desert wilderness area. Vast north–south sand dunes and salt lakes characterise the area.

Lake Eyre floods very occasionally, attracting a huge bird population. The vegetation is low stunted samphire saltbush, acacia and cassia. There are significant fossil deposits at Lake Ngapakaldi. No facilities. Bush camping at Muloorina Station waterhole. Desert park permit required. Summers can be very hot.

90 km north of Marree, or via William Creek. (08) 8648 4244.

Murray River National Park (13,250 ha)

On the floodplain of the Murray River, this park includes Katarapo Creek, Lyrup Flats, Bulyong Island and Eckert Creek. River red gums and black box woodlands grow here. Waterbirds are common, and many protected species nest on the island. Excellent canoeing, fishing and bush camping. Summers can be hot.

Close to Loxton. (08) 8585 2177.

Nullarbor National Park (230,000 ha)

In the south-western corner of the state, this large park stretches 180 km along the coast from the Western Australian border to Nullarbor. The flat, featureless plain drops 80 m to the sea in a long coastline of limestone cliffs. Rainfall is sparse, and patchy mallee forms a low ground cover over much of the park. The semi-arid landscape springs into life after rain, and the plains are covered with wildflowers.

Wildlife includes wombats, dingos, sea lions and whales, which migrate past the coast from May until October. There are sinkholes, blow-holes and caves. Enjoy spectacular sunsets and views of the Great Australian Bight. No camp-sites, but camping permitted at roadside stops.
Access along the Eyre Hwy. (08) 8625 3144.

Witjira National Park (776,900 ha)

A huge desert park of gibber plains, salt pans, sand dunes, flat-topped hills and numerous mound springs. The latter create oases with palms and melaleucas, and attract desert animals and birds. Dalhousie Springs is the largest artesian spring in Australia, and is suitable for swimming. Red mulga and gidgee trees grow around the dry river courses.

Camp at Dalhousie Springs where there are basic facilities. A desert park permit is required. Summers can be very hot.
120 km north of Oodnadatta, or via Birdsville. (08) 8648 4244.

Northern Territory

Featured National Parks

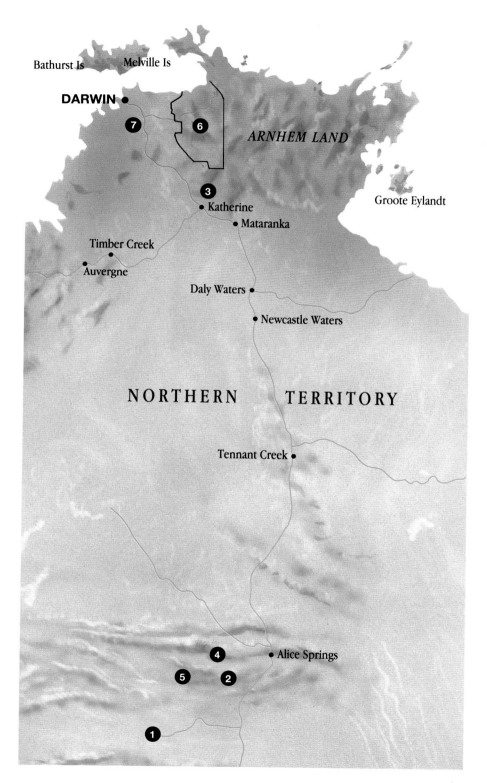

Bathurst Is

Melville Is

DARWIN ●

7

6

ARNHEM LAND

3

● Katherine

● Mataranka

Groote Eylandt

Timber Creek
●

● Auvergne

Daly Waters ●

● Newcastle Waters

N O R T H E R N T E R R I T O R Y

Tennant Creek ●

4

● Alice Springs

5 **2**

1

Uluru–Kata Tjuta National Park

In the dry heartland of Central Australia the massive monoliths of Uluru (Ayers Rock) and Kata Tjuta (The Olgas) dominate the plains, their colours shifting through blues and violets to browns and fiery reds as the burning sun arcs through the sky.

This World Heritage listed park occupies 132,566 ha on the edge of the Gibson and Great Victorian Deserts. Uluru, the world's greatest monolith, stands 348 m above the red sand plains at 862 m above sea level, and has a cir-cumference of 9.4 km. The rock is smooth and rounded with vertical fissures down the sides that channel water during the infrequent rain storms, which crashes down waterfalls into large pools feeding the semi-permanent Mutitjula spring.

Kata Tjuta, 32 km west, means "many heads", and comprises 36 red conglomerate domes separated by deep canyons and broad valleys covering an area 7 km long and 5 km wide. The largest, Mount Olga, rises 546 m above ground level.

Formation

Uluru and Kata Tjuta are the weathered tips of huge slabs of rock extending up to 6 km beneath the desert. The rock was formed over hundreds of millions of years from sediments washed from an ancient mountain range into a depression called the Amadeus Basin. At times this was a shallow sea, and the sediment compacted into layers of sandstone and conglomerate — a mixture of peb-bles and boulders cemented by sand and mud.

Between 400 and 300 million years ago the land was pushed up above sea level, folding and fracturing the rocks. The surface eventually erod-ed away, leaving the tip of a huge sandstone rock (Uluru) standing above the plains, separated by a broad valley from the rounded conglomerate hill tops of Kata Tjuta. Over the last 500,000 years the climate has become much drier and the valley has filled with a thin blanket of wind-blown sand.

Weathering has given the rocks their present form. Ongoing erosion is visible in the flakes of rock that peel from the sides of Uluru. As iron particles in the sandstone rust they expand, flaking off the outer layers of rock and giving the monolith its red colour.

Anangu

Aboriginal people, known as Anangu, have lived in the area for at least 22,000 years, and many features of the landscape were created by their ancestral beings. Uluru and Kata Tjuta are part of a wide network of significant sites linked by tracks made by different ancestral beings during their travels. Paintings in the caves and rock shelters around the Uluru's base illustrate stories of the creation period. Some of the sites are sacred and access is denied to the public, others, such as Kantju waterhole, require specific behaviour.

The land around Uluru and Kata Tjuta was too harsh for grazing, and Anangu were spared the most devastating effects of the pastoral indus-try that spread from Alice Springs in the 1870s. The area was included in a system of Aboriginal reserves, but conflict over water and hunting grounds arose when the pastoral companies began expanding south and west of Alice Springs in the 1930s. Mineral exploration began in the 1940s, opening the area to tourists, and part of the reserve was declared a national park in 1958. Many Anangu were pressured into leaving, but some remained to protect their sacred sites.

After a long and complex battle, title to the park was transferred to Anangu in 1985. The park is leased back to the Director of the Australian National Parks and Wildlife Service and managed co-operatively. In 1977 the park was accepted as a UNESCO Biosphere Reserve. In 1987 the park was inscribed on the World Heritage list for its natural values, and in 1994 it was also inscribed as a cultural landscape.

Plants and Animals

Despite the hot and harsh conditions, the area is

surprisingly rich in plants and wildlife. Some 416 plant, 178 bird, 72 reptile and 25 native mammal species have been recorded. Anangu harvested resources in a sustainable fashion, burning small patches of vegetation to create more diverse plant and animal communities. Children were taught the geography of desert waterholes, how to preserve them from pollution and evaporation, and other conservation measures such as restrictions on hunting.

Around the rocks where soil and water collect are fig trees, native plums, hop bushes, bloodwood gums, wild oats and swaying kangaroo grass, with ferns and trigger plants hidden in cracks and crevices. Spinifex dominates the plains with clumps of mulga protecting the parakeelyas and white daisies that bloom prolifically when it rains. Stands of desert oaks appear among the spinifex, while on the sandhill crests are grevilleas and small pea plants. River red gums line some of the watercourses, together with Sturt's desert rose and the unique early nancy create a pink carpet after rain.

On top of and around the rocks are euros, dingos, bats, hopping mice, the red-eared antechinus and echidnas. Among the mulga and on the plains red kangaroos and herds of introduced camels roam. Reptiles are common and include venomous king and western brown snakes, the harmless childrens python, the perentie (Australia's largest lizard, growing to 2 m or more), sand monitors, geckoes, and the unmistakable thorny devil, which, despite its fierce-looking spines, is quite harmless.

High on the rocky ledges and caves wedge-tailed eagles and Australian kestrels make their nests. Among the mulgas are honeyeaters, masked wood swallows, zebra finches, diamond doves and crested pigeons. Bustards, emus and flocks of budgerigars are often seen on the plains, while black crows scavenge.

Walks

A number of walking trails introduce visitors to the landforms and vegetation types and Anangu culture. The 2 km Liru walk from the Cultural Centre winds through stands of mulga to the base of Uluru. The 10 km Uluru Circuit around the base of the monolith is a good alternative to the climb, and takes three to four hours.

Rangers conduct the 2 km Mala walk to Kantju Gorge every morning, explaining the significance of the area to Anangu. The short Mutitjulu walk leads to a waterhole which is the home of the ancestral water snake, Wanampi.

The track to the top of Uluru follows the traditional route of the ancestral Mala men on their arrival at Uluru, and has great spiritual significance for Anangu who prefer that visitors do not climb Uluru.

There are spectacular views of Kata Tjuta from the Dune Viewing area, but to explore the surreal beauty of this landscape take the 2 km return Olga Gorge walk or the 7 km Valley of the Winds circuit. Kata Tjuta is a maze of rock formations and it is easy to become lost away from the trails. Wear a hat and protective clothing, drink plenty of water and rest in the heat.

Facilities

The Cultural Centre details aspects of Anangu life with audiovisual, artwork and other installations. There is a performance area, cafe and store. Ayers Rock Resort (08-8956 2144), 18 km from Uluru at Yulara, has hotels and apartments. The resort's camping area has around 500 camp sites, caravan sites, overnight vans, electric barbecues and all facilities including a swimming pool and kiosk. Bookings should be made during peak holiday periods. Bush camping is not permitted. Other facilities include bicycle hire, car rental, a service station, supermarket, restaurants, post office, banks, medical centre and police station.

Access

The park is 463 km south-west of Alice Springs via the sealed road from Erldunda. There are regular flights, express coaches and coach tours. Scenic flights and other tours can be arranged in Yulara. The main park roads are sealed.

Climate

The average rainfall is 200 mm. Summer is hot and temperatures reach 44 degrees Celsius. Best time to visit is May to October, when there are warm days and cool nights, although night temperatures fall below freezing in July.

Uluru – Kata Tjuta National Park, PO Box 119, Yulara, NT 0872. Tel. (08) 8956 2299.

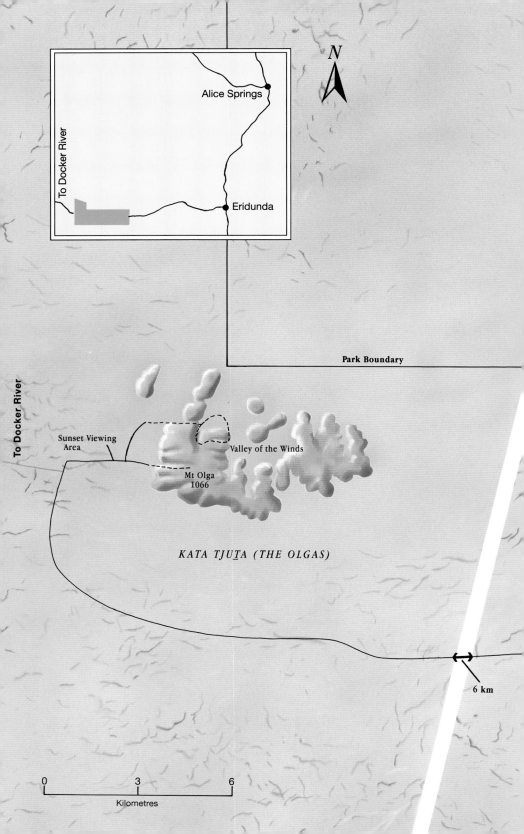

N

Alice Springs

To Docker River

Eridunda

Park Boundary

To Docker River

Sunset Viewing
Area

Valley of the Winds

Mt Olga
1066

KATA TJUṮA (THE OLGAS)

6 km

0   3   6

Kilometres

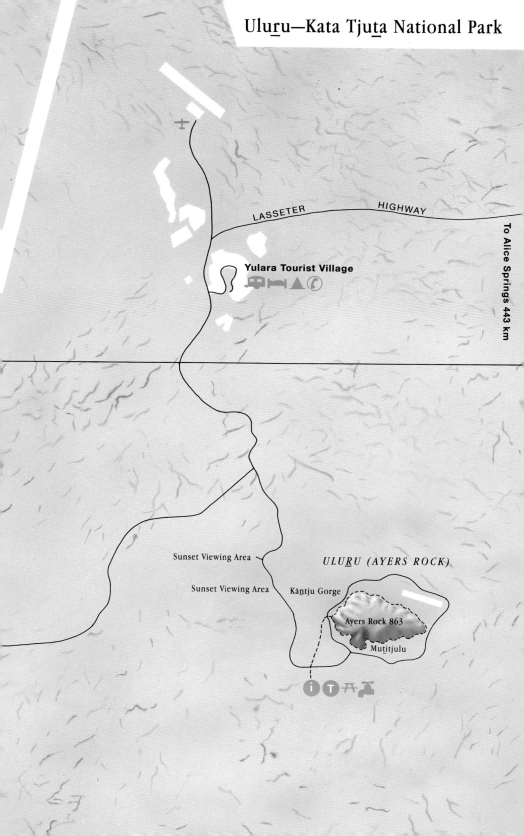

Uluru—Kata Tjuta National Park

LASSETER HIGHWAY

Yulara Tourist Village

To Alice Springs 443 km

Sunset Viewing Area

ULURU (AYERS ROCK)

Sunset Viewing Area

Kantju Gorge

Ayers Rock 863

Mutitjulu

Finke Gorge National Park

Finke River is one of the oldest watercourses in the world. For more than 100 million years it has carved its way through the ancient rocks of the James and Krichauff Ranges creating wide, sculptured gorges. Here, protected by the Finke Gorge National Park, are rare plants left clinging to life in small moist havens. The park includes Palm Valley, a lush oasis of rare red cabbage palms surrounded by rugged red cliffs.

This 46,000 ha park, set in one of the driest and most inhospitable parts of Australia, was declared in 1967 to protect the rare red cabbage palm (*Livistona mariae*). Yet the area has a strange, otherworldly feel, as though the shadowy canyons hide unfathomable secrets from the past. Carved into the sandstone are impressive formations such as The Amphitheatre (Kalarranga) and Cycad Gorge.

The major physical features of the park are the dry sandy river beds and wide shallow gorges of Finke River and Ellery Creek, winding through the worn and rounded hills of the James and Krichauff Ranges. Finke Gorge is not as deep and impressive as some of the other gorges in the area, but it has a soft, rich beauty, particularly in the early morning and late afternoon when the high cliffs, mirrored in the river pools, glow with brilliant red hues. Every few years heavy rainfalls unleash floodwaters that transform the watercourses into raging torrents. This is an awesome sight as the surging waters tear rocks from the cliffs and hurl debris high into the trees. The floods bring new life to the waterholes and replenish the water table.

Palm Valley, a tributary of Finke River, is a cliff-rimmed amphitheatre reached by a track that climbs from the sandy bed of Finke Gorge. The valley walls have been eroded into fascinating shapes, with headlands, side gorges and spires of bright red rock contrasting with the blue waterholes and lush green foliage of the stately palms. Away from the twisting gorges is a desert landscape of rugged sandstone uplands and gullies with pockets of vegetation.

Formation

The James and Krichauff Ranges are giant folds in the earth's crust, created as the land was slowly uplifted some 300 million years ago. The course of the Finke River is independent of the folding of the rocks and does not follow any faults or other natural weaknesses, indicating that the ancient river maintained its course as the ranges rose.

The river began to carve its present gorge only 20 million years ago during another period of geological uplift. Palm Valley and the Amphitheatre were formed at the same time by Palm Creek, which drains a small closed valley in the James Range. Over the past 65 million years central Australia has experienced dramatic changes in climate. As recently as one million years ago this area supported lush tropical rainforests. Crocodiles swam in the swamps and rivers and giant herbivorous marsupials roamed the land. The rhinoceros-sized Diprotodont managed to survive here despite the increasing aridity until about 7500 years ago.

History

The Finke River is of great significance to the Western Arrernte people who have lived in this area for at least 20,000 years. The springs and waterholes were the source of food and game in the long droughts, and the river was a major trading route linking the centre with South Australia. On its 600 km journey into the Simpson Desert the Finke River (known as Larapinta, meaning running waters, to the Western Arrernte people) passes through the territories of at least five Aboriginal language groups. The area is the focus of legends of the spirit beings who wandered the earth in the Dreamtime.

Early European explorers followed the river bed on their journeys into Central Australia. Ernest Giles was the first European to set foot in the area in 1872, followed by Lutheran missionaries who established the Hermannsburg Mission in 1877 in order to "civilise" the Aboriginal people. Camel teams brought supplies from the south along the Finke, and pastoralists began importing cattle, unleashing bitter and often violent conflict between the two cultures, both competing for the limited resources of the area. A police camp was established at Boggy Hole in 1889 to quell Aboriginal resistance to the settlers. It was closed four years later when the Constable-in-charge was accused of murdering Aborigines. The national park was declared in 1967.

Plants and Animals

Despite the aridity of the area the park contains a remarkably rich flora. Palm Valley has the greatest diversity of vegetation in the park, and more than 400 plant species have been recorded in this area alone, including at least 22 rare and 13 relict species. Relict plants and animals are leftovers from the time when this area was part of the wet tropics. Nowadays they survive only in a few pockets of permanent moisture.

The red cabbage palm is found nowhere else in the world, and the last 1200 adult plants are restricted to the sheltered gorges and valleys of the area. Another relict plant, the MacDonnell Ranges cycad, grows on the northern and western facing slopes of Palm Valley. To prevent damage to these remarkable plants and help to ensure their survival, visitors must not collect seeds, walk among the palms or trample seedlings.

Grey and white-barked river red gums grow along the watercourses, and white-trunked ghost gums survive on the stony ridges. The upland areas support spinifex, mulga and wattles, providing habitats for some of the 140 bird species found in the park, such as the redthroat, dusky grasswren, slaty-backed thornbill, spinifex pigeon and common bronzewing.

The permanent waterholes provide refuges for fish populations during times of drought, and attract visitors such as the pelican, black swan, osprey and occasionally waterbirds from the northern hemisphere. Spotted bowerbirds are often seen feeding on the fruits of the native fig trees growing around the waterholes.

Dingos are often heard, their howls echoing from the cliff walls. They can survive with little water, obtaining most of their needs from the small animals they kill.

Walks

Four marked walking tracks have been constructed in the Palm Valley area. From the Kalarranga car park or camping area a 1.5 km track leads to Kalarranga Lookout, an easy climb with spectacular views of the rocky Amphitheatre encircled by rugged cliffs.

The Mpaara Track takes about two hours to complete. Signs along the route tell the Dreamtime story of Mpaara, one of the fascinating Aboriginal stories associated with the land.

There are two marked walking tracks into Palm Valley, the 2 km Arankaia Walk and the 5 km Mpulungkinya Walk a two hour walk from the harsh desert into a lush oasis of slender palms before returning across the arid plateau above the valley. Those going on long bushwalks should ask the ranger for advice and be well equipped with water and protective clothing.

Facilities

The camping area at Palm Valley has water, toilets, solar-heated showers, gas barbecues and picnic tables. Rangers give campfire talks from April to October. Fuel and basic supplies are available at Hermannsburg.

Access

The park is 140 km west of Alice Springs via Larapinta Drive. Turn south at Hermannsburg Mission on a high-clearance 4WD track for the final 13 km. The track follows the sandy bed of the Finke River and may be impassable after rain. Check conditions with the ranger before taking this track. Driving into the southern section of the park requires careful planning and preparation. Regular coach tours operate from Alice Springs.

Climate

The cooler months from April to September are the most pleasant times to visit, although the nights can be very cold with temperatures sometimes below zero. Summer temperatures often reach 40 degrees Celsius.

Parks and Wildlife Commission of the NT,
PO Box 1046, Alice Springs, NT 0871.
Tel. (08) 8950 8211.
Ranger (08) 8956 7401.

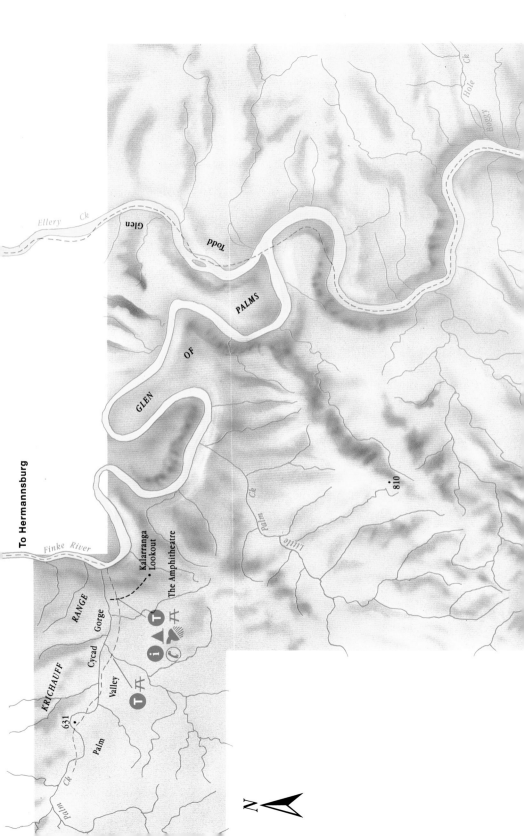

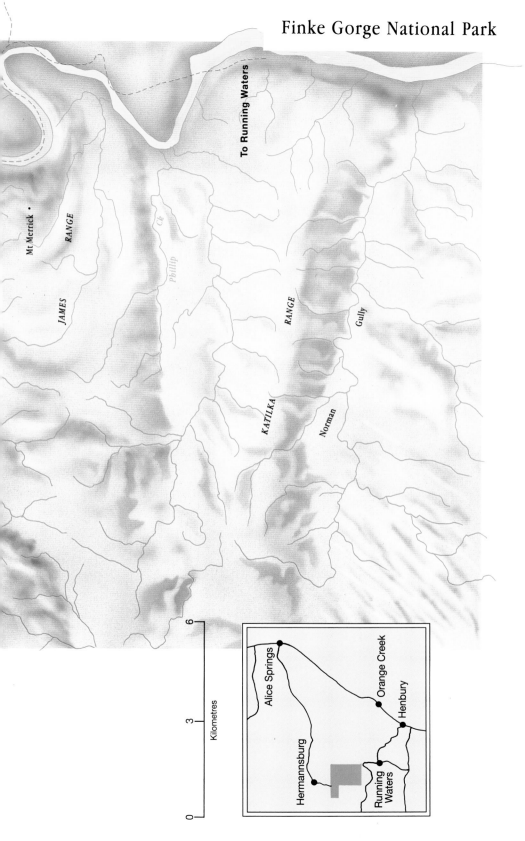

Finke Gorge National Park

Mt Merrick

JAMES RANGE

Ck Phillip

To Running Waters

KATILKA RANGE

Norman

Gully

Kilometres
6
3
0

Alice Springs

Orange Creek

Henbury

Hermannsburg

Running Waters

Nitmiluk (Katherine Gorge) National Park

A deep sandstone gorge carved through the rugged Arnhem Land Plateau by the Katherine River is the major feature of this park. North-west of the gorge, five days' hike across the plateau or a short drive from the highway, are the crystal-clear pools of Edith Falls, fringed with lush tropical greenery set against spectacular red cliffs.

Nitmiluk is one of the most popular parks in the Northern Territory and covers an area of 292,008 ha. Most of the park is a rugged sandstone plateau at an average altitude of about 250 m.

The Katherine River flows through the centre of the park in a broad valley that becomes narrower between the high sandstone cliffs of Nitmiluk (Katherine Gorge). The river has actually carved a system of 13 gorges separated by rapids. Most visitors stay within the lower reaches of Nitmiluk, and are unaware of the superb scenery upstream where the river wends its way more than 130 km through a virtually trackless wilderness area.

This is monsoon country with distinct wet and dry seasons. In the wet season torrential rains pour from the deeply dissected plateau, cascading into Katherine River to join the surging brown floodwaters that roar along the gorge, creating whirlpools and waves up to 2 m high. In the dry season the river follows a zig-zag route between vertical rock walls through a series of deep, boulder-strewn pools.

Conditions on the plateau are extremely harsh. Great expanses of undulating sandstone pavement separate one chasm from the next. Temperatures soar during the build-up to the rains, and only the toughest life forms are able to survive hidden in cracks and crevices.

Formation

Unaffected by major geological upheavals for more than 100 million years, the sandstone rocks were formed from sediments washed over the ancient bedrock by streams and river systems about 1370 million years ago.

Two major volcanic episodes spewed lava over the area creating a veneer of volcanic rock. Slight uplifting followed, cracking the volcanic veneer and forming deep parallel joints on the surface of the plateau. Watercourses followed the joints, cutting into the underlying sandstone to create the zig-zag course of the Katherine River.

Most of the volcanic rock has eroded away leaving only a few piles of rubble on the valley floors. These rocks contain various minerals, and areas near the park have been mined since 1871 when gold was discovered at Pine Creek.

History

Nitmiluk National Park belongs to the Jawoyn people, an Aboriginal tribe who, prior to the influx of Europeans in the late 1800s, occupied a large area including the upper South Alligator and Mary River systems to the north, and the Katherine River catchment area in the south.

They travelled extensively, moving with the seasons, hunting game, gathering bush food and performing ceremonies according to their Law. Jawoyn Law relates to the Dreamtime when the world was created and the rules for correct behaviour were established.

The Jawoyn were dispossessed of their lands by pastoralists who, in the 20 years following annexation of the Northern Territory in 1863, took up 92 per cent of the land. Gold miners began arriving in 1871, and the Jawoyn saw strangers populating their lands, despoiling their sacred sites and introducing cattle that fouled the waterholes. Organisations like the Eastern African Cold Storage Company hunted down Aborigines who refused to work on the stations. Others fled from some of the cattle stations where they feared for their lives, and many ended up camping around the Government Battery at Maranboy Tin Field where a small Aboriginal Reserve was declared in 1923.

In 1989 the Jawoyn Aborigines were given title

to an area of land that includes Nitmiluk National Park. The land is leased to the North-ern Territory Parks and Wildlife Commission and managed jointly with the Jawoyn people.

Plants and Animals

Conditions on top of the plateau are very harsh. There is little or no soil and few plants grow in coarse sand and leaf litter. Spinifex grasses and plants with scale-like leaves are common. The dry gorges and chasms provide more shelter and trap enough soil to support sparse trees like the scarlet gum and variable-barked bloodwood, and hardy shrubs like acacias, grevilleas and boronias.

Along the river banks and adjacent gorges where there is a constant supply of water grow paperbark trees and river pandans interspersed with freshwater mangroves, Leichhardt trees and native apple trees. In suitable sites a tree canopy provides shade for ferns and flowering shrubs. Open forests and woodlands grow on the low-lands and high level ridges where the soil is deep and water is available. The woodlands are domi-nated by eucalypts such as bloodwoods, Darwin stringybark and woollybutts, with tall grasses, scattered small trees and shrubs.

Among the few mammals living in the area are agile wallabies and black and little red flying foxes. Other mammals include the dingo, echidna, antilopine wallaroo, euro, northern nail-tailed wallaby and the common sheath-tailed bat. A variety of shy rodents such as the delicate mouse and common rock rat live in the park but are rarely seen.

The most conspicuous reptile is the freshwa-ter crocodile, often found lazing in the sun on rocks and logs along the river bank. Goulds sand goannas frequent the picnic area. Mertens water monitor, turtles, skinks and geckoes are common. Brown and green tree snakes and the venomous death adder live here.

The waterways are home to many diving birds including the darter, the little pied and lit-tle black cormorants. Around the picnic grounds are great bower birds, blue-faced honey-eaters and kookaburras. Colourful parrots, red-tailed black cockatoos, fairy martins and peregrine falcons are among the 168 bird species.

Walks

The park has more than 100 km of developed walking tracks from short strolls along the river-bank to the five-day trek from Nitmiluk to Edith Falls. Nitmiluk Tours offers a 2.5 hour bushwalk and introduction to bush food, medicine, flora and fauna with a Jawoyn guide. A four day walking tour conducted by Aboriginal guides explores parts of the gorge. Another guided walk takes nine days, following the track to Edith Falls. Visitors taking overnight walks must regis-ter and leave a deposit at the Visitor Centre to ensure they deregister at the end of the walk.

Facilities

The Visitor Centre has a restaurant, displays, videos and daily introductory talks. Close by are picnic areas, a boat ramp and the tour boat departure point. Commercially run campsites are located at the entrance to the gorge and at Edith Falls. They each have a kiosk, tolets and showers. Powered sites, laundry, fuel and hot showers are available at the gorge camping ground. Bush camping areas have been estab-lished along the gorge and some walking tracks. Water and toilets are usually available. The number of people allowed to take canoes on the river and camp in the gorges is restricted, and bookings should be made.

Boat tours operate daily in the dry season, and vary from two hours to half and full day cruises. Canoeing through the gorges is an unforgettable experience and canoes can be hired at the boat ramp. Helicopter scenic flights operate year round.

Access

Katherine is 30 km from the gorge and 60 km from Edith Falls. Both are accessed via the Stuart Highway and sealed access roads, which may be cut for short periods in the wet season.

Climate

In the dry season from May to September the days are warm and the nights cool. High tem-peratures and humidity discourage most visitors in the wet season (October to March).

Parks and Wildlife Commission of the NT, PO Box 344, Katherine, NT 0851. Tel. (08) 8972 1886.

To Katherine

Upper Falls

Sandbar Pool

Long Hole

Edith River

ARNHEM LAND PLATE

Black Hole

Sweetwate

Edith Falls

Northern Rockhole

Seventeen Mile Ck

Katherine River

Nitmiluk Visitor Centre

Jeddas Rock

Butterfly Gorge

Lilly Po
Falls

Nitmiluk
(Katherine Gorge)

To Katherine

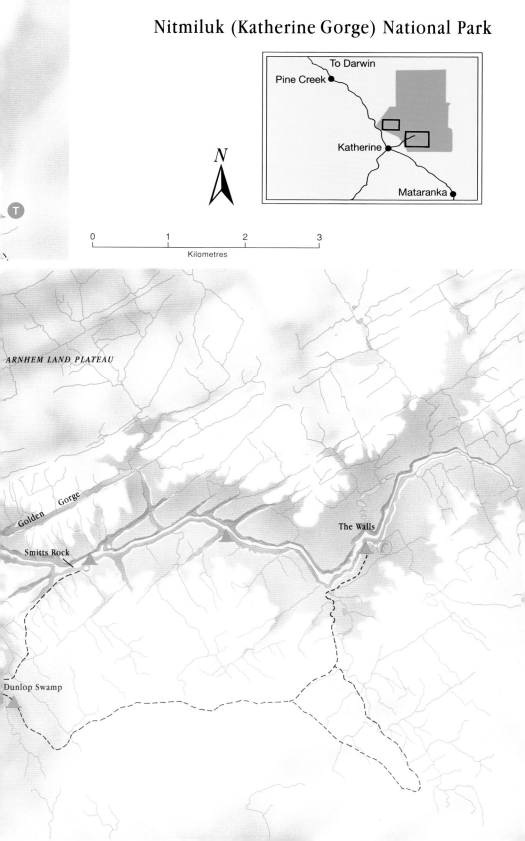

Nitmiluk (Katherine Gorge) National Park

To Darwin

Pine Creek

Katherine

Mataranka

N

0   1   2   3
Kilometres

ARNHEM LAND PLATEAU

Golden Gorge

Smitts Rock

The Walls

Dunlop Swamp

West MacDonnell National Park

Incorporating a string of parks and reserves, West MacDonnell National Park protects a vast and spectacular block of the MacDonnell Ranges west of Alice Springs. The area is a colourful world of gaps and gorges in the dry centre of the continent, a magnificent sight for the traveller who has spent hours crossing the broad, flat plains.

The MacDonnell Ranges are a series of parallel ridges separated by narrow flat valleys that arc from east to west across the plains of Central Australia. Ancient rivers have cut through mountains to create deep colourful canyons with permanent pools where plants and animals survive in isolated pockets, relics of ages past when this area was covered with lush tropical forests.

The colours in the rocks are spectacular, particularly at Ormiston Gorge where the broken rock escarpments glow with fiery red hues, deep browns, bright yellow tints, and brilliant white broken by veins of coal black. Dominating the skyline is the bulky peak of Mount Sonder. Rising to 1380 m this arid and eroded mountain forms a shimmering violet backdrop to Ormiston Pound, a huge rock-walled amphitheatre almost 10 km across.

Formation

This ancient landscape has its origins in a period of mountain building some 350 million years ago, when massive earth movements thrust up a chain of mountains several kilometres high. Before then the area was submerged beneath a shallow inland sea. Horizontal layers of sand, silt and lime mud were deposited on the underlying volcanic rocks to form quartzite, soft siltstone and limestone.

Folding and faulting of the land as it was slowly uplifted tilted the horizontal layers of rock and exposed them to the elements. The softer rocks eroded away forming valleys running east to west between ridges of hard quartzite. Freshwater lakes filled the valleys and large river systems cut their way through the ridges, taking advantage of any natural weaknesses in the rocks.

The rivers transported eroded rock fragments from the mountain range downstream to the south and south-east, decreasing their height by several thousand metres. Deep pools were scoured into the bedrock as the rushing waters emerged through the gorges they had created. Today these holes fill with water that seeps through the sands of the apparently dry river beds, or surges downstream in the occasional flood.

The major geographical features of the West MacDonnell Ranges are now incorporated in the park. Among the gorges are Simpsons Gap, Standley Chasm, Ellery Creek Gorge, Serpentine Gorge, Ormiston Gorge, Glen Helen Gorge and Redbank Gorge. They are characteristically steep-sided narrow chasms cut through the red quartzite rocks of the main range, with cool permanent waterholes surrounded by vegetation.

The Arrernte People

In this arid land the Arrernte people were blessed with an abundance of water seeping from the rocks and riverbeds of the MacDonnell Ranges. The Arrernte have lived in this area for many thousands of years, following a nomadic hunter-gatherer lifestyle within defined tribal boundaries, focussed on the waterholes where game animals and food plants are plentiful. These areas were vital to their survival and have special mythological significance.

Most of the deep waterholes are said to be occupied by a large watersnake, an uncompromising creature that will kill anyone who lingers too long at the edge of the pool or swims in the water. The first human being in a shapeless form is said to have emerged from the waterhole at Glen Helen Gorge, known as Yapulpa. Ellery Bighole is known as Udepata and was a meeting place for friends and relatives of the Arrernte.

Aboriginal people travelled great distances to obtain ochre from the ochre pits near Serpentine Gorge, renowned for the quality of the ochre mined there. Ochre was an important ceremonial and medicinal substance and was traded far and wide. It was used in rock and ceremonial body painting. Weapons were painted with ochre to improve the hunter's skill, and white ochre mixed with water and blown from the mouth was said to abate the heat of the sun or the force of the wind.

Plants and Animals

Some of the plants and animals living around the waterholes are uncharacteristic of this arid region, and are usually found in coastal districts. They are the last remaining relics of a wetter age when large river systems flowed here and lush rainforests flourished in the valleys. The fossil record shows that giant herbivorous marsupials roamed over this area and crocodiles swam in the rivers and lagoons less than one million years ago.

One relict species is the MacDonnell Ranges cycad, a slow-growing palm-like plant found on the cliffs around Ellery Bighole. This unique plant grows only in the ranges of the southern half of the Northern Territory, and has survived unchanged for at least 200 million years.

The MacDonnell Ranges are home to more than 250 plant species, from large trees to delicate ferns and beautiful wildflowers. Most species are adapted to the arid climate and are able to survive long periods of drought, while others live only in the moist sheltered gorges. Stout river red gums, willow-like ironwoods, bloodwood and whitewood trees grow along the river flats where water is trapped in the deeper soil. The sprawling native fig with its broad glossy leaves is usually found around rocky waterholes, together with reeds, bulrushes, sedges and pondweed.

In stark contrast to the damp gorges the dry, rugged hills support only the hardiest low trees like the Finke River mallee and mulga, sparse shrubs and spinifex grasses. Common trees found on the lower hills and slopes are whitewood, rosewood and the long-leaf corkwood, whose thick corky bark protects the tree from fire. Ghost gums, witchetty bushes and the native fuchsia bush are locally common on these barren rocky slopes.

The introduction of foxes, cats and cattle has had a devastating effect on the native wildlife of the area. Heavy grazing around the waterholes has compacted the soil destroying the homes of many burrowing animals, caused large-scale soil erosion and depleted the food supplies of native animals. The situation is slowly improving now that cattle have been removed from the park and the feral animals are being trapped.

The two most common large native animals in the park are the euro or common wallaroo and the black-footed rock wallaby, both found in rocky terrain and often seen at the waterholes around dawn and dusk. The desert mouse, the small carnivorous fat-tailed antechinus, the common brushtail possum and echidna live in the park but are rarely seen. The central rock rat was recently discovered on the Larapinta Trail. This critically endangered mammal was last seen in 1960. The long-nosed dragon, perentie and black-headed monitor are the most commonly seen reptiles. Among the snakes are the harmless childrens python, the venomous king and western brown snakes and the mulga. All reptiles, including snakes are totally protected.

Birds are the most noticeable of the park's fauna. Huge migrating flocks of budgerigars are common in spring and summer, and the aptly-named rainbow bee-eater is often seen catching insects over the waterholes at these times of year. Conspicuous permanent residents include the pied butcher bird, grey-crowned babbler, crested and spinifex pigeons, the white-plumed honeyeater, and two birds of prey: the peregrine falcon and Australian kestrel. Around the pools large waterbirds such as the white-faced heron, Australian pelican, black swan, darter, and pied cormorant may be seen.

The pools are full of aquatic life. Small fish such as the rainbow fish, hairback herring and spangled and striped gunters are common.

Molluscs, frogs, crustaceans, and insects such as dragonflies, beetles and bugs are well represented in and around the waterholes.

Walks

A wide range of walking tracks introduce the visitor to all the major attractions and breathtaking vistas of the ranges.

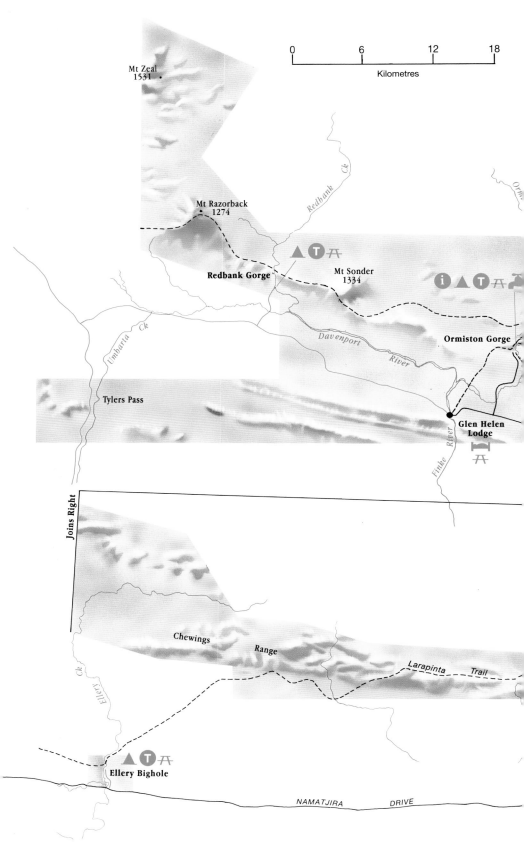

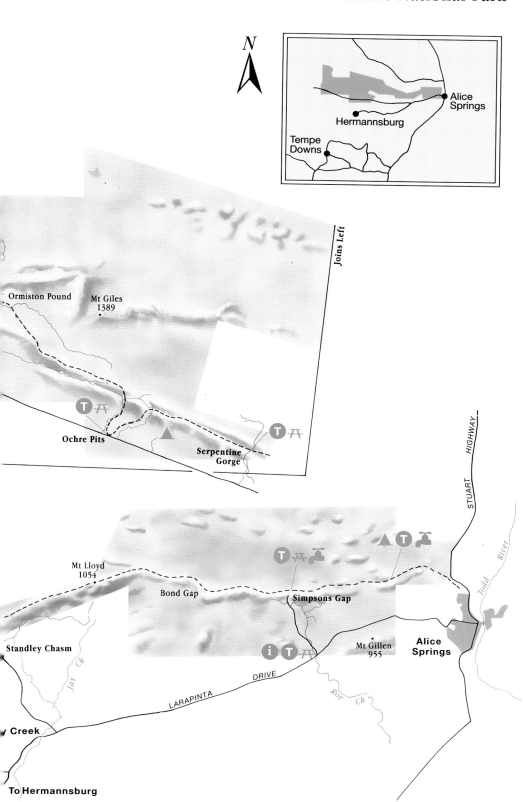

West MacDonnells National Park

N

Alice Springs

Hermannsburg

Tempe Downs

Joins Left

Ormiston Pound

Mt Giles
1389

Ochre Pits

Serpentine Gorge

STUART HIGHWAY

Todd River

Mt Lloyd
1054

Bond Gap

Simpsons Gap

Mt Gillen
955

Alice Springs

Standley Chasm

Jay Ck

DRIVE

LARAPINTA

Roe Ck

Creek

To Hermannsburg

A 500 m walk at Simpsons Gap leads through groves of witchetty bush and mulga to Cassia Hill with views over the range. A 16 km return journey goes from Simpsons Gap to Bond Gap, a narrow rocky cleft where there is an ice-cold pool.

From the Visitor Centre at Ormiston Gorge the Ghost Gum Walk is a beautiful 2.5 km walk along the western side of the gorge.

The 7 km Ormiston Pound Walk meanders around scenic slopes to the flat expanse of the pound where you are surrounded by steep multi-coloured rock walls. The track continues along Ormiston Gorge to the main pool, an excellent place for a swim on a hot day. Unmarked one to three day walks lead to the north-west corner of the Pound and to Mount Giles.

The Larapinta Trail is a major 12-stage walking trail system from Alice Springs to Mount Sonder. It has minimal facilities and is designed to be used by any well-prepared, reasonably fit person. The well-marked trail passes through the remote and rugged terrain of the Arrernte people, far from civilisation in a timeless landscape of ancient hills and valleys. Each stage has been designed as a two day walk with suggested bush camping sites along the route. Surface water is scarce, and sufficient drinking water must be carried. Water is available at the beginning of each stage, and these trackheads are accessible by vehicles. Excellent pamphlets are available detailing the route and giving safety advice.

Facilities

Visitor Centres are located at Simpsons Gap and Ormiston Gorge. Walkers should register their intentions with the staff here and take advantage of the information and displays. Ranger-guided walks, slide shows and campfire talks are given each winter between April and September.

Picnic areas and toilets are at Simpsons Gap, Serpentine Gorge, Ellery Creek Bighole, the Ochre Pits, Ormiston Gorge and Redbank Gorge. Free gas barbecues are provided at Simpsons Gap, the Ochre Pits and Ormiston Gorge. Other picnic sites have wood-burning barbecues, although firewood must not be collected in the park.

A commercial kiosk and picnic area is located at Standley Chasm. Treated drinking water is not provided in the park, and all water should be boiled or sterilised. The camp ground at Ormiston Gorge has solar-heated showers and other amenities. Other camping areas in the park have basic facilities only.

Bush campers should avoid camping near waterholes as these are frequented by snakes, wild horses and cattle. River red gums and some other trees shed branches, and flash floods can occur in creek beds at any time of year. Do not attract dingos to your camp by leaving foodstuffs lying around.

Access

Simpsons Gap is 18 km from Alice Springs via the sealed Larapinta Drive. The entrance gate to the park is only open from 8 am to 8 pm daily. Cyclists can take the sealed bicycle path from Alice Springs. Namatjira Drive is sealed as far as Glen Helen Lodge. Many of the roads within the park are unsealed, some are rough and unsuitable for conventional vehicles, and may be flooded after heavy rain.

Climate

The cooler months from April to September are the most pleasant times to visit the park, although the nights can be very cold with temperatures sometimes falling to minus ten degrees Celsius. Summer temperatures are high and make walking strenuous and potentially dangerous.

Parks and Wildlife Commission of the NT, PO Box 1046, Alice Springs, NT 0871. Tel. (08) 8950 8211.

Watarrka National Park

Located in the George Gill Range, some 130 km north of Uluru, Watarrka National Park is one of the most fascinating places in Central Australia. In this desiccated landscape of almost timeless antiquity are isolated waterholes surrounded by lush vegetation and cliff-lined gorges breaking through the low, weathered hills. Kings Canyon is the most spectacular gorge in the George Gill Range, and the major feature of the park.

The sheer cliff walls of Kings Canyon rise up to 270 m, and when it rains Kings Creek plunges over a semi-circular precipice from a smaller and longer gorge above.

The plateau surrounding the canyon is a fascinating place to explore. A maze of weathered sandstone domes, rock spires and small canyons have created a strange landscape where rock walls streaked with coloured patterns are complemented by stunted, twisted trees.

Formation

The predominant rock in the region is sandstone formed more than 350 million years ago on the floor of the ancient lakes and rivers that inundated the area.

The surface layer, known as Mereenie sandstone, is porous and soaks up rainwater like a giant sponge to form a water table above a thin, impervious shale layer. The water seeps out to produce the permanent springs and waterholes of the George Gill Range. Below this is a softer, reddish-brown sandstone some 440 million years old containing fossilised tracks of a creature similar to the Moreton Bay bug. The tracks indicate that these older sedimentary rocks were formed on the bed of a bay or estuary.

Subsequent uplifting of the land raised Central Australia high above sea level and created the George Gill Range. Millions of years of erosion have worn down the mountains into a range of rounded hills rising to 870 m at Carmichael Crag.

Subterranean movements formed deep cracks in the sandstone. In some areas they form a criss-cross pattern dividing the rock into block shapes. Wind and rain have eaten into the cracks and rounded off the corners to create the strange domes and spires seen on the plateau. In other areas the cracks have formed deep vertical fissures.

The south wall of Kings Canyon follows one of these fissures, and the canyon itself has been created by erosion of the softer lower sandstone undercutting the higher sandstone of the north wall, causing it to collapse.

History

The area is the homeland of the Luritja people, who have lived here for at least 22,000 years.

Before the arrival of the Europeans they led a nomadic hunter-gatherer lifestyle focussed on the springs and waterholes where game animals and food plants are plentiful. In times of good rainfall they would move to the plains giving the food resources around the waterholes a chance to recover. The Luritja still have strong ties to the land, and the area has many sacred sites associated with landforms in the park.

The first Europeans to see this area were members of an expedition led by Ernest Giles, who passed through in 1872. They named most of the prominent features of the area after their sponsors and friends. Thus we have the George Gill Range, Kings Creek and Carmichaels Crag. Other expeditions followed. Some, like the Horn Scientific Expedition remarked on the diversity of flora and fauna in the area, others were more interested in the potential economic gains to be had from mineral exploitation and pastoral activities.

In the late 19th century the Tempe Downs Pastoral Association introduced cattle to the district, and in 1889 some 6000 animals were grazing in the area now included in the park, causing significant damage to the native flora

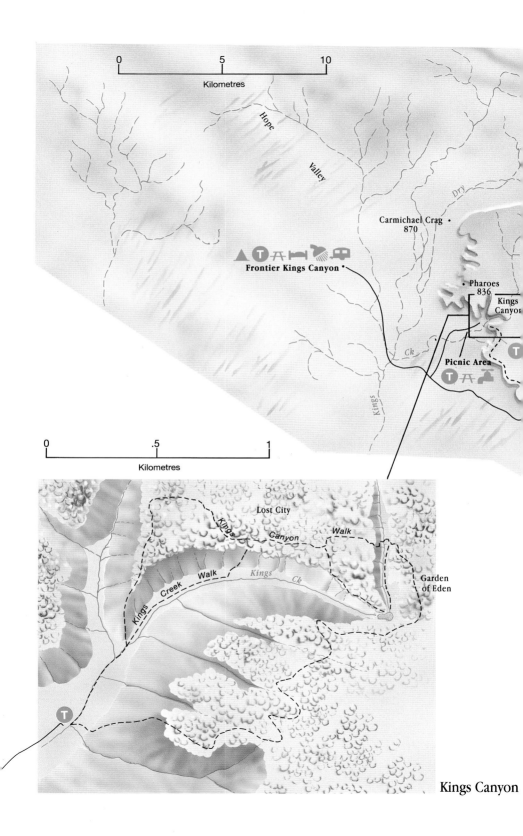

Kings Canyon

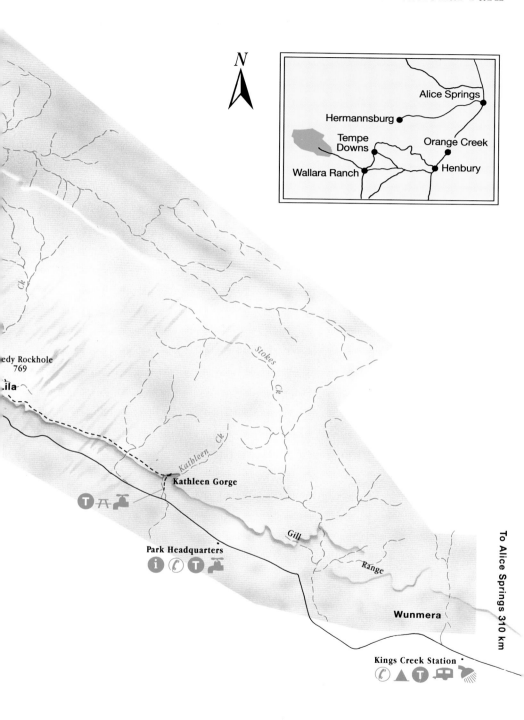

N

Alice Springs

Hermannsburg

Tempe
Downs

Orange Creek

Wallara Ranch

Henbury

edy Rockhole
769

.ila

Stokes

Ck

Kathleen Ck

Kathleen Gorge

T A

Park Headquarters

i l T

Gill

Range

Wunmera

To Alice Springs 310 km

Kings Creek Station

and polluting the waterholes. Grazing continued until 1983 when the national park was created to preserve 71,720 ha of land.

Three small Aboriginal residential areas near sites of traditional significance have been excised from the park.

Plants and Animals

Watarrka is one of the most important botanical sites in Central Australia and the area has a mixture of plants associated with the western deserts, MacDonnell Ranges and the Simpson Desert regions.

Among the 600 plant species recorded in the park more than 60 are considered to be rare or relict species, isolated from their counterparts in wetter parts of the continent as the climate became increasingly dry. Less than one million years ago this area was part of the wet tropics. Lush rainforests grew in the valleys, giant herbivores roamed the land and crocodiles swam in ancient river systems.

The MacDonnell Ranges cycad is one of the more interesting relict species, a survivor from the age of the dinosaurs. Known only from the range country of the southern half of the Northern Territory, this long-lived, slow-growing cycad may survive 1000 years or more, with a trunk only 1 m high. Relict ferns, such as the creeping swamp fern, are found in the wet refuges.

On the dry hills and associated scarps the vegetation is sparse and stunted, comprising mainly spinifex grasses, shrubs and low trees. The sand plains support a great diversity of vegetation types adapted to a cycle of drought followed by brief rain spells. They flower and seed after good rain, providing food for a host of animals.

Most animal populations crash in the drought. Some migrate to the permanently wet areas and repopulate the sand plain when the rains return. Others, like the lizards, can survive in hard times by slowing down their energy consumption.

Among the larger mammals are euros and rock wallabies, sometimes seen around the rocky ramparts of the gorges. Red kangaroos frequent the plains. Dingos, bats, hopping mice, rodents and echidnas are among the smaller native mammals in the area. Bilbies were reintroduced to the area but all were taken by feral cats and dogs.

Along the walking tracks reptiles are often seen, including the giant perentie and numerous small lizards like the ringtailed dragon. Venomous king and western brown snakes, and harmless pythons live in the park.

Australian kestrels and wedge-tailed eagles nest on rocky ledges, fairy martins, spinifex pigeons and crows are often seen, and common seasonal visitors include honeyeaters, mistletoe birds, rainbow bee-eaters and ring-neck parrots. Emus roam the plains, coming to drink from the sheltered waterholes at the foot of the range.

Walks

Two signposted walking tracks have been constructed at Kings Canyon. The Kings Creek Walk takes about one hour to complete. The track meanders along Kings Creek to a lookout where the huge multi-hued cliffs are a spectacular sight in the setting sun.

The Kings Canyon Walk is 6 km long and takes three to four hours. The track is rough and steep in sections, so take strong footwear, a hat and drinking water. Views from the rim of the canyon and of the weathered rocky domes and buttresses of the Lost City are magnificent.

In the Garden of Eden are permanent waterholes fringed by cycads and tangled vegetation. A steel bridge leads to the top of the north wall from where there are impressive views of the canyon. Timber walkways in the Garden of Eden have been constructed to protect the creek bed and plants from erosion.

A major overnight ridge top walk has been opened from Kings Canyon to Kathleen Gorge, allowing visitors to experience the wilderness area from a properly constructed track.

From Kathleen Gorge picnic area a short self-guided nature walk leads to a shady fern-fringed rock pool in the gorge.

Overnight walkers must obtain permits at the Park Headquarters and inform the ranger of their route.

Facilities

The Park Headquarters has displays, information, tap water and toilets. There are barbecues at Kings Canyon Picnic Area and Kathleen Gorge. Firewood collecting in the park is not allowed, and visitors should bring fuel stoves.

Camping areas are provided at Kings Canyon Resort and Kings Creek Station. At Kings Canyon Resort there is also a motel, backpackers accommodation, restaurant, tavern, cafe, pool, store and fuel supplies. Permits must be obtained by those wishing to camp on overnight walks.

Aboriginal cultural tours can be booked at Frontier Kings Canyon, and permission must be obtained to enter the Aboriginal living areas within the park.

Access

The park is 310 km south-west of Alice Springs via the Stuart Highway and the Ernest Giles Road, which is only sealed for the last 82 km to the park.

From Uluru the park is 290 km via the Lasseter Highway and the sealed Luritja Road. The unsealed roads are usually accessible by conventional vehicles, but great care must be taken, particularly in wet weather.

Advice on current road conditions can be obtained from the NT Emergency Services at Alice Springs, (08-8952 3833).

Off road driving causes soil and vegetation damage which is very slow to recover, and is not allowed in the park.

Climate

The area is semi-arid and has a low, highly variable annual rainfall. Summers are hot and winters mild with very cold nights when the temperature may fall below zero.

*Parks and Wildlife Commission of the NT,
PO Box 1046, Alice Springs, NT 0871.
Tel. (08) 8951 8211.
Park Headquarters (08) 8956 7460.*

Katherine Gorge, a deep gash in the Arnhem Land Plateau in Nitmiluk National Park

The rugged sunburnt landscape of the West MacDonnells National Park

Kings Canyon, a spectacular sandstone gorge in Watarrka National Park

Yellow Waters on the floodplain of Kakadu National Park

Kakadu National Park

In the far north of Australia, where the ancient rocks of the Arnhem Land Plateau give way to lowlying coastal floodplains, lies Kakadu National Park. Inscribed on the World Heritage List on the basis of both its natural and cultural values, Kakadu contains a wide range of plants and animals from both arid and wetland habitats, and is one of the most important artistic and cultural sites in Australia.

The 20,000 square kilometre Kakadu National Park extends 210 kilometres inland from the Van Dieman Gulf to the Arnhem Land Plateau. It includes virtually the whole catchment of the South Alligator River system – one of the greatest monsoonal river systems of the tropical north – and the northern edge of the plateau, known as the Arnhem Land Escarpment. The escarpment has been deeply dissected by ephemeral streams that cascade over its edge in the wet season, joining the Alligator Rivers and feeding an extensive wetland area on the lowlying coastal plain. In the long dry season the land bakes in the sun, the torrential creeks are reduced to mere trickles, and the overflowing rivers to strings of rock pools and billabongs.

Formation

The hard quartzite and sandstone rocks of the Arnhem Land Plateau are at least 1600 million years old, and were deposited by great river systems that once flowed over the area, leaving layers of sandy sediments more than one kilometre thick. Millions of years of erosion have worn down the surface of the plateau and opened up faultlines to produce a crisscross pattern of ravines and gorges.

The Arnhem Land Escarpment takes the form of an uninterrupted line of cliffs rising 300 metres above the plains and winding through the southern section of Kakadu National Park. The cliffs were created about 100 million years ago when a shallow sea lapped against the foothills of the plateau, undermining the layers of sediment, forming sandstone cliffs and cutting off large islands of rock, such as Nourlangie Rock. The seas gradually receded as the climate became drier, and for millions of years the plateau stood above a lowlying coastal sand plain hundreds of kilometres wide.

Creeks cutting through the plateau washed sand and gravel over the lowlands, a process that continued until about 10,000 years ago when the sea level rose once again and submerged the plains in muddy estuarine waters. Over the past 7000 years the sea has been gradually receding, and today the coastline is growing by 20 to 30 cm each year.

History

Archaeological research indicates that Aboriginal people have lived in this area for at least 30,000 years. Some of the rock paintings in the park are thought to be 20,000 years old, providing evidence of one of the oldest civilisations on earth. They depict beings of the Dreamtime, hunting, fighting and other social activities in X-ray, stick-figure, dot and realistic styles.

The abundant natural resources of the area, such as fish, shellfish, waterfowl, wallabies, yams, fruit and other bush foods were harvested by the Aboriginal clans who lived here, and many continued to live a traditional lifestyle well into the latter half of this century. Their spiritual beliefs are illustrated throughout the park in rock art, and passed on through stories, songs and dances.

The many sacred sites in the area are places occupied by the spirits of the Nayuhyunggi, the creation ancestors of the Dreamtime who formed the social and physical world. They are considered to be dangerous places, and access, if any, is restricted to people with responsibilities to that site under Aboriginal Law.

Many of the older inhabitants of the park worked in the buffalo industry, which flourished from 1880 until 1950. The men were skilled hunters, renowned for their horsemanship and accuracy with a rifle, while the women cleaned and salted the hides. They were usually paid with provisions such as tea, flour and sugar.

Monsoonal flooding and the rugged nature of the plateau saved the area from white settlement, and apart from the establishment of missions and remote mining ventures, white incursions have been minimal. Discovery of uranium, manganese, gold and tin deposits in the area brought the traditional landowners into conflict with mining companies, which were determined to exploit these resources despite the fact that many of the proposed mines were near sacred sites.

Legal recognition of Aboriginal ownership of the land led to a partial resolution of these conflicts, but pressures to mine the area are still great, even though the park has been declared a World Heritage Area.

Kakadu National Park was first established in 1979, with two major extensions in 1984 and 1987. Most of the area is owned by Aboriginal people who manage the park in conjunction with the Australian National Parks and Wildlife Service. The name Kakadu is derived from Gagudju, the name of the major Aboriginal language of the northern floodplains. About 300 Aboriginal people now live in the area, and some are employed by the park. Visitor numbers continue to rise, and now exceed a quarter of a million per year.

Vegetation

Most of the habitats of far northern Australia are found within the catchment area of the South Alligator River. Thin, sandy soils cover about one-third of the Arnhem Land Plateau and support little more than spinifex grasses and low, hardy heath plants. Elsewhere the plateau is a barren, rocky wilderness area relieved by small pockets of tropical rainforest plants surviving in moist, sheltered gullies where deep soils have accumulated. These oases are dominated by one large, majestic tree: the evergreen myrtle (*Allosyncarpia ternata*), believed to be a relict species at least 60 million years old, a leftover from the time when Australia was part of the supercontinent of Gondwana.

Eucalypt woodlands dominate the dry ridges below the plateau. This is one of the richest woodland habitats in Australia, with countless species of trees, shrubs, grasses and animals.

Common among the eucalypts are the Darwin stringybark, the bark of which is used for shelter and bark paintings, the orange-flowering woollybutt, dense stands of stringybark bloodwood, and attractive white-trunked ghost gums in the grassland savanna areas.

Pockets of monsoon rainforest crowd the moist lowland areas. Paperbark trees interspersed with pandanus fringe the wetlands and billabongs, while along the coast and river estuaries grow forests of mangroves. The tropical monsoonal climate causes the floodplains to change from cracked and parched earth in the dry season to lush green grasslands and sedgelands in the wet season.

Wildlife

The sparse vegetation of the plateau supports a number of mammals, including the tiny sandstone antechinus, the rare large rock-rat, the rock ringtail possum, and macropods such as the black wallaroo and the rare little rock wallaby or nabarlek. Birds and reptiles are generally better adapted to these harsh conditions, and are more visible than the mammals. Some of the birds of the plateau are unique to this area, such as the chestnut-quilled rock pigeon and the white-lined honeyeater. The Oenpelli python and burrowing blind snake are also restricted to the plateau, a habitat they share with lizards like the beautiful jewelled velvet gecko and Pamela's gecko.

On the lower southern hills and basins the habitats are quite different. Two mammals have recently been discovered here: Calabys mouse and the Kakadu dunnart. The hooded parrot, which nests in termite mounds, and the colourful Gouldian finch are among the seven rare or endangered birds living here.

The Kakadu floodplain is one of the greatest tropical wetland areas in the world, and is a refuge for migratory birds. One of Kakadu's most interesting sights is the gathering of waterbirds on the Magela and Nourlangie floodplains towards the end of the dry season. An estimated 2.5 million birds fly into the area, and the plains echo with the resonant honking of thousands of magpie geese and the shrill cries of wandering whistling ducks. Flocks of brolgas gather around

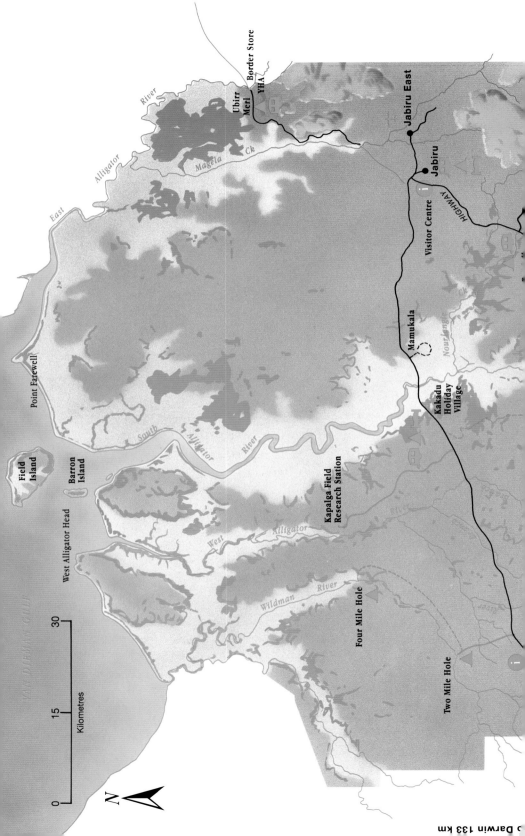

Kakadu National Park

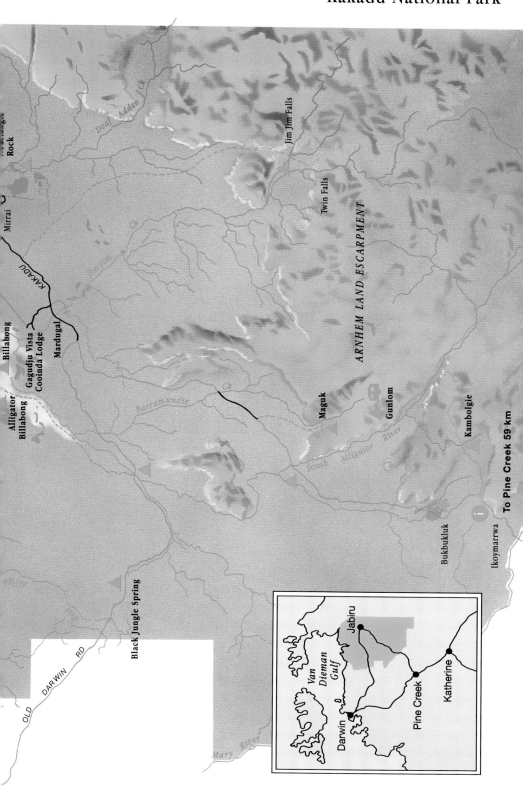

the diminishing wetlands, performing graceful and elaborate courtship dances, and the tall jabiru, Australia's only stork, can be seen striding through the shallows, probing for fish, crabs and frogs. The lagoons and billabongs teem with fish, turtles and other animals at this time of year. The rare pig-nosed turtle relies on these refuges to survive. This unusual animal has flippers like a sea turtle, grows to half a metre long, and can weigh more than 20 kg.

Crocodile attacks are possible, and visitors must obey warning signs. Both freshwater and estuarine (saltwater) crocodiles live in the park. The former grow to about 3 m and are not considered dangerous. The latter grow to more than 6 m, live in both fresh and saltwater, and are fast, ferocious, well-camouflaged hunters. Among the other reptiles are goannas, water pythons, keelback snakes, brown and green tree snakes, Mitchell's water monitor and the large frilled lizard.

Kakadu is home to one-quarter of Australia's freshwater fish species. Some dash upstream at the end of the wet season to escarpment pools where they mature.

Walks and Other Activities

A number of well-defined walking tracks have been established from nature trails (some leading to Aboriginal galleries) to long hikes along creeks, through woodlands and rainforests to caves, billabongs and the rocky escarpment. Experienced bushwalkers will find many challenging and interesting areas to explore, but rangers should be consulted beforehand, and drinking water carried. Rangers conduct walks and talks in the dry season.

Kakadu is one of the richest areas in Australia for Aboriginal paintings. Ubirr with its vivid "X-ray" studies and Nourlangie Rock, where there are dramatic series of human and mythical figures, contain excellent examples.

Fishing is allowed, but only lures may be used, and bag limits apply to barramundi. Boating on the East and South Alligator Rivers is a good way to see the landscape and wildlife, but beware of crocodiles, fast-flowing water, tidal changes and hidden snags. Safety equipment and extra fuel must be carried, and a friend or ranger advised of your destination and estimated time of return. Organised boat tours are conducted by private operators. Boating ramps are located at the Arnhem Highway bridge over the South Alligator River, Yellow Water and the East Alligator River, with unsealed ramps at Muirella Park and Mardugal.

Facilities

Camping areas with facilities are provided in beautiful settings at Merl, Mardugal, Muirella Park and Gunlom. Bookings are not required. There are also a number of undeveloped camping areas. Bush camping is allowed, but a permit must be obtained from the Visitor Centre. Beware of crocodiles if you are camping near a billabong or creek. Do not leave food or refuse lying around. Keep children away from the water's edge. Do not swim in natural waterways.

Backpacker, motel, hotel and caravan accommodation is available within the park (08-8979 2474). Jabiru has banks, a golf course and most of the facilities of a small town. The Visitor Centre has displays, an audiovisual theatre, books and information, and the Bininj people illustrate some of their creation stories at the Warradjan Aboriginal Cultural Centre.

Access

The park is 250 km east of Darwin via the sealed Arnhem Highway. From the south access is via the sealed road from Pine Creek (206 km). Most of the roads to the waterfalls are 4WD only. The Visitor Centre has up-to-date road information.

Many commercial tours are available, and a daily coach service operates from Darwin to Kakadu. There is no public transport within the park. Cars can be rented in Jabiru and Darwin, but should be booked in advance.

Climate

Kakadu has two distinct seasons: a wet, hot season from November to March, and a dry, cooler season from May to September. Most people visit in the dry season. In the wet season the park is green and very beautiful, although many find the high temperatures and humidity uncomfortable.

Kakada National Park, P.O. Box 71, Jabiru, NT 0886. Tel. (08) 8938 1100.

Litchfield National Park

Spring-fed waterfalls cascading from the Tabletop Range, weathered sandstone pillars of the Lost City, intriguing magnetic termite mounds, and pockets of dense monsoon rainforests make Litchfield one of the Northern Territory's most popular parks.

A two-hour drive from Darwin, the 143,000 ha park is dominated by the huge weathered sandstone plateau of the Tabletop Range. This is monsoon country, and the wet season downpours soak through the gently undulating surface of the plateau into a large reservoir of water trapped by a layer of underlying sandstone.

Water seeps constantly from the plateau, particularly on the western edge of the Tabletop Range, feeding the waterways and creating a number of spectacular waterfalls, including the Wangi, Tolmer, Florence and Tjaynera Falls. They cascade from the plateau rim into tranquil plunge pools surrounded by monsoon forests.

On the southern edge of the plateau near Tolmer Falls is the fascinating Lost City, an area of weathered and sculpted sandstone formations with colourful pillars and door-like arches linked by a maze of narrow passages, resembling the ruined streets of an ancient civilisation.

History

The rich natural resources of the area supported Aboriginal people for many thousands of years, providing a variety of bush food, medicinal plants and materials for shelter and tool making.

Four Aboriginal groups have long associations with the northern section of the park, where scattered art sites date back more than 10,000 years. They created rock paintings in a naturalistic style depicting simple figures in a single colour, and colourful linear and circular designs. A burial site has been identified at Bamboo Creek, and a sacred site at Wangi Falls.

Frederick Henry Litchfield explored the area in 1865. Prospectors discovered tin deposits and established small mines at Mount Tolmer and Bamboo Creek in 1869. The mines were marginal, and the remains of the Bamboo Creek mine can still be seen. Pastoralists moved in soon after, introducing cattle and logging some of the trees. Blyth Homestead was built in 1929, and in 1984

the lease owners suggested that the Territory Government protect the Tabletop Range, leading to the creation of Litchfield National Park in 1986.

Plants and animals

Tall open woodlands dominated by woollybutt and stringybark cover most of the park, with a understorey of cycads, banksias, acacias, grevilleas and sand palms. The waterways support pockets of monsoon forest, with carpentaria palms, wild nutmeg, tuckeroo, native lasiandra and a profusion of epiphytes, vines and ferns beneath the canopy. Sparse shrublands of pandanus, grevilleas and acacias colonise the sandy creek banks. Paperbarks grow in swamps and drainage depressions on the plateau and lowlands.

Some 44 mammal species have been identified. The cliff lines are home to the short-eared rock wallaby, nabarlek, euro and sandstone antechinus. Antilopine wallaroos are found in the woodlands and open monsoon forests, a habitat they share with agile wallabies, sugar gliders, brush-tailed phascogales and northern quolls. Caves and rocky overhangs are roosting sites for bats, including the endangered ghost bat, orange horseshoe bat and little cave eptesicus.

At least 73 species of frogs, turtles, snakes and lizards live here. Northern snapping turtles, marbled frogs, green tree frogs and ornate burrowing frogs are among the 15 amphibian species. Venomous snakes such as northern death adders and king brown snakes are found along with pythons and tree snakes. Sand and water goannas are commonly seen in the dry period, and frilled lizards often bask on the roads after the first rains. Freshwater crocodiles are common in the rivers and streams, and saltwater crocodiles are occasionally found in some of the pools. Visitors should stay out of the water unless it is designated safe.

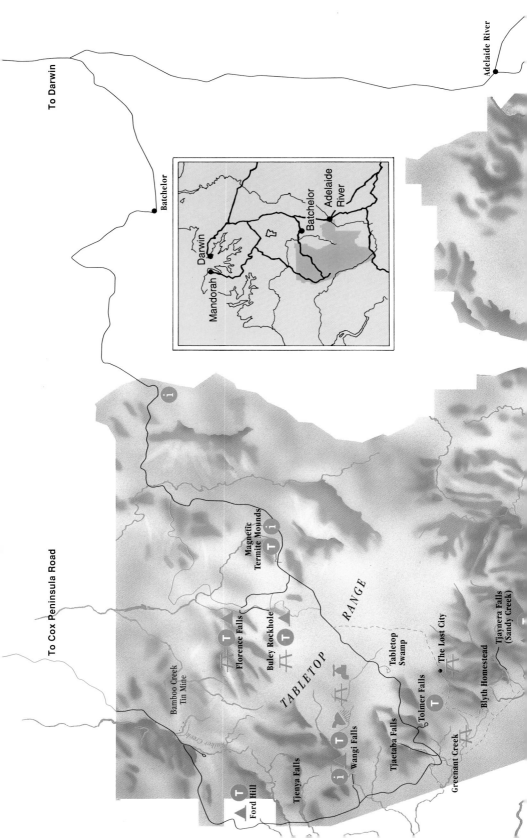

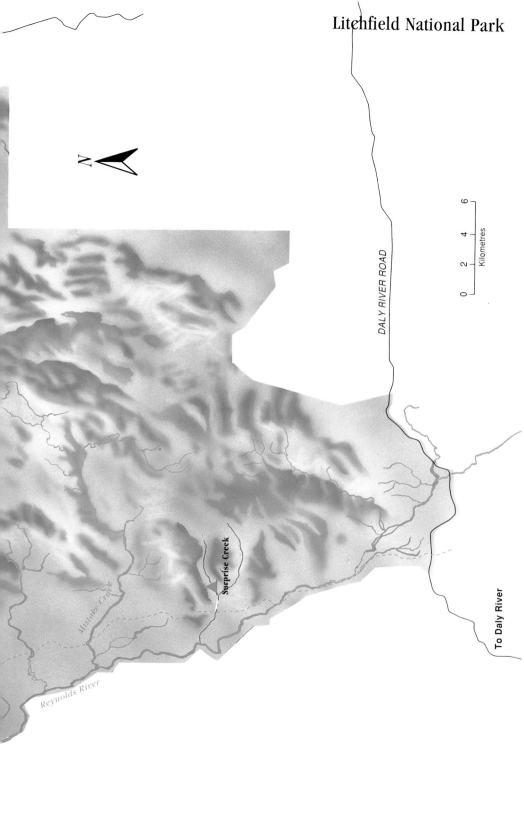

Litchfield National Park

N

DALY RIVER ROAD

Kilometres
0   2   4   6

To Daly River

Surprise Creek

Mistake Creek

Reynolds River

In the streams and pools are native fish such as barramundi, rainbow fish, grunters, catfish and archerfish (which shoot down insects with water fired from the mouth). Waterbirds fly in to feed, and grebes, cormorants, herons, egrets, spoonbills, jabirus and pelicans are common.

Wedge-tailed eagles, whistling and black kites are among the birds of prey wheeling above the escarpment. Flocks of northern rosellas, rainbow lorikeets, red-tailed black cockatoos and sulphur-crested cockatoos are common in the woodlands, together with blue-winged kookaburras and the large, noisy Torresian crow. The rare bush hen and Torres Strait imperial pigeon live in the monsoon forests.

The magnetic termite mounds of the black soil plains are unique to the region. These slab-like structures are up to 3 m tall, 3 m long and 1 m wide, and their long axes face 10 degrees east of true north. Their orientation warms the eastern face in the morning, while the midday sun hits the narrow edge. Equally spectacular are the cathedral mounds, up to 6 m high and 2 m diameter with great supporting buttresses.

Walks

The scenic terrain and waterways make excellent bushwalking, although you must protect yourself from the sun and take enough water. If you go on a long walk you must obtain a permit from rangers or the district office at Batchelor, and inform someone of your route and expected time of return.

Walking tracks have been constructed at each major waterfall. A one hour trail at Wangi Falls leads from the waterhole through monsoon forest to the top of the falls with fine views over the park, then down to the other side. The waterfall plunges 80 m into a huge, clear pool.

A network of trails at Florence Falls links the car park, lookout, camp ground and plunge pool. A two-hour return walk from the camp ground goes to the top of the falls and on to Buley Rockhole where there are spa-sized pools and cascades.

Tolmer Falls cascades over two high falls and is the most spectacular waterfall in the park. To protect the bat colonies living around the waterhole entry to the gorge is prohibited and access is restricted to a 1.6 km loop track and a short walk to a viewing point overlooking the falls.

One of the major attractions in the south is Tjaynera Falls on Sandy Creek, a 4WD track to the camp ground and a 3.5 km return walk. The creek runs through an open valley filled with paperbark trees, and the falls are in a beautiful setting surrounded by orange cliffs and tall palms with a large plunge pool. From Greenant Creek picnic area a 2.7 km return track follows the creek to Tjaetaba Falls.

A northern cross-country track network and a track to the headwaters of Walker Creek with walk-in campsites are under construction.

Facilities

Wangi Falls has a kiosk and a large camping area with good facilities and provision for caravans and large groups. Other camping areas have basic facilities only. Florence Falls has a picnic area and camp ground accessible to conventional vehicles, and a camping area at the base of the falls for 4WD vehicles. These sites should be booked in advance. About 2 km above the falls at Buley Rockhole is a small picnic and camping area. The Sandy Creek camping area is about 1 km below Tjaynera Falls, and is 4WD only. Camping is allowed off the southern access track at Surprise Creek Falls, for 4WD only.

Access

The park is 129 km south-west of Darwin via a sealed road from Batchelor or from Cox Peninsula on a gravel road unsuitable for caravans or trailers. Both roads may be closed in the wet season due to flooding rivers (08-8976 0282 for road conditions). The Southern Access Road is dry weather only for 4WD vehicles.

Climate

Most visitors choose the dry season from May to September when days are warm and the nights cool. Hot, humid conditions and heavy rains from November to March detract many people, although the park is even more spectacular.

Conservation Commission of the NT,
PO Box 496, Palmerston, NT 0831.
Tel. (08) 8989 4559.
Batchelor Office (08) 8976 0282.

Elsey National Park (13,840 ha)

The upper Roper River and the popular Mataranka thermal pool are in this park. The crystal clear waters of Roper River offer good swimming, fishing and canoeing. Walk along the river to small waterfalls and through pockets of rainforest. Mataranka thermal pool has a constant temperature of 34°C and is in a forest of paperbarks, pandanus and *Livistona rigida* palms. Picnic areas. Camp at 12 Mile Yards – good facilities and a kiosk – or at Mataranka Homestead Tourist Resort.
100 km south of Katherine and 7 km east of Mataranka off Stuart Hwy. (08) 8975 4560.

Gregory National Park (1,050,000 ha)

This large, remote park features spectacular gorges and ranges, significant Aboriginal sites and evidence of European exploration and history. In the east orange cliffs, tall palms and rock art shelters of the 50 km long Victoria River Gorge attract experienced bushwalkers. The larger western section is accessed by 4WD through rocky hills, and past waterholes to traditional camps on the old stock route beside Barra Barra Creek. The area is a transition zone between tropical and semi-arid regions, where red sands merge into green. Crocodiles occur in the Victoria River, the creeks and billabongs, making swimming unsafe. Table top ranges, sandstone escarpments and limestone hills with woodlands, spinifex grasslands and majestic boab trees characterise the landscape. Visit the karst formations at Limestone Gorge. Commercial boat tours operate on Victoria River. Camp at Big Horse Creek, Sullivans Creek, Limestone Gorge or Bullita where there are basic facilities. 4WD tracks cross the park.
160 km south-west of Katherine via the Victoria Hwy. (08) 8975 0888 or (08) 8975 0833.

Gurig National Park (220,700 ha)

At the very top of the Northern Territory on the Cobourg Peninsula, this park is on Aboriginal land, visitor numbers are limited and entry permits must be obtained well in advance from the Northern Land Council (08-8920 5100). Offshore lies the 22,900 ha Cobourg Marine Park. The area is isolated, with clear, turquoise bays, white sandy beaches and colourful cliffs. The scenic coast is perfect for walking, fishing, bird watching, boating and exploring tropical rainforests. Other habitats include tall eucalypt forests, wetlands and coastal sand dunes. Saltwater crocodiles can make swimming unsafe. Visit the ruins of Victoria Settlement and Black Point Cultural Centre. Tours are available. There is a ranger station, store, and basic camping, or stay at nearby Smith Points – cabins and a camping ground in an idyllic settings – or at Seven Spirit Wilderness Lodge. Roads are impassable in the wet season.
570 km north-east of Darwin via Jabiru by 4WD, boat or charter flight. (08) 8979 0244.

Keep River National Park (56,889 ha)

On the border with WA, this remote park offers rugged sandstone escarpments and gorges. It is the traditional home of the Gajerrong and Miriwoong people. There are fascinating Aboriginal art sites, enormous boab trees and a variety of wildlife with five kangaroo species (including the short-eared rock wallaby), crocodiles and at least 100 species of birds including the rare Gouldian finch. Walk the spectacular Keep River Gorge, camp at Gurrandalng or Jarrnarm where there are basic facilities.
469 km south-west of Katherine off the Victoria Hwy. (08) 9167 8827.

Mary River National Park (900,000 ha)

A new park on the coast east of Darwin featuring extensive wetlands, billabongs, rainforests and upland plains. Bird life on the floodplain is a major attraction towards the end of the dry season. Roads are unsealed and flood during the wet (October to April). Many are 4WD only. Good barramundi fishing. Houseboats can be rented on Corroboree Billabong, and aluminium fishing boats hired at Shady Camp. Beware of crocodiles. Camping grounds with basic facilities at Couzen's Lookout and Shady Camp, or stay at Point Stuart or Wildman River resorts.
150 km east of Darwin off the Arnhem Hwy via Point Stuart Rd. (08) 8978 8986.

Western Australia

Featured National Parks

Carnarvon •

Shark Bay

Kalbarri

Geraldto

THE KIMBERLEYS

Wyndham

Broome

Fitzroy Crossing

Margaret River

GREAT SANDY DESERT

Port Hedland

Roebourne

Marble Bar

6 HAMERSLEY RANGE

5 Wittenoom

Newman

GIBSON DESERT

WESTERN AUSTRALIA

Meekatharra

Mount Magnet

GREAT VICTORIA DESERT

NULLARBOR PLAIN

Kalgoorlie

Eucla

Northam

PERTH

Bunbury

Esperance **1** Cape Le Grand

2

3 Albany

Cape Le Grand National Park

Cape Le Grand National Park protects a wild coastline of bold granite hills and headlands interspersed with wide beaches of snow white sand and sheltered bays. The brilliant blue waters are studded with the rocky islets of the Recherche Archipelago, a seascape rivalling that of the Great Barrier Reef.

Great granite outcrops form a series of impressive peaks rising to 345 m in the south-western corner of this 31,578 ha park. Inland are undulating sand plains supporting rich coastal heaths, swamps and freshwater pools. The granite peaks are pockmarked with caves, the most significant being a huge cavern at the summit of Frenchman Peak. Lucky Bay, Thistle Cove and Hellfire Bay are particularly beautiful, their fine white sands emphasised by the sparkling blue of the Southern Ocean.

The islands of the Recherche Archipelago are protected as flora and fauna reserves. They vary in size from low rocks to islands up to 5 km long. Many have precipitous cliffs and rocky slopes making access very difficult, and permits are required to land on certain islands. Cruise boats take tourists from Esperance to the archipelago, visiting the nearby Woody Island.

Formation

The granite and gneiss rocks exposed on the hills and headlands were formed more than 1100 million years ago when molten rock rose close to the surface and cooled into great blocks. Overlying the granite on the coastal plains are sedimentary rocks formed from marine deposits laid down between 25 and 28 million years ago when the area was submerged beneath the ocean. The sea level at that time was some 300 m higher than today, and the higher peaks would have been islands isolated in a shallow sea from the highlands of the western shield. The caves and tunnels in the peaks were probably scoured out by wave action and underwater currents during this period.

The sea level eventually dropped and the islands of the Recherche Archipelago became coastal headlands. Towards the end of the last ice age between 6000 and 11,000 years ago the sea level rose, isolating the islands once again and creating the present coastline of rocky hills and headlands.

History

The park takes its name from the southern cape, named after Le Grand, an officer of L'Esperance, one of the French ships commanded by Admiral D'Entrecasteaux who visited this coastline in 1792. Matthew Flinders anchored at Lucky Bay in 1802, allowing the botanist Robert Brown to spend five days investigating the flora of the region.

The early explorers noted the frequent burning of the country by the Aboriginal inhabitants. The region was part of the territory of the Nyungar, a group of clans and bands with their distinctive languages and customs, who occupied a vast area of south-western Australia including some 1600 km of coastline. They constructed bark houses and wore cloaks of kangaroo skin. Food was plentiful and they trapped and hunted for fish and game, burning the land to flush out animals and stimulate the growth of young green shoots and fire resistant grasses. The new growth attracted animals back to their hunting grounds and encouraged the growth of food plants.

Sealers arrived in the early 1800s to hunt the New Zealand fur seal. They soon decimated the seal populations and the industry had collapsed by the 1840s. John Eyre stopped at Rossiter Bay in 1841 on his near disastrous land crossing from South Australia to Albany. Much to his relief he attracted the attention of a passing whaling boat captained by Rossiter, after whom the bay was named.

Plants and Animals

Much of the park is an undulating sand plain covered with low scrubby heath and stands of eucalypts, particularly in the valleys. The park has a mixture of plants and animals of the south-west and south-east, including the beautiful Christmas tree (*Nuytsia floribunda*) at its easternmost limit in the area. Dense thickets of *Banksia speciosa* thrive in the deep sandy soils, growing 3-4 m tall; while on the shallow, gravelly soils *Banksia pulchella* grows.

The park was one of the first collecting sites of the early European botanists, and many of the species descriptions were based on material found in the park. Robert Brown, for example, described around 100 new species when he visited the area in 1802. Some of the early explorers were poisoned by the fruit of the cycad *Macrozamia reidlei*. This ancient palm-like plant was a staple food of the Aborigines, who removed the toxins by leaching and roasting the green fruit.

Banksias, bottlebrushes and the tubular flowers of the chittick (*Lambertia inermis*) provide a vital source of nectar and insects for the tiny honey possum, a mouse-sized marsupial found only in the sand plains of the south coast. This endearing animal probes the flowers with its long tubular snout. Although relatively common it is nocturnal and rarely seen, and needs an area rich in wildflowers to survive. Among the other marsupials are the black-footed rock wallaby, tammar wallaby and southern brown bandicoot. Colonies of New Zealand fur seals and Australian sea lions have returned to the area and can occasionally be seen resting in the bays and on some of the islands.

More than 90 bird species have been recorded, including the largest and one of the smallest of the Australian birds: the emu and the southern emu wren. Other birds include the Cape Barren goose and numerous birds of prey such as the peregrine falcon, white-bellied sea eagle, marsh harrier, wedge-tailed eagle, brown falcon, black-shouldered kite and Australian kestrel. Parrots are represented by the purple-crowned lorikeet, Port Lincoln redneck parrot, elegant and rock parrot, and the white-tailed black cockatoo. The heaths attract many honeyeaters and the tiny red-eared firetail, a brilliantly coloured finch of the south-western corner of Australia.

Walks
The Coastal Trail is 15 km long and traverses the magnificent coastline from Cape Le Grand Beach to Rossiter Bay. The track passes granite headlands and sheltered sandy bays and is a good introduction to the different habitats of the park and the spring wildflower displays. The track is accessible by car at various points. From Lucky Bay camping area it is an easy 4 km stroll to Thistle Cove. The terrain becomes rugged to Hellfire Bay, a hard two hour walk, and Le Grand Beach is three hours hard walking. From Lucky Bay to Rossiter Bay is an easy two hour walk.

The Le Grand Heritage Trail takes in part of the Coastal Trail from Thistle Cove to Lucky Bay. This is a self-guiding 2 km round trip providing a closer look at the history and spectacular landscape of the park.

A track leads from the car park to the top of Frenchmans Peak, a one to two hour walk up the gentle east slope leading to magnificent views over the park and islands.

Facilities
Basic facilities such as toilets, picnic areas and fireplaces are provided at the locations shown on the map, and there are camping grounds at Lucky Bay and Le Grand Beach with septic toilets, hot showers and drinking water. Visitors should bring a fuel stove as firewood is scarce. The ranger must be consulted about bush camping. Esperance has a wide range of accommodation.

Lucky Bay is the safest boat-launching site. The beaches are notoriously treacherous and vehicles are easily bogged in the most innocent looking sand. Ask the ranger about conditions and tides.

Access
The park is 40 km east of Esperance via the sealed Merivale and Cape Le Grand Roads. There are regular tours from Esperance to the park.

Climate
The area has a mild climate with warm dry summers and cool winters. Most rain falls between April and October. Visit in spring to see the wildflower displays.

Cape Le Grand National Park, PO Box 706, Esperance, WA 6450. Tel. (08) 9075 9022.

Marbellup Hill

0   2   4
Kilometres

CAPE LE GRAND

• Frenchman Peak

Le Grand Beach

Mt Le Grand
345

Coastal Trail

Boulder

HELLFIRE
BAY

Cape Le Grand

New Is

SOUTHERN

Ram Is

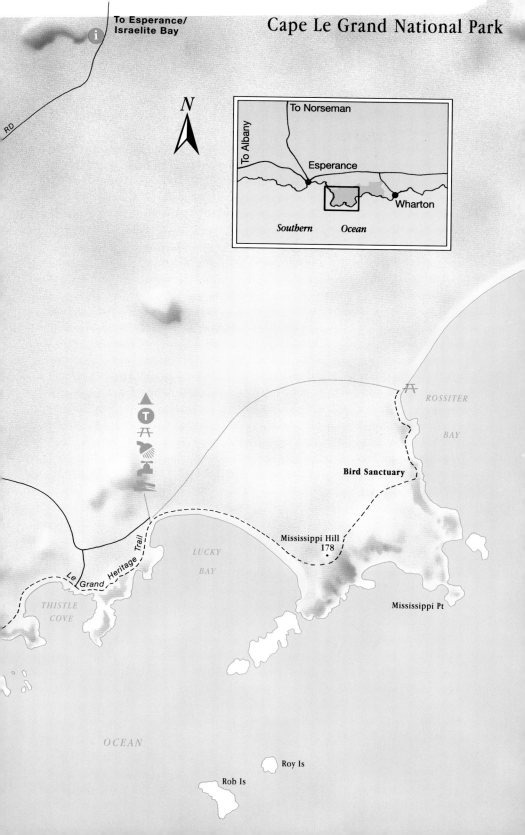

To Esperance/
Israelite Bay

RD

N

To Albany

To Norseman

Esperance

Wharton

Southern   Ocean

ROSSITER

BAY

Bird Sanctuary

Mississippi Hill
178

Le Grand   Heritage   Trail

*LUCKY
BAY*

*THISTLE
COVE*

Mississippi Pt

OCEAN

Roy Is

Rob Is

Stirling Range and Porongurup National Parks

Rising abruptly from the green coastal plains, the jagged peaks of Stirling Range and the granite-domed Porongurups are islands of outstanding ecological diversity surrounded by some of the state's richest agricultural land. Visitors from around the world come to see the astonishing variety of flowering plants of the Stirling Range and the rare karri forests of the Porongurups.

Named after Captain James Stirling, the first Governor of Western Australia, Stirling Range National Park protects 115,661 ha of rugged peaks, stacks, rough scree slopes and sand plains. The range stretches for some 65 km from east to west, with five of the peaks more than 1000 m above sea level. These are often shrouded in mist, and in winter may be dusted with snow. The creeks flowing through the gullies are intermittent, drying up during the summer months.

Some 40 km south of the Stirlings the Porongurup Range rises up to 670 m in a series of rounded granite domes. Although the mountains lack the saw-toothed profile of the Stirlings they have their own impressive cliffs and slopes, such as Castle Rock and Devils Slide. The Porongurup Range is only 12 km long, and the park covers a mere 2511 ha, but it is renowned for its beauty. Many of the slopes are clothed in karri forest with a rich understorey of wildflowers.

The first European to visit the area was Ensign Dale, who scaled Toolbrunup Peak in 1832 in search of two Aboriginal foods, kuik and quannet, which he failed to locate. The botanist James Drummond explored Stirling Range in 1843, 1846 and 1848, describing many of the area's unique plants. He noted that the Aborigines had burned areas around Toolbrunup Peak to promote new growth and flush out game.

Formation

The underlying rocks of the area are granite, formed more than 1100 million years ago when molten rock rose towards the surface and cooled into great blocks. At this time a shallow sea covered the land, and marine sediments built up over the granite. The sea eventually receded and the land that is now the Stirling Range sank into a low-lying depression. While the sedimentary rocks were eroded from the surrounding plains exposing the granite, the Stirling Range area retained its thick sedimentary rock covering. A period of uplift gradually pushed the Stirling Range and the Porongurups above the plains. Water and vegetation worked its way into the joints between the exposed granite blocks of the Porongurups, slowly opening them up and exposing them to the elements. Weathering softened their contours to leave rounded domes.

The deep sedimentary rock layers of the Stirling Range weathered to form sandy soils and jagged peaks, while rivers flowing south cut deep valleys into the soft rocks. The Chester and Red Gum passes were formed by these ancient rivers.

Around 28 million years ago rising sea levels submerged the coastal plains, leaving the peaks of the ranges and many of the coastal hills and headlands as islands. For three million years the peaks were separated by water, and this period of isolation allowed new species of plants and animals to evolve from the small island populations. The sea eventually receded and the mountains and plains once again emerged as dry land.

Plants and Animals

More than 1500 species of flowering plants have been found in the Stirling Range, and more than 80 of these are unique. Only one of the ten species of mountain bells grows outside the Stirling Range. These beautiful and unusual plants are found above 300 m on acidic soils, and each species is restricted to a well-defined area. The Mondurup bell (*Darwinia macrostegia*), its flowers hidden within white bracts with crimson veins, and the Stirling Range banksia (*Banksia solandri*) with large serrated leaves, are confined to a few peaks around Mondurup Peak.

On the stony soils of the hills are stands of jarrah and Albany blackbutt, often stunted by fire. The scrubby slopes and valleys support at least 13 species of banksias and more than 100 species of ground orchids. The most dazzling wildflower displays are seen on the sandy plains. Low heath-type plants dominate these areas, and the great diversity produces an amazing variety of flowers. Flowering gums, such as the vivid yellow-flowering bell-fruited mallee and the pink-flowering marri, add their colourful touch.

Karri trees survive in sheltered gullies and damp sites in Porongurup Range. They are the northern outliers of great forests that covered vast areas of south-western Australia in an earlier, wetter era. Karri hazel is a common understorey shrub, and in spring the forests are ablaze with the purple flowers of the tree hovea, Austral bluebells and yellow pea flowers. In drier areas are grasstrees and forests of marri and jarrah.

Purple-crowned lorikeets feed on the karri flowers and race through the treetops. Other common birds in the area include the western rosella, tree martin, grey shrike thrush, restless flycatcher, grey fantail, white-browed scrubwren, scarlet and yellow robins, and more than 14 species of honeyeaters. Among the mammals are western grey kangaroos, western brush wallabies, ringtail and brushtail possums and bush rats.

Walks

Follow the footsteps of the early botanists and climb some of the peaks in the Stirling Range for breathtaking views and a close look at some of the flora and fauna. Most of the walks are steep, so allow plenty of time and carry drinking water.

One of the most popular tracks leads to the summit of Bluff Knoll, the highest point in the Stirlings, a three hour return walk from the car park. The Toolbrunup Peak track takes three hours return and is one of the most challenging walks. The last section of the track is very rough, but the views from the summit are excellent. Mondurup Peak is a two hour moderate climb; look out for ripple patterns on the rocks along the track, formed when the waves of an ancient

sea broke against the peak. This track is closed in winter and spring and when the soil is moist to prevent the spread of dieback disease. There are precipitous rocks and caverns on Talyuberlup Peak, an interesting two hour return climb.

Bushwalkers taking overnight or long-distance hikes should leave details of their journey in the log book at Moingup Springs or Bluff Knoll at the northern entrance to Stirling Range.

The major route across Porongurup Range is the Wansborough Walk, a two to three hour return trip from Tree-in-the-Rock picnic area. Side tracks lead to Marmabup Peak and to the crest of the range where there are spectacular views. A well-graded, self-guiding 800 m loop from Tree-in-the-Rock picnic area is an excellent introduction to the park's different habitats.

Facilities

Camping is permitted in the Stirling Range at Moingup Springs, and permits should be obtained from the ranger. Camping is not allowed in the Porongurup Range. There are full facilities at the Stirling Range Caravan Park at the northern entrance to the park, and accommodation is available at Karribank Lodge at the northern junction of the entrance to Porongurup.

Access

Stirling Range is about 380 km from Perth and 64 km from Albany along sealed roads. Dieback, a plant disease caused by a microscopic fungus, *Phytophthora cinnamomi*, is a major threat to the area's wildflowers. The spores of the fungus are carried in soil, so it is essential to clean vehicles, tyres, shoes and tent pegs after leaving infected areas and before entering parks and reserves, and to keep to formed roads.

Climate

The best time to visit the park is late spring and early summer when the wildflowers are at their best and the days are warm. Winter is cold and wet, and sudden cold snaps can occur in spring.

Stirling Range National Park, Chester Pass Rd, Amelup via Borden, WA 6338.
Tel. (08) 9827 9230.
Porongurup National Park, Bolganup Rd, RMB 1310, Mt Barker, WA 6324.
Tel. (08) 9853 1095.

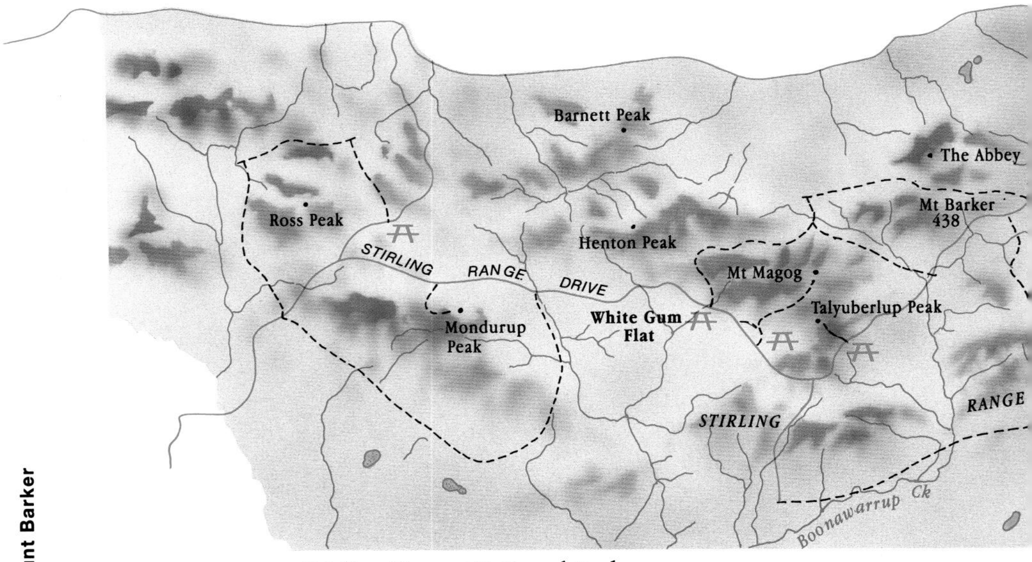

Stirling Range National Park

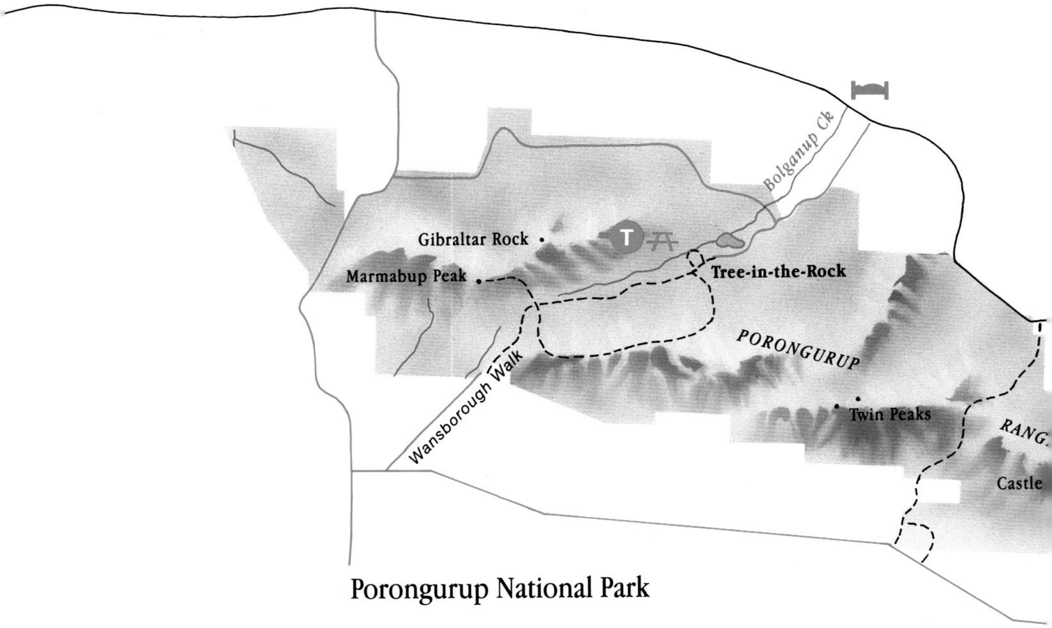

Barnett Peak

The Abbey

Ross Peak

STIRLING RANGE DRIVE

Henton Peak

Mt Barker 438

Mondurup Peak

White Gum Flat

Mt Magog

Talyuberlup Peak

STIRLING RANGE

Boonawarrup Ck

To Mount Barker

Porongurup National Park

Bolganup Ck

Gibraltar Rock

T

Tree-in-the-Rock

Marmabup Peak

Wansborough Walk

PORONGURUP

Twin Peaks

RANGE

Castle

0

Kilometres

Stirling Range and Porongurup National Parks

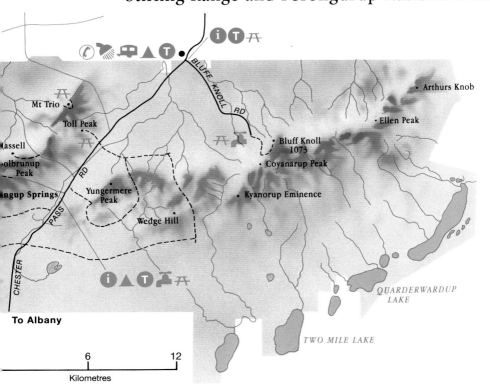

Arthurs Knob

Mt Trio

Toll Peak

Ellen Peak

assell

Bluff Knoll
1073

olbrunup
Peak

Coyanarup Peak

ngup Springs

Yungermere
Peak

Kyanorup Eminence

Wedge Hill

CHESTER PASS RD

BLUFF KNOLL RD

QUARDERWARDUP
LAKE

To Albany

TWO MILE LAKE

6   12

Kilometres

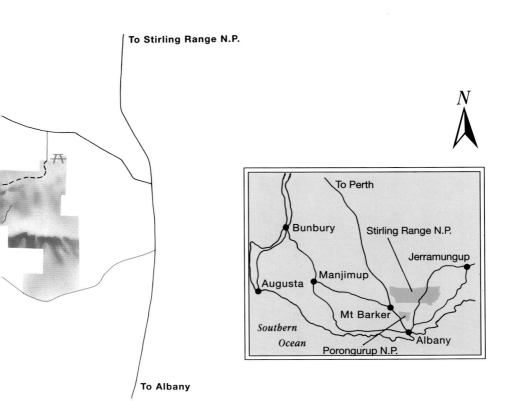

To Stirling Range N.P.

N

To Perth

Bunbury

Stirling Range N.P.

Jerramungup

Augusta

Manjimup

*Southern
Ocean*

Mt Barker

Albany

Porongurup N.P.

To Albany

Walpole-Nornalup National Park

*Surrounding the tranquil and picturesque Walpole and Nornalup Inlets, this
magnificent national park protects some of the finest remaining karri and tingle
forests in Australia. These legendary forests, with trees towering up to 90 m high,
nurture an abundant bird population and a rich floral undergrowth. Deep rivers,
waterfalls and an unspoiled coastline of sheltered bays and long ocean beaches are
just a few of the features of this great coastal park.*

The densely forested inland areas of the 15,861 ha
park are traversed by the Frankland and Deep
Rivers. These deep winding waterways are ideal
for fishing and boating, and empty into Nornalup Inlet, a broad shallow lake that opens into
the Southern Ocean. Great karri trees come right
down to the shoreline in places, and the waters of
the inlets are a haven for waterbirds. The Valley
of the Giants protects one of the few remaining
forests of giant red tingle and karri trees, some
with burned-out buttressed trunks big enough
to drive a car into.

Nuyts Wilderness is an area of heath-covered
coastal dunes, high rock-capped hills, a deep
forested gorge and spectacular rugged coastline.
Rounded granite headlands plunge in sheer
slopes to sheltered beaches and bays.

History

Sealers were the first Europeans to live in this
area. They set up a base camp at Sealers Cove at
Nornalup Inlet in 1826 and hunted New Zealand
fur seals along the coast. The Aboriginal inhabitants of the area suffered greatly at the hands of
these brutal people, yet they were friendly to the
first explorers who came from the Swan River
settlement in 1831, helping them to find food
and erect shelters.

The karri forests today are mere remnants of
those that greeted the early explorers. Timber-
getters arrived in the 1840s, cutting down the
largest trees and reducing them to useful sizes
using hand saws. The milling of karri became a
major industry of the south-west, and the forests
were managed to a certain extent by cutting out
only marked trees, allowing the forests to regenerate. This all changed when the wood chipping
industry moved into the area, clear felling vast
areas and decimating these magnificent forests.

Only small stands of old growth forests now
remain, protected in small reserves and national
parks along the south coast.

Plants

The area has higher rainfall than other parts of
the south-west, and the forests are similar to the
wet temperate forests of south-eastern Australia.

The high rainfall and rich soils of the park
support forests dominated by karri (*Eucalyptus
diversicolor*), a straight-trunked tree growing
to 90 m with a girth up to 8 m. Few trees equal
the karri, their straight smooth trunks, marked
with grey and salmon colours, soar like giant
columns unbranched for 30 m or more.

The lower levels of the karri forest are damp,
cool and shady, dominated by ferns, mosses and
shrubs such as the karri hazel and karri oak.
Along the creeks and more open areas the understorey is much denser, with flowering shrubs such
as the karri wattle, creeping holly flame pea,
blue-flowering tree hovea and cutleaf hibbertia.
In spring the understorey is ablaze with wildflowers, including many species of ground
orchids.

Hilltop Road leads to the Valley of the Giants
where there are magnificent stands of red tingle
trees (*Eucalyptus jacksonii*). Red tingle is
another massive tree growing to 70 m with a
spreading, buttressed trunk up to 5 m diameter
with persistent dark, rough bark. They loom high
above an understorey of karri oak and a forest
floor of damp humus and leaf mould. In places
tingle trees grow alongside karri to create a rare
combination of botanical and scenic interest.

The south-eastern section of the park is
known for its stands of the rare red flowering
gum (*Eucalyptus ficifolia*). Although widely
cultivated as an ornamental, this small tree with

large crimson, pink or white flowers, grows naturally only on the sandy soils of this region. The south-western part of the park supports peppermints, banksias and eucalypts, stunted by the salt-laden winds. Near the beaches the dunes are covered with hakeas, daisy bushes and creeping ground-covers.

Animals

Now that the whalers and sealers have left, southern right whales and humpback whales once again pass within sight of shore on their annual migration north, and New Zealand fur seals have returned to Saddle Island.

Kangaroos are quite common and include the western grey kangaroo, a small population of western brush wallabies, and the small, robust, quokka. Among the other marsupials are the western pygmy possum, ringtail and brushtail possums, the short-nosed bandicoot, the yellow-footed antechinus and the fat-tailed dunnart. Black snakes, dugites and tiger snakes search the area for frogs and lizards.

Around 110 bird species have been recorded in the park, and bird life is abundant in the forests. Brightly-coloured western rosellas and red-capped parrots fly beneath the canopy, and flocks of purple-crowned lorikeets feed noisily from the flowering karri trees. Black cockatoos, red-winged fairy wrens and scarlet robins are other birds of the forests. Around the inlets are resident populations of waders and seabirds, including pelicans and black swans. Sea eagles, ospreys, migratory whimbrels, bar-tailed godwits and red-capped plovers are seen along the beaches.

Walks

Walking trails lead to most of the different habitats of the park. Several short tracks cross the karri-covered hilltop near Coalmine Beach, and a number of longer tracks lead from Hilltop Road, along the Frankland River and into the red tingle forest.

One walk that should not be missed is from the campsite at Coalmine Beach around the Knoll, a small promontory covered with towering karri trees with a rich understorey of wildflowers in spring and summer. Walking through these cool mighty forests is an unforgettable experience.

Nuyts Wilderness area is accessible only by foot, and a long track leads from Shedley Drive through this area to the south coast. The track crosses a footbridge over Deep River and takes you through sand dune country and low forests to the coast. The track forks around the high headland of Point Nuyts to either Lost Beach or Thompson Cove.

The undulating coastal areas are ideal bushwalking country, comprising thickly vegetated sand dunes behind quiet beaches and bays.

Facilities

The caravan and camping area at Coalmine Beach has shady sites under peppermint trees, with fireplaces, showers, toilets, tables, a kiosk and ranger's residence.

At a number of places around the edges of the park there are commercial camping and caravan parks, chalets, cabins and motel accommodation. Bookings should be made during peak holiday periods.

Access

Walpole is 420 km south-east of Perth and 121 km west of Albany via the South-western Highway. Boat cruises operate along the Frankland River, and local tours of the park and surrounding areas can be organised in Denmark and Walpole.

Climate

Summers are warm and pleasant with cool nights. Winters can be cold, and most of the 1300 mm of rain falls in the winter months.

Walpole-Nornalup National Park, Southwestern Highway, Walpole, WA 6398. Tel. (08) 9840 1066.

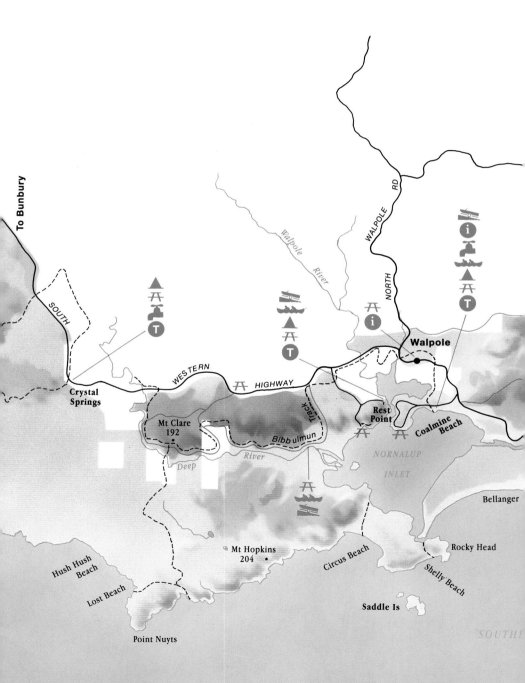

0   3   6

Kilometres

To Bunbury

SOUTH

Walpole River

WALPOLE RD

NORTH

Walpole

WESTERN   HIGHWAY

Crystal Springs

Mt Clare
192

Bibbulmun

Track

Deep

River

Rest Point

Coalmine Beach

NORNALUP

INLET

Bellanger

Mt Hopkins
204

Hush Hush
Beach

Circus Beach

Rocky Head

Shelly Beach

Lost Beach

Saddle Is

Point Nuyts

SOUTHE

Walpole-Nornalup National Park

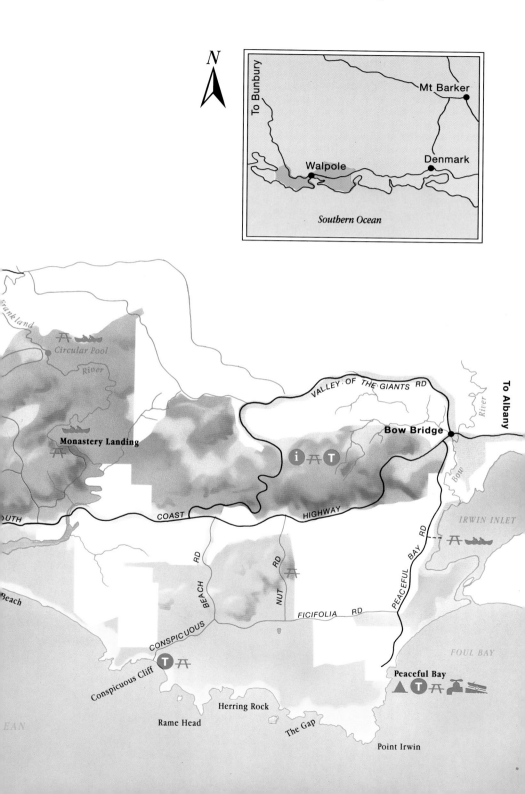

Kalbarri National Park

Kalbarri National Park protects one of the most attractive parts of the west coast of Australia, where towering sandstone cliffs form spectacular arches, deep gorges and strange offshore formations. The Murchison River winds through the park in a rugged canyon 80 km long and 170 m deep.

Proclaimed in 1963, Kalbarri National Park covers 186,050 ha and surrounds the township of Kalbarri, one of Western Australia's most popular holiday resorts. The area is famed for its multi-coloured cliffs and river gorges, and its exceptionally rich wildflower displays. The main feature is the Murchison River flowing through deep colourful gorges meandering 80 km through the park. The rocks of the gorges are in horizontal bands of red, yellow, grey and white.

Surrounding the gorges is an undulating sand plain supporting an outstanding diversity of heathland plants. The sand plain ends abruptly in deeply dissected coastal cliffs, undercut and sculpted by the pounding waves of the Indian Ocean into strange shapes and rugged headlands. The cliffs form giant steps descending more than 100 m to the ocean, and glow in shades of red and yellow as the setting sun highlights the coloured layers of the sandstone.

The Murchison River is usually a chain of long still pools fringed with trees clinging to the rocks, but when heavy rains flood the dry mulga catchment area brown floodwaters rush through the gorges, transforming the river into a roaring, raging torrent.

Formation

While other parts of the continent have been uplifted, submerged or rocked by volcanic activity, this part of Australia has been geologically stable for hundreds of millions of years. The coloured bands of rock through which the Murchison River has carved its course were formed more than 400 million years ago. At this time the park was on the edge of a broad coastal plain about 100 km wide, where it graded into wide tidal flats that sloped gently into a shallow sea. A maze of interweaving shifting rivers flowed over the plain, carrying sand from an adjacent mountain range extending north–south for

hundreds of kilometres.

The sandy sediments accumulated and compressed over millions of years into layers of thinly bedded sandstone rocks stained red by iron oxides. The resulting sedimentary rock is known as Tumblagooda sandstone. The rippled surface seen in areas such as Nature's Window was formed by waves moving over the tidal flats. The tracks of ancient marine worms are visible in places such as The Loop and along the coast where the sandstone has an organ-pipe appearance formed by burrowing worms similar to today's sand-worms. The coarser grained sandstone seen 10 to 20 m above the base of the Z Bend and on the upper part of the gorge at Hawks Head were deposited by river deltas that eventually overwhelmed the tidal flats.

Plants and Animals

The sand plains support more than 900 species of flowering plants, with massed stands of featherflowers, banksias, grevilleas, melaleucas, everlastings, kangaroo paws, pincushion plants and acacias. River red gums and native cypresses line the gorges and fringe the pools. In spring the heath plants are in full bloom and cover the sand plains in a mosaic of colour.

Many of the mammals in the park are nocturnal and rarely seen, and many have been decimated by feral predators such as cats and foxes. Rare black-footed rock wallabies have been recorded on the rocky ledges, a habitat also frequented by the euro, while red kangaroos and western grey kangaroos frequent the sand plains. Among the other native mammals are the little red flying fox, white-striped mastiff bat, little brown bat, Gould's wattled bat, ash-grey mouse, spinifex hopping mouse and Mitchell's hopping mouse. Dolphins and Australian sea-lions live in the coastal waters.

Reptiles find many habitats in the sand plains

and rocky outcrops. They include dragons such as the thorny devil, spotted dragon and dwarf-bearded dragon, monitors, skinks, legless lizards such as common and hooded scaly-foot and Burton's snake-lizard, geckoes and snakes including Stimson's python, ringed brown snake and the yellow-faced whip snake. Flat-shelled turtles and eight frog species including the green and golden bell frog live in the waterways.

More than 200 bird species have been recorded in the area. Emus are frequently seen on the sand plains. Waders, ducks and other waterbirds frequent the pools, while kestrels nest on the projecting ledges of the gorges. Parrots, finches and honeyeaters are common; peregrine falcons and white-bellied sea-eagles may be seen soaring over the coastal waters searching for fish.

Walks

The most spectacular scenery in the park is accessed by a series of walking tracks leading to lookouts over the river gorges and coastal cliffs. Those wishing to embark on long overnight hikes must notify the ranger before and after making the trip, and be well prepared for rough walking over hazardous terrain.

From Hawks Head there are magnificent views over the river gorges, and it is an easy walk down to the pools from Ross Graham Lookout. Several lookouts around The Loop give different perspectives on the winding courses of the river. The walk takes about six hours from Nature's Window, a natural rock arch framing the river view upstream. The trail is unmarked but follows the east cliff top to the first river bend, then descends to the flood plain and back up to Nature's Window.

From Ross Graham Lookout to The Loop is a strenuous 38 km hike taking three to four days along the river bed. There are no marked trails and several river crossings must be made. Temperatures soar here in the summer as heat is reflected from the surrounding rock, and even experienced bushwalkers may suffer from heat exhaustion. Shorter two day gorge hikes may be made from Ross Graham Lookout to Z Bend, or from Z Bend to The Loop (although the first 5 km of this walk is difficult).

Along the coast a number of short walks lead from car parks to lookouts over the coastal formations, and down to a tranquil beach at Eagle Gorge. Island Rock and Natural Bridge are rock formations created by constant undercutting of the soft sandstone to form sea stacks and arches. The Coastal Trail is a three hour one-way walk from Eagle Gorge to Natural Bridge along the cliffs, with magnificent seascapes. Arrange to be dropped off at the beginning of the walk and picked up at the end. A self-guiding nature trail at Mushroom Rock takes a leisurely two hours, and introduces you to some of the botanical features and geological formations of the park.

Facilities

There are no camping areas in the park, but a full range of accommodation, shops and services is available at Kalbarri township. Within the park there are toilets and picnic areas at the places marked on the map, and a Ranger Station at the Kalbarri entrance on the Ajana Kalbarri Road. Drinking water is not available; you must carry sufficient for your needs.

After heavy rain the Murchison River is deep enough to navigate by canoe or raft. This hazardous journey and should only be attempted by well equipped and experienced people. A park ranger should be contacted for advice.

Access

The park is about 590 km north of Perth via the sealed North-west Coast Highway. Turn off to Kalbarri approximately 155 km north of Geraldton. The unsealed roads within the park are suitable for all traffic. Commercial flights and coaches service Kalbarri, and park tours operate from the township.

Climate

Summers are hot, reaching 40 to 50 degrees Celsius in the gorges, and often dry and windy. May to September are the cooler months wiith temperatures from 10 to 25 degrees Celsius, and most rain falls during June and July. Wildflowers bloom from August to October, and this is the most comfortable time to explore the park.

Kalbarri National Park, PO Box 37, Kalbarri, WA 6536. Tel. (08) 9937 1140.

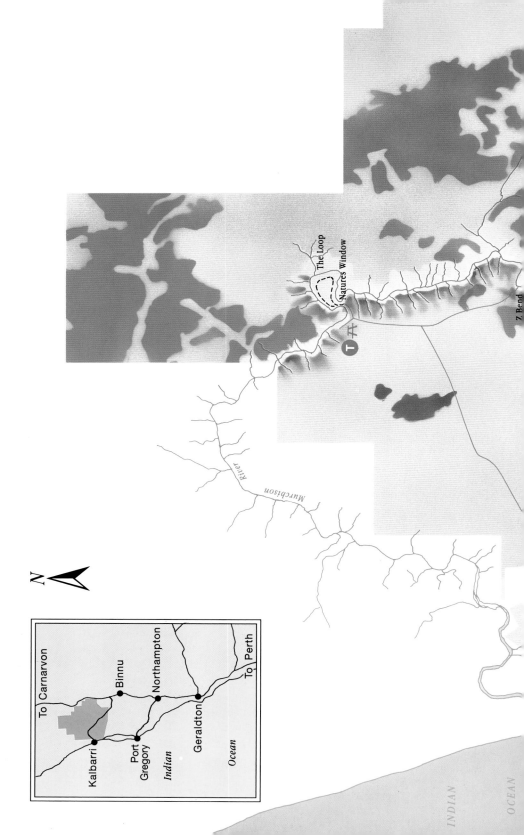

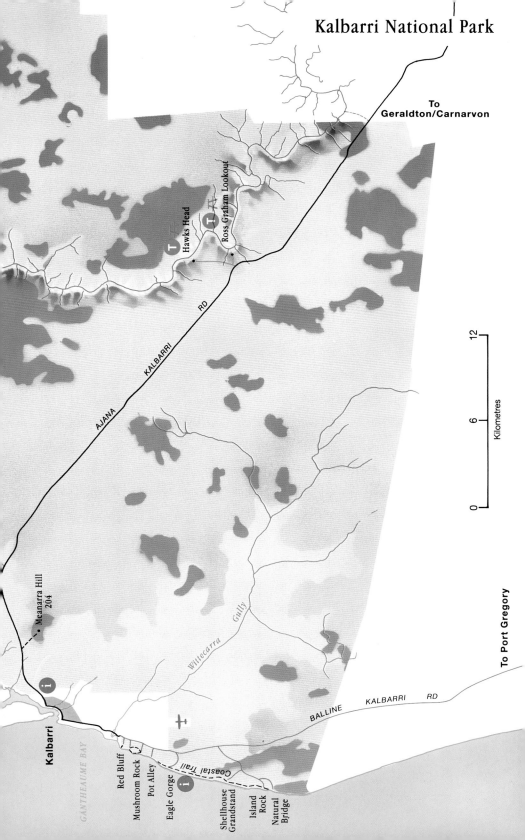

Kalbarri National Park

To Geraldton/Carnarvon

Hawks Head

Ross Graham Lookout

RD

KALBARRI

AJANA

12

6

Kilometres

0

Meanarra Hill 204

Wittecarra Gully

To Port Gregory

BALLINE   KALBARRI   RD

Kalbarri

GANTHEAUME BAY

Red Bluff

Mushroom Rock

Pot Alley

Eagle Gorge

Coastal Trail

Shellhouse Grandstand

Island Rock

Natural Bridge

Karijini (Hamersley Range) National Park

Karijini National Park lies in the heart of the Pilbara on the Great Plateau, a huge rock mass that juts out into the Indian Ocean. The park is famed for its spectacular rugged scenery, deep gorges blazing with rocks of incredible colours, ancient geological formations and a variety of arid-country ecosystems.

Karijini occupies 627,445 ha and is Western Australia's second largest national park. The most striking characteristic of the landscape is its dry, barren nature. The bare rocks reveal every fold, ridge and contour of the landscape, and their colours blaze in shades of red, brown and coal-black, contrasting the bright green oases surrounding the waterholes. Yet after rain the plains and hills are briefly carpeted by beautiful wildflowers, and when the cyclones rage water pours from the sky, transforming the creeks into surging brown torrents.

The most dramatic features of the park are the gorges in the northern section. Narrow chasms up to 100 m deep have been cut into the plateau by creeks that are now dry for most of the year. From their cliff tops dark red rock walls plunge vertically to permanent pools of cold water or floors polished smooth by the flood-waters. Downstream the valleys widen out and the stream beds emerge as alluvial fans in the Fortescue Valley.

Each gorge has its own unique character. Some are so narrow and precipitous that the sun never penetrates their depths. In others the rock walls glow with bands of red and mauve, and lush green vegetation grows around their rock pools. Some of the most spectacular are Joffre, Knox, Red, Kalamina, Hamersley, Hancock and Weano Gorges. Dales Gorge is one of the most unexpected and impressive sights of the Ranges. A deep gash cut into the spinifex-dotted plateau reveals tranquil sunken gardens, cascading waterfalls and deep pools fringed with palms, ferns and tall rushes.

Elsewhere massive rounded mountains rise from the plateau, reaching 1235 m at Mount Bruce, the second highest mountain in Western Australia. Escarpments fall into flat valleys, and stony tree-lined watercourses wind their way across the parched spinifex plains. Most of the southern area is inaccessible, and the park is so vast that visitors are generally unaware of the great open-cut mines in the area. Blue asbestos is present in Yampire Gorge, and visitors should refer to the park's warning brochure before entering this area.

Formation
The north-western corner of Australia is one of the most ancient landforms on earth. While other parts of the continent have been submerged beneath oceans, uplifted, faulted and buckled, or have erupted in volcanic activity, this ancient rock mass appears to have remained stable for some 600 million years.

Many of the rocks in the gorges have bands of iron running through them. These originated more than 2500 million years ago as sediments of iron and silica deposited on the floor of an ancient ocean. Further sediments forced out the trapped water, gradually turning them into layers of rock. The youngest rocks in the area are 600 to 1000 million years old.

Massive subterranean movements gradually lifted the land high above sea level, folding and buckling the rocks, creating vertical cracks and faultlines. Rivers cut deep into the faults forming sheer-sided gorges while millions of years of erosion has rounded the hills and sculpted the rocks to form the present landscape.

Plants and Animals
Clumps of sharp, stiff spinifex grasses are the dominant vegetation on the shallow soils of the plateau. After rain wildflowers such as Sturt's desert pea, white dragon tree, green bird flower,

mauve and pink parakeelyas and numerous everlasting daisies brighten the landscape. Low mulga woodlands and eucalypts grow on the slopes, and in the cooler months the land is covered with yellow-flowering cassias and wattles, purple mulla-mullas and northern bluebells.

The gorges offer shade and shelter from the harsh sun. Small, white-trunked ghost gums and tenacious rock figs grow from fissures in the cliff faces, while below, beside the river pools are great river red gums, huge paperbarks known as cadjeputs, and occasional palms. In the cool depths where water seeps from the rocks are banks of delicate ferns and mosses.

Wildlife is inconspicuous in this harsh and arid land where most animals hide by day. Around dawn and dusk you may see red kangaroos, euros, dingos or the rare Rothschild's rock wallaby. Ghost bats live in the caves and abandoned mine shafts, and many species of native rodents and marsupial carnivores, such as the Pilbara ninguai and the red antechinus, are resident. Rock piles of the pebble-mound mouse and huge termite nests are common beside some of the tracks.

Reptiles are often seen. They include pythons, venomous western brown snakes, legless lizards, the large knob-tailed gecko, goannas and dragons. Frogs such as the desert tree frog are found around the waterholes.

Birdlife is varied, and near the pools and streams you are likely to see kingfishers, reed warblers, wrens, rock pigeons and the beautiful star finch. Peregrine falcons, wedge-tailed eagles and kites soar above the watercourses and rocky outcrops searching for their prey.

Walks

Many short walks or climbs lead into the gorges or follow the cliff lines to lookouts. A three hour return walk into Kalamina Gorge is an excellent introduction to the gorge country. This easy walk follows the stream past rock pools to Rock Arch Pool. Dales Gorge is reached from the parking area by following the rim or descending by a steep trail to Fortescue Falls (one hour return) or the fern-fringed Circular Pool (two hours return). A trail follows the creek from Fortescue Falls to Circular Pool.

Narrow passages, banded iron rock formations and precipitous cliffs await the visitor to the Hancock and Weano Gorge area. A steep narrow path (three hours return) leads into Hancock Gorge where the rocks have been polished by the water. A shorter, one hour return walk, follows a steep winding track into Weano Gorge: a narrow crevice of coloured banded rock formations. Deep pools block the gorge and you must swim and wade through these to reach the river bed of Red Gorge.

From Oxers Lookout you can look down over the junction of four gorges, a spectacular sight in the early morning and late afternoon. Short tracks lead to Knox Lookout and Joffre Lookout where there are views over the natural amphitheatre created by Joffre Falls.

Facilities

Camping is only allowed at designated sites at Joffre, Weano and Fortescue. There are bush toilets, gas barbecues and picnic tables. Drinking water is scarce and available from tanks at locations indicated on the map. Carry plenty of water at all times. Accommodation and supplies can be found at Auski Roadhouse, Wittenoom and Tom Price.

Access

The park is 1400 km north of Perth via the Great Northern Highway. Turn off along the unsealed road to Wittenoom, 10 km from the northern border. An unsealed road leads from Wittenoom to Millstream-Chichester National Park. Roads within the park are unsealed and reasonably good except after rain. Many tourist coaches visit the park, and commercial flights operate to Wittenoom.

Climate

The ideal time to visit the park is in winter and spring when the days are warm and clear, although the nights are cold and sometimes frosty. Summers are hot with a highly variable rainfall of 250–350 mm associated with dramatic thunderstorms and cyclones.

Karijini National Park, PO Box 29, Tom Price, WA 6751. Tel. (08) 9189 8157.

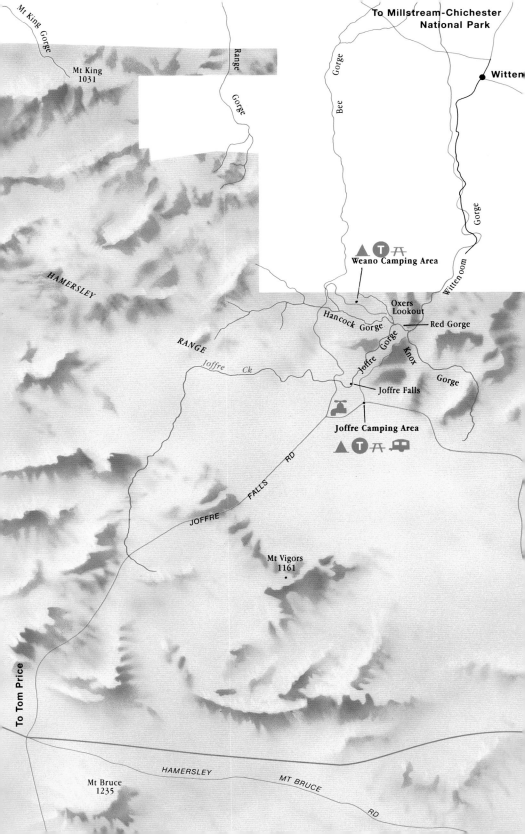

To Millstream-Chichester National Park

Mt King Gorge

Mt King
1031

Range

Gorge

Bee Gorge

Witten

Gorge

HAMERSLEY

Wittenoom Gorge

Weano Camping Area

RANGE

Oxers
Lookout

Hancock Gorge

Red Gorge

Joffre Ck

Joffre Gorge

Knox Gorge

Joffre Falls

Joffre Camping Area

FALLS RD

JOFFRE

Mt Vigors
1161

To Tom Price

HAMERSLEY

MT BRUCE

Mt Bruce
1235

RD

Karijini (Hamersley Range) National Park

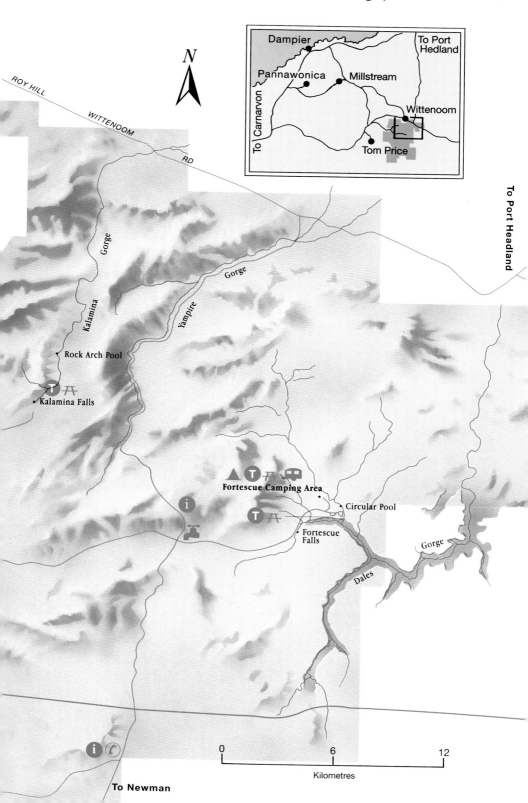

Millstream-Chichester National Park

Millstream is a green oasis set in the parched rolling spinifex hills and spectacular escarpments of the Chichester Range. The spinifex-clad rocky ranges provide a golden backdrop to the massive bare black hilltops, the forested wetlands and the string of clear, spring-fed pools along the Fortescue River.

The Chichester Range rises sharply from the coastal plain to form a stony plateau sloping gradually to the bed of the Fortescue River. Tumbled masses of black boulders form a jumble of rocky peaks, while tranquil gorges and cool hidden rock pools await the visitor. The Fortescue River flows only after heavy downpours. Normally it is a dry watercourse in a broad flat valley until it reaches Millstream where it surfaces in a string of deep, spring-fed pools fringed by sedges, palm groves and paperbark forests.

Python Pool is a beautiful natural rock pool fed by a semi-circular, crater-like waterfall, set in a rugged and beautiful section of the Chichester Range. Views from the nearby Mount Herbert look out over the coastal plains and the hills and valleys of the Chichester Range.

Most of the 199,736 ha Millstream-Chichester National Park is an inhospitable, hot, parched land where the occasional rainfall brings a sudden ephemeral existence to a host of desert plants and animals. The downpours are soaked up by a mass of porous rock, some 2000 square kilometres in extent, beneath the bed of the Fortescue River. This aquifer, thought to hold 1700 million cubic metres of water, feeds the string of pools of the Millstream oasis and the surrounding wetlands.

Huge volumes of water are pumped from the underground reserves to supply the mining and industrial towns in the area. This has begun to lower the water table, killing trees and affecting some of the pools. A dam has been proposed for the Fortescue River. If this is constructed it will irrevocably damage the delicately-balanced ecosystem and flood many Aboriginal art sites.

History

Millstream was known as Ngarrari to the Aboriginal people who lived here for many thousands of years before the arrival of the Europeans. Ngarrari was an important meeting place for members of the Jindjibandji tribe, who led a nomadic lifestyle centred around the waterholes between the Hamersley Range and the Chichester escarpment. Visitors camped beside Chinderwariner Pool, harvesting edible plants, fishing, crafting spears and performing ceremonial rites.

The Ngarrari pools are said to have been formed by the Barrimindi, a great water snake living beneath the Fortescue River, where it forced its way to the surface in search of initiates. The snake's presence is still felt by Aboriginal people of the area, who regard Barrimindi as the protector of the permanent waterholes along the river.

Ngarrari was renamed Millstream by the explorer F.T. Gregory in 1861. He commented on the grazing potential of the area and the abundant water supply. The first pastoral lease at Millstream was taken up in 1865. The Jindjibandji, who fought in vain to drive the squatters away, were obliged to work for the station or starve. Those who resisted were killed or dragged off to a hastily-constructed jail at Roebourne and forced to work in chain gangs.

Kangaroos were shot in their thousands to make room for sheep, and by the turn of the century the land was badly overstocked. Some 55,000 sheep grazed the arid plains and hills around Millstream, damaging the fragile ecosystem and polluting the waterholes. In the late 1960s the squatters were obliged by law to pay their Aboriginal workers award rates. Unwilling to do this they simply evicted them. After a century of working for no more than food and clothing, they were obliged to live in overcrowded government camps.

The Millstream lease was purchased by the Department of Conservation and Land Management, and combined with Chichester National Park in 1982. A few Jindjibandji people are employed as rangers and contract workers in the park, and older members of the tribe are keeping their culture alive by passing on their unique knowledge to the younger generations.

Plants and Animals

After rain the normally barren hills are covered with blankets of mulla-mulla and Sturt's desert pea, interspersed with yellow wattle flowers, everlasting daisies and parakeelyas. Most days, however, only golden spinifex, mulga woodlands and scattered eucalypts are visible in the harsh sunlight. Plants typical of the tropical north grow near the permanent waterholes. The Millstream pools are bordered by huge river red gums and forests of cadjeput paperbarks. Of special interest is the Millstream Palm (*Livistona alfredii*), unique to the Pilbara. Date palms and cotton palms have spread through the area, and weeds and the water lily are common.

Wildlife is seldom seen during the hot, dry days, although colonies of black flying foxes live in the dense clumps of date palms. Red kangaroos, dingos and emus roam the plains, and the common wallaroo lives in the rocky hills. Small mammals, such as Forrest's mouse and the fat-tailed antechinus, are at home in this arid environment.

Reptiles are widespread and include side-necked tortoises, geckoes, dragons, skinks, goannas, the olive python and little spotted snake.

More than 100 bird species have been recorded, including wrens and warblers, kingfishers, black swans, pelicans, cormorants, rock pigeons, and birds of prey such as wedge-tailed eagles, kites and peregrine falcons. Twenty-two species of dragonfly and damsel fly live around the wetlands, some are found only in this area.

Walks

In the Millstream area the Murlunmunyjurna Track links the homestead with Crossing Pool. This two hour return walk passes through most of the habitats of the area: spinifex hills, wattle thickets, groves of Millstream palms, a tall paper-bark forest and riverine vegetation. Signs along the trail explain the importance of some of the plants to the Jindjibandji people.

The Chichester Range Camel Trail follows part of a road built in the 1870s to enable camel drivers to transport stores from the coast to inland sheep stations and mining towns. The trail is an 8 km walk through a beautiful section of the Chichester Range. From Mount Herbert the track goes downhill to McKenzie Spring, a watering hole for camels, and continues through rugged country to Python Pool, an excellent spot for a swim and rest. Allow two hours to walk from Mount Herbert and three hours walking uphill from Python Pool. Carry plenty of water, wear protective clothing and sturdy shoes.

Facilities

The Millstream Homestead Visitor Centre has displays dedicated to the Jindjibandji people, the early settlers and the environment. Shady camping areas with pit toilets are provided at Crossing Pool and Deep Reach Pool in the Millstream area, and at Snake Creek near Python Pool. The Millstream sites have gas barbecues or fireplaces, and Crossing Pool has a generator-free camping area. Gas barbecues are provided at the Homestead and Deep Reach Pool picnic areas. Accommodation, fuel and supplies are available at Roebourne, Pannawonica and Wittenoom.

Access

The park is 250 km south-west of Port Hedland via the North-west Coastal Highway. Turn off along the sealed Roebourne to Wittenoom Road. Local thunderstorms can flood roads and watercourses. Snappy Gum Drive in the Millstream area is unsuitable for caravans or trailers.

Climate

Summers are hot and the temperature often exceeds 40 degrees Celsius between October and April. Cyclones and thunderstorms may occur at this time of year. Little rain falls between May and August, when days are warm and nights are cool.

Millstream-Chichester National Park, PO Box 835, Karratha, WA 6714. Tel. (08) 9143 1488.

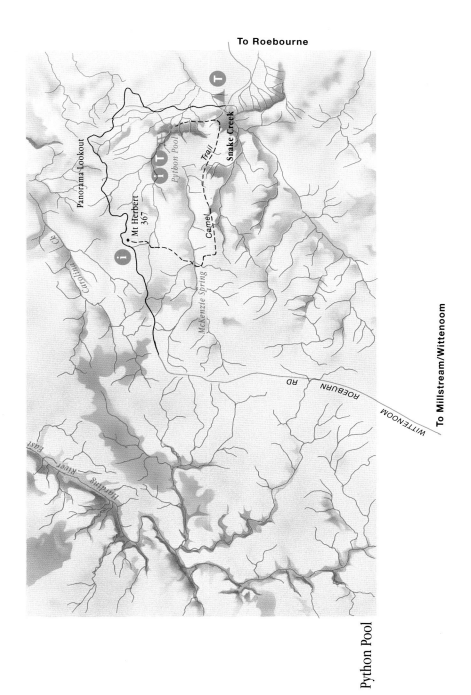

To Roebourne

To Millstream/Wittenoom

Python Pool

Millstream-Chichester National Park

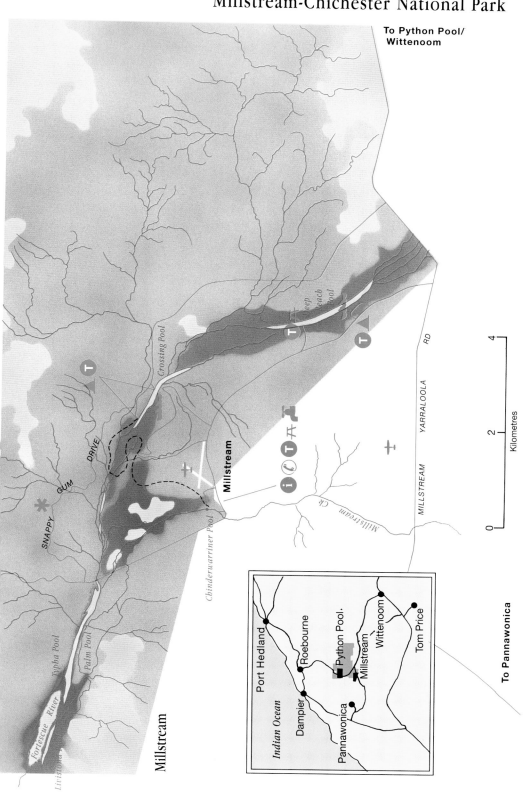

Alexander Morrison National Park (8501 ha)

On the coastal plain inland of Jurien Bay, this park is renowned for its wildflower displays in late spring and early summer. The sand heathlands and banksia woodlands of the area support species such as *Banksia laricina*, *Verticordia nitens*, the golden kangaroo paw and the Western Australian Christmas tree. There are no facilities in the park.

260 km north of Perth off Midlands Scenic Way along Green Head Rd. (08) 9652 7043.

Avon Valley National Park (4366 ha)

Located in the steep hilly country of the Darling Ranges, this park protects part of the course of the Avon River and its tributaries. The river only flows intermittently, reaching its peak from June to August when it is ideal for canoeing.

The woodlands and heaths provide beautiful wildflower displays in spring. Walk to the top of Bald Hill for extensive views over the winding course of the river. There are picnic areas with barbecue facilities and designated bush camping sites.

80 km north-west of Perth. (08) 9574 2540.

Badgingarra National Park (13,121 ha)

This is one of the best of the west coast wildflower parks. The undulating hills and sandy valleys of the area support heath and banksia woodlands rich in wildflowers, including many black kangaroo paws. Visit in spring and summer for magnificent wildflower displays. No facilities.

200 km north of Perth. (08) 9652 7043.

Beedelup National Park (1786 ha)

Located on the south-western corner of the state this park surrounds Beedelup Brook and includes the beautiful Beedelup Falls. Walks lead through dense karri forests and mixed forests of karri, jarrah and marri. Visit in spring for wildflower displays. No facilities.

340 km south of Perth and 16 km west of Pemberton. (08) 9771 1988.

Boorabbin National Park (26,000 ha)

An inland park straddling the Great Eastern Hwy protecting an area typical of the sand plain heaths of the eastern wheatbelt, rich in wildflowers and birdlife. No facilities.

450 km west of Perth between Southern Cross and Kalgoorlie. (08) 9021 2677.

Brockman National Park (49 ha)

A tiny park on the south-west corner of the state protecting some fine stands of karri forest with magnificent towering trees. Visit in spring for good wildflower displays. No facilities.

340 km south of Perth and 12 km south of Pemberton. (08) 9776 1200.

Cape Arid National Park (279,382 ha)

This large coastal park, located between Israelite Bay and Cape Le Grand on the south coast, is known for its sweeping beaches, clear blue seas and ancient granite headlands. Sand plains and heaths cover most of the area. Thomas River, Seal Creek, Poison Creek and Mount Ragged are well-known attractions. Whales are often seen and seals sometimes visit local beaches. The endangered ground parrot survives here, and the rare Cape Barron Goose is a regular visitor. There are camping and caravan sites and a number of walking trails.

120 km east of Esperance. (08) 9075 0055.

Cape Range National Park (50,581 ha)

Located on the western side of North-west Cape, the park includes the rocky mountain range with its canyons and sandy beaches. Yardie Creek contains the only permanent water in this hot, dry area, and resembles a fjord trapped between vertical cliffs. The range tops support eucalypt woodlands and shrubs, with spinifex grasses on the slopes of the gorges and ridges. Kangaroos are very tame. Rock wallabies, euros, 80 species of reptiles and more than 100 bird species live in the area. Good fishing and camping.

400 km north of Carnarvon via Exmouth. (08) 9949 1676.

Collier Range National Park (235,162 ha)

Located in a remote wilderness area close to the headwaters of the Ashburton River between Meekatharra and Newman, this arid park includes the high land between the upper reaches of the Gascoyne and Ashburton Rivers. There are red rocky ranges and sand dunes supporting spinifex and mulga. No facilities.

960 km north of Perth via the Great Northern Hwy. (08) 9143 1488.

D'Entrecasteaux National Park (115,787 ha)

On the south coast and accessible by 4WD vehicle only, this park protects a coastline of rocky headlands and dune-backed beaches. There are wildflower heathlands, pockets of tall forests and wetlands. Basic camping.

380 km south of Perth via Manjimup and Northcliffe. (08) 9776 1200.

Drovers Cave National Park (2681 ha)

Located on the west coastal plains, this small park features a number of limestone caves. Drovers Cave has spectacular stalactites, while Hastings and Moorba Caves are important fossil sites. The undulating sand plains support heath and banksia woodlands with excellent wildflower displays in spring and summer. No facilities.

258 km north of Perth, just north of Jurien Bay. (08) 9652 7043.

Drysdale River National Park (448,264 ha)

The largest of the Kimberley's national parks it includes open woodlands, the wide waters of Drysdale River, waterfalls, pools, creeks, rugged cliffs and gorges. Tall trees fringe the waterways and pockets of rainforest dot the Carson Escarpment and Worriga Gorge. More than 600 plant species have been identified and 129 bird species, many found nowhere else. Short-eared rock wallabies, sugar gliders and bats occur here. No facilities.

150 km west of Wyndham. (08) 9168 0200.

Eucla National Park (3342 ha)

On the south-east corner of the state this small coastal park protects the vast Delisser Sandhills and Wilson Bluff, a high limestone cliff that provides extensive views of the coastal cliffs extending for hundreds of kilometres to the east. The vegetation is mostly mallee scrub and heathlands. Whales, seals and albatrosses may be seen. No facilities.

Near Eucla township. (08) 9071 3733.

Fitzgerald River National Park (329,039 ha)

Given a Biosphere rating by UNESCO in 1970, this coastal park includes the rugged Barron Range cut through by the Fitzgerald River. Magnificent views along the coast are obtained from the peaks. There are extensive sand plains, low coastal scrub, heaths, mallee, stunted eucalypts and banksia woodlands. 200 bird species have been recorded as well as tamar wallabies, honey and ringtail possums, emus and many reptiles. The 1700 wildflower species include 81 orchids (almost half the state's total), 70 of which are unique. Whales migrate along the coast. Camping is allowed at certain times of the year.

240 km west of Esperance off the South Coast Hwy. (08) 9835 5043.

Francois Peron National Park (52,529 ha)

Located on the Peron Peninsula north of Denham in Shark Bay, the park comprises undulating sandy plains interspersed with gypsum claypans. One of these is open to the sea and is known as the Big Lagoon. Wildflowers and birds are abundant, and dolphins, dugongs, turtles and manta rays are often seen from the cliffs of Cape Peron. Bush camping only.

4 km from Denham by 4WD only. (08) 9948 1208.

Frank Hann National Park (67,550 ha)

This southern park protects a representative cross section of the heath flora of the inland sand plain. The park is rather flat and supports eucalypt woodlands and mallee scrublands in an area of low rainfall. Bushwalks lead to lookouts and rich wildflower habitats. No facilities.
150 km north-east of Ravensthorpe.
(08) 9076 8541.

Geikie Gorge National Park (3136 ha)

Part of the ancient Devonian Reef, the park protects the 30 m deep Geikie Gorge cut through the limestone by the Fitzroy River at the junction of the Oscar and Geikie Ranges. The cliffs are scoured white by floodwaters 16 m above the normal water level, exposing marine fossils. Sawfish, stingrays and freshwater crocodiles live in the river, and the archer fish may be seen shooting down insects from the foliage with a jet of water. Take a tour boat up the river and walk to the gorge wall. No camping.
16 km north-east of Fitzroy Crossing.
(08) 9191 5121.

Goongarrie National Park (60,356 ha)

In the heart of the Western Australian desert country, north of Kalgoorlie, this park protects a large area of mulga-dominated vegetation at its southern limit. Visit in spring when the temperatures are mild and there is a brilliant display of ephemeral wildflowers. No facilities.
90 km north of Kalgoorlie, turn east off the Kalgoorlie-Menzies Rd. (08) 9021 2677.

Gooseberry Hill National Park (33 ha)

A tiny park on the Darling Ranges east of Perth. The scenic Zig-Zag Rd leads to a scenic lookout on the western edge of the escarpment. The area supports eucalypt woodlands, and is known for its spring wildflower displays. No facilities.
20 km east of Perth. (08) 9298 8344.

Greenmount National Park (58 ha)

Located on the Darling Ranges east of Perth, this small park protects an area of eucalypt forest with jarrah, marri, wandoo and banksia. Wildflowers are prolific in spring. There are panoramic views over the coastal plains and the Swan river. No facilities.
25 km east of Perth. (09) 298 8344.

Hassell National Park (1265 ha)

A roadside reserve in an area of gently undulating heathlands and low mallee, north-east of Albany. Birdlife is prolific, and the spring and early summer wildflower displays are beautiful. No facilities.
50 km north-east of Albany via the South Coast Hwy. (08) 9841 7133.

John Forrest National Park (2676 ha)

Located on the crest of the Darling Range escarpment, there are outstanding views over Perth and the coastal plains from lookouts on the scenic drive through the park. A popular escape from the city, the park is in a virtually untouched jarrah forest with wildflowers, abundant birdlife, kangaroos, bandicoots and the chuditch, a small native cat. Walk to Hovea and National Park Falls, or ride a horse on the special trails. There are tea rooms, a restaurant, rock gardens and a large natural swimming pool. No camping.
26 km east of Perth off the Great Eastern Hwy. (08) 9298 8344.

Kalamunda National Park (375 ha)

Located in the Darling Rages east of Perth, this park protects an area of natural bushland with dry eucalypt forest, good wildflower displays and prolific birdlife. No facilities.
25 km east of Perth. (09) 298 8344.

Leeuwin-Naturaliste National Park (19,143 ha)

A coastal park along the lower west coast between Cape Naturaliste and Cape Leeuwin. The scenery is spectacular. Ridges of granite, gneiss and lime-

stone form a rugged coastal area with rocky headlands, limestone caves and magnificent beaches offering excellent surfing. There are heathlands and karri forests. Hiking, boating, fishing, swimming and surfing are popular. Camping and caravan sites are provided.
260 km south of Perth via Busselton. (08) 9752 1677.

Lesmurdie Falls National Park (56 ha)

One of a cluster of parks on the Darling Range overlooking Perth, Lesmurdie Falls is located on the western edge of the scarp in an area of open forest of jarrah, marri and wandoo gums with a low undergrowth that blooms prolifically in spring. There are good picnic facilities and walking tracks to the waterfall and lookouts. No camping.
22 km east of Perth. (08) 9298 8344.

Mirima (Hidden Valley) National Park (2068 ha)

Often described as a mini Bungle Bungle, the park is in an area of rugged sandstone hills, valleys and gorges. Boab trees cling to the sheer rock faces, their seeds carried there by rock wallabies. The area is of great significance to the Miriuwung people who still live in the region, and some good examples of rock art can be seen in the park. There are spectacular views from walking trails along the valley and ridges. No camping.
2 km north of Kununurra. (08) 9168 0200.

Moore River National Park (17,540 ha)

Located on the coastal sand plains inland of Ledge Point, this park protects an area of outstanding wildflower displays. The sand heaths and banksia woodlands support such species as the Western Australian Christmas tree, golden verticordias, golden and black kangaroo paws. Visit in spring and summer for the wildflower displays. No facilities.
120 km north of Perth. (08) 9561 1004.

Mount Frankland National Park (30,830 ha)

Mt Frankland is a granite monadnock standing above the surrounding eroded landscape supporting majestic karri, tingle and jarrah forests. A walking track leads around the base of the mountain and to the peak, a steep path offering sweeping views over the park and ocean. There are exceptional wildflower displays in spring. Canoe on the Frankland River and camp at the base of the mountain.
29 km north of Walpole. (08) 9840 1027.

Nambung National Park (18,362 ha)

Features The Pinnacles, a strange, unique formation comprising thousands of limestone pillars up to 4 m tall rising out of the flat yellow sand plains. Other parts of this coastal park are rich in wildflowers. Low mallee and heathlands scattered with stunted eucalypts and banksias characterise the vegetation. Visit in spring and summer for the wildflower displays. Walk through The Pinnacles. Coastal fishing is popular. No camping.
4 km south of Cervantes. (08) 9652 7043.

Neerabup National Park (1069 ha)

Prolific springtime wildflower displays are the main attraction of Neerabup, an undeveloped area of slightly undulating sand plains on the west coast just north of Perth. The sandy soils support an open forest of eucalypts and banksias with a low understorey that includes a great variety of wildflowers. No facilities.
30 km north of Perth. (08) 9561 1004.

Peak Charles National Park (39,959 ha)

Located in the south-east goldfields the park protects a pristine area of dry woodlands, sand plain heaths and salt lake vegetation. The spectacular granite outcrops of Peak Charles (651 m) and Peak Eleanora (501 m) rise above the plains. A difficult walk to the summit of Peak Charles provides extensive views over Peak Eleanora and the surrounding countryside. No facilities or freshwater. Bush camping only.
70 km south-west of Norseman. (08) 9076 8541.

Purnululu (Bungle Bungle) National Park (239,723 ha)

The park is part of a soft sandstone plateau rising more than 200 m above the plains, intersected with sheer-sided gorges. It features a number of huge, striped, beehive-shaped sandstone domes rising dramatically from the surrounding Kimberley wilderness. A delicate skin of orange silica and black lichen protects the rocks from erosion. Permanent springs support rainforest pockets, the unique Bungle Bungle fan palm clings to the rocks, while tough eucalypts, acacias, grevilleas and spinifex grow on the undulating yellow and red sand plains. Walk into the gorges. Basic camping at Bellburn Creek or Kurrajong Camp.
164 km north-east of Halls Creek. Difficult access by 4WD only. (08) 9168 7300.

Rudall River National Park (1,283,706 ha)

The largest national park in Western Australia, this remote wilderness park is on the edge of the Great Sandy Desert, a land of salt lakes, rugged hills and sand dunes. The area is scenically very attractive and has a diverse range of flora and fauna, but access is difficult and should only be attempted by well-equipped and experienced travellers. No facilities.
1350 km north-west of Perth. 4WD only. (08) 9143 1488.

Serpentine National Park (4360 ha)

The park is best known for the waterfall that cascades over a sheer granite cliff, dropping 15 m to a large, very deep pool. Located on the rugged western escarpment of the Darling Range, the scenic beauty of the ancient landforms and the views over the coastal plains attract many day-visitors from Perth. The forests of jarrah, marri and wandoo are ablaze with colour during the wildflower season. Birdlife is prolific and western grey kangaroos are common. Camp at Gooralong where there are basic facilities.
60 km south of Perth via Armadale the South-western Hwy and Falls Rd. (08) 9525 2128.

Sir James Mitchell National Park (497 ha)

In undulating country along the South-western Hwy between Manjimup and Walpole, this park protects a narrow, 64 km stretch of jarrah, marri and karri forest alongside the road. The area has beautiful springtime wildflowers. No facilities.
340 km south of Perth. (08) 9771 1988.

Stokes National Park (9726 ha)

A coastal park surrounding Stokes Inlet on the south coast, this park protects the heaths, wetlands and lake systems of the area and the wildlife habitats. There are long beaches and rocky headlands. Dense low forests of yate, swamp yate and paperbarks support a rich birdlife. Look for the yellow flowers of the beautiful bell-fruited mallee. Follow the Heritage Trail for magnificent views over Stokes Inlet. Canoeing and boating are popular. Camp at Stokes Inlet, Skippy Rock or Fanny Cove where there are basic facilities.
70 km west of Esperance off the South Coast Hwy. (08) 9076 8541.

Tathra National Park (4322 ha)

Preserves an area of undulating sand plains, sand heaths and banksia woodlands on the west coastal plain inland of Green Head. The wildflowers of the sand plains are exceptional in their variety. Visit in late spring and early summer. No facilities.
42 km east of Carnamah. (08) 9652 7043.

Torndirrup National Park (3936 ha)

This southern park includes some of the most spectacular coastal scenery in the state. There are high cliffs and sweeping beaches between rocky headlands. Features include The Gap, Natural Bridge (a huge granite suspension), Jimmy Newells Harbour, Bald Head and Frenchman's Bay. The undulating coastal hills support stunted vegetation rich in wildflowers, honeyeaters and possums. Good fishing and boating in King George Sound. No camping.
Just south of Albany. (08) 9844 4090.

Tunnel Creek National Park (91 ha)

Features a 750 m long tunnel carved out of the ancient limestone reef by Tunnel Creek. In the dry season you can walk through the tunnel to the other side of the Napier Range. There are cave paintings and permanent pools of fresh water. Five species of bats and the occasional freshwater crocodile live in the tunnel. The Aboriginal hero Jundumurra used the tunnel as a hideout late last century during his battle with the settlers. No camping.

117 km north-east of Fitzroy Crossing. (08) 9191 5121.

Walyunga National Park (1812 ha)

On the hills of the Darling Range just east of Perth, Walyunga includes the beautiful upper reaches of the Swan River and its river pools, and an important Aboriginal campsite containing a number of stone artefacts. The area supports open eucalypt forests with a low understorey rich in wildflowers. There are good picnic areas. Swimming, bushwalking and canoeing are popular. No camping.

30 km east of Perth. (08) 9571 1371.

Warren National Park (2982 ha)

Straddling the Warren River in the south-west of the state this park protects a small but magnificent area of untouched Karri forest where the trees reach up to 90 m in height. Walking trails lead through the forest to the river, giving excellent views over the Warren Valley. Visit in spring for the wildflower displays. The roads are steep and unsuitable for caravans or trailers. There are camping areas with basic facilities.

345 km south of Perth, 10 km south of Pemberton. (08) 9776 1207.

Watheroo National Park (44,474 ha)

Protects an important area of sandstone country of the inland coastal plains. A number of rare plant species grow among the sand heaths and the banksia and eucalypt woodlands. It is also the site of Jingamia Cave, an important archaeological site. Magnificent wildflowers in late spring and early summer. No camping.

50 km north of Moora. (08) 9652 7043.

William Bay National Park (1738 ha)

Located in the south of the state this coastal park protects a superb landscape of rocks, reefs, sandy beaches and headlands. Scenic spots include Green Pool, Elephant Rocks, Tower Hill, Madfish Bay and Waterfall Beach. The coastal hills support a sandy heath flora with good spring wildflower displays. No camping.

14 km west of Denmark. (08) 9840 9255.

Windjana Gorge National Park (2134 ha)

Protects the 3.5 km gorge formed by the Lennard River as it winds through the ancient limestone reef. The walls of the gorge rise abruptly from the wide alluvial floodplain forming a narrow canyon up to 100 m high. The river flows only in the wet season, otherwise it is a series of pools surrounded by trees and shrubs supporting freshwater crocodiles and an abundance of fish and birds. A walking trail winds through the gorge. The camping and caravan area has good facilities.

150 km north-east of Fitzroy Crossing. (08) 9193 1411.

Wolfe Creek Meteorite Crater National Park (1460 ha)

On the edge of the Great Sandy Desert, the park protects the second largest meteorite crater in the world: 800 m wide and 50 m deep. Among the broken rocks of the crater wall brown ring tail dragons stalk insects in the flowering shrubs. In the centre of the crater are stands of wattles and paperbarks. Red kangaroos and cockatoos are sometimes seen. Walk around the rim of the crater. Camp at Carranya Station 7 km from the park.

145 km south of Halls Creek via the unsealed Tanami Rd. (08) 9168 0200.

Yalgorup National Park (13,001 ha)

Located on the west coast between Mandurah and Bunbury, this park incudes coastal dunes, heaths, paperbark wetlands and tuart forest with an understorey of banksias and wattles. Lakes Preston and Clifton are located in the park. In summer they are home to large numbers of waterbirds. There are good beaches and a number of historical farms. Visit in spring for the wildflower displays. No camping.

120 km south of Perth. (09) 9739 1067.

Yanchep National Park (2842 ha)

One of Perth's most popular recreation areas, the park has freshwater lakes, tuart and banksia woodlands, kangaroos, waterbirds and spring wildflower displays. Alongside the natural bushland are manicured lawns and gardens surrounding Tudor-style buildings. Located on the Swan coastal plain, the landscape is flat with eroded limestone crags rising above the sands and wetlands. A vast network of caves, potholes and underground streams lie beneath the park. There are boats for hire, a museum, bushwalking trails and a koala colony. No camping.

50 km north of Perth. (08) 9561 1004.

Index